Connections

Empowering College and Career Success

• • •

Paul A. Gore
Xavier University

Wade Leuwerke
Drake University

A.J. Metz
The University of Utah

Bedford/St. Martin's
A Macmillan Education Imprint

Boston • New York

For Bedford/St. Martin's

Vice President, Editorial, Macmillan Higher Education Humanities: Edwin Hill
Publisher for College Success: Erika Gutierrez
Senior Executive Editor for College Success: Simon Glick
Senior Developmental Editor: Christina Lembo
Senior Production Editor: Deborah Baker
Senior Production Supervisor: Joe Ford
Marketing Manager: Kayti Corfield
Market Development Manager: Katherine Bates
Associate Editor: Bethany Gordon
Copyeditor: Linda McLatchie
Indexer: Mary White
Director of Rights and Permissions: Hilary Newman
Senior Art Director: Anna Palchik
Text Design: Maureen McCutcheon
Cover Design: John Callahan
Cover Art: Kudryashka/Shutterstock
Composition: Jouve
Printing and Binding: RR Donnelley and Sons

Manufactured in the United States of America.

0 9 8 7 6 5
f   e   d   c   b   a

For information, write: Bedford/St. Martin's, 75 Arlington Street, Boston, MA 02116
   (617-399-4000)

ISBN 978-1-4576-2840-5 (Student Edition)
ISBN 978-1-319-01234-2 (Loose-leaf Edition)
ISBN 978-1-319-01236-6 (Instructor's Annotated Edition)

Acknowledgments

letter to students

Dear Student,

Congratulations and welcome to college! If this class marks the beginning of your college experience, welcome to a new chapter in your life. If you're returning to college, welcome back as you continue your educational adventure. We're excited for you to start this class, and we've written this book to help you develop the skills you'll need to succeed in school right now and in your career for years to come.

As educators we've spent many years focused on helping college students succeed. We've had the wonderful privilege of working closely with students as they learn inside and outside of class. It's always a tremendous thrill to help students explore their passions, nurture their talents, learn about themselves, overcome challenges, and ultimately discover their life path. Now as authors, we're excited to join you on this journey.

You'll soon discover that *Connections* is different from your other textbooks. Rather than simply presenting information to you, we encourage you to engage with the material, act on it, and make it your own. Along with traditional textbook features — like facts, research, stories, and diagrams — the following pages are filled with ideas, activities, questions, tips, and exercises. With this book and in this class, you'll not only learn, you'll *use* what you learn to develop as a student and as a person. You'll have the chance to reflect, think critically, make connections, try new things, and set goals. At every stage, we'll help you figure out what works, change what doesn't, and celebrate your successes.

We wrote down the ideas and activities in *Connections* so that you might take them, shape them in a way that works for you, and use them to succeed. We promise that we put a ton of time, energy, brain power — and even some creativity! — into this book, and we ask that you put your own time, energy, brain power, and creativity into trying out the ideas in each chapter.

In our experience, the exact combination of strategies that helps each student succeed is unique to that student. We hope that the ideas in *Connections* will spark in *you* the creation of new skills and practices that help you accomplish your goals — both during your time in college and beyond.

Wishing you all the best,
Paul, Wade, and A.J.

about the authors

Christina Rodriguez

Paul A. Gore

Paul's efforts to promote college and career readiness, high school and college student persistence, and academic success are informed by more than 20 years of research, program development, implementation, evaluation, and teaching. Paul currently serves as the dean of the College of Social Sciences, Health, and Education at Xavier University in Ohio. Paul earned his Ph.D. in Counseling Psychology from Loyola University–Chicago with an emphasis in student career development, academic success, and transition. He has held academic and administrative responsibilities at the University of Missouri–Kansas City, Southern Illinois University–Carbondale, ACT, Inc., and the University of Utah.

Paul's research and practice efforts focus on noncognitive and motivational aspects of academic and career success. In particular, he is interested in how secondary and postsecondary institutions use data describing the noncognitive strengths and weaknesses of their students to promote student success and retention. He regularly consults with secondary and postsecondary institutions in the United States and abroad on developing and evaluating student academic and career success programs.

Paul has authored more than 50 peer-reviewed journal articles and book chapters. He is the past chair of the Society for Vocational Psychology, served as an Advisory Board member for the National Resource Center for the First-Year Experience and Students in Transition, and is the current editor of the *Journal of the First-Year Experience and Students in Transition*. During the 2013–2014 academic year, Paul was the recipient of an American Council on Education Emerging Leadership Fellowship.

MRogalla Photography

Wade Leuwerke

Wade is an associate professor of Counseling and Chair of the Leadership and Counseling Department at Drake University. He earned his Ph.D. in Counseling Psychology from Southern Illinois University–Carbondale. Wade has authored over 50 journal articles and book chapters, as well as national and international conference presentations. One of his areas of research is the assessment and development of student and employee noncognitive skills. He cocreated the Student Strengths Inventory, a measure of noncognitive skills used with secondary and postsecondary students to identify students' skills and drive interventions for students at risk of academic failure or dropout. Wade also studies factors that predict college retention, the impact of computer-assisted career guidance systems on academic planning and career exploration behaviors, and the role of technology in career development processes.

Wade has experience examining school counselors' roles and working with professional school counselors to positively impact students' academic development, career and college exploration, and the acquisition of personal and social skills that will prepare them for college and life beyond. He has worked with dozens of secondary and postsecondary institutions on a range of factors related to student success and persistence, including evaluation of institutional practices, use of data to drive student interventions, creating individualized student success plans, training, strategic planning, resource allocation, and collaboration to promote student success. He has also worked as a research project manager focusing on academic and career development research for Kuder, Inc.; ACT, Inc.; Career Cruising; and intoCareers. Wade provides executive and career coaching to corporations and the federal government.

A.J. Metz

Photo courtesy of Andy Brimhall

A.J. is an assistant professor in the Department of Educational Psychology at the University of Utah. She earned an M.Ed. in Vocational Rehabilitation Counseling in 1997 and a Ph.D. in Urban Education (specialization in Counseling Psychology) in 2005 from the University of Wisconsin–Milwaukee. Her research examining factors related to academic and career success in underrepresented and underserved student populations has led to numerous journal articles, book chapters, conference presentations, workshops, and faculty in-service trainings.

A.J. has extensive teaching, counseling, and career advising experience in high schools, community colleges, and four-year public and private institutions of higher education. She is passionate about mentoring students and recently received a University of Utah Early Career Teaching Award. She is the head Core Values judge for the Utah FIRST LEGO League and has been on the board of directors of the Utah Psychological Association for six years, most recently serving as president.

brief contents

contents

1 Building a Foundation for Success   *1*

Thinkstock/Getty Images

© Mike Theiss/National Geographic Creative

2 Thinking Critically and Setting Goals 21

3 Motivation, Decision Making, and Personal Responsibility *49*

©John Lund/Blend Images/Corbis

David Freund/
Getty Images

4 Learning Preferences 73

©Rudy Sulgan/Corbis

5 Organization and Time Management 99

Helena Schaeder
Söderberg/Getty
Images

6 Reading for College Success 125

7 Taking Effective Notes *151*

Asia Images Group/
Getty Images

Ammentorp Photography/ Shutterstock

8 Memory and Studying *177*

⑨ Performing Well on Exams *201*

Paul Thomas/
Getty Images

Maciej Noskowski/
Getty Images

10 Information Literacy and Communication 227

11 Connecting with Others 253

Hector Mandel/
Getty Images

145/Eunice Harris/
Ocean/Corbis

12 Personal and Financial Health 281

13 Academic and Career Planning *307*

Willie B. Thomas/ Getty Images

© Kevin Dodge/
Corbis

preface

As educators, we've had the great privilege of interacting with students during our time as instructors at two- and four-year schools, as advisers and mentors, as student success administrators, and as researchers in the area of student transition and success. It's because of our fascinating and fulfilling experiences with students that we wrote *Connections*, giving us the opportunity to put in one place the combined knowledge, experience, and expertise we've garnered over many years of working with college students and studying the factors that impact their success. To help increase student satisfaction, retention, and completion, we built the book from the ground up and integrated an exciting new student self-assessment tool called **ACES, the Academic and Career Excellence System.** Available to be packaged with the text, ACES focuses on noncognitive as well as cognitive factors.

As counseling psychologists, we've come to believe—and have seen the research to support—the idea that there's more to student success than academic achievement alone. That's why we use a holistic, strengths-based approach in *Connections* that integrates a balance of motivational skills, study skills, and life skills. Our goal is to help students understand themselves as individuals who appreciate their own strengths, acknowledge where their challenges lie, and work to strengthen current skills and build new ones. Our experience has shown us that one of the best ways to accomplish this is through an emphasis on personal reflection and self-assessment—an emphasis that has its foundation in positive psychology, concepts from which are woven throughout this text. While research has shown us that past academic performance is a good predictor of future academic performance, recent and compelling research also clearly establishes the role of motivational—*noncognitive*—factors in promoting college and career success.[1] These noncognitive factors include attitudes, behaviors, and skills such as critical thinking, self-efficacy, resilience, and working with others, and they form the scaffolding for achievement. Colleges and universities across the country are increasingly using noncognitive measures to better understand their students so they can provide them with the support they need to succeed.

Because we believe that noncognitive skills, in concert with cognitive skills, are crucial to student success, we have devoted a significant portion of our life's work to developing noncognitive assessments and creating strategies that empower students, instructors, and administrators. And that's why we jumped at the chance to create a student self-assessment platform, **ACES, the Academic and Career Excellence System**, that can be packaged with *Connections*.

ACES is a powerful, norm-referenced self-assessment that helps students pinpoint their strengths and challenges. Students can take ACES at the start of this course to better understand their own abilities and attitudes in twelve critical areas, both cognitive and noncognitive, that correspond to specific chapters in the book. They can then use the information in *Connections* to help them develop and strengthen their skills in each area. Callouts throughout the book also prompt students to reflect on their ACES results.

The idea to pair *Connections* and ACES comes from our shared experience in counseling and assessment. Rather than a self-assessment that serves as an "add on," we wanted to develop one that was woven into the fabric of the book, thereby providing two valuable resources that are even more beneficial when used together. Our goal was to ensure that information would lead to action. We achieved this goal by creating a powerful and easy-to-use assessment, along with tools and guidance that students can use to act on their results.

The idea of translating information into action also prompted us to develop another one of the key features of this book: the **Personal Success Plan (PSP)** goal-setting tool. It has been our experience that the act of responding to questions has zero value in and of itself. What *does* have value is what you *do* with or how you *act* upon that information. And that's where the PSP comes in. Students learn about themselves through ACES and then can apply that knowledge in each chapter using the PSP to create SMART goals and purposeful, personalized action plans to achieve those goals. Students can track their PSPs throughout the term, helping them document the action steps and goals they've achieved, and demonstrate the specific ways they're building important skills for college, career, and life.

As crucial as self-reflection and self-assessment are to the identity of *Connections*, there is another driving force behind the text that is just as crucial: making the connection between college and career success meaningful to today's students. Throughout the book we emphasize specific ways that the attitudes, habits, and skills needed to succeed in college—such as persistence, communication, critical thinking—are the exact same attitudes, habits, and skills needed

---

[1]S. B. Robbins, K. Lauver, K., H. Le, D. Davis, R. Langley, and A. Carlstrom. (2004). Do psychosocial and study skill factors predict college out-comes? A meta-analysis. *Psychological Bulletin*, 130, 261–288. W. J. Camara. (2005). Broadening predictors of college success. In W. J. Camara and E. W. Kimmel (Eds.), *Choosing students: Higher education admissions tools for the 21st century*. Mahwah, NJ: Erlbaum. N. Schmitt, J. Keeney, F. L. Oswald, T. J. Pleskac, A. Q. Billington, R. Sinha, M. Zorzie. (2009). Prediction of four-year college student performance using cognitive and noncognitive predictors and the impact on demographic status of admitted students. *Journal of Applied Psychology*, 94, 1479–1497.

to succeed in the workplace. Our goal is to help students see how the material they are learning now can be applied directly in any work environment.

Creating this book has been a five-year journey for us, with lots of hard work and many sleepless nights, and has proven to be the culmination of so many of our professional and personal passions. In the process, we've been gratified by very positive feedback and reviews from instructors at two- and four-year institutions across the United States. We hope that *Connections* and ACES prove as meaningful and effective for you and your students as they have been for us and for our reviewers. We hope that you, too, find this program a powerful mix of engaging content, practical strategies, effective activities, thought-provoking research, and useful self-assessment data that will help students build the skills they need to succeed in college, in their careers, and in life.

Using ACES (the Academic and Career Excellence System) with *Connections*

ACES gives students, instructors, and administrators the data they need to succeed. Available to be packaged with *Connections*, the ACES online self-assessment helps students develop a thoughtful, strengths-based understanding of themselves. ACES measures student strengths in twelve critical areas, both cognitive and noncognitive. Norm-referenced reports indicate whether students are at a high, moderate, or low skill level in these areas, as compared to students in other schools across the country.

- **Students** take ACES at the start of the term to get a snapshot of their own attitudes, skills, habits, and opportunities for improvement. Throughout the book, students reflect on their results, which they can use to set and achieve goals with the Personal Success Plan.

- **Instructors** can use ACES data to start conversations with students—individually and as a class—about how to achieve excellence in college and in their careers. ACES data can also help instructors prioritize the topics they teach, highlight relevant programs or events outside of class to provide additional support for addressing students' weaknesses, and identify strong students who might be willing to report on the ways they practice a skill.

- **Administrators** can use aggregate information about student performance from ACES to track progress within the program and individual classes, and to determine the type and level of resources needed to help students succeed.

ACES has been designed with ease-of-use in mind. It takes students about 20 minutes to complete and offers intriguing questions in a clean, appealing interface, helping ensure high student satisfaction and participation rates.

ACES works in concert with *Connections*. Students answer questions about twelve areas, or scales, that match the chapter topics in *Connections*. They reflect on their results throughout the book, and use what they've learned to strengthen their strengths and use challenges as opportunities for growth.

Students respond to 80+ empirically supported, statistically valid statements. Questions have been thoroughly tested in a national pilot study and are organized to obtain the clearest possible picture of students' attitudes and skills. Reverse scoring on select questions helps ensure that students are honest with their responses.

Targeted, thorough feedback helps each student take his or her own next steps. Students get feedback on their responses in each of the twelve skill areas. Each area is correlated as higher, moderate, or lower compared with the national sample. Feedback offers students an assessment of their current skills, encouragement to improve, and concrete suggestions for activities and resources to help them achieve their goals.

Individualized and class-level reports give students and instructors the information they need to understand student strengths and weaknesses, and to formulate realistic plans for improvement. Data can be organized in several ways and output for use in standard quantitative programs like Excel and Qualtrix.

ACES is available in the LaunchPad for *Connections*. To give your students access to ACES, assign the text with LaunchPad for *Connections*—which includes ACES. LaunchPad brings together all the media content for the textbook, curated and organized for easy assignability and assessment, and presented in a powerful, yet easy-to-use interface.

- LaunchPad is available at a significant discount when packaged with the book. To package the paper text with LaunchPad, use ISBN 978-1-319-06245-3. To package the loose-leaf edition with LaunchPad, use ISBN 978-1-319-06246-0.
- LaunchPad is also available as a standalone resource purchased separately. To order LaunchPad standalone, use ISBN 978-1-319-01239-7.

Key Features in *Connections*

The holistic, strengths-based approach provides a balanced integration of motivational, study, and life skills. The text is built on a foundation in positive psychology and a strengths-based approach, covers all topics typically taught in the course, and seamlessly integrates motivational skills, study skills, and life skills—all backed by research.

Prominent coverage of critical thinking and goal setting helps students develop key skills necessary for success. Chapter 2, Thinking Critically and Setting Goals, presents these essential skills up front, and self-assessments and activities throughout the text encourage students to think critically about their work and themselves. Included at the end of Chapters 2–14, the **Personal Success Plan** (PSP) goal-setting tool provides students with a structured platform for SMART goal setting and action planning. It encourages students to think metacognitively about the skills they develop as they set and achieve goals, and to consider how those skills might be useful in a future career. Instructors can assign as many or as few PSPs as desired based on the structure and needs of the class.

A strong emphasis on college and career connections points students in the right direction. Each chapter illustrates how topics apply to the world of work; Chapter 13 on academic and career planning helps students begin creating their own personal roadmaps to success; "College Success = Career Success" activities at the end of each chapter emphasize the college/career connection; and an in-depth appendix focuses on conducting a job search.

Content and features in each chapter illustrate the connection between students' academic and life plans. Students often wonder how the material they learn in this class connects to what they're doing in their other classes—and their careers. *Connections* addresses this question head on:

- **"Connect" prompts integrated throughout each chapter.** These brief exercises encourage students to think about how the chapter's ideas connect to their personal experiences, current coursework, career goals, and available resources.

- **"Voices of Experience" narratives included in each chapter.** These first-person stories show the real-world effects of chapter concepts in the lives of college students and graduates.

- **A strong foundation in research.** Research backs the authors' guidance to students throughout the book; the "Spotlight on Research" feature introduces original research to students in an accessible way and includes reflection questions that help students connect the findings to their own experiences.

Chapter Activities reinforce key themes, prompt self-reflection, and strengthen skills. Each chapter concludes with four activities that instructors can assign as homework or use to prompt class discussion and student engagement.

- The **Journal Entry** encourages written reflection on a wide array of topics.

- **Adopting a Success Attitude** focuses on positive psychology concepts.

- **Applying Your Skills** helps students apply the skills they've learned in the chapter.

- **College Success = Career Success** helps students connect what they're learning in college with skills they'll need in their careers.

Key Chapter-by-Chapter Content

Chapter 1, Building a Foundation for Success, introduces the text's unique themes using a clear and approachable narrative style. It makes a strong case for the benefits of a college education to students in our society and lays the foundation for the book's balanced emphasis on motivational, academic, and life skills. Topics include the benefits of personal reflection, the power of positivity, the importance of recognizing one's own strengths and weaknesses, and the strong connection between skills needed to succeed in college and in one's career.

Chapter 2, Thinking Critically and Setting Goals, presents these essential topics earlier than in most competing texts, and prompts students to focus on them as they read the chapters that follow. The chapter examines what it means to be a critical thinker and covers higher-level thinking skills, critical thinking processes, and Bloom's taxonomy. The chapter then shows how critical thinking connects to goal setting, gives step-by-step goal-setting guidance, and introduces the powerful Personal Success Plan (PSP) goal-setting tool, which students can use throughout the term to map out their goals and build a plan for achieving them.

Chapter 3, Motivation, Decision Making, and Personal Responsibility, offers a strong emphasis on noncognitive skills, ensuring that students learn key motivational topics early in the term. And *Connections*, unlike a number of competing texts, devotes a full chapter to these crucial concepts. Students learn concrete ways to stay driven and focused; make effective decisions; adopt active learning and metacognitive principles to take responsibility for their success; and develop a growth mindset. In this chapter, as in all chapters, the discussion concludes by examining how the major topics apply in the working world.

In **Chapter 4, Learning Preferences**, students assess their own approaches to learning—via self-analysis, and an introduction to the Myers-Briggs Type Indicator and the VARK model—and use what they read to become stronger learners, work more effectively with others, and excel in a wide variety of environments. While some books offer lists of strategies but no context within which to view them, here students see the principles of active learning and metacognition applied firsthand.

Chapter 5, Organization and Time Management, explores ways that students can take control of their environment and manage their lives effectively. This chapter helps students take ownership of their time, and use this valuable resource in a way that fits their priorities and helps them meet their very personal goals. It also includes a unique section on strategies for getting (and staying) organized and examines ways to beat procrastination and deal with distractions.

Chapter 6, Reading for College Success introduces a three-step process for getting the most out of college reading—preparing to read, reading with focus, and reviewing what's been read. Unlike many competing texts, which fail to make the connections among different academic skills clear to students, this chapter illustrates the relationship between reading and other key study skills. And because students are hungry for suggestions they can use to excel in math, science, and online classes, this content is also included.

Chapter 7, Taking Effective Notes, introduces note taking not as a mechanical activity, but as a method of working with—and mastering—information. In addition to presenting a clear, four-step strategy for participating in class and recording information effectively, the chapter spotlights methods and strategies students can use to take notes in a variety of settings. And to emphasize that note taking is a lifelong skill, the chapter focuses on the importance of taking notes in the workplace.

Chapter 8, Memory and Studying, spotlights strategies students can use to study effectively and remember what they've learned. Based on current research, the chapter discusses memory basics, including the processes of encoding, storage, and retrieval. Students are introduced to a wide variety of study strategies they can use to stay focused and productive, and retain the information they've learned.

Chapter 9, Performing Well on Exams, provides students with the information they need to know to take tests of all kinds—and to do so successfully. In addition to specific test-taking strategies, other key topics include managing test anxiety and taking tests with integrity. And unlike other texts, the chapter illustrates how good test-taking skills—a seemingly academic topic—come in handy in the working world.

Chapter 10, Information Literacy and Communication, connects these key academic skills to broader approaches to critical thinking and explores three essential components of information literacy—locating information, evaluating its quality, and communicating that information through writing and speaking. The chapter also discusses how to navigate the writing process, avoid plagiarism, and give strong class presentations.

Chapter 11, Connecting with Others, focuses on key skills that students need to build and sustain relationships, with special emphasis on active listening and effective speaking. The chapter explores how to strengthen emotional intelligence and manage conflict, and examines how connecting with others can enhance existing relationships, help students build new ones, and strengthen their relationships with people from different backgrounds.

Chapter 12, Personal and Financial Health, offers a unique combination of content and draws important connections between the discrete but closely related topics of stress, personal health, and financial health. Through a self-management lens, the chapter introduces a variety of strategies that students can use to promote physical well-being and mental health, maintain sexual health, and take control of their finances—all of which can help them manage stress and live happier, more fulfilled lives.

Chapter 13, Academic and Career Planning, continues the text's strong emphasis on the college/career connection. It provides information students need to think critically about their academic and career options—whether they've chosen a major or not. Far more than a laundry list of available degrees and careers, the chapter helps students personalize academic and career planning by considering their own interests, values, skills, and goals. Topics include making an academic plan; conducting career research; and managing important milestones in the academic and career development processes.

Chapter 14, Celebrating Your Success and Connecting to Your Future, a chapter unique to *Connections*, serves as a capstone chapter for the course. Both active and metacognitive, this chapter encourages students to revisit and reassess their ACES results, complete activities designed to solidify what they've learned over the term, and identify strategies they can use to sustain their success in the years to come.

Instructor Resources

LaunchPad for *Connections* with ACES and LearningCurve

LaunchPad combines an interactive e-book with high-quality multimedia content and ready-made assessment options, including the ACES student self-assessment and LearningCurve adaptive quizzing. Prebuilt units are easy to assign or adapt to your material, such as readings, videos, quizzes, discussion groups, and more. LaunchPad also provides access to a gradebook that provides a clear window on performance for your whole class, for individual students, and for individual assignments.

- **Unique to LaunchPad: ACES (The Academic and Career Excellence System).** See the earlier discussion of ACES for more detail.
- **Unique to LaunchPad: LearningCurve for *Connections*.** LearningCurve is an online self-quizzing program that quickly learns what students already know and helps them practice what they haven't yet mastered. LearningCurve motivates students to read and engage with key concepts before they come to class so that they are ready to participate, and it offers reporting tools to help you discern your students' needs.
- **Ordering information.** Please note that *Connections* is not automatically packaged with LaunchPad. To package the paper text with LaunchPad, use ISBN 978-1-319-06245-3. To package the loose-leaf edition with LaunchPad, use ISBN 978-1-319-06246-0. To order LaunchPad stand-alone, use ISBN 978-1-319-01239-7.

Instructor's Annotated Edition

A valuable tool for new and experienced instructors alike, the Instructor's Annotated Edition includes the full text of the student edition along with abundant marginal annotations that include activity suggestions, writing prompts, topics for discussion, resources for further reading, and notes about using the book's key features.

Instructor's Manual

The Instructor's Manual, available online, is packed full of activities and resources. Content includes sample syllabi; chapter objectives and summaries; class activities, topics for discussion, and writing assignments for each chapter; and a guide to using the ACES self-assessment in class.

Computerized Test Bank

The Computerized Test Bank contains more than 700 multiple-choice, true/false, short-answer, and essay questions designed to assess students' understanding of key concepts. A midterm and final exam are also included, and all questions are accompanied by an answer key. A digital text file is also available.

Lecture Slides

Available online for download, lecture slides accompany each chapter of the book and include key concepts and art from the text. Use the slides as provided to structure your lectures, or customize them as desired to fit your course's needs.

French Fries Are Not Vegetables

This comprehensive instructional DVD (ISBN 978-0-312-65073-5) features multiple resources for class and professional use.

Custom Solutions Program

Macmillan Education's custom publishing program offers the highest-quality books and media, created in consultation with publishing professionals who are committed to the discipline. Customize *Connections* to fit your course and goals by integrating your own materials, or including only the parts of the text you intend to use in your course, or both. Contact your Macmillan Education sales representative for more information.

TradeUp

Bring more value and choice to your students' first-year experience by packaging *Connections* with one of a thousand titles from Macmillan publishers at a 50 percent discount off the regular price. Contact your local Macmillan Education sales representative for more information.

Student Resources

LaunchPad for *Connections* with ACES and LearningCurve

LaunchPad is an online course solution that offers our acclaimed content, including an e-book, the ACES self-assessment, LearningCurve adaptive quizzes, videos, and more. For more information, see the Instructor Resources section.

- **Unique to LaunchPad: ACES (the Academic and Career Excellence System).** See the earlier discussion of ACES for more detail.
- **Unique to LaunchPad: LearningCurve for *Connections*.** LearningCurve is an online, adaptive, self-quizzing program that quickly learns what students already know and helps them practice what they haven't yet mastered.
- **Ordering information.** Please note that *Connections* is not automatically packaged with LaunchPad. To package the paper text with LaunchPad, use ISBN 978-1-319-06245-3. To package the loose-leaf edition with LaunchPad, use ISBN 978-1-319-06246-0. To order LaunchPad standalone, use ISBN 978-1-319-01239-7.

E-book Options

E-books offer an affordable alternative for students. You can find PDF versions of our books when you shop online at our publishing partners' sites. Learn more at **macmillanhighered.com/ebooks**.

Bedford/St. Martin's Insider's Guides

These concise and student friendly booklets on topics that are critical to college success are a perfect complement to your textbook and course. One Insider's Guide can be packaged with *any* Bedford/St. Martin's textbook at no additional cost. Additional Insider's Guides can also be packaged for additional cost. Titles include: *Insider's Guide to Academic Planning*; *Insider's Guide to Beating Test Anxiety*; *Insider's Guide to Career Services*; *Insider's Guide to Getting Involved on Campus*; *Insider's Guide to Time Management*, 2e; and many more. For more information on ordering one of these guides with the text, go to **macmillan highered.com/collegesuccess**.

The Bedford/St. Martin's Planner

Everything that students need to plan and use their time effectively is included, along with advice on preparing schedules and to-do lists, blank schedules, and monthly and weekly calendars for planning. Integrated into the planner are tips and advice on fixing common grammar errors, taking notes, and succeeding on tests; an address book; and an annotated list of useful Web sites. To order the planner standalone, use ISBN 978-0-312-57447-5.

Journal Writing: A Beginning

This writing journal is designed to give students an opportunity to use writing as a way to explore their thoughts and feelings, and includes inspirational quotes throughout the pages, tips for journaling, and suggested journal topics. To order the journal standalone, use ISBN 978-0-312-59027-7.

Acknowledgments

We wish to express our gratitude to all the people who have helped to make this book a reality. Paul would like to thank his parents, who taught him balance between critical reflection and creativity; his mentors Waded Cruzado, Steve D. Brown, Virginia Rinella, and Michael Anch, who have supported his personal and professional development for almost thirty years; and the staff of the National Resource Center for the First-Year Experience and Students in Transition for embracing his passion for promoting student success. Wade wishes to thank his wonderful partner Lesley and his three great yahoos at home. They put up with a lot over the past few years and he couldn't have done this without their support. A.J. wishes to thank her parents (Kay and Jerry), brothers (Mike and Dave), and friend Janice for their continuous interest, support, and encouragement through the course of writing this book. Together, we'd like to thank our students—especially Ali Pappas, Natalie Noel, Keith Gunnerson, Alex Kelly, Laken Shirey, Jenna Leishman, Derek Smith, Qin Hu, and Summer Hickam—who helped bounce around ideas and gave thoughtful feedback. We'd also like to thank all of the students and new professionals who shared their stories with us and made the "Voices of Experience" feature possible. The richness and variety of their stories helped bring the book content alive, and we hope that you find their wisdom and advice as helpful as we do.

At Bedford/St. Martin's, thanks to Edwin Hill, Vice President, Editorial, for taking a chance on new authors; we wouldn't have gotten this project off the ground without your support. To Simon Glick, Senior Executive Editor, thank you for providing insight and encouragement along the way. To Christina Lembo, Senior Editor, thank you for steering us through this long and challenging process. The book is a testament to your guidance, patience, and skill at helping us make our vision a reality. Our appreciation also goes out to Deb Baker, Senior Production Editor, for her invaluable attention to detail; Erika Gutierrez, Publisher, and Susan McLaughlin, Development Manager, for their ideas and leadership; Tom Kane and Melissa Graham Meeks, Media Editors, for their work on ACES; Bethany Gordon, Associate Editor, for managing the accompanying ancillaries; and Katherine Bates, Market Development Manager, and Kayti Corfield, Marketing Manager, for their enthusiasm in sharing this new book with instructors across the country.

Finally, we would like to thank the reviewers, survey participants, and focus group attendees who took the time to provide detailed, thoughtful feedback on the book throughout all stages of the development process. Your comments and suggestions were instrumental in creating both *Connections* and ACES:

Sandra Albers, Leeward Community College; Fred Amador, Phoenix College; Holly Andress-Martin, Culver-Stockton College; Bonnie Bailey, Central New Mexico Community College; Christopher Barker, Miami Dade College; Wesley Beal, Lyon College; Jennifer Beattie, Tri-County Technical College; Ashley Becker, Florida Institute of Technology; Sheila Bedworth, Long Beach City College; Kristine Benard, Bryant & Stratton College, Eastlake Campus; Edie Blakley, Clark College; Dustyn Bork, Lyon College; Jennifer Boyle, Davidson County Community College; Beverly Brucks, Illinois Central College; Alim Chandani, Gallaudet University; Rebecca Coco, Massasoit Community College; Colleen Coughlin, University of Massachusetts; Melanie Deffendall, Delgado Community College; Erika Deiters, Moraine Valley Community College; Susan Delker, The Community College of Baltimore County; Bob DuBois, Waukesha County Technical College; Denise Dufek, Bay de Noc Community College; Kim Dunnavant, Martin Methodist College; Darin Eckton, Utah Valley University; Carly Edwards, Campbell University; Shawna Elsberry, Central Oregon Community College; Annette Fields, University of Arkansas at Pine Bluff; Stephanie M. Foote, Kennesaw State University; Karen Frost, University of Arkansas at Little Rock; Kate Frost, Arizona State University; Susan Gaer, Santa Ana College; Cathy Gann, Missouri Western State University; Linda Gannon, College of Southern Nevada; Margaret Garroway, Howard Community College; Nicole Gilbertson, Mt. Hood Community College; Carlen Gilseth, Minot State University; Tracey Glaessgen, Missouri State University; Joselyn Gonzalez, El Centro College; Tymon Graham, Coker College; Barbara Granger, Holyoke Community College; Laurie Grimes, Lorain County Community College; Betsy Hall, Illinois College; Timothy Hare, Morehead State University; Angie Hatlestad,

Ridgewater College; Robin Hayhurst, Western Nebraska Community College; Teresa Hays, DeVry University; Lorraine M. Daniels Howland, NHTI, Concord's Community College; Cedric Jackson, University of Arkansas at Pine Bluff; Barbara Jaffe, El Camino College; Jody Kamens, Jacksonville University; Kim Keffer, Ohio University Southern; Alice Kimara, Baltimore City Community College; Stacy Kirch, Orange Coast College; Ray Korpi, Clark College; Fatina LaMar-Taylor, Prince George's Community College; Teresa Landers, Lee College; Christopher Lau, Hutchinson Community College; Kristina Leonard, Daytona State College; Andrew Logemann, Gordon College; Judith Lynch, Kansas State University; Malinda Mansfield, Ivy Tech Community College; Melanie Marine, University of Wisconsin Oshkosh; Lisa Marks, Ozarks Technical Community College; Mickey Marsee, University of New Mexico–Los Alamos; Patrick McConnell, Rio Hondo College; MaryAnn McGuirk, North Lake College; Maureen McMahon, Paul Smith's College; Ryan Messatzzia, Wor-Wic Community College; Pat Missad, Grand Rapids Community College; Pamela Moss, Midwestern State University; Jodi Murrow, Fort Scott Community College; Tami Mysliwiec, Pennsylvania State University Berks; Nicole Nagy, Madonna University; Chaelle Norman, Cedar Valley College; Scott O'Leary, University of Saint Mary; Ellen Oppenberg, Glendale Community College; Taunya Paul, York Technical College; Elizabeth Price, Ranger College; Cynthia Puckett, Eastern Florida State College; Linda Refsland, William Paterson University; Leigh-Ann Routh, Ivy Tech Community College; Danielle Rowland, University of Washington Bothell and Cascadia College; James Rubin, Paradise Valley Community College; Carolyn Sanders, University of Alabama in Huntsville; Sarah Sell, Wichita State University; Mark Shea, Buena Vista University; Barbara Sherry, Northeastern Illinois University; Sarah Shutt, J. Sargeant Reynolds Community College; Cheryl Spector, California State University Northridge; Charlene Stephens, Wesley College; Pamela Stephens, Fairmont State University; Chris Strouthopoulos, San Juan College; Brenda Sudan, Georgia Perimeter College; Susan Sullivan, Louisiana State University Alexandria; Ricardo Teixeira, University of Houston–Victoria; Kim Thomas, Polk State University; Virginia Thompson, Grayson County College; Althea Truesdale, Bennett College; Adanta Ugo, San Jacinto College; Dominick Usher, University of Massachusetts Amherst; Sherri VandenAkker, Springfield College; Jodie Vangrov, Chattahoochee Technical College; Angela Vaughan, University of Northern Colorado; Melanie Wadsworth, Western Nevada College; Jacob Widdekind, Miami Dade College; Cheryl Wieseler, Luther College; Margaret Williamson, Dillard University; Cornelia Wills, Middle Tennessee State University; Leslie Wilson, Chestnut Hill College; and Marguerite Yawin, Tunxis Community College.

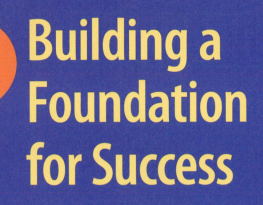

1 Building a Foundation for Success

Why Go to College?

Learn about Yourself

Stay Positive, Even When It's Tough

Embrace Your Strengths — and Learn from Your Weaknesses

College Success Leads to Career Success

Welcome to college! Are you a recent high school graduate? Did you put your education on hold to raise a family, and now you're returning to school? Are you a veteran beginning college after a tour of duty in the military? Did you take a gap year after high school to get some work experience or to travel, and now you're ready for college? Regardless of your personal situation, congratulations! Starting college is a huge accomplishment that you can be proud of. And it's a major step toward your future success—not only in your academic life but also in your personal and professional life.

We wrote this book to help you take that step. As educators and authors, we've worked with thousands of college students, and we've found that almost all of them want to succeed. We've met students who had a hard time defining their goals or who didn't feel confident that they could achieve them. We've also met students who struggled to translate their goals into action and who had trouble finding help when they needed it. But no matter what their challenges, these students were all in school with one objective in mind: to improve their lives. We assume that you have this same objective, and we're committed to helping you meet it.

But wanting to improve your life is only the beginning. Getting through college requires effort and persistence, and colleges and universities understand that. That's why so many schools have developed courses like this one to equip you with the attitudes, skills, and resources you need to achieve your goals. Research from hundreds of experts over the last thirty years shows that students who complete these courses achieve higher grades, are more likely to stay in school, graduate faster, and make better decisions than students who don't.[1] So the good news is, you're in the right place! With the help of your instructor, this book, and other resources available on your campus, you'll develop the tools you'll need to excel in college and embark on a satisfying career.

As you go through this course and this book, keep in mind that successful people don't succeed on their own. Rather, they draw on connections to advance toward their goals—connections with other people, with new knowledge they encounter along the way, and with their own strengths and intentions. Now that you're in college, a great way to set the stage for your success is to make similar connections. By doing so, you'll gain a new understanding of yourself and help to maintain your motivation in school. For example, when you connect the skills you learn in college with those you'll use in your career, every course you take will have more meaning and value to you. That means you'll be more motivated to do well in these courses. And by making connections with the people around you — instructors, classmates, college staff — you'll build a network of supporters who can help you through tough times and join you in celebrating your successes.

Connections are a big theme in this book — and in this course. As you'll discover, *nothing* you do or learn is isolated: The information you read about in one chapter relates to topics in other chapters; what you learn in this class will be useful in your other classes; and the skills you build here will be the same ones that will help you excel at work.

In this chapter you'll learn about the critical components of your success: recognizing why college is important, deep thinking and personal reflection, the power of positivity, a detailed understanding of your strengths and weaknesses, and connecting college and career. In fact, this chapter introduces all the big ideas you'll learn more about as you go through this class. We'll expand on those big ideas later in the book, and you'll have plenty of time to get your head around the details. For now, as you read, ask yourself: How does the material in this chapter apply to my other classes? How does it relate to my current or future career? How can I use what I learn in this chapter to create my own success?

Why Go to College?

Life is full of choices, and you've already made an important one: to attend college and further your education. Now that you've made this choice, ask yourself a basic question: Why are you here? All students have their own reasons for going to school, whether it's training for a specific occupation, pursuing a love of learning, or searching for their life's purpose. You may not even be sure why you're here, other than to give yourself a chance for a better life.

No matter what your reasons, it's crucial to understand one thing: By pursuing your education, you're making a smart investment in your future. Half a century ago, fewer than 50 percent of adults in the United States had a high school diploma.[2] Today, that number has risen to 88 percent, and almost 42 percent of all adults have an associate's degree or higher.[3] What prompted the change? Think of everything that's happened in the past fifty years: We've landed on the moon, sent scientific equipment to Mars, invented the Internet and smartphone, advanced civil rights, and made countless gains in medicine, communications, agriculture, and energy. Improving any society in these ways requires education, and the more sophisticated our society becomes, the higher the demand will be for educated people — people like you.

Education not only strengthens societies but also pays off for individuals — and in more ways than one. For example, a recent report by the College Board suggests that compared to high school graduates, college graduates

- are more engaged in their communities
- lead healthier lifestyles

CONNECT TO MY EXPERIENCE

Write down three adjectives that describe how you feel about being in college. It's okay if you have mixed emotions. You may feel excited and hopeful, but also scared or nervous. Has anything about the college experience so far surprised you?

- participate more actively in their children's education
- earn higher salaries (as much as $20,000 more a year)
- are more likely to have jobs[4]

In fact, by the time you graduate, more than 60 percent of all jobs will require some form of college education.[5] As you can see, you're in the right place at the right time.

So now that you're in college, what should you expect? And what will be expected of you? First and foremost, you'll encounter challenges. More so than in high school, your instructors will expect you to participate actively in your learning, not just look to them for all the answers. They'll expect you to figure out *how* and *what* to study, to determine how to apply what you've learned to new situations, and to think critically about concepts you might have just accepted as fact in high school. They'll also assume you'll ask for help when you need it, schedule your own study time, and keep up with your assignments.

If this responsibility feels difficult at times, that's okay. College is designed to push you out of your comfort zone. It's about growing intellectually and personally so that when you graduate, you're ready to launch a career that meets your needs. Fortunately, this book is packed with tips that can help you become an active, successful learner. So as you progress through this class and others, remember that you're in college for great reasons and that the rewards of completing your education will make all that hard work worthwhile.

Learn about Yourself

Though everyone's path to success looks different, there's one skill that we all need to succeed: critical thinking. When you engage in *critical thinking*, you consider information thoughtfully, understand how to think logically and rationally, and apply those methods of thinking in your classes and your life.[6] Critical thinking helps you examine information in a careful, unbiased way so that you can use that information to make good decisions.

In college, academic success and critical thinking go hand in hand. As you'll see throughout this book, you can use critical thinking in your classes to analyze information, answer questions on exams, and write papers, among many other pursuits. But you can also use it in a more personal way, to better understand yourself. This kind of critical thinking involves reflection, which is a time for *you* to think about your hopes, wishes, and what you're looking for from college and from life. Reflection helps you pinpoint your goals (what you want to achieve) and your motivations (what drives you to keep working toward your goals). When you recognize your goals and motivations, classes have more meaning for you, you find it easier to stay focused, and you feel more confident when you're making important decisions, such as what major to declare or certificate to pursue.

Throughout this book you'll have many opportunities to learn more about yourself. To get started, think critically about two personal attributes that powerfully influence your goals and motivations: your values and your interests.

Discover Your Values

Your values are what you consider important—really important. They stem from your experiences with your family, your community, or your faith. For example, your values may include getting a good job, taking care of your family, or playing an active role in your community. Values are essential because they can influence your behavior and your choices. You're more likely to pursue goals and activities that are consistent with what you care about most.

What Do You Value Most?
When you know what your values are and how each of your courses connects with those values, you'll feel far more motivated to work hard to excel in each course. You'll also seek out experiences that let you express your values. And those experiences can help you gain new skills and knowledge essential for succeeding in your chosen career. Tim Pannell/Corbis

CONNECT TO MY EXPERIENCE

(1) What is the most important thing in your life right now? (2) What single goal would you most like to achieve? (3) What would most motivate you to achieve that goal? Write your answers on a separate sheet of paper.

Consider Tasha, a first-year student who is picking elective courses to fulfill her general-education requirements. Her values include the importance of treating people fairly and helping those in need—values she learned from growing up with parents who behaved in these ways with others. Tasha's adviser suggests that she take a political science and a U.S. history course. In these classes Tasha will learn how the United States has, over time, developed legal systems as well as political and social support structures aimed at treating people fairly and helping those in need. Because the subject matter in these courses connects to ideas that mean a lot to Tasha—it connects to her values— she'll likely find the classes interesting. And she'll be motivated to complete assignments, master the material, and do her best on exams.

What are your values? For starters, the fact that you're in college means you value education. Perhaps you and your family make sacrifices so that you can attend school. Maybe you juggle commitments, taking out loans and cutting back on your work hours to free up time and energy for class. You're making these sacrifices because you appreciate what a college education has to offer.

Take a moment to think about what other values you hold dear. All of these values affect the decisions you make. For example, if you want to build a meaningful career after you graduate (and most students do[7]), reflecting on your values can help you pick a major that will help prepare you for such a career. Suppose that taking care of others is one of your values. In this case, majors like nursing or teaching might be the perfect fit for you. If achieving financial independence is among your values, then majors that lay a foundation for lucrative careers—such as finance or business administration—might be good matches. The more you know about yourself, the more meaningful your chosen goals will be—and the more motivated you'll be to keep working toward those goals.

More Than Just Hobbies. Your interests matter. If you connect them to your coursework, you'll be more likely to stay motivated even when you encounter challenges. And who knows where your interests could lead you? You might find yourself gravitating toward a career that's not only stimulating but also financially rewarding and personally meaningful. *Left:* Hannamariah/Shutterstock *Right:* Alexander Raths/Shutterstock

Follow Your Interests

Like your values, your interests powerfully influence your goals and motivations. Interests are your preferences for activities, things, people, and places—everything from exercise to animals to cars to music. Why are interests so important? When you define goals that connect with your interests, you're more likely to feel motivated to achieve those goals. For instance, if you're interested in the outdoors, physical activity, and nature, you'll be motivated to complete assignments in courses that incorporate these elements, such as wilderness management and forestry. Finding ways to connect your coursework with your interests—even when the connection isn't obvious—is a great way to stay motivated.

You'll learn more about your interests later in the book, but don't wait until then to start thinking about them. Consider what you like and don't like as you evaluate the courses you're taking, interact with your fellow students, and reflect on your past academic and work experiences. The more you're interested in the work you're doing in school, the more energized you'll feel as you pursue your goals.

Table 1.1 shows examples of how values and interests can connect with goals.

TABLE 1.1 Connecting Values, Interests, and Goals

Sample student	Values	Interests	Possible academic and career goals
Liza	• Supporting my family financially • Continually developing my knowledge and skills	• Writing • Working with people	Take some courses that involve assignments like written reports and group projects. Pursue careers that offer a good starting salary, a clear advancement path, and opportunities to use my writing skills and work on team-based projects.
Theo	• Helping to foster a more inclusive society • Helping people in need	• Taking part in campus activities • Spending time with members of my community	Join volunteer organizations on campus. Learn about career opportunities at organizations that address problems affecting my community, such as poverty, crime, or mental illness.
Ahmed	• Spending time with my family • Being recognized for my accomplishments	• Being outdoors • Working with my hands	Take daytime courses that involve outdoor, hands-on projects (such as taking water samples for an ecology class). Explore careers that let me work reasonable hours while also building a professional reputation (such as publishing articles about field research I conduct).

Courtesy of
Megan Jackson

LEARNING ABOUT YOURSELF

NAME:	**Russell Jackson**
SCHOOL:	*Iowa State University*
MAJOR:	*Psychology*
CAREER GOALS:	*Professor, Counselor*

" I thought critically about myself and found my calling."

I've struggled to find my purpose in life, mainly because I'm terrified of making big decisions. I've been worried that I don't know myself well enough to make the right decision, and I don't want to travel down a road, taking my family with me, if it's not meant for me. I used to go to someone I trusted, listen to *his* suggestion about my future, and run with it.

About a year and a half ago, I ended a career that just didn't fit me. My situation was frustrating and stressful, and I was running out of steam with no idea where to go or what to do. I needed to create some happiness. I realized then that I had never sat down and considered what *I* wanted, what *I* loved, and where *I* wanted to go. I knew I couldn't simply follow everyone else's desires for me anymore. I had to take charge of my destiny and mold it to meet my needs. I had to make changes that would help me prepare for a different career.

For the next year, I worked on finding my purpose in life. I put aside what others thought I should do and focused on my own thoughts, desires, talents, and goals. I thought critically about myself and found my calling. It didn't come all at once, but it did finally develop into a recognizable goal: I want to be a counseling psychologist.

Once my goal was set, everything else fell into place. I enrolled in school, registered for classes, spoke with professors, and found opportunities like volunteering, working in research labs, and helping at the Student Counseling Service. Granted, it's still difficult; I battle most days with thoughts that I can't do it. Sometimes I have to fight off doubts that I made the right decision. However, I'm able to overcome those fears and doubts by remembering that *I know what I want from my life*. My life is bright and fulfilling, simply because I finally found my purpose.

YOUR TURN: Do you have a sense of what your purpose might be? If so, what is it? Does it influence the goals you define for yourself? If you don't yet know your purpose, how might learning more about your values and interests help you find clarity?

Stay Positive, Even When It's Tough

Have you ever heard the song "Happy" by Pharrell Williams? If so, you may know that it's about deciding to be happy, rather than letting negativity bring you down. The song has resonated with many people—not only because it's a catchy tune but also because the lyrics touch on an important concept: the power of positivity. If you maintain a positive attitude, you're more likely to achieve your goals and lead a fulfilling life.

The idea that positivity can lead to success forms the foundation of **positive psychology**, a branch of psychology that focuses on people's strengths rather than on their weaknesses and that views weaknesses as growth opportunities.[8] Positive psychology has become a major influence in educational and workplace settings, and it plays an important part in this book.

The positive psychology movement emphasizes four central concepts: self-efficacy, resilience, hope, and personal responsibility (see Figure 1.1). All four will play a large role in your academic and professional success.

FIGURE 1.1
Four Key Concepts in Positive Psychology

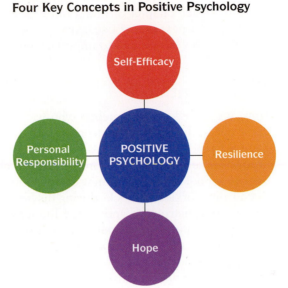

Positive Psychology:
A branch of psychology that focuses on people's strengths rather than on their weaknesses and that views weaknesses as growth opportunities.

Build Self-Efficacy

Self-efficacy is your belief in your ability to do the things required to achieve your goals. Students with a stronger sense of self-efficacy perform better on tasks and persist in those tasks even when things get rough. But not all self-efficacy is created equal. Self-efficacy works best when it's based on a *realistic* assessment of your skills and abilities—and on evidence from your past performance, such as grades and instructor feedback. If your sense of self-efficacy is based more on self-deception than on evidence from your actual experiences, it can be overinflated. That can be dangerous: If you don't live up to your own expectations of yourself, you could experience a painful "reality check." But you also don't want to underestimate your skills and judgment. If you lack confidence in your ability to do something you're actually good at, you probably won't perform your best.

Many students arrive at college with a strong sense of self-efficacy, only to have it shaken by poor grades or unexpected setbacks. For instance, Kathleen went to a small high school, where she easily got straight A's and graduated near the top of her class. She enrolled in a large college and quickly discovered that it was much harder to stand out as an excellent student in such a large population and that the courses were much more challenging than in high school. She got some B's and even a C in her first-term classes and started asking herself, "Can I really succeed in college?"

If you have similar experiences, understand that they can present you with valuable learning opportunities. Use those opportunities to turn setbacks into success. For example, if you do poorly on your first accounting test, don't think of it as a failure; think of it as a starting point for improving your performance. How did you study for the exam? Did you complete all the practice problems at the end of each chapter or find a tutor? If not, would it be worth taking those steps for your next exam? Use learning opportunities like this to develop realistic self-efficacy beliefs and to improve your future performance.

Be Resilient

Have you ever known someone who went through a rough patch in life but came out of the experience stronger and more driven to succeed? Perhaps you have a friend who was devastated when she lost her job but turned things around by getting support from her family, obtaining financial aid, and going back to school to train for a new career. Or maybe you know someone who suffered from workload "shock" during his first college term but got help from his adviser and instructors and ended the term with strong grades and a better approach to time management. Both of these people displayed **resilience**, the ability to cope with stress and setbacks.[9]

Resilience: The ability to cope with stress and setbacks.

College students often face challenges, and between balancing academic work and personal responsibilities, at times you may find yourself stressed out or overwhelmed. During these times, you can demonstrate resilience by getting support and making positive changes. If you receive a D on a biology exam, for example, you can use the experience to improve your study strategies for future exams. Resilience helps you manage challenges, big and small, and stay motivated to achieve your goals.

Resilience in Action. Resilience helps you cope with the stresses you'll experience in your college career and your work and personal life. While the 2013 Boston Marathon bombings were devastating, many spectators and runners who suffered injuries or lost loved ones in the attack developed potent strategies for rebuilding their lives. For some, their resilient response made them stronger than ever. AP Photo/Michael Dwyer

Keep Hope Alive

Hope is the feeling that you can achieve your goals and that events will turn out for the best. Hope is strong when you have realistic self-confidence and a goal that you're motivated to achieve—one that's personally relevant to you. Charles Snyder, a specialist in positive psychology, offers another definition of hope: "the sum of the mental willpower and waypower that you have for your goals."[10] *Willpower* is the mental energy that drives hopeful thinking—the sense that through focus and motivation you can create a positive outcome. Snyder sometimes refers to willpower as *agency*. *Waypower* is having resources and plans—sometimes referred to as *pathways*—to achieve the positive outcome you believe in. For example, suppose you've always wanted to be a veterinarian. You know that getting into a school that awards a doctorate of veterinary medicine is tough—there's a lot of competition for the few schools that offer this degree. You used your willpower to research colleges that offer a pre-veterinary curriculum through a department of animal science, and you applied to several schools and got accepted at one of your top choices. Your waypower enabled you to take this first major step toward the career of your dreams. That waypower includes critical resources like the time and energy you expended to research possible colleges, as well as your ability to learn about and apply for financial support to help pay your college tuition.

According to Snyder, it's not enough to believe that good fortune awaits us. We also need a plan and the skills to make that good fortune become real. In other words, we have to transform our thoughts and intentions into actions, a process that you'll have many opportunities to practice throughout this book. For more on the benefits of hope, see the Spotlight on Research.

Take Personal Responsibility for Your Success

Positive psychology is about personal responsibility—taking charge of defining your goals, creating plans for accomplishing them, and seeking out resources that can help you achieve them. Personal responsibility gives you control: *You* have the power to turn negative results into positive ones by treating disappointments as learning opportunities. After all, most of your instructors aren't going to approach you and say, "I see you got a bad grade on the exam; here's what I think you should do about it." It's up to you to come up with strategies for doing better on the next exam. You'll get a chance to think about this topic more fully later in the book, but for now, just remember: When it comes to your success, *you're* the boss.

"Really, only you can tell yourself to giddyup."

Horse Sense. Why is it so important to take personal responsibility for your success? Because it puts *you* in charge. You don't have to wait for someone else to define your goals, tell you how to reach them, and explain what you can learn from setbacks. You can do it yourself. Personal responsibility: It just makes sense. Bruce Eric Kaplan/ The New Yorker/© Conde Nast

Embrace Your Strengths— and Learn from Your Weaknesses

If someone asked you to describe your strengths, what would you say? Maybe you'd point out that you can negotiate a subway system like a pro, give great advice, or play guitar. You might explain that you're a strong swimmer, you know how to design Web pages, or you can cook meals like a gourmet chef. What about your weaknesses? Would you find it harder to acknowledge that you have poorly developed writing skills or that you're shy around people you don't know? If so, you're not alone: Many people feel far more comfortable talking about where they excel than revealing where they struggle.

But everyone has strengths and weaknesses, and a key to success and happiness is knowing what these are. Armed with this understanding, you can *use*

HOPE PROMOTES ACADEMIC SUCCESS IN COLLEGE

When it comes to success in college, your intelligence and academic ability are only part of the equation. In a study published in the *Journal of Educational Psychology*, researchers demonstrated that *hope* was also an important element of student success.

The researchers followed more than two hundred students from their first year of school through graduation. They measured levels of hope when the students entered college and then examined student grade point averages, college dismissal rates because of poor grades, and graduation rates over the next six years. The researchers discovered the following:

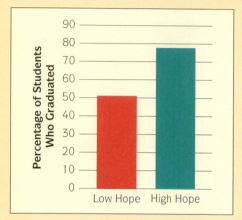

Nearly 80 percent of the students with high hope graduated, while only about half of those with low hope graduated.

- Students with lower levels of hope were dismissed from college at a rate three times higher than were students with high levels of hope.
- Students with high levels of hope graduated at a much higher rate than did those with lower levels of hope.

This research suggests that hopeful students can identify their goals (such as graduating from college) and stay focused on pursuing them. Hope allows you to roll with the punches and achieve the goals that have meaning for you.

THE BOTTOM LINE

Being hopeful can help you focus on the positive and stay motivated to keep working toward your goals.

REFLECTION QUESTIONS

1. **What goals do you look forward to achieving this term? Are they related to your academic performance, your performance at work, or something more personal?**
2. **How hopeful are you about achieving these goals? Rate your hopefulness on a scale from 1 to 10, with 10 being "extremely hopeful" and 1 being "extremely lacking in hope."**
3. **What actions can you take to become hopeful, strengthen your hopefulness, or remain hopeful about achieving your goals?**

C. R. Snyder, H. S. Shorey, J. Cheavens, K. M. Pulvers, V. H. Adams III, and C. Wiklund, "Hope and Academic Success in College," *Journal of Educational Psychology* 94 (2002): 820–26.

your strengths, while also improving areas you find challenging.[11] Using your strengths and working on your weaknesses takes effort. You need those four key ingredients of positive psychology: self-efficacy, resilience, a sense of hope, and a willingness to take personal responsibility.

As you think about building your strengths, consider basketball. Every team has players with different specialties. For example, the point guard has long-range shooting skills, understands the opponent's defenses, and has the best ball-handling skills. The center is typically the tallest and most athletic player on the court and can secure rebounds. The coach makes sure each player uses his or her best skills while also addressing weak areas. Everyone has to practice ball handling, free throws, rebounding, and distance shooting—regardless of whether it comes naturally— because these skills are necessary for the team to succeed.

When it comes to the game of college, you're your own coach. You need to take advantage of your strengths and play to them regularly, but you also need to work on your weak areas. This book, your instructors, and the resources available on campus will help you build winning attitudes and skills. But ultimately, it is your responsibility to put those attitudes and skills into action. By focusing on using your strengths *and* addressing your weaknesses, you'll become as versatile in the classroom as professional athletes are on the court.

Coach Yourself to Success. To succeed in college, you have to play to your strengths while working on your weaknesses. Athletes know this, and their coaches help. So think of yourself as your own success coach in school. Where should you start? Be honest with yourself about what you're good at — and where you need to improve.
© USA Today Sports

Identify Your Strengths and Your Weaknesses: ACES and Other Tools

Before you can use your strengths and address your weaknesses, you need to know what they are. Figuring this out isn't always easy. It requires a healthy dose of self-reflection (and often a reality check) to acknowledge what you do well and where you struggle. It also involves collecting concrete information about yourself, which can come from the following sources:

- **The Academic and Career Excellence System (ACES).** Did you know that with this book you likely got access to an online self-assessment that will help you understand yourself better? It's called ACES (which stands for Academic and Career Excellence System). Have you taken ACES already? If not, you probably will soon. ACES helps you identify your strengths and weaknesses and use that information to establish goals. You'll revisit different ACES scores at the beginning of each chapter in the rest of this book and reflect on how you might better use a strength or improve a weak area. By engaging in such reflection, you can read each chapter with a better understanding of what you want to accomplish.

You're Only Human. It's more fun listing your strengths than writing down your weaknesses. But to succeed in college, you have to know both sides of yourself. What's your best strength? Your most frustrating weakness? Be honest! somchai rakin/Shutterstock

- **Past successes and failures.** Reflecting on your past successes and failures can provide a wealth of useful information. For example, can you recall a time when you were well prepared for an exam and another time when you weren't? How did your grades reflect your preparedness? What lessons can you gain from these contrasting experiences? How can you apply those lessons so that you do better on future exams?

- **Class experiences.** Think about your current classes. Are some more difficult for you than others? What do you think makes them harder for you? Reflecting on where you struggle can help you identify which skills you need to strengthen.

- **End-of-chapter activities.** The activities at the end of each chapter often require you to consider how the chapter material relates to your strengths and weaknesses. You'll also have further opportunities to practice developing your skills.

Once you've consulted these sources, then what? Learning about your strengths and weaknesses is great, but this information is useless if you don't use it to create positive change. That's what this book and this class are for: to help you achieve the necessary changes. In each chapter, you'll work on developing a new skill—such as setting goals, managing your time, reading a wide range of course materials, taking notes, and studying for exams. As you build these skills in this class, you can use them to succeed in your other classes, too. Why? Because as we pointed out earlier, all your learning is connected.

CONNECT TO MY RESOURCES

When things get tough in school, at work, or in your personal life, who's there to support you? Write a thank-you note to one special person, letting that person know why he or she is such a great support to you.

Recruit Help

There are many ways to build skills on your own, but you don't have to "fly solo" in this effort: You can recruit a team of supporters to help you when you struggle. According to a growing body of research, seeking help can *increase* your level of success.[12] Also, getting help is a form of taking personal responsibility: When you identify what challenges you face, what resources exist, and how to use them, you take charge of your own success.

Help is everywhere, once you know what's available and where to look for it (see Figure 1.2). Off campus, you can find help from family members, friends, and community resources. On campus, you can find help from instructors, classmates, advisers, and support services like the math lab, writing center, and career center. To take advantage of the support resources around you, follow these three steps:

1. **Know what resources exist.** You can choose from countless resources, so find out which ones are available to you. If you're not sure which resources exist at your school or in the surrounding community, seek help from your instructor, an adviser or a counselor, or the campus Web site.

2. **Know which resources you need.** Think about which resources you need in a particular situation. If you're struggling in English class, for example, you won't get much help from the financial aid office. If you don't know which resources to seek out, ask your instructor or an academic adviser. They're skilled student-success specialists and will point you in the right direction.

3. **Use available resources.** Once you know which resource is appropriate for a particular need, take action. For example, find out how best to contact the tutoring center (do you need to make an appointment, or can you just walk in?); then do it. If you don't know how to approach campus resources, ask your instructor or adviser for advice, or search your school's Web site for information. Table 1.2 provides examples of questions you can ask to get help from several key sources.

FIGURE 1.2   **Examples of Supports**

TABLE 1.2   Sample Questions You Might Ask When Visiting Support Services on Campus

Advising center	May I please meet with an adviser? I have some questions about scheduling my classes for next term.
	I'd like to find classes that will help me decide on my major. Can you help with that?
	I want to declare a major in psychology, but my adviser is in the English department. Can she still be my adviser?
	I'm having difficulty in my algebra class. Can you suggest where I can get some help?
Financial aid office	I missed the deadline for applying for aid this year. What are my options for paying for classes this term?
	I need to work while I'm in school. Are there any opportunities to work on campus?
	I don't want to take on too much debt. Can you help me create a plan for managing my finances?
	What scholarships are available in my field of study?
Instructors	I'm really struggling in this class. Can you recommend some additional reading materials or support services that can help me?
	Do you know of an advanced student who might be interested in helping me understand this material?
	I'm very interested in what we're covering in this class, and I'm thinking about majoring in this area. Can you give me the name of someone I can discuss this with?

College Success Leads to Career Success

In this chapter we've talked a lot about connections—between self-knowledge and your success, between a positive attitude and meeting your goals, and between embracing your strengths and weaknesses and growing as a learner. But another type of connection is equally important to your future: the connection between college and career. The skills, attitudes, and behaviors you're developing in class will be just as valuable in the working world. It's the ultimate two-for-one deal: When you invest in your education, you also succeed at work.

Transferable Skills:
Skills that can be applied in many different settings, such as work, home, and school.

Take critical thinking. Not only is it important to your academic success and your self-knowledge, but it's also something employers look for in potential hires.[13] Critical thinking is known as a **transferable skill** because it's useful in many different settings—not just school. Attitudes and behaviors—including motivation, resilience, personal responsibility, and self-efficacy beliefs—can also be transferable. According to surveys, many of the skills you're building in college and in this class are valued by employers—including communicating, working in teams, making decisions, and staying organized.[14]

We'll discuss transferable skills in more detail throughout this book, and you'll see how the skills you develop in school will serve you well in your chosen profession. To get you started, Table 1.3 shows how specific skills might transfer from one environment to another. Whether you're sure of your career path now or are still considering your options, building skills like these will help you succeed in your career—whatever it turns out to be.

TABLE 1.3   **Examples of How College Success Skills Transfer to Work Settings**

Skill	Application at school	Application at work
Goal setting	Decide to meet with your instructor during office hours at least once a week	Decide to improve your on-time arrival at weekly staff meetings
Communication	Deliver a well-researched presentation to your history class	Deliver a presentation explaining employee health benefits to your team
Critical thinking	Gather facts supporting the argument in your essay	Review a patient's medical data to determine how a new medication would interact with his current medications
Personal responsibility	Recognize that your low test score may have resulted from not studying enough	Take responsibility for submitting a report too late, and develop strategies to better manage your time
Teamwork	Complete a small-group experiment in your biology lab	Work with representatives from other branch offices to prepare a regional sales report
Listening	Pay attention to your instructor's comments and classmates' questions	Consider the concerns expressed by a high school student's parents about courses you've recommended for her senior year

PERSONAL RESPONSIBILITY
IN THE WORKPLACE

NAME:	**Chris Cline**
PROFESSION:	*Creative Services Director*
SCHOOL:	*Modesto Junior College*
DEGREE:	*Associate of Arts*
MAJOR:	*Graphic Communications*

Courtesy of
Christopher A.
Cline

In my job as Creative Services Director for a local newspaper publishing group, I oversee the graphics production for our printed publications and manage our newspaper's Internet presence. The newspaper industry is facing tremendous upheaval right now, with shrinking revenue from ads and competition from free content online. There's a lot of pressure to adapt, particularly on the digital side of the industry.

I've had to face these same challenges in my career, needing to continually develop technology skills for a changing workplace. I've always been confident in my computer skills, but I didn't know much about building Web sites when I graduated, as most of my educational training was print-based. I needed to build up those digital skills to succeed in the evolving newspaper business.

It took several months of self-directed learning on the job, but eventually I reached my goal: I created our newspaper's Web site without hiring an outside consulting firm. Not only did this save our company a substantial amount of money; it also helped me to further my own career. Now, as the newspaper industry continues to change, I feel confident that I'm prepared to adapt.

YOUR TURN: If you have a job now or have had one in the past, did you take personal responsibility for using your strengths and addressing your weaknesses? If so, how? What happened as a result?

> " As the newspaper industry continues to change, I feel confident that I'm prepared to adapt."

CHAPTER SUMMARY

In this chapter you learned about the book's key themes: the importance of college, self-awareness, thinking positively, and recognizing your own strengths and weaknesses. You also saw how these themes connect to one other and to your college and career success. Revisit the following points and reflect on how this information can support your success now and in the future.

- College is important. You're at the right place at the right time. By getting your degree or certificate, you'll have more career options, earn more money, and be more likely to get involved in your community.

- Critical thinking involves considering information in a thoughtful way, understanding how to think logically and rationally, and applying those methods of thinking in your classes and your life.

- Thinking critically will help you succeed academically, as you analyze information, respond to questions on exams, and write papers.

- Personal reflection is a type of critical thinking. By reflecting on your values and interests, you can use the resulting self-knowledge to set goals that are personally meaningful, and you can stay motivated to achieve them.

- According to positive psychology, when things don't go your way, you can maintain a positive attitude by reframing negative results as opportunities for improvement. Four key ingredients of positive psychology are self-efficacy, resilience, a sense of hope, and a willingness to take personal responsibility.

- You're your own success coach — it's up to you to identify the skills you have and those you need to develop. Use every opportunity to play to your strengths while also addressing your weaknesses.

- Many resources are available to help you meet your goals. You can seek help from family, friends, instructors, and support services on campus and in your community.

- There's more to college than learning class material. You'll also develop transferable skills and attitudes that you can apply in whatever career you choose. Succeeding at school is directly connected to succeeding in your work life.

CHAPTER ACTIVITIES

Journal Entry

ESTABLISHING AN ACADEMIC PURPOSE

The perfect way to begin your college journey is to reflect on why you're here and what you hope to accomplish. Having a purpose will help you set meaningful goals, overcome obstacles, stay motivated, and make changes if needed. Write a journal entry answering the following questions:

- What are your reasons for attending college?
- What made you select this particular college?
- What skills, personal characteristics, relationships, and experiences would you like to develop during your time here?
- How will developing those skills, characteristics, relationships, and experiences help you succeed in college? How will they help you succeed in your career? How will they help you lead a more satisfying personal life?

Adopting a Success Attitude

COACHING YOURSELF TO MOTIVATION

One aspect of personal responsibility is self-motivation. How can you motivate yourself to keep working toward your goals if you're discouraged or overwhelmed? This chapter has a great suggestion: Be your own success coach. A coach is a source of moral support and inspiration when the going gets tough. To be your own success coach, identify a *mantra*: a quotation, saying, or poem that you find meaningful and that can inspire you when you encounter challenges this year. Why did you select this particular mantra? Where will you place it so it's easily visible or accessible? How will you use it to stay motivated?

Applying Your Skills

ENGAGING PERSONAL SUPPORTS AND RESOURCES

Successful people know when to ask for help or use resources to accomplish their goals, and they're not ashamed to seek support. In college, people across campus — advisers, career counselors, tutors — are employed specifically to help you. Find out who they are and what forms of support they can offer. Resist any temptation to think that asking for help reflects negatively on you. Remind yourself that successful students and employees surround themselves with personal supports to keep them motivated and to help them improve and succeed. In this exercise you'll learn more about available resources — both in your personal life and on campus.

Personal Supports

1. On a separate sheet of paper, list three people in your life you interact with regularly. (They can be friends, roommates, parents, siblings, a significant other, children, bosses, coworkers, and so forth.)
2. Next to each name, identify three to five ways this person could support you in your quest to be a successful student. For instance, "My roommate could allow me quiet time to study," "My mom could call me once a day, not three or four times a day, to see how I'm doing," or "My older sister could share the study strategies that she used during her time in college."
3. After you graduate, will any of these people remain personal supports for you as you launch a new or different career? If so, how might they support you in the future? If not, who else could support you, and how?

Campus Resources

1. Visit your college's Web site.
2. Search the Web site and identify five available resources that could help you succeed in school or plan your career.
3. Write down the name of each resource. Describe how you think it could help you, where it's located, and contact information.

College Success = Career Success

IDENTIFYING AND EMBRACING YOUR STRENGTHS

Acknowledging the strengths you bring to college will lay the foundation for your success. These strengths will serve as a source of self-esteem, help you accomplish your academic goals, and provide you with ideas for career paths that might interest you. Moreover, knowing your strengths will help you write a résumé, interview effectively for jobs, and advance your career. Identify the strengths (skills, talents, and personal qualities) you already possess, and write them in the blank spaces below. Then describe how they will help you succeed in school and at work.

Hint: If you need help, search for examples of strengths on the Internet, or ask family, friends, and coworkers what they see as your strengths.

PART 1:

Skills: abilities you have become good at through practice (such as handling customer complaints or computer programming)

_____   _____   _____

Talents: abilities that come easily or naturally for you (like drawing, math, or writing poetry)

_____   _____   _____

Personal Qualities: adjectives describing your attitude, work style, work ethic, or ways of interacting with others (for instance, optimistic, friendly, and hardworking)

_____   _____   _____

PART 2:

How will the strengths you identified in Part 1 help you succeed in college?

_____

_____

How will these strengths help you succeed in your career?

_____

_____

2 Thinking Critically and Setting Goals

Build Your Critical Thinking Skills

Use Bloom's Taxonomy

Think Critically to Set Goals

Create Your Personal Success Plan

Critical Thinking and Goal Setting in Your Career

Everyone thinks, but not everyone thinks critically — that is, in a careful, unbiased way. Take Christopher, a first-year student majoring in criminology who wants to become a forensic crime-scene investigator. He's watched a lot of crime shows and visited several Web sites related to crime-scene investigation, so he's sure he's found the perfect path for him. He believes that majoring in criminology will prepare him for his dream job and that after he graduates, he'll easily find work in his chosen field. He also expects that he'll work in exciting locations, interact regularly with police and witnesses, and make lots of money.

But if Christopher thought critically about his choices, he would realize that his assumptions were off base. For one thing, many forensic specialists start out as forensic science technicians and major in chemistry or biology — not in criminology. Moreover, technicians often work in laboratory environments and interact mostly with other scientists and technicians — not with police and witnesses. Starting salaries for technicians are modest, often less than $45,000 a year. Finally, according to the U.S. Department of Labor, job growth for forensic specialists is slower than the national average for all occupations.[1]

These facts don't mean that Christopher shouldn't pursue his interests — he may do so and have a successful, rewarding career. But he *does* need to think critically about his goals and expectations using accurate information — not TV shows. Critical thinking will help him make informed decisions based on solid facts and analysis.

In fact, critical thinking is a fundamental element of success in college and the workplace, and that's why we highlight it in this chapter and address it throughout the rest of this book. Critical thinking helps you learn new course content so that you can succeed academically. It also helps you learn about yourself so that you can set meaningful personal goals. In addition, it helps you keep learning and growing as an employee and sets you up for workplace success: Most employers highly value strong critical thinking skills.

In this chapter you'll explore how critical thinking influences your learning (spoiler alert: it helps you learn more deeply) and how it helps you set goals. You'll also try out the Personal Success Plan, a tool you can use to map out your goals and build a plan for achieving them. Finally, you'll discover how necessary critical thinking is in whichever career you decide to pursue.

© Mike Theiss/National Geographic Creative

Reflect

On Your Critical Thinking and Goal Setting

Self-knowledge gives you the power to make positive change. That's why you're using the Academic and Career Excellence System (ACES): to learn more about your strengths and areas where you could improve. By knowing what you're good at, you can use those skills to master course content and build other skills. By acknowledging your weaknesses, you can target areas for improvement.

At the beginning of most chapters in this book, you'll review your score on the related section of ACES. Then you can use that information to focus on the chapter content that will best help you become a stronger student.

Let's start: Retrieve your Critical Thinking and Goal Setting score on ACES, and add it in the circle to the right. This score measures your beliefs about how well you think critically and set goals. How do you feel about your score? Do you think it accurately reflects your skills? No matter what your score is, you can use the results to become a more effective critical thinker and goal setter. Here's how to *act* on what you've learned about yourself.

■ **IF YOU SCORED IN THE HIGH RANGE** on ACES, strengthen your strengths. Take pride in your results, but remember that even if you're good at something, you can always build up that skill even more. A swimmer might win first place at a swim meet, but she'll be back at practice the next morning to improve her time and refine her stroke. That way, she can keep working toward her goal of competing against more advanced swimmers. As you read this chapter, use what you learn about your strengths to build them up even more — so you can further expand your learning in every course.

■ **IF YOU SCORED IN THE MODERATE OR LOW RANGE** on ACES, don't worry; instead, target ways to improve. You'll have many opportunities to build your skills in this chapter and throughout the term. Can you think of an activity that you found difficult the first time you tried it but that you got better at with practice? The same is true here: Many people don't have well-developed critical thinking and goal-setting skills at first, but they get better at these skills with practice. This chapter shows you how.

MY ACES SCORE

☐ **HIGH**

☐ **MODERATE**

☐ **LOW**

LaunchPad

To find your **Critical Thinking and Goal Setting score,** go to the LaunchPad for *Connections*.

Build Your Critical Thinking Skills

Critical Thinking:
The ability to consider information in a thoughtful way, understand how to think logically and rationally, and apply those methods of thinking in your classes and your life.

As noted in the chapter on building a foundation for success, **critical thinking** is the ability to consider information in a thoughtful way, understand how to think logically and rationally, and apply those methods of thinking in your classes and your life.[2] You use critical thinking in all kinds of situations: For instance, when you're making the tough decision of figuring out how many college loans you should apply for. You also use it to assess whether information—such as a candidate's political position, an article you've read online, or claims made in a product advertisement—makes sense or is trustworthy.

In this section we'll look at key elements of critical thinking, including the skills involved and tips for mastering those skills.

The Higher-Level Thinking Skills behind Critical Thinking

Critical thinking is made up of a collection of skills that help you assess information, answer questions, and make decisions. These skills are also known as *higher-level thinking skills* because they require you to think in sophisticated ways, such as evaluating and synthesizing information. Yet all higher-level thinking is based on lower-level thinking skills, such as remembering facts, dates, and definitions or describing an object or idea. One way to think of lower- and higher-level thinking is to consider the six questions journalists typically ask: *Who?*, *What?*, *Where?*, and *When?* are lower-level questions because they focus on basic facts and information, while *How?* and *Why?* are higher-level questions because they require you to connect and work with those basic facts.

Table 2.1 shows a few examples of higher-level thinking skills. As you read through the rest of this chapter and the book, you'll use these and other critical thinking skills to make smart decisions about your coursework, life, and career.

Truth or Myth? When you think critically, you assess whether information is trustworthy: Does it make sense? Does it come from a credible, unbiased source? Critical thinking helps you avoid the mistake of blindly accepting whatever you see, hear, or read. So it saves you from reacting to information in a knee-jerk way — like driving for days to see a supposed UFO crash site.
AP Photo/Eric Draper

TABLE 2.1   Examples of Higher-Level Thinking Skills

Skill	Definition	Examples
Comparing and contrasting	Identifying similarities and differences between two or more concepts	• To prepare for a sociology exam, you identify similarities and differences between Marxism and socialism. • You want a new smartphone, so you compare and contrast data plans and other terms offered by several vendors to see which vendor offers the best deal.
Deducing	Arriving at a conclusion using reason and logic	• You notice that all your friends who take time to study for exams get better grades than those who don't study. You deduce that you can improve your grades if you study more. • Someone you've dated several times has stopped responding to your texts and avoids looking at you in class. You conclude that this person has lost interest in spending time with you.
Synthesizing	Combining facts into a larger understanding of a concept	• In your computer programming class, you learn that different techniques for finding and fixing software bugs all have limitations. You figure out a way to combine several techniques to compensate for their various limitations so that you can find and fix more bugs. • As a marketing assistant, you review and synthesize comments from a focus group assembled to examine a new product. Participants' comments suggest that the product name is intriguing but that it doesn't communicate the product's key benefits clearly.
Evaluating	Judging the authenticity or soundness of an argument	• For a journalism class assignment, you read an article arguing against vaccinating children and adults against influenza (the flu) because the vaccine can have side effects and doesn't guarantee immunity. You judge the argument weak because the author doesn't address the fact that vaccination significantly lowers hospitalization rates for the flu.[3] • Your boss says you can't have a raise because the company is having financial troubles. After evaluating the situation, you question this explanation because the company is hiring new employees.
Prioritizing	Determining the order of importance of tasks	• To complete a term paper on the American Revolution, you list all the tasks involved (such as reading source materials, preparing an outline, and writing and revising the paper). You decide that the most important tasks are those that all the others depend on, such as reading sources, and those that will take the most time, such as preparing an outline. • Your manager has just given you several new responsibilities. You prioritize those that directly support an important goal your manager has set for the team: increasing sales.

How to Use Your Higher-Level Thinking Skills

Now that you have a sense of the types of higher-level thinking skills involved in critical thinking, let's explore how to *use* them. The next time you have a decision to make, a question to answer, or an argument to consider, follow these guidelines to reach careful conclusions.

Gather and Evaluate Information. To think critically, you need information. The kind of information you need depends on what you're trying to accomplish. If you want to choose a major, you'll need information about your interests, values, strengths, and possible career goals. If you're writing a term paper, you'll need information found in books, your class notes, or readings on reserve in the library.

Having good information can steer you in the right direction and help you avoid mistakes. Imagine you're a doctor treating a sick patient. If you diagnose the person's medical problem using information that isn't accurate, you could end up treating him for, say, an earache when he really has the flu. That's why you have to *evaluate* how reliable your information is. If a source is questionable or hard to assess—maybe you overheard something from a friend's cousin's dog walker—you'll need another source to back up the claims before you can trust the information. Remember Christopher? His sources—TV shows and Web sites—left out important facts and even distorted information, so they weren't very reliable. Better sources lead to better choices.

Keep an Open Mind. Critical thinking involves keeping an open mind. To do this, be open to new possibilities presented by information you gather. Think about old information in new ways, and consider information from different angles. For example, if Christopher approaches his career decision with an open mind, he might identify possibilities other than crime-scene investigation that interest him and provide the benefits he's looking for.

Strange Idea? Or Strangely Brilliant? Critical thinkers see new possibilities in the information they gather. For instance, who'd ever get the strange idea that old shipping containers could serve as student housing? Architects in France did. They created this student-housing complex by stacking one hundred recycled containers, with each one serving as a different student's room. Not so strange after all. © Robert Kluba/VISUM/The Image Works

Apply What You've Learned. To be an expert critical thinker, you need to *do* something with the information you have—either disregard it because it didn't pass your evaluation, or apply it in your life and work. For instance, use new knowledge about your strengths to set a goal for yourself, or use information you gained in a class to complete an assignment correctly.

Another way to apply information is to connect something you learned in the past to what you're learning now. What do you already know about mathematics that you can use to learn college algebra? If you've worked on a construction crew, how can you apply knowledge gained from that experience in your architectural design class?

Review Your Outcomes. Reflection is part of critical thinking, so make time to review the outcomes of your decisions and actions. Ask yourself whether your decisions and actions are built on strong critical thinking— or whether you need to improve your thinking process. For example, if your instructors have been skeptical about arguments you've made in several writing assignments, consider whether you need to improve your ability to evaluate your sources' reliability. View such experiences as opportunities for positive change, and get help if you need it to strengthen your critical thinking skills.

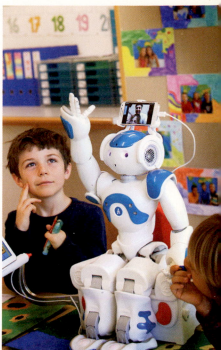

Critically Cool Creations. Critical thinking can spark critically cool inventions. Take Nao, the robot that can stand in for a sick child in the classroom during the child's hospital stays. From the hospital the child uses a tablet computer to control the robot and follow along with the lessons. Here a boy tests this use of the Nao robot, drawing on his own critical thinking skills to evaluate the robot's abilities. © Amelie-Benoist/BSIP/ Science Photo Library

Use Bloom's Taxonomy

Now that you've read about the basics of critical thinking, let's explore how you can apply these skills to learning—which is, after all, your core reason for being in college. Just as there are different levels of *thinking*, there are different levels of *learning*—and some of them require more critical thinking skills than others.

To get a sense of how the different learning levels work together, think about your experiences in school over the years. When you were in elementary school, you focused mostly on the fundamentals, such as learning how to spell, do simple arithmetic, and remember facts (like names and dates for historical events). But you may not have thought deeply about what you were learning. For example, you probably knew that Christopher Columbus sailed the ocean blue from Europe to the Americas in 1492, but you may not have pondered why he made the trip or what impact his arrival had on the peoples already living in the Americas.

As you've progressed in your education, though, you've used critical thinking skills more and more. You've likely learned that some questions have more than one right answer and that there can be multiple opinions on a topic. For instance, you and others may have come up with different answers to the question of whether Columbus's arrival in the Americas benefited the people already living there. To deal with such ambiguities, you used critical thinking skills (maybe without even knowing it) to compare, contrast, and evaluate information. Now that you're in college, these sophisticated, higher-level thinking skills are more important than ever.[4]

FIGURE 2.1   **Bloom's Taxonomy**

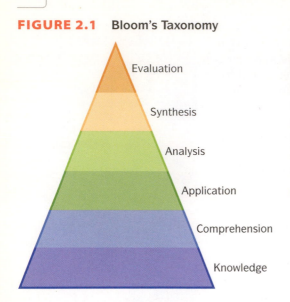

To better understand how learning moves from a simple to a more complex form, consider the work of educational psychologist Benjamin Bloom.[5] Bloom's taxonomy (Figure 2.1) shows how critical thinking relates to different levels of learning. The lowest level represents learning in its simplest form. At the higher levels, learning becomes more complex—and that's when you really start needing critical thinking skills. Not everything you learn in college will involve these higher levels of learning, but much of it will. Let's explore each level in more detail.

- **Knowledge.** Knowledge is the most basic level of learning. When you learn a set of facts and recall them on a test, you demonstrate knowledge. Perhaps you know that the American Revolution ended in 1783 or that the Cuban missile crisis happened in 1962. Think of these facts as forming a foundation you can build on to better understand a topic.

- **Comprehension.** At this level, you can restate facts in your own words, compare them to each other, organize them into meaningful groups, and state main ideas. For example, in your communications class, you may learn two facts: Facebook was launched in 2004, and the current CEO is Mark Zuckerberg. You might categorize Facebook as a type of social media platform, a group that also includes Twitter, LinkedIn, Instagram, and Flickr. You might further organize these platforms into groups that focus on sharing pictures and those that don't.

- **Application.** At this level, you use knowledge and your comprehension of it to solve new problems. For example, if you need to hire a new employee, you might read articles about how to attract top candidates and then use the information to conduct your search and to evaluate applicants for the job. In this way, you apply what you read to a real-life challenge.

  In some college majors, including business, economics, the sciences, health care, and engineering, you're expected not only to understand a topic but also to apply your understanding to real problems. In a science class, for example, you may learn how various metals react when subjected to high heat. Later, when asked to identify a mystery metal in science lab, you might heat the metal to test whether it behaves more like magnesium, aluminum, or nickel.

- **Analysis.** At this level of learning, you approach a topic by breaking it down into meaningful parts and learning how those parts relate to one another. You may identify stated and unstated assumptions, examine the reliability of information, and distinguish between facts and educated guesses or opinions.

  You'll be expected to use this level of learning frequently in college. For essay exams, group projects, debates, and term papers, you'll formulate arguments based on data. In a modern history course, for example, you may analyze how conflict in the Middle East influenced the foreign and domestic policies of President George W. Bush.

- **Synthesis.** When you synthesize, you make connections between seemingly unrelated or previously unknown facts to understand a topic. As you weave new information into your existing understanding of a topic, you'll understand that topic in new and more sophisticated ways. You can think of synthesis as advanced analysis.

  Here's an example of synthesis: To develop a research question for a psychology class, you review research findings on altruism (doing good things for others). You learn that people are less likely to help others when they don't feel a personal sense of responsibility or when there are many other people around who could also help. You use this information to propose a new study on the likelihood that students in the college cafeteria would help a person who slipped and spilled her tray.

- **Evaluation.** At this highest level of learning, you develop arguments and opinions based on a thorough understanding of a topic and a careful review of the available evidence. For instance, an essay question might ask you to establish a position for or against the current U.S. strategy to combat global terrorism. Evaluation is the "expert" level of learning—a level you'll want to achieve in college, especially in your chosen major. After all, would you want to cross a bridge built by an engineer who hadn't reached the expert level of engineering? We wouldn't either.

Your college instructors want you to remember facts (knowledge) and understand concepts (comprehension). But they will also encourage you to apply, analyze, synthesize, and evaluate information on tests, papers, and projects—in other words, to think critically. This book will help you practice learning at each of the six levels. For instance, later chapters provide tips on how to remember information, read textbooks strategically, take good notes, and study for exams, among other things. For now, review Table 2.2 to see examples of test questions associated with each level of learning.

CONNECT TO MY CLASSES

Select two questions from a textbook reading or homework assignment you completed in another class this term. If possible, choose questions for which you've received feedback. Carefully examine each question and identify which level of learning in Bloom's taxonomy it falls under.

TABLE 2.2 Sample Test Questions Based on Bloom's Taxonomy

Level in Bloom's taxonomy	Sample key words in test questions for this level	Sample test questions
Knowledge	who what where when choose list label match	• In what year did the Battle of Gettysburg take place? • List the two dominant models of nursing care.
Comprehension	compare contrast rephrase summarize classify describe show	• Classify the following molecules based on their state (gas, liquid, or solid) at room temperature. • Describe the safety steps to be followed during arc welding.
Application	apply organize plan develop model solve	• Apply your knowledge of chemical compounds to identify the unknown white solid in your tray. • Use health education principles to develop a curriculum for middle school students.
Analysis	analyze categorize examine theme relationships assumptions conclusions	• Drawing on your understanding of *Beowulf* and *King Lear*, examine how the theme of heroism is treated in these two works. • Pick two criminal justice policy theories described in your book. Explain the assumptions each theory makes about the relationship between U.S. crime rates and the health of the nation's economy.
Synthesis	synthesize propose predict combine adapt test discuss	• Using your understanding of motivation theory, propose a program that will help high school dropouts return to school. • Predict how U.S. fiscal policy might change if unemployment dropped below 5 percent and inflation increased.
Evaluation	critique judge prove disprove opinion	• Based on your review of the evidence presented during the mock trial and your understanding of U.S. law, critique the defense's argument. • Now that you've completed your reading for the term and conducted research in the community, give your opinion about the value of the arts in education.

Learning on All Levels. Even though evaluation represents the highest level of learning in Bloom's taxonomy, your college instructors will want you to be able to operate effectively at each of the six levels. If you master all six levels, you'll get maximum value from your courses.
Ammentorp Photography/ Shutterstock

Think Critically to Set Goals

A **goal** is an outcome you hope to achieve that guides and sustains your effort over time. When you set goals, you think critically about yourself and the information you gather, using many of the skills you've just read about. Thus goal setting represents critical thinking in action. For instance, to set a goal, you evaluate your options. And as you work toward a goal, you analyze your progress and any obstacles facing you so that you can develop strategies for overcoming the obstacles.

The goals you set provide a roadmap for your success—in college and in your personal and professional life. For instance, to achieve your longer-term goal of entering a particular profession, you need to meet another longer-term goal: graduating from college. And to graduate, you need to achieve shorter-term goals like passing required courses. Accomplishing these goals requires you to reach other shorter-term goals, such as completing assignments and class projects. So knowing how to use critical thinking to set and achieve your goals is vital. In this book you'll have the opportunity to set many goals—many of them short-term ones that will support your longer-term goals.

Setting any goal involves a five-step process (see Figure 2.2), and each step requires you to apply critical thinking skills. Let's take a closer look at how the process works.

Goal: An outcome you hope to achieve that guides and sustains your effort over time.

FIGURE 2.2 The Steps of Goal Setting

1
Gather Information

2
Set a SMART Goal

3
Make an Action Plan

4
List Barriers and Solutions

5
Act and Evaluate Outcomes

Step 1: Gather Information (about *You*)

The first step of goal setting isn't actually *stating* your goal. Rather, it's gathering information about yourself (like what you want to achieve and what your strengths are) so that you can define goals that are realistic and meaningful for you.

You can start by gathering information about your strengths and weaknesses. Review your ACES results and reflect on the classes you find challenging, the grades you've received, and past experiences you've had. Then consider whether you want your goal to focus on addressing a weakness or strengthening something you're already good at. For instance, if you're a chronic procrastinator, you may want to set a goal of improving your time-management skills. If you're a masterful note-taker, you might want to set a goal of becoming a tutor, since teaching a skill to others often makes you even better at it yourself.

Step 2: Set a SMART Goal

SMART Goal: A goal that is specific, measurable, achievable, relevant to you personally, and time-limited.

Once you've gathered information about yourself, the next step is to set a goal that expresses what you want to achieve. Express it as a **SMART goal**—one that is *specific*, *measurable*, *achievable*, *relevant to you personally*, and *time-limited*. Avoid stating your goal in vague terms, such as "I'm going to study more" or "I want to get good grades." Such goals are weak, because you'll have a hard time knowing whether you've achieved them. (For instance, what does "to study more" actually mean?) By contrast, the SMART approach helps you create strong goals that you can realistically achieve by taking concrete steps to achieve them (see Table 2.3).

♦ CONNECT TO MY EXPERIENCE

Think about a personal, professional, or academic goal you set but never achieved. Write down elements from the SMART goal system that might have helped you achieve your goal, and explain why they would have been useful.

Specific. When you express a goal in specific terms, you know exactly what you're trying to achieve. Contrast the specific goal "Get a GPA of 3.0 or higher this term" with the vague goal "Get good grades." The vague goal doesn't say what qualifies as a good grade (an A? a B+?), so you don't have a clear idea of what you're working toward.

TABLE 2.3   **Weak Goals versus SMART Goals**

Weak goal	SMART goal
Get good grades in class	Get a B or better in my algebra class this term
Spend more time studying for biology	Study my biology class notes and textbook at least five hours each week this term
Make some new friends	Attend a meeting of at least two on-campus clubs or organizations in the next month
Get some help writing my term paper	Meet with a tutor at the writing center each week for the next three weeks

Measurable. When a goal is measurable, you know when you've reached it. For instance, it's easy to determine if you've earned a GPA of 3.0 or higher by the end of the term. Your school calculates your GPA, so one quick look at your grades for the term tells you whether you've met your goal.

Achievable. Nothing is more frustrating than establishing a goal that's beyond your reach. What is and isn't achievable differs from person to person. For example, if you're working full time and raising two kids while attending college, setting a goal that involves taking five classes and studying four hours a day probably isn't achievable. On the other hand, taking one or two classes and studying one and a half hours a day on weekdays and two hours a day on weekends may be a more reasonable goal.

If you have doubts about whether a goal is achievable, consider revising your goal to increase the chances you'll reach it. Then, once you succeed, you can set the bar higher for yourself. The key is to set goals that are challenging enough to inspire you but not *so* challenging that you can't reach them.

The Achievability Advantage. Defining a goal? Make sure it's achievable — for you. When this chocolatier was in culinary school, he probably didn't set out to create a dragon of this size and complexity. Instead, he first aimed to master the basics of working with chocolate. So as you're defining goals, remember this helpful saying: "Don't bite off more than you can chew." AP Photo/Jens Meyer

Relevant to You. When you set goals that matter to you personally (for example, they reflect your values, interests, and career plans), you'll be more motivated to achieve them. So if you enjoy learning about science and want to become a pharmacist, it will be easier for you to reach a goal of studying chemistry three additional hours a week. And if you plan on a career in the food services industry and believe that hunger is a pressing social problem, volunteering once a week at a food pantry would be relevant to you.

Time-Limited. SMART goals include deadlines by which you aim to achieve the goals (such as earning a GPA of 3.0 or higher by the end of the term). Take care in setting deadlines. If the deadline is too far in the future, you may procrastinate on working toward the goal. But if you set a deadline that's too soon, the goal may start to seem unachievable, and you might feel too overwhelmed and discouraged to tackle it. Setting a time limit for achieving a goal helps you assess whether you've actually accomplished what you intended.

Step 3: Make an Action Plan

To achieve your goals, you need an **action plan**, a list of the steps you'll take to accomplish a goal and the order in which you'll take them. Think of your action plan as a to-do list for achieving your goal.

❞ CONNECT TO MY CAREER

Imagine that you've just accepted a job offer for a position in your chosen field or a field that you're considering. Write down the name of the position and create a career goal for yourself, using the SMART criteria.

Action Plan: A list of steps you'll take to accomplish a goal and the order in which you'll take them.

Write Down Your Actions. The first step in developing a good action plan is to write down the actions you'll take to achieve your goal. You might be tempted to make a mental list of these actions, but writing them down is a *much* better idea. In a recent study at Dominican University, participants who didn't write down their goals and plans achieved only 43 percent of their goals, whereas those who wrote them down achieved more than 76 percent of their goals.[6] Don't worry about making the list perfect or recording the steps in a particular order—just write them down as they pop into your mind. For example, if your SMART goal is to submit your English term paper on the day it's due, you might brainstorm a list of action steps like this:

Action Steps
• Submit final term paper by due date
• Prepare rough draft of term paper
• Submit rough draft to writing tutor
• Buy a dictionary
• Schedule appointment with writing tutor
• Incorporate feedback from writing tutor into final version

Prioritize Your Action Steps. Once you've brainstormed action steps and written them down, determine which steps are critical and which aren't. (Noncritical steps are those that, if ignored, wouldn't jeopardize your goal.) In this example, you might decide that buying a dictionary isn't a top priority—after all, there's one on your computer—so you cross that off the list. The items that remain should be those that are most important.

Put Your Steps in Order and Set Deadlines for Them. Once you've eliminated noncritical steps from your list, arrange the remaining steps in the order in which you'll complete them. For example, if you need feedback from the writing center before editing your paper, put a visit to the writing center higher on your list. Also, add a deadline for each step so you can track your progress.

Here's how your action plan might look now:

Action Plan Steps (in Order)	*Deadlines*
1. Schedule appointment with writing tutor	*This Friday*
2. Prepare rough draft of term paper	*Three weeks before due date*
3. Submit rough draft to writing tutor	*Same day as above*
4. Incorporate feedback from writing tutor into final version	*Within one week of due date*
5. Submit final term paper	*On due date*

THE ACADEMIC BENEFITS OF GOAL SETTING

Hundreds of research studies have established the importance of goal setting in the workplace. Recently, a group of researchers conducted a study to see if goal setting also promotes college success. They took eighty-five undergraduate students who were having trouble with their studies and divided them into two groups:

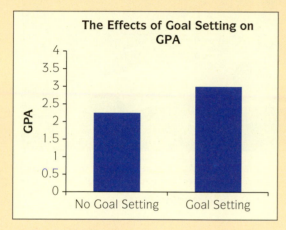

The Effects of Goal Setting on GPA

Research suggests that setting goals helps you earn higher grades.

- **Group 1:** These students completed surveys measuring their career interests, curiosity, and initiative. They also listed past accomplishments that they were proud of. They received no training on setting and achieving goals.

- **Group 2:** These students participated in a Web-based program introducing them to a process for setting and achieving personal goals. They wrote down seven or eight goals, prioritized them, and described how meeting those goals would improve their lives.

On average, students in group 1 achieved GPAs of 2.25. On average, those in group 2 achieved GPAs of almost 3.0. They also completed more academic credits. And compared to the group 1 students, they said they felt less anxious, less stressed, and more satisfied with life.

THE BOTTOM LINE

When you learn how to set goals, you'll likely improve your grades, feel more satisfied with your life, and achieve more of your goals.

REFLECTION QUESTIONS

1. How often do you write down your goals and the steps needed to achieve them?
2. Do you ever stop to evaluate your progress toward your goals? Why or why not?
3. Which of the five SMART criteria do you think will be the most difficult to follow in defining your goals?

D. Morisano, J. B. Hirsh, J. B. Peterson, R. O. Pihl, and B. M. Shore, "Setting, Elaborating, and Reflecting on Personal Goals Improves Academic Performance," *Journal of Applied Psychology* 95 (2010): 255–64.

Oops! Even if you've built an action plan for achieving a goal, you can still encounter barriers: Your car breaks down, so you're late for a group-project meeting. Your boss needs you to work extra hours, so you have less time to study than you had hoped. By anticipating possible barriers, you can craft strategies for overcoming them if they do arise. Mikadun/Shutterstock

Step 4: List Barriers and Solutions

Barrier: A personal characteristic or something in your environment that prevents you from making progress toward a goal.

Even when you have an action plan for achieving a goal, you can still encounter barriers. A **barrier** is something that prevents you from making progress toward your goal. It might be a personal characteristic (like a tendency to procrastinate) or something in your environment (like too many family commitments). Some barriers (such as poor time management) are under your control. With others (like family or work demands), you might have less control.

As you set your goals, write down the types of barriers you may face. By acknowledging potential barriers, you won't get blindsided if you actually encounter them. Also, you can brainstorm in advance how to overcome them. For example, suppose you're worried that your job will get very busy during midterms and interfere with your study time. By anticipating this barrier, you can figure out ways to avoid it—such as trading hours with a coworker.

And remember that you don't have to face barriers alone. Many helpful resources are available to provide support and encouragement. Faculty members, tutors, and academic and career advisers, for example, can work with you to overcome common barriers. To get help, you just have to ask.

◗ **CONNECT TO MY RESOURCES**

Write down two barriers that might prevent you from achieving your goals this term. Then list at least two resources on campus or in your community that could help you overcome these barriers.

Step 5: Act and Evaluate Outcomes

As you start taking the steps in your goal-setting action plan, regularly evaluate your progress. Are the steps you're taking effective? Are you completing them on time? Are they helping you get closer to meeting your goal? If you're not

FOCUSING ON SOLUTIONS

Courtesy of
Kerry Maxime

NAME:	**Thamara Jean**
SCHOOL:	*Broward College*
MAJOR:	*Pre-Nursing*
CAREER GOAL:	*Nursing*

Since I was seven years old, I've wanted to be a doctor — I think my goal was influenced by my parents and from watching lots of doctor shows on TV. With that goal in mind, I arrived at college and really struggled with courses like organic chemistry and pre-calculus. It wasn't until I attended a required advising meeting that I realized I wasn't thinking very critically about my goal. I didn't have much information about what was required to get through pre-med and medical school. I realized that semester that choosing medicine was probably a mistake but that making mistakes doesn't mean failure, unless you fail to learn from your mistakes. My adviser and I discussed creating a backup plan that included switching to pre-nursing, getting experience in health care settings, and continuing to gather information about medical school.

That same semester I attended a leadership and goal-setting workshop where I learned about SMART goals and was encouraged to get more involved in campus leadership activities. It was part of a campus initiative called QEP — Questioning Every Possibility. I learned to question, assess, analyze, and even research everything, because my future depends on me!

I immediately set a number of specific goals, like joining Phi Theta Kappa and the campus Honors Committee, passing my classes the next semester, and researching information about how to get into nursing school. To support my goal of passing classes, I set additional goals like getting tutoring in math and science and getting feedback on my papers before submitting them in literature classes. I feel back on track. I recently transferred to Florida Atlantic University, where I'm applying for acceptance into the nursing program, and I'm looking forward to a successful career in nursing.

YOUR TURN: Have you ever set a goal and then discovered significant barriers blocking your way? If so, what did you do to overcome those barriers or adjust your goal to make it more realistic?

> **"Making mistakes doesn't mean failure, unless you fail to learn from your mistakes."**

making the progress you'd hoped for, evaluating your outcomes helps you know this immediately so that you can change your action plan or find resources to get you back on track. Also, evaluation can help you stay motivated to keep working toward your long-term goals. By recording and celebrating your progress on the short-term goals that support your long-term ones, you build up proof that you're getting closer to your long-term goals.

If your evaluation shows that you've experienced a setback, stay positive. The point of evaluating your progress is to identify and deal with setbacks. Each time you do so, you'll get even better at achieving your goals, and you can seek out help if you need it. Remember: Setting and achieving goals takes practice. You didn't learn how to ride a bike on the first try either!

Create Your Personal Success Plan

Personal Success Plan (PSP): A tool that helps you establish SMART goals, build action plans, evaluate your outcomes, and revise your plans as needed.

Now that you've explored how to set and achieve goals using critical thinking skills, put your learning into action with the **Personal Success Plan (PSP)**. This tool guides you through the five steps of the goal-setting process. You can use it to establish SMART goals, build action plans, evaluate your outcomes, and revise your plans as needed as you go through this course. You can also use the PSP to set and achieve goals in other courses or in your personal and professional life.

The PSP's major sections mirror the five goal-setting steps you just learned:

1. Gather Information
2. Set a SMART Goal
3. Make an Action Plan
4. List Barriers and Solutions
5. Act and Evaluate Outcomes

An additional section—Connect to Career—helps you consider how a goal you've defined using the PSP can help prepare you for success in your chosen career or a career you're considering.

As you start using the PSP, you'll become a stronger critical thinker and a more independent learner. You'll use critical thinking to gather information, make decisions, and evaluate what you've learned about yourself so that you can get better and better at setting and achieving goals. In short, you'll discover that *you're* in the driver's seat when it comes to defining and meeting your goals—and you'll gain much practice taking personal responsibility for your own learning.

The PSP in Action

In this section, you'll get a firsthand look at how the PSP functions. You'll read about the experience of one student, Kayden, as he sets up his PSP, and you'll see the steps he takes to create and accomplish his goal. This is goal setting in action!

Gather Information. Kayden has enrolled in a first-year seminar course, and one of his assignments is to establish a specific goal and action plan. As a first step, Kayden gathers information about himself by reflecting on his strengths and weaknesses. He knows that he's a very motivated student but that he also struggles to manage his time. Therefore he decides that setting a regular study schedule will help him stay on track.

Set a SMART Goal. Kayden decides on his SMART goal: "I'll study for my first-year seminar at least one hour each weekday." This is a *specific* and *measurable* goal. Based on his existing schedule, Kayden believes that this goal is *achievable*. He's motivated to get good grades this term, so it's also personally *relevant* to his success. Finally, the goal has a clearly established *time limit*, which will help him check his progress within a day or two.

Make an Action Plan. To identify the steps he must take to meet his goal, Kayden considers his class and work schedules and upcoming personal commitments. He knows that his brain doesn't kick into gear until noon, so studying after lunch is best. He also knows that he prefers studying in his own apartment, but only when it's quiet. With this information in mind, he makes a plan.

- By Friday, he'll meet with his roommate to plan quiet, afternoon study time in their apartment.
- By Sunday, he'll enter his study schedule into his smartphone calendar.
- By Sunday night, he'll develop a log to record how much he studies.

List Barriers and Solutions. On his PSP, Kayden lists several barriers that might prevent him from achieving his goal and brainstorms solutions for overcoming those barriers. For example, his roommate may need to use the apartment when Kayden wants to study. (Perhaps his roommate is a music major

Turn It Down! Building flexibility into your action plan helps you keep barriers from standing between you and your goal. For instance, if your neighbor is an aspiring deejay, take that into account when designing your study plan: Identify a quiet location where you can study in case your neighbor decides to crank up the volume just as you crack open your textbook. Maxim Blinkov/Shutterstock

and needs to practice his tuba.) As a backup plan, Kayden decides to look for alternative study areas in the school library. Also, Kayden might not always be able to follow his set schedule or might feel pressure to socialize when he's supposed to be studying. In case these things happen, he develops strategies for staying on track.

Act and Evaluate Outcomes. For the next two weeks, Kayden implements his action plan and records his results in the PSP. He does the following:

- works with his roommate to set aside quiet study time at their apartment
- identifies a backup study location just in case the apartment becomes noisy
- enters his study schedule into his smartphone to remind himself when to study
- creates a log to record how much he studies

He experiences a setback in week 2, when he misses two study periods. But he doesn't give up; instead, he makes up his study time over the weekend and revises his schedule to make it more realistic. And he's so pleased with how useful this study strategy has been that he decides to build a study schedule for his other courses, too.

Connect to Career. On his PSP, Kayden has identified three skills he is learning as he works toward his goal:

- managing his time
- prioritizing his action steps
- mastering his new smartphone app

These are skills he can use in any current job or any future employment. By recording these skills on his PSP, he can refer to them when he prepares a résumé, writes cover letters, and describes his qualifications during job interviews.

my personal success plan

Kayden Davis

1 my information

Sometimes it's hard for me to manage my time.

I need a regular study schedule to stay on track.

2 my SMART goal

I'll study for my first-year seminar at least one hour each weekday.

✓**S**PECIFIC ✓**M**EASURABLE ✓**A**CHIEVABLE ✓**R**ELEVANT ✓**T**IME-LIMITED

3 my action plan

1. I'll discuss apartment quiet time with my roommate (by Friday).
2. I'll enter study times into my smartphone calendar (by Sunday).
3. I'll make a log to record how much I study (by Sunday night).

4 my barriers/ solutions

1. If my roommate has a conflicting schedule, I'll find a place to study in the library.
2. If I miss a scheduled study session, I'll find a makeup time.
3. If family and friends want to get together during study time, I'll find a different time for us to meet.

5 my actions/ outcomes

1. My roommate and I set quiet hours for the apartment. I also found a good place to study in the library, just in case.
2. I entered my study schedule into my smartphone and created a study log.
3. In week 2, I missed two study periods. I'll make up this study time over the weekend and revise my schedule to be more realistic!

6 my career connection

1. I'm learning to manage my time, which will help me meet deadlines on the job.
2. I'm setting priorities, and I can use this skill to focus on the most important tasks at work.
3. I've mastered my new smartphone app, which I can use to schedule appointments during the workday.

Create Your First Personal Success Plan

Kayden is off to a great start this term, and now it's time for you to create your first Personal Success Plan. To begin, follow the steps below and sketch out your ideas on the following page. Or visit the LaunchPad for *Connections* to access the PSP online.

1. **Gather information.** What are your strengths and your weaknesses? Review your ACES results to identify a strength (high score) you want to develop further or a low score suggesting an area in which you could improve.

2. **Set a SMART goal.** Define a short-term goal that meets the SMART criteria. You can always revise it later, so don't worry about making it perfect.

3. **Make an action plan.** List steps you'll need to take to achieve this goal, and arrange them in an order that makes sense to you. Give each step a deadline.

4. **List barriers and solutions.** Identify possible barriers to your action steps and brainstorm solutions for overcoming each barrier. If these barriers occur, you'll be ready.

5. **Act and evaluate outcomes.** It's up to you to put your plan into action and to record the completion of each action step and any problems you encounter. Do this to track your progress.

6. **Connect to career.** List the skills you'll develop as you progress toward your goal. Then identify how those skills will help you succeed on the job.

Once you've filled out your Personal Success Plan, you'll have set your first academic success goal of the term. Congratulations—this is a great first step! Remember, though, that goal setting is an ongoing process that takes practice, and that's why you'll get the chance to set multiple goals over the course of the term. How many goals should you set? Your instructor may provide guidance on the number required for your particular class. Some instructors may ask you to set one goal for each chapter, while others may require only a few goals over the course of the term. Either way, we have included a sample PSP at the end of each chapter to inspire you and to walk you through the goal-setting process. If you aren't setting a goal in a particular chapter, the PSP will still be there to offer suggestions and serve as a model.

You might need some time to get used to the PSP, but as you progress through this course, you'll become an expert goal-setter. By the end of the term, you'll have set and achieved a number of goals, and you'll be well on your way to academic and career success.

my personal success plan _____

1 my information
_____
_____
_____
_____
_____

2 my SMART goal
_____
_____
_____

☐ **S**PECIFIC ☐ **M**EASURABLE ☐ **A**CHIEVABLE ☐ **R**ELEVANT ☐ **T**IME-LIMITED

3 my action plan
_____
_____
_____
_____

4 my barriers/ solutions
_____
_____
_____
_____

5 my actions/ outcomes
_____
_____
_____
_____

6 my career connection
_____
_____
_____
_____

Critical Thinking and Goal Setting in Your Career

Using critical thinking to set and achieve goals helps you not only to succeed academically but also to launch and maintain a successful, satisfying career. In the workplace you'll stand out if you use reliable information to make decisions, consider all points of view, set meaningful goals, and brainstorm innovative solutions to problems. You can do all of these things by *applying* the information you've learned in this chapter to your current or future job.

Learn on the Job

When you graduate from college, you don't stop learning. In fact, to advance in your career, you'll be expected to keep learning new skills and acquiring new knowledge. Some professions even require you to take continuing education credits each year to maintain your credentials or license. In other professions you'll need to stay current on the latest technologies to remain productive in your work and competitive in the job market. For example, after only two weeks at his first job working for a transportation consulting firm, Sweeny was asked to review three transportation dispatch software platforms and recommend one for the company to adopt. Sweeny relied on critical thinking skills like synthesis and evaluation to weigh the options and make his recommendation.

Set Goals on the Job

The goal-setting strategy you're learning in this course can also help you set career goals. Let's say you want to take on more responsibility at your job, communicate more effectively with colleagues, or complete tasks more efficiently. You can reframe these general statements as SMART goals and use the PSP to achieve them.

As you develop your own work-related goals, also consider how they support your organization's goals. For example, as a licensed practical nurse, you might decide to increase the number of patient charts you review each hour by 10 percent in the next month. This goal demonstrates enthusiasm and a desire for self-improvement. However, consult with your supervisor about which goals would best support both the organization's success and your own professional development. If your employer prefers that you focus on learning to use a new piece of equipment instead, you might have to modify your original goal to support your employer's top priorities. Developing goals in consultation with your supervisor is a win-win situation and a great way to show your enthusiasm and your ability to take the initiative.

Never Stop Learning. You'll want—and need—to keep learning on the job so that you can excel at your work and advance in your career. For instance, teachers often need continuing education credits to maintain their teaching certification. No matter where you work, critical thinking can help you keep building your skills and knowledge. michaeljung/Shutterstock

SETTING GOALS FOR WORKPLACE SUCCESS

Courtesy of Chris Funderburk

NAME:	**Chris Funderburk**
PROFESSION:	*Branch Manager, Car Rental Office*
SCHOOL:	*Indiana University*
DEGREE:	*Bachelor of Science*
MAJOR:	*Biology*

Back in college, I had some difficulty — in fact, I was asked to leave my university due to low grades. It took me some time, but I went back to school and improved my GPA. Failing in college gave me a new perspective. It gave me purpose and made me stronger, and goal setting helped. I refocused on my ultimate goal of graduating and used a lot of short-term goals to stay motivated. Having specific, achievable goals was critical to this success.

Now that I'm working, I use the goal-setting skills I developed in college all the time. We have monthly sales and customer service targets to meet each month. Having a very clear, concrete goal helps me focus on what I need to do each day to achieve my goals for the month. Not every month is perfect, and it's easy to get down when I don't meet a personal goal or my team doesn't meet its goal. However, that's when I take a minute to reflect on what was happening during that month.

Sometimes I reach out to successful colleagues and ask them for input. Other times I return to strategies that worked in the past. I get back to the basics of making sure I put both customers and my employees first. When I combine reflection with perseverance and a strong work ethic, I can ramp up to make my goals the next month.

I've faced huge challenges in the past, but I'm able to build upon everything I learned to keep pushing forward.

YOUR TURN: Have you ever experienced difficulty achieving work-related goals? If so, what did you do about it? What results did you get?

> " Having a very clear, concrete goal helps me focus on what I need to do each day."

CHAPTER SUMMARY

This chapter introduced you to one of the most fundamental factors in your college and career success: critical thinking. You can use critical thinking to learn and set goals — in school and at work. Revisit the following key points and reflect on how you can use this information to support your success now and in the future.

- Critical thinking is the process of approaching information in a thoughtful way, understanding how to think logically and rationally, and applying those methods of thinking in your classes and your life. It involves using higher-level thinking skills such as synthesis and evaluation.

- You can use critical thinking to learn in every course you're taking. Bloom's taxonomy helps you identify the level at which you're learning and think about how that learning will be assessed on exams or assignments.

- You can use critical thinking to set and achieve goals through a five-step process: (1) gather information about yourself, (2) set a SMART goal, (3) make an action plan, (4) list possible barriers and solutions, and (5) act and evaluate your outcomes.

- The Personal Success Plan can help you set and achieve goals. The steps in the PSP mirror the five goal-setting steps, with one additional step, connecting to career. You can use the PSP to list your goals and action steps, document which steps you've completed, evaluate your progress, and revise your plan if needed.

- Thinking critically helps you launch and maintain a successful career. You can use the techniques you read about in this chapter to continually acquire new knowledge and skills and to set goals in the workplace.

CHAPTER ACTIVITIES

Journal Entry

THINKING CRITICALLY IN EVERYDAY LIFE

You'll certainly have to think critically in college, but it's also a vital skill in everyday life. One way to practice your critical thinking skills is to pay attention to *how* you think about the world around you. You probably don't need to think critically about the things you do every day, such as eating breakfast or commuting. But some things do require much deeper thought — for instance, learning a new skill, taking a course about an unfamiliar subject, setting a goal, or making a decision.

1. Describe something in the last six months that was challenging for you and required you to think critically. What approach did you take? What challenges did you face, and how did you overcome them?

2. Were you able to maintain an open mind during the process, or did something get in the way (like strong feelings, ideas about how things *should* be, or difficult material)?

3. Were you satisfied with the outcome of your thinking? Why or why not? If you could do it over, would you do anything differently? Explain.

Adopting a Success Attitude

PERCEIVING SETBACKS AS LEARNING OPPORTUNITIES

Regardless of how realistic your goals are and how many barriers you anticipate, at some point you won't accomplish something you want to. Dealing effectively with your emotions when you experience setbacks and maintaining a positive attitude separates successful students from unsuccessful ones. Let's use reflection to turn a goal-setting setback into a learning opportunity.

1. Describe a goal you set (something that was important to you) but never achieved. Evaluate it using the SMART criteria described in this chapter. Was the goal specific, measurable, achievable, relevant to you, and time-limited? If not, how could you have redefined the goal so that it met all of those criteria?

2. Describe how you felt when you didn't achieve this goal. Did you experience negative feelings? Did these feelings affect your motivation to continue pursuing your goal?

3. Reflect on what made it difficult to achieve your goal. Try not to place blame, but do consider the ways in which you may have been responsible for the setback.

4. Identify what you could do differently to achieve this goal now and how you could maintain your motivation and stay positive. Also, who could help you reach this goal? List the names and contact information for personal or campus resources who could provide support if you experience this setback again.

Applying Your Skills

CONSTRUCTING SMART GOALS

This activity gives you practice turning broad, general goals into specific, measurable, and time-limited goals. We aren't focusing on the *A* (achievable) and the *R* (relevant to you) of the SMART acronym, because only you can determine if a goal is achievable or relevant.

First, review the Set a SMART Goal section of this chapter. Then rewrite the following goals to make them specific, measurable, and time-limited.

1. Goal: *Look for a job soon.*

   SMarT Goal: _____

2. Goal: *Figure out my major.*

   SMarT Goal: _____

3. Goal: *Make some networking contacts before I graduate.*

   SMarT Goal: _____

4. Goal: *Lead a healthier life.*

   SMarT Goal: _____

5. Goal: *Do well in class.*

   SMarT Goal: _____

College Success = Career Success

APPLYING CRITICAL THINKING ON THE JOB

In the workplace you'll need to think critically and innovatively about procedures, customers, solutions, and new products. Consider the following four scenarios, which require critical thinking. Explain in writing how you'd respond to each scenario.

1. You're hiring a new employee. You've reviewed résumés for two applicants and conducted interviews with them. Both seem friendly and competent. Applicant A has a college degree but very little work experience related to the open position. Applicant B has no degree but a lot of relevant work experience. A college degree is not required for the job. Whom would you select? Why?

2. You're marketing a new breakfast cereal. Do you package and market your product to appeal to children or to parents? Explain your answer and how you would put your marketing strategy into action.

3. You're a customer service agent for a major utility. A customer calls and asks if you can extend the due date of his bill, for which his payment is overdue. (You have the authority to do this.) How would you respond to him, and why? Would any additional information or something about this customer's attitude cause you to be more or less likely to extend the due date? If so, explain your answer. Is it okay to treat one customer differently from another? Why or why not?

4. You own a manufacturing company, and you're considering moving your operations to a country where wages are lower so that you can cut your costs. Describe the factors you'd need to consider before deciding whether to outsource operations to that country. Who would be affected if you did outsource, and how? Who would be affected if you kept the operations in your home country, and how?

3 Motivation, Decision Making, and Personal Responsibility

What Keeps You Motivated?

Make Good Decisions

Take Personal Responsibility for Your Education

Motivation, Decision Making, and Personal Responsibility at Work

My Personal Success Plan

© John Lund/Blend Images/Corbis

Meet Nadia, a veteran who recently returned from a tour of duty and began her first year of college. Nadia has been in school a few months now, and she's surprised at how different college life is from her previous experiences. In the military Nadia's life was highly structured, and her commanding officer and other superiors often determined what she needed to do, when, and with whom. In college Nadia's instructors don't provide as much structure. They expect Nadia to schedule her own time and figure out how — and how much — to study. Nadia finds this new freedom and responsibility for managing her life not only exciting but also intimidating. She knows it's up to her to stay motivated, make good decisions, and take responsibility for achieving her own goals.

Like Nadia, you may be surprised, excited, and intimidated by aspects of college life that seem unfamiliar, even if your background differs from hers. As a result, you may be having difficulty staying motivated, making smart choices, and taking charge of your learning. By understanding more about these important college survival skills, you can restore the initial enthusiasm you felt as you looked ahead to your first term at school. And you can truly *own* your college experience. As a result, you'll get the most value from your classes — including new knowledge and skills that will help you excel in your career.

In fact, motivation, decision making, and personal responsibility will be just as critical in your work life as in your college life. Why? Recent college graduates can't expect to stay with their first employer for a lifetime. They need to develop marketable skills, be flexible, and prepare to find new jobs if necessary. Doing this involves seeking out mentors for guidance, regularly assessing your abilities and needs, and creating action plans to build new skills and strengthen others. In short, to be competitive in today's work world, you need to assume responsibility for your own success.

In this chapter you'll learn how to activate three forces that will keep you motivated in school: believing you can succeed, viewing all your coursework as important to your goals, and cultivating a positive attitude. In addition, you'll learn strategies you can use to make careful decisions and take personal responsibility for your education. Finally, you'll learn ways to stay motivated, make good choices, and assume responsibility in your professional life.

Reflect

On Your Motivation, Decision Making, and Personal Responsibility

Take a moment to reflect on your Motivation, Decision Making, and Personal Responsibility score on ACES. Find your score and add it in the circle to the right.

This score measures your beliefs about how well you stay motivated, make decisions, and take responsibility for your learning. Do you think it's an accurate snapshot of your current skills in these areas? Why or why not?

■ **IF YOU SCORED IN THE HIGH RANGE** and you think this score is accurate, you may be very good at staying motivated, making careful decisions, and taking responsibility for your education. This is great news! Now, though, look for new ways to improve. As you read this chapter, focus on developing even better ways to stay motivated, make decisions, and actively drive your own learning. The more strategies you build up, the better prepared you'll be when you run into those inevitable moments of feeling discouraged or overwhelmed. Use your new insights from this chapter to enhance your strengths and upgrade any skills needing improvement.

■ **IF YOU SCORED IN THE MODERATE OR LOW RANGE**, don't be discouraged. You *can* strengthen your motivation, learn how to make good decisions, and take more responsibility for your learning. This chapter is filled with ideas you can begin using now. Read on to get started!

MY ACES SCORE

☐ **HIGH**

☐ **MODERATE**

☐ **LOW**

LaunchPad

To find your **Motivation, Decision Making, and Personal Responsibility score,** go to the LaunchPad for *Connections*.

What Keeps You Motivated?

Imagine it's Friday night, and you have five chapters to read in your biology textbook to prepare for a test on Monday morning. Let's say that you're not very confident in your reading abilities; you don't think you'll spend much time reading in your career; and you often feel frustrated when you have to read long passages. Given these feelings and thoughts, you probably won't feel motivated to work through the chapters this weekend.

Now imagine a different scenario. Once again, it's Friday night, but this time you have an investigative story due Monday for your journalism class. You believe you're a good writer, and you think you have a meaningful and important story to tell—plus, you love this class. Given these thoughts and emotions, you'll probably feel motivated to work hard on the story over the weekend.

Why? You believe you can do a good job, meaning you have strong *self-efficacy* in your journalism skills. You see this writing task as *relevant* to what matters most to you. And you have a positive *attitude* about the task facing you. These are three key components of motivation (see Figure 3.1).

Let's begin by taking a closer look at each component. Then we'll compare two types of motivation—and explore which is more powerful.

FIGURE 3.1
Three Key Components of Motivation

Self-Efficacy

Self-Efficacy: Your belief in your ability to carry out the actions needed to reach a particular goal.

Self-efficacy refers to your belief in your ability to carry out the actions needed to reach a particular goal. In other words, you *believe* you can be effective. The stronger your sense of self-efficacy, the more likely you'll do what's needed to achieve your goals and to keep trying even when you encounter setbacks.

Take Moira, who always struggled in her high school Spanish classes. She didn't believe she could improve, so she gave up easily on projects. Her grades suffered as a result. If Moira had believed that she could do what was needed to master Spanish—such as finding a tutor or joining a study group—she would have taken action to make it happen. Her grades would have ultimately improved. Her sense of hope that she could succeed in school would have been restored. And she would have built new knowledge that would have equipped her for jobs that require Spanish speaking and writing skills.

How can you strengthen your sense of self-efficacy? Try the following tactics, suggested by psychologist Albert Bandura.[1]

Self-Efficacy Secrets. These music students are building self-efficacy by experiencing successes gained through practice. They can strengthen their self-efficacy even more by observing each other's best techniques and sharing suggestions. Hill Street Studios/Getty Images

- **Experience success.** One important component of a SMART goal is that it's achievable. Achieving a desired goal enhances your self-efficacy beliefs and spurs you to take on your next challenge. In that way, success builds on success. By proving to yourself that you're making progress (as you do on the PSP), you strengthen your sense of self-efficacy and are more likely to succeed in your next goal.

- **Observe others who are successful.** You can strengthen your self-efficacy beliefs by watching other people complete a task successfully. Psychologists call this process *modeling*. For instance, join a study group and see how students who get the best grades take notes during lectures. Or ask tutors at the math and writing centers to show you the strategies they use to master the subject matter. Stronger self-efficacy beliefs for these activities will help motivate you to try them in the future.

- **Seek support and encouragement.** Being supported and encouraged in your pursuits helps you believe more strongly in your ability to achieve goals. So surround yourself with people who want you to succeed. Let them know not only when you're struggling but also when you're making progress toward your goals. Their encouragement will help you feel even more confident in your abilities.

- **Turn stress into a motivator.** Stress is natural—everyone feels it—and it isn't *always* bad. In fact, a little bit of it can energize you to tackle a challenge. Too much stress, however, can sap your motivation. The key is to find a middle ground—just enough stress to inspire you, but not so much that it paralyzes you.

Relevance

If you think that a goal has relevance for you—that achieving it will make a positive difference in some way—you'll feel more motivated to work toward that goal. (Remember the *R* in SMART?) Relevance can even motivate you to achieve a goal that seems boring or unpleasant in the short term, because you know that by meeting this challenge now, you'll get something that's important to you in the long term. For instance, maybe you dread your English composition class. Still, you force yourself to work at the class assignments because you understand that knowing how to write well will help you in your professional life, no matter what career you choose to pursue.

If a subject or an assignment seems irrelevant to your life at first, connect it to something that *is* relevant. If your motivation for a particular task starts to wane, try out these strategies.

- **Find something interesting in every class.** Almost all academic topics relate to one another in some way. For example, if you're a psychology major taking a history class, you might be able to write a paper on the history of psychoanalytic thought. Even though the paper is for your history class, the topic connects with something that interests you. If you remind yourself of such connections, seemingly irrelevant projects will become more relevant than you thought at first—and you'll be more motivated to do a good job on them.
- **Connect coursework to your long-term goals.** Doing well in college can give you the knowledge and skills needed to achieve your long-term goals—such as going to graduate school, getting into a highly competitive program like nursing, or effectively managing family or community responsibilities. Always try to keep the big picture in mind.

CONNECT TO MY EXPERIENCE

Write down two goals you set for yourself in your personal life: one with strong personal meaning and one with weak personal meaning. Did your motivation to achieve these goals vary based on how relevant they were to your life?

The Power of Relevance. When your goals have relevance to you, you'll stay motivated to achieve them—even in the face of serious setbacks. Take Malala Yousafzai, the Pakistani activist for female education and the youngest person to ever receive the Nobel Peace Prize. After a gunman shot and nearly killed her and the Taliban threatened her life and her father's, her commitment to education only grew stronger. AP Photo/ Susan Walsh

- **Build transferable skills.** Use general-education courses to develop transferable skills like note taking, writing, time management, and critical thinking.

- **Focus on practical benefits.** Remind yourself of the practical benefits of achieving a goal—for instance, "If I can maintain a 3.5 GPA, I can keep my scholarship" or "If I pass this class, I'll avoid the cost of retaking it."

- **Focus on a love of learning.** The feeling of accomplishment you get from mastering new material—even if that material isn't your favorite—can give a task meaning.

Attitude

A positive attitude is a beautiful thing: It makes you more resilient in the face of difficulties, helps you learn from your mistakes, and increases your enjoyment when you succeed. It's also a powerful motivator that can keep you energized and focused on your goals. Use the following strategies to stay positive, even when a project, an assignment, or a class leaves you feeling uninspired.

- **Identify something positive resulting from the work you're doing.** Even little rewards can make difficult tasks more pleasant. Look for those small moments of enjoyment or positivity, and take time to appreciate them. For instance, if you're reading your art history textbook, you might unexpectedly find a photo of a painting that takes your breath away. Or if you're working with a classmate on a calculus assignment, you might realize that you have a lot in common and that this person could become a good friend.

Fake It 'Til You Make It. Maintaining a positive attitude can help you remain motivated to work toward your most challenging goals. So practice thinking positive thoughts and making positive statements about yourself and your studies. Does positive self-talk feel awkward or contrived to you? If so, remind yourself that sometimes you have to "fake it 'til you make it." marekuliasz/ Shutterstock

- **If possible, take at least one course in your intended major each term.** That way, you can spend some time each week focused on the content you most enjoy.

- **Think and speak positively.** Monitor your *self-talk*: what you tell yourself about the courses you're taking, the assignments you're working on, and your goals. Positive self-talk—thinking positive thoughts and making positive statements—protects you from stress, promotes creative thinking, and can help you stay motivated.[2] Practice turning negatives into positives by reframing what you think and say. For instance, if you're unhappy about taking a required math course, you may find yourself muttering, "This course is a waste of time—smartphone apps can do these calculations." Instead, try telling yourself, "I'd like to become less dependent on my smartphone. Learning how the math actually works will help me do calculations, rather than always having to rely on technology to do them for me."

When your self-efficacy is strong, your task is relevant, and you have a positive attitude, you'll feel especially motivated to work toward a goal. See Table 3.1 for examples of how these components fit together to help you achieve what is important to you.

TABLE 3.1 **How Key Components of Motivation Help You Achieve Goals**

Goal	Strong self-efficacy	High relevance	Positive attitude
Conduct research in the library for an English composition paper	I used the online catalog successfully last week, so I should be able to find the materials I need this week.	This isn't my favorite class, but I'll need to conduct research in other classes, too. If I build my skills now, I can apply them in my other classes.	Instead of telling myself that this project will be boring, I'll think about how good it will feel to check this task off my to-do list.
Read three chapters in my textbook for Foundations of Education	I've worked with a tutor to create a reading schedule, so I know what I have to do to finish the chapters on time.	I want to become a teacher, so this reading is relevant to my long-term goal.	I feel too tired to read all these chapters this weekend, but I do like the boxes in the chapter where real people share their stories. I'll read those first to energize myself.
Do a group marketing campaign project for my business class	Last spring I worked with some neighbors to design a fundraising campaign for our local after-school program. I can apply what I learned about working in a group to this assignment.	I want to do creative work and eventually manage a team. This project will let me create something I can show employers as part of my portfolio.	One of my classmates on this project seems especially creative. I think it'll be fun to work with her on this assignment.

Tap into Your Internal Motivation

In your school, work, and personal life, multiple motivations underlie the choices you make. Maybe you decided to go to college because you enjoy learning new things, but also because you need to build skills that will get you a good job. Perhaps you've joined a study group because you'll meet friendly people, but also because it will help you get better grades. Each of these decisions reflects the two kinds of motivation identified by psychologists: intrinsic and extrinsic motivation. **Intrinsic motivation** stems from your inner desire to achieve a specific outcome. **Extrinsic motivation** derives from forces external to you, such as an expected reward or a negative outcome that you want to avoid. If you study hard because you enjoy the feeling of success, then you're motivated for intrinsic reasons. If you study hard because you need to maintain a 3.0 GPA to keep your scholarship, then you're motivated for extrinsic reasons. Sometimes you'll be influenced by both intrinsic and extrinsic motivation. For example, you may genuinely enjoy the subject you're studying, but you also work hard to keep up your GPA.

Both types of motivators can prompt you to meet your goals, but intrinsic motivation has some special benefits over extrinsic motivation. First, intrinsic motivation is usually more reliable because you control it. How? You stay focused on the positive feelings you'll experience when you achieve the goal, and that keeps you motivated. Also, intrinsic motivation is especially helpful in unfamiliar or confusing situations—like your first year in college. Your professors assign course material, but they may not tell you *how* to learn it. You have to figure that out, and intrinsic motivation can spur you on.

The more you know about yourself—your goals, interests, and values—the more you can tap into your intrinsic motivation by seeing how a goal or task is relevant to who you are and what you want. For instance, let's say you've always loved solving puzzles. After your first month at school, you feel overwhelmed by all the coursework. You decide to look at your situation as a big puzzle that you *know* you can solve, and that motivates you to identify resources that can help you manage the workload—such as a tutor or a study group. When you understand what makes *you* tick, you can figure out how to keep yourself moving forward.

But how can you find an approach to building intrinsic motivation that works for you? There are many approaches and lots of people giving advice about the best ways. Many techniques are covered in this chapter: using positive self-talk, identifying positive aspects, and finding something interesting in challenging situations. Leaders of industry, professional athletes, psychologists, salespeople, Navy SEALs, and others often use another powerful technique—visualization.[3] In visualization you imagine the outcome you'd like to happen and the steps in getting there, using all your senses, including sight, sound, smell, and feel. Visualizing a desirable outcome can stir positive emotions and

The $1.00 CEO. Why did Facebook CEO Mark Zuckerberg ask for a $1.00 salary in 2013? He's worth almost $28 billion, so he doesn't need a big paycheck. But this might also have shown shareholders that he values his work for its own sake. Such intrinsic motivation can inspire you to reach your goals more than can extrinsic motivators (such as a big salary).
AP Photo/Jeff Chiu

STAYING MOTIVATED IN COLLEGE

Courtesy of
J. Altdorfer
Photography

NAME: **Erin Smith**

SCHOOL: *Chatham University*

MAJOR: *Foundations of Higher Education and Student Affairs*

CAREER GOAL: *Working in a college or university to support student success*

I'm in my sophomore year, and I'm currently feeling unmotivated in some of my classes. I want to pursue a master's degree that will prepare me to work with college students at a university. I'm so happy that I found my passion early in my undergraduate years, but sometimes it makes it hard for me to focus on classes that seem unrelated to my professional goals.

For example, it's sometimes difficult for me to see how my Shakespeare class relates to my interest in higher education institutions and student learning. However, even if I don't immediately recognize a connection between each course and my professional goals, gaining new knowledge intrinsically motivates me. I know that I'm learning important skills in every class, such as how to manage my time, take notes, think critically, and reduce stress. In addition to developing these skills, I'm learning more about complicated issues such as gender, race, class, and identity. I can then apply what I've learned about these issues to my work with college students. In the future I'll appreciate what I learned in these classes and how I've developed as a well-rounded, lifelong learner.

It can be tough to stay disciplined and remain focused in classes that don't strongly capture your interests. But if you connect your passions to each of your courses, it's easier to find something meaningful in every class you take.

YOUR TURN: Do you use particular strategies to connect seemingly irrelevant courses to something you're passionate about? If so, what are those strategies?

> " If you connect your passions to each of your courses, it's easier to find something meaningful in every class you take."

motivate you to work hard. It prompts you to think about your values, the importance and relevance of your goals, and the steps needed to reach them. To visualize effectively, relax and clear your mind. Imagine your future self accomplishing the goal you set out to achieve. Where are you? Who are you with? What are you doing? How do you feel? Use these images and feelings to maintain motivation. You'll have a chance to try a visualization activity at the end of the chapter.

Make Good Decisions

In your school, work, and personal life, you might make hundreds of decisions every day. Some choices are straightforward and quick, like selecting tuna over turkey for lunch. Others are more complex, with higher stakes. For example, should you stay in school even if your spouse isn't supportive? Should you buy a car to get to class even though you're already carrying heavy credit card debt? What major will you declare? The outcomes of the choices you make, along with the complexity or difficulty of such choices, can affect your motivation. And your level of motivation can ultimately influence whether you achieve the goals that have personal meaning for you.

With tough choices, you need to weigh your options carefully, but you also have to make reasonable decisions that help you move forward. If you obsess about making a "perfect decision," you can fall victim to "analysis paralysis," which can sap your motivation and leave you feeling hopeless about selecting a course of action.

How do you make a reasonable decision even when you're feeling over-whelmed or frightened by a choice you're facing? Try the following steps, which have a lot in common with the steps in the Personal Success Plan.

◗ CONNECT
TO MY EXPERIENCE

Select one choice you've made recently—personal, academic, or professional—and reflect on the decision-making process you used. In a brief paragraph, answer these questions: What decision-making steps did you take? Which steps *didn't* you take? How could the steps you didn't take have been helpful to you?

1. **Identify the decision to be made.** Articulating the decision sets the stage for the rest of the process.

2. **Know yourself.** Identify your strengths, weaknesses, interests, and values. This self-knowledge helps you think broadly about your options.

3. **Identify your options.** With a friend, colleague, or family member, brain-storm options available to you and write them down on a sheet of paper.

4. **Gather information about each option.** Research the details of each option you've listed, such as what actions you'd need to take if you chose that option and who could help you take those actions.

5. **Evaluate your options.** List the pros and cons of each option. Rate each option based on how attractive it is to you and how it will affect the people who are important to you.

6. **Select the best option.** The option with the highest rating is your most reasonable choice. If you feel nervous about committing to this choice, remind yourself that you can always change your mind later if the deci-sion doesn't work out as well as you had hoped.

7. **Develop and implement an action plan.** List the actions you'll take to fol-low through on your decision. Then take those actions.

8. **Evaluate the outcomes of your decision.** Determine whether your decision has worked out. If not, follow this eight-step process again to arrive at a new decision.

Making complex, high-stakes decisions will always be challenging, but this process can help you take a systematic approach (see Figure 3.2 and Table 3.2). Also, the more you practice using it, the easier it gets.

FIGURE 3.2   The Decision-Making Process

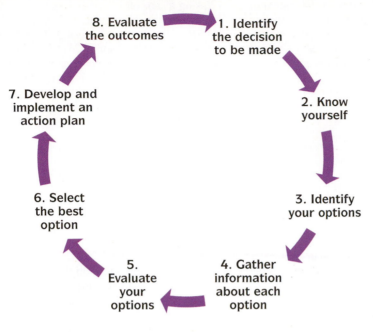

TABLE 3.2   Examples of the Decision-Making Process

Step	Example 1	Example 2
Identify the decision to be made	I need to select a major.	My mom is sick in another country. Should I leave school to take care of her, or should I continue my studies?
Know yourself	I love history, art, music, and literature, but I'm not an artist or a musician. I enjoy interacting with people. I value family, so I don't want to work sixty hours a week. I may want to work in an art museum or possibly in arts management.	I value my family and my education. I'm the oldest of three, so my mom relies on me a lot. I'm also the first in my family to go to college, which is a point of pride for my loved ones. I'm torn between these responsibilities.
Identify your options	I'm considering a major in art history, finance, business, or psychology. Taking various electives is also an option.	I called my brother back home and discussed options: Take a year off from school to help Mom; stay in school and my brother will care for Mom; move Mom to a medical facility near home; or hire a visiting nurse to care for Mom twice a day.
Gather information about each option	I'll learn more by meeting with my academic adviser, visiting the career center library, and interviewing recent graduates who are working in museums and the entertainment industry.	I'll research the answers to some key questions: If I take time off from school, when do I have to come back? Could I keep all my credits? How much would care in a medical facility cost?

TABLE 3.2   (continued)

Evaluate your options	The information I gathered suggests that art history and business could prepare me for jobs in the arts. But with both majors, I'll have to study aspects of art that don't interest me and take two accounting courses.	Taking a year off from school would make things tough for me. My brother works full-time to support our family, so it will be hard for him to care for Mom. Mom loves her home, so it would be difficult for her to move to a medical facility. Hiring a visiting nurse would let me stay in school and ensure regular care for Mom. It's pricey, though, and two visits a day may not be enough.
Select the best option	I'll major in art history but take electives in business and management.	Balancing all these factors, we'll have a nurse visit Mom twice a day.
Develop and implement an action plan	I'll declare my major and meet with my new art history academic adviser to create a course plan.	My brother lives near Mom, so he'll interview nurse candidates. My brother and I will split the costs. We'll both ask several of Mom's friends to check in on her at least once a day.
Evaluate the outcomes of your decision	I've taken courses in my major for one term and I like them, but my gut tells me that declaring a business major will give me the most options after graduation. I'll need to do more career research before I'm comfortable with my decision.	This arrangement has worked out well. Mom's nurse and friends check in on her during the day, and my brother comes by after work whenever he can. I'm doing well in school, but I really miss Mom—I can't wait to visit her during the next school break.

Take Personal Responsibility for Your Education

Taking personal responsibility for your education is empowering. It puts *you* in control of maintaining your motivation and making smart choices. For instance, if you don't see why a particular assignment is important, *you* can find reasons to care. If you keep missing class, *you* can set two alarms so you'll wake up on time. If friends want you to go out the night before a test, *you* can say no.

By taking responsibility in these ways, you drive your learning and your personal growth. You also prove to yourself that you value your education, and show respect for your instructors and the classmates who depend on you to complete group projects and assignments. Taking responsibility for our actions isn't always easy, but every college student—and every professional in the workplace—needs to do it.

In the next section, we'll explore four ways you can take responsibility for your own education: cultivating a growth mindset, taking an active approach to your learning, navigating the transition to college life, and reflecting on how you think and learn.

Growth Mindset: The belief that one can improve and further develop one's skills.
Fixed Mindset: The belief that one cannot improve one's talents, skills, and abilities.

Develop a Growth Mindset

Stanford University psychologist Carol Dweck proposes that there are two types of students. Those with a **growth mindset** believe they can improve and further develop their skills.[4] They assume personal responsibility for their success and learn as much as they can from their failures.

By contrast, students with a **fixed mindset** believe they can't improve their talents, skills, and abilities, and they tend to see themselves as victims of circumstance. Take Maya, who turned in a project late and was penalized one letter grade. She blamed work and family demands (she has three young children) for missing the deadline. She didn't reflect on her behaviors or learn how to manage her time more effectively; as a result, she continued to struggle to meet her deadlines.

When you have a growth mindset, you take responsibility for setbacks rather than blame others for them. You examine the behaviors that led to the failure, identify what you could have done differently, and apply those lessons to the next situation. For example, if Maya had adopted a growth mindset after losing a letter grade, she might have identified behavior changes to make in the future, such as exchanging work shifts as a deadline approaches or working on assignments when her children are in school.

If you blame others for setbacks, you miss an opportunity to become more competent by learning how you can improve in the future. Adopting a growth mindset is a win-win situation: When you fail, you take steps to improve, and when you succeed, you get the credit for making a positive change. Either way, you become a better student and get more value from your education.

Cross That Finish Line. No matter what your goals are, only you can cross the finish line and reach them. By taking personal responsibility in college, you drive your own learning and growth, rather than look to others to lead you. That's real power — but you have to embrace it. © Rana Faure/Corbis

Keep a Growth Mindset. When you have a growth mindset, you're willing to see setbacks and disappointments from a whole new angle. Instead of coming up with excuses or blaming others for failures, you look for the lessons hidden in these experiences — such as what you can do differently in the future to get a better result. serg_debrova/Shutterstock

Take an Active Approach to Your Learning

If your high school was like many, it had a passive learning environment. Teachers were considered experts who imparted knowledge, and students memorized the information that was presented. By contrast, most colleges encourage *active learning*, in which instructors create a learning environment but students are expected to think critically about course material, engage in classroom discussion and debate, and apply their knowledge and skills to real-world problems and settings. To foster a growth mindset, embrace active learning. Instead of simply attending class and listening to your instructor, identify and use *learning strategies*—methods for mastering important course material.

Consider Cody's experience. Cody is studying to become a certified medical assistant and is taking a course in medical terminology. While studying one evening, he encounters an unfamiliar term: *neuropathy*. He decides to puzzle out the meaning rather than Google the term. To do that, he recalls information he learned in his biology and anatomy courses: *Neurology* is the study of the nervous system, and *pathology* means "disease." He combines these two pieces of information and determines that *neuropathy* means "a disease of the nerves." By doing this, he has adopted an active learning approach: connecting past learning to this new term to figure out its meaning.

As you read this book, you'll find dozens of active learning strategies—from the best ways to schedule your time and preview your textbooks to tactics for effective note taking and paper writing. Not all strategies work in all situations, but if you experiment, you'll figure out which ones work best for you with each course and assignment. In the meantime, get a head start by giving these strategies a try.

❥ **CONNECT**
TO MY CLASSES

Pick an active-learning strategy described in this section and explain how you'll apply it in a class this week or next.

"What Do *You* Think This Term Means?" Joining a study group can help you take an active approach to your learning in college. You can discuss assignments with other group members, brainstorm possible test questions, or debate concepts from class. wavebreakmedia/ Shutterstock

1. **Get involved.** Asking questions in class can help clarify content you find confusing. Briefly summarize what you do understand about the topic: Then ask about the parts that are unclear. For instance, "You said that alternative energy sources, like solar or wind, have influenced the debate about global warming. But can you please describe the scientific research going on in those areas?" Form or join study groups to discuss assignments, brainstorm possible test questions, or debate ideas you're learning about in class.

2. **Look for connections.** What you learn in one class often relates to something you're learning in another or to an experience you've had in the past. As Cody discovered, connecting new, unfamiliar material to other material is a powerful active learning strategy. When you make such connections, you're more likely to remember what you've learned, allowing you to use your new knowledge long after the class ends.

3. **Seek applications for your new knowledge.** Look for ways you can apply what you're learning to your personal life, your current job, or your future career. As we discuss

in the critical thinking and goal-setting chapter, applying what you've learned is an important critical thinking skill and makes the concepts you're learning more concrete.

Navigate the Transition to College Life

We're all accustomed to some degree of personal responsibility in our lives, but in college, personal responsibility is a whole new ballgame. For one thing, in college you probably have a lot more independence—and therefore more responsibility—than you had in high school. (See Table 3.3 for common differences between these environments.) Take Theo. In high school his parents woke him up each morning, and his school days were highly structured. In college it's up to him to set his alarm, go to class, and study for tests. Theo—not anyone else—must structure his own time and make choices that keep him on a path to success.

If you entered college a number of years after graduating from high school, you're probably used to personal responsibility. You may have several years of

⟩ CONNECT TO MY RESOURCES

List your *most* important responsibilities this term. Identify two resources, either on campus or in your community, that can help you build a plan for managing these high-priority responsibilities.

TABLE 3.3   **Common Differences between High School and College**

In high school	In college
Your time and schedule was structured by others.	You must manage your time and choose how to spend it.
You were told what to learn and often how to learn it. Learning was teacher-focused.	You must figure out what to learn and how to learn it. Learning is student-focused.
You needed your parents' permission to participate in extracurricular activities.	You must choose whether to participate in co-curricular activities, and which fit best with your academic, personal, and other goals.
You could count on parents and teachers to remind you of your responsibilities and to give regular guidance in setting priorities.	You must set your own priorities and take responsibility for achieving them.
You attended class 5 days a week and proceeded from one class directly to another.	You often have hours between classes and may not attend classes every day. Much of your work will happen outside of class time.
Most of your classes were determined by school counselors.	You must choose which classes to take in consultation with faculty and academic advisers. Your schedule may look easier than it actually is.
Students are not responsible for knowing what is required to graduate or tracking their own progress.	Students are expected to select their own majors and/or minors and are expected to learn the graduation requirements for their programs of study.
Summary: Students are told what to do and corrected if their behavior is not in line with expectations.	**Summary: Students are expected to take responsibility for their path and academic success, as well as the consequences and rewards of their actions.**

Credit: "Common Differences between High School and College." Used by permission of the Altshuler Learning Enhancement Center at Southern Methodist University.

employment under your belt and have a family to help support. Still, you'll likely find yourself accountable for new kinds of decisions when you start college. Vicky is a good example. A first-year student, Vicky has a job and two young children. She's used to caring for her kids and earning a living, but now she has another responsibility: staying focused on her studies. Only she can decide how to balance her various responsibilities as she pursues her degree.

Think about Thinking and Learning

Metacognition:
Thinking about thinking or about learning.

If you're an active learner, you monitor your learning and adjust your strategies based on your results. You're also aware of how you think and learn. Scholars call this awareness **metacognition**, which means "thinking about thinking" or "thinking about learning." For instance, you're engaging in metacognition if you notice that you have an easier time learning biology than learning European history, if you discover that one study strategy works better for you than another, and every time you reflect on your ACES results.

To get a better sense of how metacognition works, consider Cholena's experience. She just got her first writing assignment back in Freshman Composition, on which she got a C–. Instead of getting frustrated or losing hope, Cholena reflected on her instructor's comments and how she had approached the assignment. She asked herself, "How did I approach writing the paper, and how did that work out for me?" She also took the paper to a tutor in the writing center. Together, they discussed her writing strategies, the instructor's comments, and approaches she might take to get better grades. All of these actions involve metacognition.

Research shows that metacognition promotes learning.[5] Students who reflect on their approach to coursework remember more information, apply that information to new situations more effectively, and get higher grades. To make use of metacognition to improve your performance in school, try these strategies.

Think Your Thoughts.
How do you usually think through class assignments? What study strategies work best for you? When you explore these kinds of questions, you're using metacognition — thinking about how you think and learn. And the more you use it, the greater the chance you'll improve your performance in school.
Snvv/Shutterstock

- **Plan and organize.** Set learning goals, and preview assignments so you can decide how best to approach them.

- **Monitor your progress.** Check your progress against time lines you set for yourself. Troubleshoot problems. Ask yourself whether you're doing your best work or whether you could improve your effort.

- **Evaluate your results and make adjustments.** Consider how well your learning strategies helped you achieve a goal. If you weren't as successful as you had hoped, plan how to change your strategy the next time.

These metacognitive strategies may seem familiar because you've seen many of them before. Critical thinking, goal setting, and decision making also call for you to evaluate your learning, apply new knowledge, reflect on your results, and make changes as needed to get better results. Since these skills are all connected, you can use them over and over again, in any setting.

Take a moment now to assess your metacognitive skills. What are you thinking about as you read this section of the chapter? Are you daydreaming, contemplating all the assignments that are due in your other classes, or pondering what to make for dinner? Or are you considering how these concepts can benefit you, be useful in other courses and assignments, and help your future career? If you reflect on both the *content* you're studying and the *processes* you're using to understand and apply material, you're on your way to becoming an active learner who makes good use of metacognition.

ACTIVE LEARNING AND PERSONAL RESPONSIBILITY LEAD TO SUCCESS!

As you've discovered by now, your instructors expect you to complete assignments outside of class on a regular basis. Homework assignments help you learn course content. They also encourage you to become a more *independent* and *active* learner. And research suggests that being this kind of learner can boost your odds of succeeding in school.

In fact, researchers Anastasia Kitsantas and Barry J. Zimmerman set out to answer a key question about types of learners: Are students who take responsibility for their homework and who believe in their ability to complete assignments more successful than those who don't? Their research findings suggest that the answer to that question is yes. In their study they surveyed more than two hundred university students to see how responsibly the students made plans to complete homework assignments and how strongly they believed in their ability to finish the assignments. Students with high self-efficacy who actively planned how to complete their assignments earned significantly higher grades than the other students in the study.

How did those successful students demonstrate responsibility? They took a series of steps — steps that *you* can take — to set themselves up for success:

- Designating a regular place to study
- Estimating the time needed to complete assignments
- Prioritizing tasks
- Completing assignments on time

In addition, the most successful students believed in their ability to

- Take notes
- Find help when they needed it
- Use many different learning strategies

Students with high self-efficacy who took personal responsibility for their homework got better grades than students who didn't.

THE BOTTOM LINE

When you take responsibility for completing assignments and believe in your ability to complete them, you'll get the best results.

REFLECTION QUESTIONS

1. **When you receive a homework assignment, what steps do you take to prepare to complete it?**
2. **Where do you prefer to study, and why?**
3. **What steps can you take this term to make sure you turn in assignments on time?**

A. Kitsantas and B. J. Zimmerman, "College Students' Homework and Academic Achievement: The Mediating Role of Self-Regulatory Beliefs," *Metacognition and Learning* 4 (2009): 97–110.

Motivation, Decision Making, and Personal Responsibility at Work

Imagine that you're a manager who needs to fill an open position. What qualities would you look for in a job candidate? If you're like many employers, you'd hunt for someone who can stay motivated, make good choices, and take responsibility for his or her actions—all characteristics you'll develop by taking this course and applying what you learn in this textbook. So keep up the good work! If you do, you'll be more likely to get a rewarding job, perform well in that job, and advance quickly in your career.

Apply Motivational Strategies on the Job

Staying motivated is just as important in your work life as it is in college. In fact, psychologists who focus on workplace success study the role of motivation closely.[6] Look at Table 3.4 to see how workplace motivational strategies relate to staying motivated in school.

Make Good Choices at Work

On the job, you make choices every day that can impact your career and your organization. Sometimes choices are tough. If a salesperson on your team gives a friend an unauthorized discount, what do you do? If you own a restaurant and revenues decrease, do you lay off employees or raise prices? In such cases, the decision-making process in this chapter can help you make sensible choices.

Of course, not every decision will work out the way you had hoped. When that happens, stay positive and rethink strategies that aren't working. *Choose* to own your successes and bounce back from your mistakes.

Take Responsibility to Boost Career Success

Taking responsibility on the job can enhance your career prospects. In fact, research shows that employees who have more independence—and therefore more responsibility—experience greater job satisfaction, better performance evaluations, and more success.[7]

TABLE 3.4 Staying Motivated in School and at Work

Staying motivated in school	Staying motivated at work
Take a variety of courses so that at least a few each term motivate you.	With your boss, design your job so that you can use a variety of skills.
Establish goals in each class that feel relevant to you.	Find aspects of your job that relate to your passions.
Develop active-learning strategies.	Take responsibility for your workplace choices.
Evaluate the results of your learning strategies, and if needed, adjust your strategies to get better results.	Reflect on the results of your work efforts, and if needed, change your strategies to get better results.
Identify your strengths and take advantage of them. Find ways to address your weaknesses. Graduate!	Seek out opportunities for growth and advancement at work.

MAKING DECISIONS ON THE JOB

Courtesy of
Tiona Blyden

NAME:	**Tiona Blyden**
PROFESSION:	*Entrepreneur*
SCHOOL:	*Morgan State University*
DEGREE:	*Bachelor of Science*
MAJORS:	*Communications and Broadcast Journalism*

As an entrepreneur and small business owner, decision making is critical for my success as well as my family's livelihood. While I make lots of small decisions every day, major decisions about my business can make a difference in success or failure. I recently had a critical decision to make regarding staffing in my business. I was spending a lot of time working and wasn't seeing much income for all of my efforts. I knew it was time to make a decision about how to move the business forward.

I started with a self-evaluation. Through this process of introspection and gathering information about myself, I laid out the fact that I've always had lots of ideas and tons of passion to give back to the world. I also discovered that I'm sometimes short on execution, or seeing my ideas through to the end. I was also spending three to four hours a day conducting administrative tasks for the business—not a good use of my time and creative energy. Using this information, I evaluated my options and made the major decision to hire a personal assistant to free up time. This was a significant expense for my small business, but I believed that it was the best choice.

Looking back on the past few months, this has turned out to be a wonderful choice. I'm working fewer hours and my income has increased. To be an effective leader and catapult your business to success, you have to make tough decisions. Knowing the facts and the options available can help you make the best decision. Often the best option requires a leap of faith.

YOUR TURN: Have you had to make a tough decision in a work situation? If so, how did it turn out? What did you learn from the outcome of your decision?

> " **Knowing the facts and the options available can help you make the best decision.**"

Taking responsibility can also help you deal with work challenges. Psychologist Marla Gottschalk describes one common challenge: feeling as though you don't have enough time to complete all the tasks facing you.[8] Many people blame others for this problem: "My coworkers interrupt me" or "We have too many meetings." Gottschalk suggests another response: acknowledging your role in the problem. Ask yourself, "Do I value my own time and communicate that to my coworkers?" or "What am I going to do to remedy this situation?" With this approach, you make yourself part of the solution to your problem. And that means *you* can control your own effectiveness at work.

my personal success plan

MOTIVATION, DECISION MAKING, AND PERSONAL RESPONSIBILITY

Are you inspired to set a new goal aimed at improving your motivation, decision-making skills, or ability to take personal responsibility? If so, the Personal Success Plan can walk you through the goal-setting process. Read the advice and examples; then sketch out your ideas in the space provided.

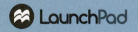

To access the Personal Success Plan online, go to the LaunchPad for *Connections.*

1 GATHER INFORMATION

Think about your strengths and weaknesses related to motivation, decision making, and personal responsibility. What strategies have worked for you in the past? What could you do differently? Revisit your Motivation, Decision Making, and Personal Responsibility score on ACES and review the relevant sections of this chapter for ideas.

2 SET A SMART GOAL

Use the information you've gathered to create a SMART goal, making sure to use the SMART goal checklist.

SAMPLE: I'm struggling to stay motivated in my sociology class. By the end of the week, I'll figure out how to make the course content more relevant to my interests and goals.

3 MAKE AN ACTION PLAN

Outline the specific steps you'll take to achieve your SMART goal, and note when you'll complete each step.

SAMPLE: Tomorrow, I'll ask my instructor if I can write my term paper on a topic I'm passionate about: factors that cause economic inequality.

4 LIST BARRIERS AND SOLUTIONS

Think about possible barriers to your action steps; then brainstorm solutions for overcoming them.

SAMPLE: My instructor might reject my term paper idea. If she does, I'll explain my areas of interest to see if there's another topic that I'm just as passionate about that would meet the course requirements.

5 ACT AND EVALUATE OUTCOMES

Now that your plan is in place, take action. Record each action step as you take it. Then evaluate whether you achieved your SMART goal, and make any adjustments needed to get better results in the future.

SAMPLE: My instructor and I were able to identify several alternative topics that interest me and would meet the course requirements.

6 CONNECT TO CAREER

List the skills you're building as you progress toward your SMART goal. How will you use these skills to land a job and succeed at work?

SAMPLE: I'm learning more about my interests and how to incorporate them into my coursework. These skills could help me work with a supervisor to design job responsibilities that appeal to these interests.

1 my information

2 my SMART goal

☐ **S**PECIFIC ☐ **M**EASURABLE ☐ **A**CHIEVABLE ☐ **R**ELEVANT ☐ **T**IME-LIMITED

3 my action plan

4 my barriers/ solutions

5 my actions/ outcomes

6 my career connection

CHAPTER SUMMARY

In this chapter you learned how motivation, decision making, and personal responsibility affect college and career success. Revisit the following key points, and reflect on how you can use this information to support your success now and in the future.

- Three key components of motivation are *self-efficacy*, or your belief in your ability to carry out the actions needed to reach a particular goal; the *relevance* of a goal to you; and your *attitude* toward the goal. The stronger these components are, the more motivated you'll feel to work toward the goal.

- You can be motivated by either intrinsic rewards (for example, a feeling of accomplishment) or extrinsic rewards (such as praise from others). But intrinsic motivators are more powerful than extrinsic motivators.

- The eight-step decision-making process can help you transform your motivation into action by making carefully considered choices.

- To take personal responsibility for your learning in college, you can develop a growth mindset, take an active approach to learning, successfully navigate the transition to college, and reflect on how you think and learn and make the changes needed to improve (metacognition).

- Motivation, decision making, and personal responsibility set the stage for career success as well as college success. By acquiring or strengthening these skills now, you'll make an attractive candidate for jobs that interest you, and you'll perform better in those roles.

CHAPTER ACTIVITIES

Journal Entry

BUILDING SELF-EFFICACY

Self-efficacy — your belief in your ability to carry out the actions needed to reach a particular goal — powerfully affects how you approach a task and deal with obstacles. You can increase your self-efficacy for a particular activity by experiencing success, observing others who are successful, seeking support and encouragement from others, and turning stress into a motivator.

In this journal entry, identify an activity that you initially didn't believe you could do but went on to complete successfully. Describe how achieving small successes, observing successful people, seeking support and encouragement, and using stress as motivation increased your sense of self-efficacy for that activity.

Then identify an activity you would like to perform more confidently. How could you build feelings of self-efficacy for this activity? What small tasks might you complete successfully to build your confidence? Who could encourage and support you, or be a good model? How can you manage your stress so you can continue to make progress?

Adopting a Success Attitude

VISUALIZING SUCCESS

Visualization is a powerful success strategy that can instill positive emotions, help you assess the relevance of your goals, and motivate you to follow through on your intentions. Try a short visualization activity designed to help you reflect on your motivation for being in college.

1. Find a quiet, peaceful place where you can be alone. Close your eyes and breathe in deeply through your nose. Hold for a count of three, and then breathe out through your mouth. Repeat this process until you feel your body relaxing and your mind clearing.

2. Imagine yourself in a graduation gown walking across the stage to receive your diploma. You shake hands with the college president, and as you walk off the stage you notice a video camera pointed at you. A reporter asks if she can interview you for a "graduation success story." You agree. Think about how you would respond to her questions: "How are you feeling right now? What does this accomplishment mean to you? What explains your success? How did you stay motivated when the going got tough? How will your life change now that you have this degree?" The reporter thanks you for your time, and you walk back to your seat.

3. Translate your thoughts and feelings about getting your degree into action steps. What three actions could you take this week to ensure that you're on the right path and to make this graduation scenario come true?

Applying Your Skills

MONITORING, EVALUATING, AND ADJUSTING FOR COLLEGE SUCCESS

When you monitor your progress, evaluate the results of your strategies, and adjust your strategies as needed, you take responsibility for your learning. Practice each of these skills in the following activity.

Monitoring Your Progress

Pretend that you're the instructor of this course and that you have to assign yourself a letter grade as a student. Give yourself a grade that honestly reflects three class-performance criteria: your attitude, effort, and results up to this point in the term. You may use + or – designations such as A– or C+.

Letter grade: _____

Evaluating Results

Explain why you gave yourself this grade by responding to the following questions:

1. How would you describe your attitude toward this class? How might you consciously or unconsciously convey this attitude toward your actual instructor?

2. What kind of effort have you put into this course so far? Such effort might include reading, taking notes, completing assignments, participating in

classroom discussions, reflecting on course material, and applying your new knowledge.

3. What results have you achieved in this class up to this point? Results can include quiz grades, written feedback on a journal entry, points for completing an assignment, and your instructor's verbal acknowledgment of a thoughtful response you provided, as well as class attendance, participation in discussions, and assignments turned in on time.

Making Adjustments

Give yourself both positive and constructive feedback on your attitude, effort, and results. What are you doing well? What could you improve? What adjustments will you make in the next week to improve your performance (or maintain outstanding performance) in this class?

College Success = Career Success

LEVERAGING INTRINSIC MOTIVATION IN YOUR CAREER

In this chapter you've learned about intrinsic motivation, which in some cases can be more powerful than extrinsic motivation. To explore how intrinsic motivation can affect your career success, respond to the following scenarios.

1. You've won the lottery, but one condition of receiving the money is that you have to work forty hours a week. What three occupations would you consider pursuing? Why? (Don't worry if they require more education—you'll have the money to pay for it.)

2. A company offers you a job with an annual salary of $2 million. You're asked to create a unique job title for yourself and outline five job responsibilities based on activities you most enjoy doing. What title and responsibilities would you select?

3. Identify the worst job you've ever had (or could imagine having). Besides an inadequate salary, what made (or would make) it the worst job?

Based on your responses to these three scenarios, create a list of intrinsic rewards that motivate you. How might you use this list to make career-related decisions, such as choosing a major, identifying a career path, applying for a job, accepting a job, or leaving a job?

4 Learning Preferences

Learning Preferences: The Basics

Identify Your Learning Preferences

Use Learning Preferences in Your Courses

Use Learning Preferences in Your Career

My Personal Success Plan

David Freund/Getty Images

f your stomach starts growling, would you rather feast on pizza or on tacos? After a long day in class, would you rather watch TV or go for a run? Your responses to these questions show your preferences — even if you answered "neither." Although your preferences in these kinds of choices may be clear, your preferences in how you approach learning new course material may be less obvious. Do you prefer to learn by reading a book or by listening to a lecture? By talking over ideas with your classmates or by studying on your own? By looking at the big picture or by examining the details first?

Thinking about your learning preferences gives you several important advantages. First, it makes you more self-aware and self-directed. As a result, you make better decisions about how to study, and you can seek out courses that align with how you like to learn. For instance, if you're a hands-on learner, you might thrive in courses in chemistry, nursing, dance, and education. If you love theories and concepts, you might prefer philosophy, psychology, and business courses. Second, thinking about your learning preferences helps you identify and overcome your "blind spots." For example, if you realize you focus so much on the big picture that you tend to miss important details, you can catch yourself before you make that mistake again. Finally, thinking about your learning preferences helps you understand your instructors' teaching preferences — they do have them — so you can figure out how to thrive in your courses, even when your preferences and your instructors' don't match.

Learning on the job is just as important as learning in the classroom, so understanding your preferences will also prove useful in your career. Your preferences affect how you approach work tasks or projects. And understanding how your coworkers and supervisors learn allows you to fine-tune your interactions with them — especially when you're working in teams.

There are many ways to classify learning preferences. In this chapter we look at two: the Myers-Briggs Type Indicator (MBTI) and VARK (Visual, Aural, Read-Write, and Kinesthetic) model. For each model you'll identify your preferences and discover actions you can take if your learning strategies don't work well in specific settings. Finally, you'll consider how understanding your preferences and others' can help you in your career.

David Freund/Getty Images

Reflect

On Your Learning Preferences

MY ACES SCORE

☐ **HIGH**

☐ **MODERATE**

☐ **LOW**

LaunchPad

To find your **Learning Preferences score,** go to the LaunchPad for *Connections*.

Take a moment to reflect on your Learning Preferences score on ACES. Find your score and add it in the circle to the right.

This score measures your beliefs about how well you understand your learning preferences. Do you think it's an accurate snapshot of your understanding? Why or why not?

■ **IF YOU SCORED IN THE HIGH RANGE** and you feel that this score is accurate, you may have a solid understanding of how you learn. Put that information to good use in your classes and when you study. As you read this chapter, be on the lookout for new techniques you can use to learn information. Seize the opportunity to hone your existing learning strategies *and* develop new strategies.

■ **IF YOU SCORED IN THE MODERATE OR LOW RANGE**, now is the perfect time to discover more about your learning preferences. Let's say you took up juggling as a way to relieve stress. Though you probably couldn't keep all the balls in the air the first time, chances are that the more you practiced, the better you got. Most people don't fully understand their learning preferences right away, but with time and practice they become more self-aware. Use this chapter to learn more about yourself and which strategies can work for you.

Learning Preferences: The Basics

A **learning preference** (also called a *learning style*) is a person's preferred method of learning. It refers to how you like to acquire and work with information, including how you prefer to gather, interpret, evaluate, organize, and draw conclusions about the information. If these concepts sound familiar, you're already one step ahead of the game because they're also components of critical thinking. In fact, you can think of your learning preferences as your preferred ways of engaging in critical thinking.

In college every student acquires and works with information — for instance, through classroom learning, reading textbooks, conducting experiments, and studying for quizzes and tests. But students differ in *how* they prefer to acquire and work with information. Take Dylan and Elizabeth. They're in a first-year seminar course, and their instructor has just challenged them to think critically about how they learn best. Dylan realizes that he loves classes in which he can take part in discussions and find out what other students know and think. This way of learning keeps him energized and engaged. By contrast, Elizabeth finds it difficult to learn new information while she's also expected to participate in

Learning Preference: Your preferred method for acquiring and working with information. Also called a *learning style*.

discussion. She likes lecture classes best and enjoys discussing material later in her study group once she feels ready to contribute to the conversation. By thinking *metacognitively* about how they prefer to learn, Dylan and Elizabeth will take a more active approach to mastering course material and develop more effective learning strategies. Learning about your own preferences will help you do the same.

As you think about ways of learning, remember the word *preference*. Your learning preferences are the ways that you prefer to learn, when given the choice, and these preferences strongly influence the learning strategies you develop. However, your preferences aren't the only ways you *can* learn. Although most of the time you'll probably use learning strategies that make you most comfortable—those that reflect your preferences—you can also develop other techniques with effort and practice. Why would you bother? Because doing so makes you more flexible: You can make adjustments if a particular approach isn't working or the learning situation demands a strategy that you don't typically use. For instance, though Dylan prefers to learn through discussion, he can still learn by reflecting on material on his own—and sometimes he may need to. It will just take more effort for him to use this way of learning.

To see for yourself how preferences work, try a quick activity. Start by signing your name on the line below:

_____

Can You Change Your Colors? When it comes to how you approach learning, think of yourself as a chameleon: You can change your "colors" (how you learn) depending on your learning environment. The more adaptable you are in how you learn, the more you can adjust to changing circumstances—and get the most from your classes. Dr. J. Beller/Shutterstock

How long did it take you to sign your name? Is your signature recognizable to you and others? How much effort and thought did you put into writing your signature?

Now sign your name on the line below using your *other* hand:

_____

Was anything different this time around? How much time, effort, and thought did you put into writing your signature on the second try? How does your signature look?

If you're like most people, you found it easier to sign your name with one hand than with the other. The signature using your nonpreferred hand probably took more time, thought, and effort, and maybe it looks a bit messy. When given the choice, you'll continue writing with your preferred hand because you get a better result. But suppose something happens—let's say you break your arm—and you have to write with your nonpreferred hand. At first you'd likely find it harder to do, but the more you practiced, the easier it would get.

The same is true for learning strategies: Most of the time, you'll rely on the strategies that feel most natural and familiar. After all, if something works, why change it? But if needed, you can adjust to different conditions by using learning strategies that lie outside your comfort zone. Doing so takes time, effort, and an open mind—but the results will be worth the investment.

Identify Your Learning Preferences

In the following sections, we explore two popular instruments for understanding how you prefer to learn: the Myers-Briggs Type Indicator (MBTI) and the VARK (Visual, Aural, Read-Write, and Kinesthetic) model. You can use each of these instruments, or both in combination, to identify your learning preferences. In fact, evaluating your results from both can give you valuable insights that can, in turn, help you develop effective learning strategies. As you read about both models, think about which preferences you identify with most. How might these preferences influence the way you tackle new and challenging material? How might they help explain why you like some classes more than others? How might understanding your preferences help you do well in classroom environments that challenge you to step outside your comfort zone?

Use the Myers-Briggs Model

Katharine Briggs and her daughter Isabel Myers created the Myers-Briggs Type Indicator (MBTI) based on the work of psychologist Carl Jung. In Jung's theory, four dimensions of our personalities guide our behavior, influencing where we focus our energy, the kinds of information we prefer working with, how we make decisions, and how we organize our time and activities. Each of the four dimensions can be thought of as a continuum: Extravert/Introvert, Sensing/Intuitive, Thinking/Feeling, and Judging/Perceiving.[1] As you read the following descriptions, consider where you fall on each dimension's continuum. You may explore this content in even more detail if you take the MBTI in class or if it's available at your campus career center.

Extravert/Introvert. The Extravert/Introvert dimension describes where you tend to focus your energy. Extraverts are action-oriented and like spending time with others. Being with people energizes them. Extraverts like Dylan, whom you read about at the beginning of the chapter, often learn best by interacting and discussing their learning with others or by applying their learning to real-life problems. Dylan's preferred learning strategies may include forming study groups and working on group projects.

By contrast, Introverts are more thought-oriented and are energized by spending time alone. Introverts like Elizabeth prefer to learn through reflection and feel most comfortable discussing ideas once they've had a chance to think about them. Elizabeth can still work effectively in groups, but she may want time to process new information before she feels prepared to discuss it with others. Both Extraverts and Introverts can operate in their nonpreferred environments, but they may find it more draining than energizing.

Sensing/Intuitive. The Sensing/Intuitive dimension relates to the kind of information you prefer working with: the details and facts or the big picture. Sensing learners prefer working with information as it comes to them through their senses. They love details and facts and have an easy time remembering and organizing such information. They choose to focus on "what is" rather than on "what might be," and they enjoy making connections between seemingly unrelated pieces of information.

Sensing learners use the facts to build an understanding of the big picture. For example, Jonah isn't sure what career he wants to pursue after graduation (the big picture). During his first two years at school, he chooses courses from the list of requirements and electives that interest him most. By the end of his

❧ CONNECT TO MY EXPERIENCE

When you're learning something new, do you focus on details and facts or on the big picture? Think about the advantages and disadvantages of each preference. Then, in writing, describe a time when focusing on details caused you to miss out on the big picture, or when focusing on the big picture caused you to overlook important details.

What's Your Sense of Snow? Suppose you've never seen snow before. If you're a Sensing learner, you'd probably look at the snowflakes (the details) first as a way to understand the concept of a snowstorm (the big picture). If you're an Intuitive learner, you'd pay attention to the snowstorm and then use your understanding of it to grasp the concept of individual snowflakes.
Left: Kichigin/Shutterstock *Right:* Creative Travel Projects/Shutterstock

second year, he sees that many of the courses he has gravitated toward concern human nature and relationships, such as psychology, sociology, and public health. Putting these details together, he concludes that he may enjoy careers in social work, psychotherapy, and health administration.

By contrast, Intuitive learners prefer to pay attention to facts and details only long enough to understand the big picture—the theory behind the concept or how the concept connects to other material. They focus on the possibilities ("what might be") rather than on just the facts. They like to get an overview of a topic before digging into the specifics and want to know answers to broad questions such as "How does this topic relate to the last topic presented in class?"

Intuitive learners use the big picture to help themselves organize details and facts. For example, Leah has always seen herself going into some type of helping profession. Having this big picture in mind, she selects courses that specifically relate to these types of professions.

Thinking/Feeling.   The Thinking/Feeling dimension relates to how you make decisions. Thinking decision makers prefer to use analysis and logic to arrive at a decision. By contrast, Feeling decision makers tend to make choices that maintain harmony or that demonstrate concern about human values and needs.

Take Tyler and Maria, who are in the same philosophy class, and are given an assignment to debate whether ethics or profits matter more in business. As a Thinking decision maker, Maria chooses to gather data, consider the pros and cons of both sides, and present an argument that making a profit is the primary goal in business and leads to social good. Tyler, who is a Feeling decision maker, chooses to focus on how a business's decisions affect the well-being of people and communities. He prepares a more emotional argument that putting ethics at the forefront of business can lead to more profitable operations.

"Is It Logical?" Since the *Star Trek* TV series began in 1966, Spock—the pointy-eared Vulcan who is second in command to the starship *Enterprise* captain James T. Kirk—has represented the Thinking learning style. Spock makes decisions based on facts and logic rather than on emotion. His Thinking approach complements Kirk's Feeling approach to decision making, so the two make a powerful team. © Paramount Pictures/Photofest, Inc.

Being a Thinking or a Feeling learner can influence how you react during the various steps in the decision-making process (see the chapter on motivation, decision making, and personal responsibility). When evaluating the available options and weighing the pros and cons of each alternative, Thinkers may focus on the option that has more pros, while Feelers may concentrate on how the decision will affect the important people in their lives.

Judging/Perceiving. The Judging/Perceiving dimension describes how you organize your time and activities. Judging learners plan the details of their actions before proceeding, focus on actions that directly contribute to achievement of a goal or task, and generally have structured routines. They prefer making decisions and sticking with them and like to complete one project before starting another.

Perceiving learners are more comfortable taking action without first developing a plan. They multitask and juggle different projects at once, and prefer keeping their options open rather than committing to a decision.

When you study organization and time management in the corresponding chapter of this textbook, you may get a better sense of where your organizational preferences lie on this dimension. If you're a Judger, you'll likely appreciate the material on scheduling in that chapter. If you're a Perceiver, you may cringe at the thought of organizing your life so systematically.

Your Preferences. Now that you're familiar with the four dimensions of the MBTI (see Table 4.1 for a review), take a moment to record where you think you fall on each dimension. Using Figure 4.1, place an X on each line to designate your preference and how strong you think it is. For example, an X far to the right on the Extravert/Introvert line would indicate that you have a strong Introvert preference, while an X far to the left would show a strong Extravert preference. An X somewhere in the middle would suggest a more moderate or a neutral preference.

TABLE 4.1   Myers-Briggs Dimensions

Extravert/Introvert: Where you focus your energy
E: Externally in the world of people I: Internally in your head
Sensing/Intuitive: The kind of information you prefer working with
S: Facts and details N: The big picture
Thinking/Feeling: How you make decisions
T: Analysis and logic F: Human values and needs
Judging/Perceiving: How you organize your time and activities
J: Planned actions and structured routines P: Action taken without a plan, options kept open

FIGURE 4.1 **Myers-Briggs Self-Rating Chart**

	Strong Preference	Moderate Preference	Neutral	Moderate Preference	Strong Preference	
Spend time with people Learn through discussion Share ideas in the moment	**Extravert**				**Introvert**	Prefer time alone Learn through reflection Think about ideas before sharing
Focus on details Prefer facts Focus on "what is"	**Sensing**				**Intuitive**	Focus on big picture Prefer concepts Focus on "what might be"
Consider facts when making decisions Make decisions based on logic Decide with my head	**Thinking**				**Feeling**	Consider people when making decisions Make decisions based on values Decide with my heart
Like coming to decisions Like structure Like to plan	**Judging**				**Perceiving**	Avoid decisions in favor of exploring options Go with the flow Comfortable without a plan

Use the VARK Model

The VARK is another model that can help you understand how you prefer to learn. Proposed by Neil Fleming, a high school and university teacher, the VARK describes what types of information people prefer to work with while learning.[2] According to this model, learners have a preference for working with one or more of the following types of information: **V**isual, **A**ural (auditory), **R**ead-Write, and **K**inesthetic (hands-on, action-based). Many people feel comfortable working with more than one of these types of information. As you read the descriptions of each preference, consider which one(s) fit you best.

Visual (V). Visual learners prefer working with information that comes in such forms as charts, diagrams, maps, and graphs. They may translate material presented in class into concept maps, flowcharts, or other graphic forms to better understand course concepts and see how they relate to each other. For example, Marla, a Visual learner, made a map of concepts and arguments related to vegetarianism in her health class. The map helped her understand and organize various aspects of this lesson, including the history of vegetarianism; health, economic, environmental, and moral reasons for choosing this lifestyle; and possible health benefits and dangers associated with it.

Aural (A). Aural learners prefer working with information that comes in auditory forms, such as lectures, podcasts, and discussions with others. For instance, after listening to a lecture in her health class, Shoko talked about what she was learning with her vegetarian friend Becca. Through this conversation she found out why Becca decided to give up meat and what health benefits she experienced as a result of her choice.

EXAMINING MBTI DIFFERENCES IN ONLINE LEARNERS

Are you taking an online course? If so, you know that the online educational experience differs from the traditional face-to-face experience. For example, in an online course you use technology to exchange ideas, rather than talk in person with your instructor and classmates. You also have time to reflect as you formulate responses to discussion postings.

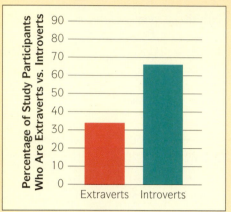

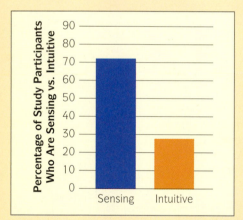

In this study more Introverts and Sensing students took online classes than did Extraverts and Intuitive students.

Because online and traditional learning environments differ, do students who choose to take online courses have different learning preferences than students who don't? To answer this question, Dr. Davison Mupinga and his colleagues examined the Myers-Briggs types of 131 students enrolled in online courses in the Department of Industrial Technology at Indiana State University. They found that twice as many Introverts and almost three times as many Sensing learners enrolled in these courses, compared to Extraverts and Intuitives. This suggests that the vast majority of students in these online courses prefer having time alone to reflect on course content, and they prefer learning that focuses on factual information rather than on the big picture.

What do these results mean for you? Understanding your preferences will help you assess which learning environments you'll feel more *and* less comfortable in. However, you shouldn't avoid courses in learning environments where you're less comfortable. Rather, the trick is to identify which environments are challenging and then actively seek out strategies that can help you succeed in those classes.

THE BOTTOM LINE

Understanding your learning preferences can help you find learning environments that best suit you — *and* succeed in environments where you're less comfortable.

REFLECTION QUESTIONS

1. Where do you think your preference lies on the Extravert–Introvert continuum? How does the strength of this preference influence your comfort level when interacting with others in face-to-face courses?

2. Where do you think your preference lies on the Sensing–Intuitive continuum? How does the strength of this preference help explain your comfort level with details and facts versus theories and big concepts?

3. If you're taking an online course now, how has your experience been? If you've never taken an online course, what aspects of that environment do you think would be most enjoyable and most challenging for you?

D. M. Mupinga, R. T. Nora, and D. C. Yaw, "The Learning Styles, Expectations, and Needs of Online Students," *College Teaching* 54 (2006): 185–89.

Read-Write (R). Read-Write learners prefer learning from the written word. They may read a lot, use text-heavy slide presentations, and seek out books and journal articles using popular online sources such as Google Scholar. They may prefer to study by rereading important material, revising and reorganizing class notes, or preparing brief written responses to anticipated essay questions. Mateo, for example, decided to supplement the lecture on vegetarianism by reviewing Web sites and books on the topic in the college library. In these resources he learned more about the practice of vegetarianism in various religions, a topic that the lecture covered only briefly. These written resources reinforced material presented in the lecture and extended his learning in ways he found interesting.

Learning by Doing. The people hanging from these poles are taking a climbing course offered by a utility company. They're students at a workforce institute affiliated with a nearby community college. The three-week course supports kinesthetic learning — learning by doing. Students master skills that will prepare them to compete for jobs in the utility industry, such as pre-apprentice lineworker.
Justin Sullivan/Staff/Getty

Kinesthetic (K). Kinesthetic learners prefer experience and practice as a means of learning. They learn by doing or by watching others, and they enjoy watching demonstrations, trying their hand at simulations, and analyzing case studies. For example, Terrell decided to interview different types of vegetarians, including vegans and macrobiotics. After conducting these interviews, he spent a week on a vegan diet to see if he could detect any health-related benefits and challenges.

The VARK Questionnaire. Now that you understand the VARK model, you can assess your preferences using the VARK dimensions. Take a few minutes to respond to the items on the following page and score your assessment. Place a check mark next to all the answers that apply to you; you can choose more than one response per question, or you can leave the question blank if none of the responses apply to you.

Keep in mind that your score in each learning preference category (V, A, R, and K) represents the strength of your preference for that type of information. Some students have clear preferences (for example, **V = 11**, A= 3, R = 1, K = 1), while other students' preferences are more evenly distributed (for instance, V = 2, A = 1, **R = 6, K = 7**).

Once you have your results, reflect on them. What is your highest score? Does that learning preference make sense to you, based on your understanding of yourself? Do you have two or three scores that are relatively close together? If so, what are they? Do you use learning strategies from each of these categories?

VARK Questionnaire

1. You are helping someone who wants to go to your airport, the center of town, or a railway station. You would:
   - [ ] **A.** go with her.
   - [ ] **B.** tell her the directions.
   - [ ] **C.** write down the directions.
   - [ ] **D.** draw, or show her a map, or give her a map.

2. A Web site has a video showing how to make a special graph. There is a person speaking, some lists and words describing what to do, and some diagrams. You would learn most from:
   - [ ] **A.** seeing the diagrams.
   - [ ] **B.** listening.
   - [ ] **C.** reading the words.
   - [ ] **D.** watching the actions.

3. You are planning a vacation for a group. You want some feedback from them about the plan. You would:
   - [ ] **A.** describe some of the highlights they will experience.
   - [ ] **B.** use a map to show them the places.
   - [ ] **C.** give them a copy of the printed itinerary.
   - [ ] **D.** phone, text, or e-mail them.

4. You are going to cook something as a special treat. You would:
   - [ ] **A.** cook something you know without the need for instructions.
   - [ ] **B.** ask friends for suggestions.
   - [ ] **C.** look on the Internet or in some cookbooks for ideas from the pictures.
   - [ ] **D.** use a cookbook where you know there is a good recipe.

5. A group of tourists wants to learn about the parks or wildlife reserves in your area. You would:
   - [ ] **A.** talk about, or arrange a talk for them about, parks or wildlife reserves.
   - [ ] **B.** show them maps and Internet pictures.
   - [ ] **C.** take them to a park or wildlife reserve and walk with them.
   - [ ] **D.** give them a book or pamphlets about the parks or wildlife reserves.

6. You are about to purchase a digital camera or mobile phone. Other than price, what would most influence your decision?
   - [ ] **A.** Trying or testing it.
   - [ ] **B.** Reading the details or checking its features online.
   - [ ] **C.** It is a modern design and looks good.
   - [ ] **D.** The salesperson telling me about its features.

7. Remember a time when you learned how to do something new. Avoid choosing a physical skill, e.g., riding a bike. You learned best by:
   - [ ] **A.** watching a demonstration.
   - [ ] **B.** listening to somebody explaining it and asking questions.
   - [ ] **C.** diagrams, maps, and charts — visual clues.
   - [ ] **D.** written instructions — e.g., a manual or book.

8. You have a problem with your heart. You would prefer that the doctor:
   - [ ] **A.** gave you something to read to explain what was wrong.
   - [ ] **B.** used a plastic model to show what was wrong.
   - [ ] **C.** described what was wrong.
   - [ ] **D.** showed you a diagram of what was wrong.

9. You want to learn a new program, skill, or game on a computer. You would:
   - [ ] **A.** read the written instructions that came with the program.
   - [ ] **B.** talk with people who know about the program.
   - [ ] **C.** use the controls or keyboard.
   - [ ] **D.** follow the diagrams in the book that came with it.

10. I like Web sites that have:
    - [ ] **A.** things I can click on, shift, or try.
    - [ ] **B.** interesting design and visual features.
    - [ ] **C.** interesting written descriptions, lists, and explanations.
    - [ ] **D.** audio channels where I can hear music, radio programs, or interviews.

11. Other than price, what would most influence your decision to buy a new non-fiction book?
    - [ ] **A.** The way it looks is appealing.
    - [ ] **B.** Quickly reading parts of it.
    - [ ] **C.** A friend talks about it and recommends it.
    - [ ] **D.** It has real-life stories, experiences, and examples.

12. You are using a book, CD, or Web site to learn how to take photos with your new digital camera. You would like to have:
    - [ ] **A.** a chance to ask questions and talk about the camera and its features.
    - [ ] **B.** clear written instructions with lists and bullet points about what to do.
    - [ ] **C.** diagrams showing the camera and what each part does.
    - [ ] **D.** many examples of good and poor photos and how to improve them.

VARK Questionnaire

(continued)

13. Do you prefer a teacher or a presenter who uses:
    - ☐ **A.** demonstrations, models, or practical sessions.
    - ☐ **B.** question and answer, talk, group discussion, or guest speakers.
    - ☐ **C.** handouts, books, or readings.
    - ☐ **D.** diagrams, charts, or graphs.

14. You have finished a competition or test and would like some feedback. You would like to have feedback:
    - ☐ **A.** using examples from what you have done.
    - ☐ **B.** using a written description of your results.
    - ☐ **C.** from somebody who talks it through with you.
    - ☐ **D.** using graphs showing what you had achieved.

15. You are going to choose food at a restaurant or cafe. You would:
    - ☐ **A.** choose something that you have had there before.
    - ☐ **B.** listen to the waiter or ask friends to recommend choices.
    - ☐ **C.** choose from the descriptions in the menu.
    - ☐ **D.** look at what others are eating or look at pictures of each dish.

16. You have to make an important speech at a conference or special occasion. You would:
    - ☐ **A.** make diagrams or get graphs to help explain things.
    - ☐ **B.** write a few key words and practice saying your speech over and over.
    - ☐ **C.** write out your speech and learn from reading it over several times.
    - ☐ **D.** gather many examples and stories to make the talk real and practical.

Your VARK Score

Use the following scoring chart to find the VARK category that each of your answers corresponds to. Circle the letters that correspond to your answers. For example, if you answered B and C for question 3, circle V and R in the question 3 row.

Responses to Question 3:	A	B	C	D
VARK letter	K	(V)	(R)	A

Question	A category	B category	C category	D category
1.	K	A	R	V
2.	V	A	R	K
3.	K	V	R	A
4.	K	A	V	R
5.	A	V	K	R
6.	K	R	V	A
7.	K	A	V	R
8.	R	K	A	V
9.	R	A	K	V
10.	K	V	R	A
11.	V	R	A	K
12.	A	R	V	K
13.	K	A	R	V
14.	K	R	A	V
15.	K	A	R	V
16.	V	A	R	K

MY HIGHEST SCORES

Total number of Vs circled =

Total number of As circled =

Total number of Rs circled =

Total number of Ks circled =

Use Learning Preferences in Your Courses

Now that you understand more about your learning preferences, apply that understanding! Use it to select learning strategies that will help you succeed in all kinds of classes and environments—from labs and lectures to discussion groups and solo research in the library. Mix it up a bit, too; find strategies that make sense based on your learning preferences, but also try out strategies that nudge you outside your comfort zone. Remember: You don't have to be limited by your strongest learning preferences. In fact, it's better to stretch yourself beyond those preferences. The more you experiment with different strategies, the more flexible you'll become as a learner.

Use Your MBTI Preferences

As you saw earlier, the MBTI model contains four separate dimensions: Extravert/Introvert, Sensing/Intuitive, Thinking/Feeling, and Judging/Perceiving. In Table 4.2 study tips are paired up with each of these dimensions. Use these tips to strengthen the learning strategies that align with your existing preferences or to develop alternative learning strategies.

TABLE 4.2   **Learning Strategies for the Myers-Briggs Dimensions**

Extravert	• Ask a family member, friend, or classmate to listen as you explain concepts from class. • Find a study group of other Extraverts and meet regularly. • Meet with your instructor, teaching assistant, or tutor to discuss important concepts from class.
Introvert	• Set aside quiet study time. • If you join a study group, learn topics in advance so you're prepared to discuss them. • After class, write a summary of what you've learned. Refer to your summary when sharing your thoughts in the next class.
Sensing	• Study with an Intuitive learner who can help you understand the big picture. • Outline the details of your study goals and strategy. • Combine facts in ways that help you tell a story about the big picture.
Intuitive	• Study with a Sensing learner so you don't miss details. • Focus on the what-ifs, possibilities, or applications associated with the material you're learning as a way to help you organize the facts. • Rather than feeling frustrated by the repetitive tasks associated with some classes, consider how these tasks help you better understand the big picture.
Thinking	• Go with your preference to focus on the logic of arguments and theories. But in group work, remember that Feeling learners prefer to focus on how arguments or theories affect people. • If class material seems unorganized and illogical, reorganize it so it makes sense to you. • Identify principles in material you're learning, and apply them systematically to new situations.

TABLE 4.2 (continued)

Feeling	• Go with your preference to focus on the impact of arguments and theories on the people involved. But in group work, remember that Thinking learners prefer to focus on the logic of arguments and theories. • You're most comfortable in study groups in which students agree with one another, but disagreement and debate are a natural part of learning. Step out of your comfort zone, and learn from different perspectives. • To feel personally connected to course material, find ways to make it relevant to your life.
Judging	• Create binders for each of your classes. Help other students (especially Perceivers) by sharing your organizational plan with them. • Create structured study schedules based on deadlines. • When you finish a task, reward yourself by doing something enjoyable.
Perceiving	• Instead of putting off studying until the last minute, use spare moments to review class notes and headings in your textbook chapters. • Break down large assignments into smaller, more manageable chunks. • If you start many projects, prioritize them, and deal with the most important ones when deadlines are approaching.

Use Your VARK Preferences

According to VARK, do you have a strong Visual, Aural, Read-Write, or Kinesthetic preference? Review your VARK scores from earlier in the chapter; find the strategies in Table 4.3 that correspond to your strongest preferences. How might you use these to learn more effectively? Also see the suggestions paired with your less preferred categories. Would you like to test any of these tips?

TABLE 4.3 **Learning Strategies for VARK Learning Preferences**

Visual (V)	• Underline, highlight, or use other tactics to mark up printed course materials. • Draw pictures or diagrams in your notes to illustrate examples. Reference these images when you study. • Ask your instructor for copies of visually complex materials presented in class.
Aural (A)	• Study in groups, and discuss concepts with others. • Record lectures (with your instructor's permission), and listen to them later. • Use word associations to learn terms, and repeat newly learned terms out loud.
Read-Write (R)	• Revise and reorganize your notes after every class to understand and remember concepts. • Find alternative written resources on a topic to supplement class-assigned reading. • Write out answers to possible test questions before taking exams.
Kinesthetic (K)	• Find hands-on ways to learn course content (such as trying computer simulations or conducting lab experiments). • Incorporate movement into your note taking by drawing charts or diagrams of important relationships covered in class. • Take breaks from studying and move around. Use the exercise to review or rehearse material that you've already learned.

USING LEARNING STRATEGIES IN COLLEGE

Courtesy of Terri Baskin Photography

NAME:	**Brittnee Nicole Baskin**
SCHOOL:	*Western Carolina University*
MAJOR:	*Motion Picture and Television Production*
CAREER GOAL:	*Director or Cinematographer*

" Sometimes you have to use more than one resource to make it through a class successfully."

I definitely have a learning style. I learn best from classes with lots of group discussions and visual aids. I like group discussions because they give me a chance to hear other people's opinions and understand where they're coming from. It can be difficult for me to stay focused in large lecture classes, so I sit close to the front and try to get to know the other people that I'm sitting around. That way, when there's time, we can have group discussions about the class material.

I'm a visual learner. It doesn't matter what subject it is, ever since elementary school I've needed pictures or diagrams to help me understand concepts. When I'm writing a paper, I like to start by drawing a diagram. I use arrows to help me understand what is going on and what direction I want to go in. In classes where teachers don't use lots of visuals, I've had to supplement with other material. Sometimes you have to use more than one resource to make it through a class successfully. I often use YouTube videos or find other visual information on the Internet. I've also found tutors who can help explain things using visuals.

One day I'd like to be a director or cinematographer. When I read books or hear things, I always visualize them in my head just like a movie. I hope my career will give me the opportunity to use my learning preference to help other visual learners see things in a way that they will appreciate and understand.

YOUR TURN: Brittnee's strongest VARK preference is Visual. Have you ever used any of the learning strategies that Brittnee describes? If so, which ones? If not, will you try any of these in your classes this term?

Work in a Group

Many instructors are big fans of group projects, and with good reason: Research has shown that group work contributes to learning and success in college.[3] An added benefit is that many jobs require you to work effectively in groups. As beneficial as it can be, though, group work can also be challenging—you'll be collaborating with other students, and many of them will have learning preferences that differ from your own. The good news? The more you understand your own learning preferences and those of other group members, the more you'll all be able to leverage each person's strengths. For instance, suppose your

Team Effort. In every group project you're involved in during your college and professional career, group members will have different learning preferences and adopt different learning strategies based on those preferences. When all group members understand their own and other members' preferences, they can take advantage of diverse strategies and work more effectively as a team. Roy Mehta/Getty Images

group includes Fadi, who's a Visual, Intuitive, and Judging learner. Fadi gladly takes responsibility for creating a project plan during the kickoff meeting. This "big picture" takes the form of a chart outlining which tasks have to be done when, and by whom, so that the group can submit a high-quality project on time. Fadi would likely do a great job with this responsibility.

When the inevitable difficulties arise, group members can also use their understanding of one another's learning preferences to resolve issues. For example, suppose you notice that Anatole, a Read-Write and Perceiving learner, has missed deadlines on some tasks he's responsible for. To make it easier for him to fulfill his responsibilities, you translate the project plan chart into a written list of tasks for him to complete each day until the project is done. As a Perceiving learner, he's comfortable without a plan, but you believe that the written list will appeal enough to his Read-Write preference that he'll then complete the parts of the project he's responsible for.

Diversity in learning preferences and strategies can greatly benefit group work—especially when all group members understand their own and other members' preferences.

Adapt to Differences in Teaching and Learning Preferences

In a perfect world, all instructors would teach in a way that matches your learning preferences. If you love listening, they would lecture. If you like talking, they would encourage class discussion. But in reality, teaching and learning

Multimodal Learner: Someone who uses many different learning strategies to adapt to the situation at hand.

CONNECT TO MY CLASSES

Identify the teaching preferences of the instructors you have this term. Which instructor's teaching preference is *least* aligned with your learning preferences? Why? Write down two strategies that could help you learn successfully in that instructor's class.

preferences don't always match up. You may want to work in groups or listen to guest speakers, but your instructors may have other ideas. You may wish that every test was multiple-choice, but your instructors may assign essay exams and term papers. To manage such a mismatch, become a **multimodal learner**: a learner who uses different strategies (even those outside his or her comfort zone) to adapt to different situations.

By developing the ability to use different learning strategies, you boost your chances of doing well in all your classes—not just the ones you like best. You also demonstrate personal responsibility: Instead of passively expecting instructors to change their approach to suit your preferences, you take charge of your own education.

To see how becoming a multimodal learner leads to academic success, consider Jamar, an art major who prefers lectures combined with visual aids. Most of his art instructors teach in a way that matches his learning preferences, and he's happy with the strategies he has developed to excel in these classes. But Jamar is also taking courses in mathematics, science, history, and the social sciences to fulfill his general-education requirements. Instructors in these classes want students to read large amounts of material and to do a lot of writing on exams. Jamar isn't fully comfortable with these teaching approaches, and he sometimes struggles to understand the course content. He decides to build up his strength in the Read-Write learning preference from the VARK model. He also tries some of the strategies for adopting a Judging style from the

Flex Your Learning Muscles. How your instructors prefer to teach course content won't always match how you prefer to learn. So you may need to go outside your comfort zone to adapt to your teachers' styles. This takes practice—but it also makes you a flexible learner who can switch learning strategies as needed to get the most from your courses. © DisabilityImages.com

MBTI so he can develop more structured plans for completing his reading assignments.

As Jamar discovered, a time may come when the learning strategies you rely on limit your effectiveness in particular learning environments. To increase your range of learning strategies, try the following tactics.

- **Refer to the tips in Tables 4.2 and 4.3** and pick learning strategies different from the ones you typically use. Remember: Just like signing your name with your nonpreferred hand, applying new strategies may take time and practice.

- **Talk with students in your classes** who have learning preferences that match the instructors' teaching preferences. Use these students as models. Ask them to share what works for them; then try the strategies they recommend.

- **Visit a tutor** associated with a course you find difficult. Ask for advice on how to develop learning strategies that work for that course.

- **Talk to your instructors.** They won't change the way they teach to match your learning preferences, but they don't want you to struggle. Visit them during office hours and have a conversation. They may be able to suggest ways to master the course content using your preferred learning strategies. For example, Jamar's math instructor recommended computer programs and supplemental resources that help explain math concepts in visual ways.

Seek Help for Learning Challenges

As you realize by now, we all learn in different ways. Beyond differences related to learning preferences, however, some people experience differences in how their brain receives or processes information—differences that can cause significant difficulty in listening, speaking, reading, writing, spelling, and interacting socially. In such cases, these people may be diagnosed with what's called a *learning disability*. Don't let this term fool you: People with learning disabilities still learn—just not in the same way as someone without one. A learning disability is really a learning *difference*.

Because learning disabilities can affect how people work with course material, students with diagnosed learning disabilities may be eligible to have their learning environment adapted (or *accommodated*) to suit their learning needs. For example, a student might be able to record lectures or receive extended time in which to complete an exam. The purpose of these adaptations is not to provide an advantage but rather to "level the playing field." That way, all students have an equal chance to learn the material and demonstrate their new knowledge and skills.

If you have a learning disability and need academic accommodations, visit your school's disability services office. The staff will review documentation of your disability and determine your eligibility for services. You can also visit the disability services office if you suspect you have an undiagnosed learning disability. The staff will help you seek appropriate testing, which will determine if you meet specific criteria to be diagnosed with a learning disability. The disability services office is a valuable resource you can use to better understand learning disabilities—and to get any help you might need.

❦ CONNECT TO MY RESOURCES

Do you need to register for accommodations in the classroom? Do you know a friend who does? On your college Web site, find the name and location of the campus office that provides these services. Write it down. Then record the steps a student would need to follow to set up accommodations.

Use Learning Preferences in Your Career

Understanding your learning preferences and adapting your learning strategies can help you excel on the job. In fact, most companies want employees who can adjust to different work environments as needed to build new skills and perform new responsibilities.

Work in a Team

To succeed in many careers today, you need to work in teams.[4] As in school, members of a work team will likely have different learning preferences. When team members understand their own and one another's preferences, they can build on each person's strengths and adapt their interactions to address issues that arise.

Roger, for example, is a Sensing and Perceiving learner. He likes to work on several projects at once and focus on details. Sometimes he misses the big picture, and he juggles so many projects that none move forward as fast as his supervisor wants. Roger has been teamed with Katarina, an Intuitive and Judging learner, to manage a new project: developing a training program for orienting student nurses on the hospital floor. Katarina prefers to move one project forward at a time and readily grasps the big picture associated with each, but she's less effective at tracking details. Roger and Katarina understand each other's learning preferences and use that understanding to manage their project. For instance, Katarina uses her grasp of the big picture to help Roger understand the project's overall goals: ensuring that student nurses understand policies and procedures and provide high-quality care without jeopardizing licensed professionals' work. Roger uses his grasp of the details to suggest steps they must take to execute the project, including identifying policies to cover, teaching the students the roles and responsibilities of health care providers on the floor, and providing detailed descriptions of tasks student nurses are permitted to do. Together, Roger and Katarina cover each other's blind spots, making their joint effort more successful than either of them would have been alone.

This flexibility is equally important for cultivating a good working relationship with your boss. The more you understand your preferences and your supervisor's, the more you can customize how you work together. For instance, you learn that your boss prefers to receive status updates by e-mail every Monday, rather than by informal chats in the hallway, so you adapt your communication to his preference. One of your weekly reports alerts him to the possibility of a missed deadline on a project. He meets with you to discuss solutions, such as finding someone to help you meet the deadline. Both you and he benefit.

Supervise and Train Others

As you advance in your career, your job may include supervising or training less experienced employees. Understanding their preferences can help you tailor your approach to each employee to support their learning and development.

Consider Juanita, who has asked her assistant Derek to learn how to use a new inventory-tracking system. She has given him the printed instruction manual, but he's struggling to make sense of it. By observing Derek at work, Juanita

Supercharged Teamwork. Good teamwork matters in every work setting — whether you're a member of a pit crew, a carpenter helping to build a house, or a data analyst in a team charged with identifying new customer segments. When teammates understand their learning preferences, they can leverage one another's strengths while also adapting to each other's styles. Result? Supercharged team performance. Martin Barraud/Getty Images

USING LEARNING STRATEGIES
ON THE JOB

NAME: **Grace Ku**

PROFESSION: *Social Media Manager*

SCHOOL: *University of Utah*

DEGREE: *Bachelor of Science*

MAJOR: *Business Marketing*

While I was in college, I developed learning strategies that worked great for me. Once I got into the working world, I discovered that I needed to rely on a range of learning styles to interact effectively with my boss and the people I supervise.

When I started as a Social Media Intern, one of my first tasks was to create reports for my boss. I used the skills I built in college to organize and write reports. Then I'd e-mail them to my boss, and when she had questions I'd refer her to the report that I wrote. I discovered very quickly that this wasn't working for her. She wanted me to boil down the information in the report so it fit onto a sticky note, and to give her answers myself when she had questions. I basically had to adapt to her learning style and get out of my comfort zone. Instead of writing and submitting reports like I had been, I needed to summarize information and be prepared to provide verbal answers on the spot.

After ten months on the job, I was promoted to Social Media Manager. When this happened, I had to find ways to communicate effectively with the whole team I supervise. I regularly send out information to my team members about what we need to get done that week. I quickly discovered that one of my team members is an Aural learner — I need to tell him what I expect face-to-face. If I send it in an e-mail, it won't get done, but if I take a moment to discuss things verbally, he does great work. Using different learning styles and adapting to the styles of others has been critical to my success.

YOUR TURN: Have you ever had to adopt an unfamiliar learning strategy to work more effectively with a boss, a coworker, or an employee? If so, which strategy? What was the outcome?

" **Using different learning styles and adapting to the styles of others has been critical to my success.**"

realizes that he's a strongly Visual and Kinesthetic learner. He's struggling with the instruction manual because it's text-heavy. She enrolls him in a workshop where he can practice using the new system and gives him access to an online tutorial featuring diagrams and process flowcharts. Derek soon masters the new system—demonstrating the benefits that come when supervisors understand their employees' learning preferences.

my personal success plan

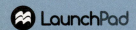
1 GATHER INFORMATION

Think about your learning preferences, the learning strategies you use based on those preferences, and your Learning Preferences score on ACES. Would you like to learn more about how you learn? Would you like to try a new learning strategy — either because it fits with your preferences or because it challenges you to go outside your comfort zone?

2 SET A SMART GOAL

Use the information you've gathered to create a SMART goal, making sure to use the SMART goal checklist.

SAMPLE: I'll organize a study group for my science class (I'm an Extravert!) and schedule the first meeting by this Friday.

3 MAKE AN ACTION PLAN

Outline the specific steps you'll take to achieve your SMART goal, and note when you'll complete each step.

SAMPLE: During tomorrow's lecture, I'll ask three students sitting near me if they're interested in studying together.

4 LIST BARRIERS AND SOLUTIONS

Think about possible barriers to your action steps; then brainstorm solutions for overcoming them.

SAMPLE: If none of my classmates in lecture can meet or their schedules conflict with mine, I'll ask my lab partners if they'd like to meet instead.

5 ACT AND EVALUATE OUTCOMES

Now that your plan is in place, take action. Record each action step as you take it. Then evaluate whether you achieved your SMART goal, and make any adjustments needed to get better results in the future.

SAMPLE: I arranged the first group meeting as planned. One person didn't show up, but the rest of us decided to meet weekly. I'll text everyone a reminder the day before we meet.

6 CONNECT TO CAREER

List the skills you're building as you progress toward your SMART goal. How will you use these skills to land a job and succeed at work?

SAMPLE: In forming and managing a study group, I'm using communication skills. In whatever career I end up pursuing, these skills will help me develop strong working relationships with coworkers — even those whose learning preferences differ from mine.

1 my information

2 my SMART goal

☐ **S**PECIFIC ☐ **M**EASURABLE ☐ **A**CHIEVABLE ☐ **R**ELEVANT ☐ **T**IME-LIMITED

3 my action plan

4 my barriers/ solutions

5 my actions/ outcomes

6 my career connection

CHAPTER SUMMARY

As you saw in this chapter, thinking critically about your learning preferences can help you succeed in college and your career. Revisit the following key points, and consider how you can use this information to support your success now and in the future.

- A learning preference is the way in which a person prefers to acquire and work with information. When you understand your learning preferences, you can further develop the skills and techniques associated with those preferences to "play to your strengths."

- According to the Myers-Briggs Type Indicator (MBTI), four dimensions affect our behavior: Extravert/Introvert, Sensing/Intuitive, Thinking/Feeling, and Judging/Perceiving. These dimensions influence where we focus our energy, the kind of information we prefer working with, how we make decisions, and how we organize our time and activities.

- The VARK (Visual, Aural, Read-Write, Kinesthetic) model provides another way to understand how people prefer to take in and process new information.

- Knowing your MBTI type and VARK preferences helps you develop and use effective study strategies.

- Using learning strategies outside your comfort zone gives you the flexibility that can help you succeed, no matter what teaching styles your instructors have.

- Learning doesn't end at graduation. Your employer will expect you to learn new information, master new processes, and work effectively with team members who have different ways of building new skills and knowledge. Using your understanding of learning preferences, you can improve your relationship with your supervisor and teach and supervise others more effectively.

CHAPTER ACTIVITIES

Journal Entry

ADAPTING TO DIFFERENT LEARNING ENVIRONMENTS

Learning environments and learning preferences don't always match up. If you ever experience a mismatch between your learning environment and your preferences, you can find ways to adapt to the situation. You'll practice doing so in this journal entry.

Begin by describing your learning preferences. How do you learn best? Next, describe a situation in which you might have to learn, study, or interact with others using a less preferred approach. Feel free to imagine an academic-related scenario, a career-related scenario, or an example from your personal life (like learning how to calculate car payments, cook a new dish, or use a computer program). Finally, respond to the following questions:

1. How could you think about this situation in a positive way?

2. What things could you tell yourself?

3. What personal supports or college resources could you use to adapt to the learning environment?

4. Knowing what you now know (learning strategies for your preferred and nonpreferred learning styles), what could you do to enhance your learning in this situation?

Adopting a Success Attitude

ENSURING A POSITIVE GROUP WORK EXPERIENCE

As you think about working with your classmates on a group project, what's your initial reaction? If it's worry, dread, or annoyance, you may have had a negative experience working with others in the past, or you may be anticipating conflict over differences in group members' learning preferences. You can use your knowledge of the MBTI to make your future group-work experiences positive and productive.

Imagine you've been assigned to work in a group, and your task is to determine whether college athletes should be paid for playing their sport. The group has to research each position in the debate and put together a presentation in which you argue for one side or the other. Respond to the following scenarios:

1. You don't know anyone in the group. What could you do to get to know your group members and feel more comfortable working with them?

2. The group has four Extraverts and four Introverts. How could you ensure that everyone has a voice in the group process?

3. The group has four Sensing and four Intuitive people. How could you best use everyone's strengths in doing the research and writing the presentation?

4. The four Thinkers in the group disagree with the four Feelers as to whether college athletes should be paid. The group needs to choose one position. What do you say to your fellow group members? How do you make a decision that will make the greatest number of people happy?

5. The four Judgers want the group to create a plan for meeting, distributing tasks, and setting deadlines. Three of the Perceivers aren't comfortable with so much structure. Although you're a Perceiver, you see the benefits of creating a plan. What can you say to the other Perceivers to help them understand these benefits?

6. The group creates a plan for managing the tasks involved in this assignment. At the next meeting, two students arrive without having completed their assigned tasks. Those who completed their tasks are angry. How do you bring the group together and refocus everyone's attention on the goal?

Applying Your Skills

BECOMING A MULTIMODAL LEARNER

Your learning preferences are the ways you *prefer* to learn, but they aren't the only ways you *can* learn. With some effort and practice, you can become a multimodal learner, which involves using many different strategies to learn.

Revisit the Use the VARK Model section, and review your score on the VARK. Which score was the *highest*? Are you more of a Visual (V), Aural (A), Read-Write (R), or Kinesthetic (K) learner? If your scores were high on two or more modes of learning, choose just one. Based on this preference, what are two strategies you can implement this week to enhance your learning? You can revisit Table 4.3 for ideas.

1. _____

2. _____

Which score on the VARK was the *lowest*? What are two learning strategies you could develop for your lowest-scoring VARK preference this week? Again, you can revisit Table 4.3 for ideas.

1. _____

2. _____

Now that you've identified strategies that interest you, use them during the week and reflect on your experience. Which strategies were most effective? What challenges did you encounter? Will you use these strategies regularly?

College Success = Career Success

APPRECIATING DIFFERENCES IN THE WORKPLACE

The Myers-Briggs Type Indicator is commonly used in the workplace to promote employee success. Think about how you could use your knowledge of the four MBTI dimensions to address the following situations:

1. **Extravert/Introvert:** You run a weekly meeting in which your sales team brainstorms new leads. The Extraverts in your group comment on or ask questions about everything you say. You can't seem to make it through your agenda. At the same time, the Introverts rarely speak up, but you know they have good ideas. In fact, you often get e-mails from them days after the meeting. Although their comments are useful, you've already moved on to something else. How can you make these meetings more productive while appreciating the strengths and weaknesses of Extraverts and Introverts?

2. **Sensing/Intuitive:** Your employees need to learn a new office procedure. How do you present the information to maximize learning for both Sensing and Intuitive types?

3. **Thinking/Feeling:** The hiring committee has just completed candidate interviews. Two committee members want to choose someone based on the facts, such as résumés and responses to questions. Two others want to base their decision on the impression they formed of each candidate through eye contact, posture, appearance, and personal interactions. You've been asked to help the committee reach a resolution. What do you do?

4. **Judging/Perceiving:** Would you prefer to work with someone who likes to focus on only one project before starting another (Judging) or with someone who can multitask but may become distracted if he or she juggles too many projects (Perceiving)? What benefits and challenges would this type of coworker bring to your working relationship and job effectiveness?

5 Organization and Time Management

Get Organized

Take Control of Your Time

Overcome Procrastination and Minimize Distractions

Use Organization and Time Management at Work

My Personal Success Plan

D o you know people who are *very* organized—people who label every drawer in their house, arrange their socks by color, or schedule each week down to the minute? If so, you may be tempted to dismiss those behaviors as excessive or over the top. After all, taken to extremes, any behavior can be unhealthy. But to a degree, the skills of being organized and managing your time are not only healthy, they're essential for succeeding in college. These skills help you take control of your environment by clarifying what tasks you have to do, when you have to do them, and what resources you'll need. When you're in control, it's easier to stay focused on your goals and minimize distractions that threaten to derail your plans.

Take Marcus and Tim. Marcus puts all of his classes and study times, his work schedule, and even his regular pickup basketball game into the calendar on his smartphone. When he and Tim meet to study chemistry, Marcus has a neatly organized binder full of notes, practice problems, and the assignment due each week. Tim is always a few minutes late to their study sessions and sometimes even forgets to show up. Occasionally he can't find the assignment in the jumble of papers in his backpack. He often leaves his notes at home and asks to share Marcus's notes.

In this scenario Marcus is more likely than Tim to succeed in college and in the workplace. By staying organized and managing his time, Marcus keeps his academic life on track. And he'll make an attractive job candidate because managers want employees who arrive at work on time, show up for meetings, and keep track of important documents.

With these realities in mind, this chapter examines how you can take control of your environment and manage your life effectively. We start with organization—how you can get a handle on your course materials. Then we explore strategies for improving your time management, including reflecting on how you spend your time, setting priorities, and using a scheduling system. Next, we discuss how to deal with procrastination and distractions. Finally, we look at how organization and time-management skills translate into a successful career.

Reflect

On Your Organization and Time Management

MY ACES SCORE

☐ **HIGH**

☐ **MODERATE**

☐ **LOW**

LaunchPad

To find your **Organization and Time Management score,** go to the LaunchPad for *Connections*.

Take a moment to reflect on your Organization and Time Management score on ACES. Find your score and add it in the circle to the right.

This score measures your beliefs about how organized you are and how well you manage your time. Do you think it's an accurate snapshot of your current skills in this area? Why or why not?

■ **IF YOU SCORED IN THE HIGH RANGE** and you feel this score accurately reflects your skills, you're probably quite organized and manage your time well. That's great news! As with all skills, however, you can improve on your strengths. For instance, if you already use a weekly schedule to organize your time, you might add a to-do list for each day so that you can track your progress and stay on target. Trying new organization and time-management strategies will keep you at the top of your game.

■ **IF YOU SCORED IN THE MODERATE OR LOW RANGE,** don't be discouraged. You *can* get more organized and manage your time more effectively. This chapter is filled with ideas for getting a better handle on your class materials and your commitments. Read on to get started!

Get Organized

Think about your life: Does it sound more like Marcus's or like Tim's? If you have to fish through piles of papers to find a syllabus, a class assignment, or a project file, you may identify more with Tim. If that's the case, consider how you feel when you can't find a book when it's time to study, or when you show up at a meeting without the documents you were supposed to bring. Do you feel out of control? Embarrassed? Incompetent? If so, you can make positive changes. Getting organized can be challenging, particularly if you're juggling competing demands of school, work, and family. But with practice and commitment, you can learn to manage your many priorities. And once you do, you'll feel calmer—and you'll be more productive.

Create a Clean Study Space

The first step in getting organized is to find a clean space where you can study. When your study space is clutter-free, you can concentrate better on what

Choices, Choices. You're ready to sit down and read a textbook chapter, and you have two choices: the room on the left or the room on the right. Which room will you pick? Better go for the neat one. A clean, organized space helps you stay focused when you're studying. © Richard Morrell/Corbis

you're doing and quickly find documents and other items that you need. There's no one "right" way to create a clean work area—pick what works best for you.

Do you have an office space at home or a quiet room in a residence hall? If so, fix it up to make it inviting. Find a place to stash your books and papers, and give yourself plenty of room for your computer. Set aside a drawer or some cups for pens and pencils, and pick an area to spread out books and notes. Does your study space serve as the kitchen table during the day and then become your desk when the kids go to bed? If so, consider using totes or a rolling cabinet to organize everything you need to study. When the dishes are done and the kitchen table is clear, you can pull out your materials and get to work.

Do you study in the break room at work? In the coffee shop between your job and school? In the library because things are too chaotic at home? If you study in any or all of these places, organize your backpack so you can easily find your pens, highlighters, notebooks, and other tools and still have room for your laptop, books, and class assignments.

Organize Your Documents

To keep your study space clean, you'll need to keep track of all the documents you collect and generate for your classes. If you set up a system for organizing and storing your documents, you can easily find what you need, instead of wasting time hunting for things and getting stressed out. Pick a storage system that's easy to use and that works with your personal preferences. Do you like to pull up documents on your smartphone or tablet? Would you rather have documents in paper form? Many people use some combination of electronic and paper storage systems.

Cloud: A place on the Internet where you can store your files.

Electronic Systems. You'll create most of your school papers and projects electronically, and you'll need a way to organize them. You can save these documents in folders on your computer, or you can use a **cloud**-based system. Available on the Internet, cloud systems let you store files online and access them from your laptop, tablet, or smartphone or even from an on-campus computer lab. You can also save documents and other materials in an *electronic portfolio*. Many colleges use portfolio systems as a way for students to store and showcase documents and projects they create for their courses, including papers, blogs, and videos of classroom presentations. Keep your next job interview in mind if you develop an e-portfolio of your coursework; showing an electronic version of a stellar project could help you stand out in a field of applicants for the job of your dreams.[1]

Paper Systems. Depending on your preferences or those of your instructors, you might also want a system for organizing documents in paper form. Many instructors hand out syllabi on the first day of class, and a paper-based system helps you store these syllabi so you can find them easily. Also, people often feel secure using a paper-based system because they don't have to worry about computer problems. (Paper files can't get viruses.) To store paper documents, use an alphabetized filing cabinet or tote, or binders and folders that you can carry with you. Pick something that works with how you've arranged your study space and how mobile your materials need to be.

Labeling and Color-Coding. Whether your system is electronic, paper, or a combination, develop a labeling system for your documents. Here are some ideas.

- **Use color.** Differentiate materials for different courses by using colors—for instance, green folders, highlighters, and notebooks for biology; yellow for sociology; blue for English; and so on. You can also use colors to signify priority: for example, a red font or pen color for your highest-priority to-dos; yellow for moderate priority; and green for low priority.

- **Create meaningful file and folder names.** Use file and folder names that are consistent and easy to decode. For example, for each class, create folders with the names "Syllabus," "Notes," "Exams," "Papers," and "Projects," and then name your files based on the folder in which they belong: "Notes from Sept 5," "Project—Voting Rights," and so on. This way, you can easily track down documents when you need them.

- **Create "In Progress" and "Complete" folders.** In the "In Progress" folder, store documents for projects you're actively working on. As you finish an exam or a paper, move it to the "Complete" folder so you can focus on documents that need your active attention.

File Backup. If you've ever spilled coffee on a document or crashed your computer, you know how crucial it is to back up your files. Your syllabi, papers, and presentations demonstrate what you've learned in school, and you'll want to retrieve them when you apply for jobs or internships. To keep paper files safe, scan your documents and save them in an electronic format you can access if the originals get lost or destroyed. For electronic files, use an external hard drive or a thumb drive to store backup files separately from your computer or cloud system.

Whatever system you create to get organized, take time each day to keep it working smoothly. For instance, spend just five minutes every night putting papers into folders or organizing your electronic files. Keep clutter and confusion from creeping back into your life!

Take Control of Your Time

Organizing your class materials is a great first step, but to really set the stage for success in college and work, you also have to take control of your time. To see why these two skills make a powerful combination, picture yourself in the following two scenarios.

Scenario 1: You check your calendar and see that you've planned to spend two hours tonight working on a paper that's due in four days. You walk into your study space, pull the exact course materials you need from a shelf, and sit down to begin working. Clearly, you've organized your course materials and taken control of your time.

Scenario 2: You never scheduled time to work on an assigned paper. The night before it's due, you suddenly remember that you haven't even started on it. You paw through a mound of papers on your desk, searching for the syllabus to see what the assignment is. When you finally find it and read the instructions, you realize that you're unprepared and have little hope of finishing the paper on time. You're so stressed out that you try to distract yourself by playing your favorite online game. An hour slips by before you force yourself to start working on the paper.

What can you do to avoid scenario 2? Get organized using the strategies in this chapter, and master the art of time management using the four-step process shown in Figure 5.1: First, track your time, by documenting how you spend your time during the course of a week. Second, identify your priorities—the activities that matter most to you—based on your values and goals. Third, build a schedule that focuses on your priorities. And fourth, use tools to track your progress on all of your assignments.

Let's explore each of these steps in detail.

Step 1: Track Your Time

If you're like most college students, you sometimes (maybe even often) feel as though you have too much to do and not enough time to do it. That's not surprising: You're probably juggling lots of different demands, such as going to class, caring for kids or elderly parents, or holding down a job. If you're just out of high school, you might also be setting your own schedule for the first time, a responsibility that can feel overwhelming. Whatever your situation, before you can take control of your time, you have to figure out where your time is currently going. What do you actually do as the hours tick by every day?

To get a complete picture of how you're spending your time, you need to record—in writing—what you do every day and how long each activity takes. Why bother writing all this down? Your perceptions about how much time you spend on daily activities could be quite different from reality. By recording specifics, you'll build a more accurate picture of where your time goes.

FIGURE 5.1 Four Steps to Effective Time Management

**1
Track Your Time**

**2
Identify Your Priorities**

**3
Build Your Schedule**

**4
Use Tools to Track Your Progress**

To begin, use a calendar or write down on a piece of paper exactly what you do each day and how long each activity takes (see Figure 5.2). Do this for an entire week. As you collect this information, ask yourself:

- What activities are taking up most of my time?
- Am I spending too much time on unproductive or distracting activities? If so, what are they?
- When am I most productive? Least productive?

Then give your critical thinking skills a workout: Examine the patterns you see in your time tracker, and analyze your responses to the questions. Use all this information to draw conclusions about how you're spending your time and how you might manage it more effectively. For example, let's say that before you started this exercise, you believed that your many obligations left you little time to study. As you evaluate the information you've gathered, you realize that you spent twenty-five hours gaming. Because you're studying English literature, not video-game design, you conclude that you could (and should) free up time to study by cutting back on your gaming. You've uncovered a wealth of time that you didn't realize was available.

Once you understand where your time is going, you can start thinking about better ways to allocate it. After all, there are only so many hours in a day (and a night). It's up to you to spend this precious resource wisely.

Step 2: Identify Your Priorities

Once you've tracked your time for a week and analyzed the results, consider whether you're allocating enough time to the things that matter to you most. Are trivial tasks eating up too many hours each week? Does your current use of time reflect how important your education is to you? With numerous obligations and activities competing for your attention, you have to make choices about where to focus your energies. In other words, you have to **prioritize** your

Prioritize: To give an activity or a goal a higher value relative to another activity or goal.

FIGURE 5.2 Sample Time Tracker

Look at this excerpt from one student's time tracker. On Monday, the student had some down-time — just the right amount. But on Tuesday, she streamed a long TV show, had a leisurely lunch, and texted *a lot*, even while she was reading. When it finally came time to study that night, she fell asleep. Had she made different choices earlier in the day, she could have finished studying and still made it to bed at a reasonable hour. Now she has the information she needs to make a change.

	Monday	Tuesday
7:00 am		
:30	woke up	woke up
8:00 am	drove to campus/breakfast	breakfast/streamed TV show
:30	↓	
9:00 am	Biology 101	
:30	↓	drove to campus
10:00 am	coffee, texting	Algebra 115
:30	read for Algebra class	
11:00 am	First-Year Experience 100	↓
:30	↓	Biology study group
12:00 pm	surfed online	↓
:30	lunch	lunch with friends
1:00 pm	Economics 125	
:30	↓	↓
2:00 pm	drove to work (10 min)	went to library to study
:30	work	texting
3:00 pm		read for Econ (10 min)/texting
:30		texting
4:00 pm		Biology lab
:30	↓	↓
5:00 pm	drove home	read for Algebra/did problems
:30	dinner	↓
6:00 pm	TV	texting
:30	read for Biology	↓
7:00 pm		dinner/drove to work
:30	↓	work
8:00 pm	did problems for Algebra	
:30		
9:00 pm	↓	↓
:30	read for First-Year Exp.	
10:00 pm	↓	drove home
:30	down-time/texting	studied for Econ quiz (10 min)
11:00 pm	↓	crashed — fell asleep on couch
:30	went to bed	

commitments and use these priorities to decide how much of your time an activity deserves.

Prioritizing commitments is a deeply personal process that depends on your values and goals. For one person, earning a degree while also spending time with family may be top priorities. For another person, completing college and getting a promotion at work may be most important. When you're clear about your priorities, you make smarter choices about how to use your time. For instance, if doing well in your classes is a top priority, you'll probably choose to study for an exam the night before, instead of going out with friends who don't have a test tomorrow.

To practice prioritizing, review your one-week time tracker, and write down the activities that currently take up most of your time (see Figure 5.3). Describe these activities in broad terms, such as "attending class," "studying," and "working." Determine how important each activity is to you personally, and indicate that importance using the following four-point scale:

- 4 = critically important
- 3 = highly important
- 2 = moderately important
- 1 = of little or no importance

Critically important activities (those you've rated 4) are those that you've decided you must do because they relate directly to your values and responsibilities. For instance, each week you may need to go to work, attend all of your classes, and be home by 3:00 p.m. when your children get off the bus. Highly important activities (rank = 3) will also have an impact on your success—such as doing five extra problems for math each evening. Activities you've rated 4 and 3 may not always be fun or exciting, but you consider them crucial for achieving your goals or living your values. Activities you view as moderately important (rank = 2) or of little or no importance (rank = 1) are less essential to your values or goals.

To define your priorities, you need to think critically about what's most important to you. And to honor your priorities, you sometimes have to make tough decisions, such as giving up activities that you enjoy or disappointing someone who wants some of your time. For example, what if your niece's school play is the same day as your statistics exam? What if your boss needs you to work Tuesday night, but you're supposed to meet with several classmates from your history course to start a group project? These kinds of choices are never easy, but we all face them and have to learn how to manage them. If you know what your priorities are, you can make the tough calls and be at peace with your decisions.

FIGURE 5.3 **Prioritizing Your Commitments**

When you prioritize, you identify what's most important to you, a process that helps you allocate more time to your top priorities. For this student, attending class, working, studying, and spending time with family are critically important.

Activity	Importance
Attending class	4
Working	4
Studying	4
Spending time with family	4
Coaching daughter's softball team	3
Exercising	3
Meeting with study group for biology class	3
Regular Saturday lunch with friends	2
Watching TV	1

4 = Critically important
3 = Highly important
2 = Moderately important
1 = Of little or no importance

Step 3: Build Your Schedule

CONNECT TO MY RESOURCES

Many time-management apps are available for smartphones and tablets. Find the three highest-rated options in the Apple or Android app store. Write a pros-and-cons list for each one; then try out your preferred option for a week. In writing, explain how well this tool worked for you. Will you use it again?

Once you've tracked your time and clarified your priorities, you can build a schedule that reflects the most important commitments in your life. Find a scheduling method and tools that work for you—whether it's a paper planner, an app on your phone, a calendar tied to your e-mail system, a calendar hanging in your kitchen, or a mix of these. You can also create schedules that cover different time frames—terms, months, weeks, and days. (For an example of a five-day schedule, see Figure 5.4.)

The activities you put on your schedule will depend on your priorities, but because you're in college, we assume that one of your top priorities is graduating. So you'll need to think about and plan for the following responsibilities:

- **Classes.** Include class time in your schedule. If your class is on campus rather than online, plan to arrive a few minutes early so that you can get settled and prepare to learn.

- **Study time.** Set aside two hours of study time for each hour of class time. The most common college class format is about three hours of class time a week, which involves six hours of studying outside of class. If you're taking four three-hour classes this term, you should budget twelve hours of class time and twenty-four hours of study time each week. Research shows that full-time students spend an average of a little less than fifteen hours per week studying.[2] That's not nearly enough time. If you can find two hours to study for each hour of class time and if you use that study time wisely, you'll likely get much better grades than students who invest less time in studying. Also, arrange your study time in a way that maximizes your learning. Spacing out your study time across multiple days and studying in small blocks of time is the most productive way to learn new material.[3]

- **Exams and assignments.** In your schedule, include the time needed to take exams, to complete regular assignments and major projects, and to develop presentations for class.

- **Work.** Add your work hours to your schedule. If you commute between home, work, and school, factor in travel time.

- **Family.** Include high-priority family time in your schedule, such as having dinner together each evening or blocking off an afternoon to celebrate a loved one's birthday. These relationships can be a source of support as you manage the many demands of being a college student.

- **School events.** Schedule time for high-priority events at school, such as attending tutoring sessions and study groups for difficult classes, going to important cultural events, or participating in student organizations. While it can be difficult for busy students to make time for these activities, it's worth it: Active involvement on campus can strengthen your commitment to college and help you develop teamwork and communication skills.

- **Exercise and leisure.** To do well in college, you have to be healthy—both physically and mentally. So be sure to schedule time for regular exercise and leisure activities to balance out the great amount of time and effort you'll be devoting to your coursework.

FIGURE 5.4 Sample Schedule

Building a complete schedule — including time for classes and studying, as well for exercise, work, and relaxation — helps you take control of your time. Hold yourself accountable for sticking to your schedule, and celebrate when you accomplish everything you planned each day.

	Monday	Tuesday	Wednesday	Thursday	Friday
7:00 am	BREAKFAST	DRIVE TO CAMPUS	BREAKFAST	DRIVE TO CAMPUS	BREAKFAST
:30	DRIVE TO CAMPUS	YOGA	DRIVE TO CAMPUS	YOGA	DRIVE TO CAMPUS
8:00 am	CHEMISTRY 101		CHEMISTRY 101		CHEM LAB
:30		COFFEE/BREAKFAST		COFFEE/BREAKFAST	
9:00 am	STUDY: CHEM 1 HR. ENGLISH 1 HR.	ALGEBRA II (QUIZ!)	STUDY: CHEM 1 HR. FYE 1 HR.	ALGEBRA II	
:30					
10:00 am					DRIVE TO WORK
:30		FREE TIME		STUDY: ALGEBRA 1 HR. 15 MIN. SOCIOLOGY 45 MIN.	WORK
11:00 am	ENGLISH 124		ENGLISH 124		
:30					
12:00 pm					
:30	LUNCH	LUNCH	LUNCH	LUNCH	
1:00 pm	FIRST-YEAR EXPERIENCE (FYE) 102	SOCIOLOGY CLUB MEETING	FIRST-YEAR EXPERIENCE (FYE) 102	STUDY: CHEM, ENGLISH, FYE 1 HR. EACH	
:30					
2:00 pm		STUDY: FYE 1 HR. 30 MIN. SOCIOLOGY 1 HR. 30 MIN.	STUDY: ALGEBRA 1 HR. 30 MIN. SOCIOLOGY 1 HR.		
:30	CHEM STUDY GROUP				
3:00 pm					
:30					
4:00 pm	DRIVE HOME			FREE TIME	
:30	FREE TIME				
5:00 pm		DRIVE HOME	DRIVE TO WORK		
:30		DINNER		DINNER	
6:00 pm	DINNER WITH COUSINS	STUDY: ALGEBRA 1 HR. CHEM 30 MIN.	WORK		DINNER
:30				SOCIOLOGY 105	
7:00 pm	STUDY: ALGEBRA 1 HR. CHEM 30 MIN.				TIME WITH FRIENDS
:30					
8:00 pm		EDIT ENGLISH PAPER			
:30	FREE TIME		DRIVE HOME		
9:00 pm		FREE TIME	DINNER	DRIVE HOME	
:30			FREE TIME		
10:00 pm				FREE TIME	
:30		BED	BED		
11:00 pm	BED			BED	DRIVE HOME
:30					BED

■ **Rewards.** Schedule time to reward yourself for your successes in college. For instance, schedule a movie with friends or family members the night after an exam. These rewards don't have to consume a lot of time, but they can help recharge your batteries so you can stay motivated for another round of hard work at school.

As you create your schedule, try to build some flexibility into it, in case something goes wrong. For instance, suppose you commute to school, and one of your classes starts at 8:30 a.m. on Tuesdays and Thursdays. You know traffic can be heavy at that time, so when you schedule time for commuting on those days, you add a "cushion" in case you get stuck in traffic. Or let's say you're scheduling time to study for a final exam. You pencil in a few hours of study on an alternative night, in case an emergency comes up and you can't study on the original night you planned for. When you build flexibility into your schedule, you can shift gears more easily if surprises come up. If you schedule your time too tightly, it will be much harder to make these adjustments.

Step 4: Use Tools to Track Progress on Your Projects

Tracking your progress helps you evaluate how effectively you're managing the time allocated to your priorities. By doing this, you hold yourself **accountable**, or responsible, for completing the tasks and meeting the obligations that are connected to your priorities. Here are some tools that can help you keep your projects on track and help you meet your goals.

Accountable:
Responsible for completing tasks and meeting obligations.

Project Plan. Your schedule will include time to work on major school projects, and when you create a project plan, you can track your progress on each of these projects. A project plan helps you break down an assignment into smaller, more manageable steps and budget time to complete each step. This tool builds on key concepts in the chapter on thinking critically and setting goals, such as identifying action steps, prioritizing them, and giving each step a deadline. To create a project plan, you estimate how much time will be required to complete each step in the project. That way, you can build enough time into your schedule to complete all the steps by the assignment's due date.

Consider Mia, who has six weeks to write a major paper on Greek architecture. Figure 5.5 shows how Mia has broken down the tasks involved in completing this paper. She starts with the due date and adds a goal statement for this assignment. She lists the steps needed to complete her paper. Since Mia is a new college student, she isn't sure how much time each task will take, but she wrote papers in high school and often pulls together documents for her boss. She draws on these experiences to estimate how much time she'll need for each task.

One advantage of creating a project plan is that you can use the deadlines in your plan to hold yourself accountable. Also, crossing off tasks as you complete them gives you a feeling of accomplishment, which can be crucial for maintaining momentum throughout the project.

To-Do List. A to-do list helps you manage time and activities on a daily basis, by reminding you of key tasks (see Figure 5.6). For example, in the Student Voice of Experience later in this chapter, Amni lists the tasks she wants to complete each day and crosses them off as she finishes them.

FIGURE 5.5   Project Plan

Project:	Greek architecture paper		
Due date:	October 31		
Goal:	Demonstrate new knowledge of Greek architecture through written work		
Action steps	**Estimated time**	**Deadline**	**Done**
Read assigned textbook chapters	5 hours	September 20	**X**
Find and read three additional resources	18 hours	October 3	**X**
Find six images of architecture	4 hours	October 5	
Write an outline for the paper	3 hours	October 10	
Write first draft	12 hours	October 20	
Revise to create second draft	6 hours	October 24	
Revise to create third draft and polish the paper	4 hours	October 28	
Hand in the paper and celebrate!		October 31	

CONNECT TO MY CAREER

In many careers, people have to manage projects, write reports, or complete major assignments. Explain how you might use a project plan to manage a project in your current job or, if you're not currently working, a project that you may have to do in a career you're considering.

Try creating a to-do list for the next day each night before you go to bed or for the current day when you get up in the morning. It takes only a couple of minutes. You can make your list using an e-mail program, the calendar on your smartphone, apps on your tablet, or a piece of paper. Experiment with color-coding or numbering the tasks on your to-do list by priority. Try different methods to discover which strategies work best for you.

CONNECT TO MY EXPERIENCE

Think about everything you have to accomplish tomorrow, and create a to-do list—either just before you go to bed tonight or just after you get up tomorrow morning. What are your main tasks for the day?

FIGURE 5.6   Sample To-Do List

To-Dos
Date: Wednesday
1. ~~Read for history class.~~
2. ~~Complete biology lab write-up.~~
3. Read book on reserve in the library for literature class.
4. Go running.
5. Go to dinner with the kids.
6. Follow up with Sasha about group project.
7. Make dentist appointment.

TOOLS FOR TIME MANAGEMENT

NAME: **Amni Al-Kachak**

SCHOOL: *University of California, Irvine*

MAJOR: *Biological Sciences*

CAREER GOAL: *Ph.D. in Biological Sciences*

> **"I can't live without schedules and lists."**

When I started college, I knew I'd have to work even harder than I did in high school. To be proactive, I started a scheduling system; now I can't live without schedules and lists. I make special timelines that include goals and when I want them done by. I make a list for the year, a list each week, and a daily list and keep them all on paper. Seeing it written down makes it feel more achievable for me, and I love the feeling I get when I can cross something off my list!

I've always believed that academics come first, then work, then fun. Whenever I schedule things, I put them in that order. For example, if I have a homework assignment due, I get it done first. After that, if I have any work for my job that needs to get done, I'll do that. Then, if I'm done with my immediate academic and work priorities, I squeeze in study time. I like to make a habit of studying every day, just so the information stays fresh in my head without having to stressfully cram it in during test time. After I've completed all of the tasks on my list, I can reward myself by having fun with my friends. I always do things according to deadline and importance.

It can be hard to stick to my schedule. One day I was reading my biology textbook, but then my friend texted me. We started a conversation that lasted for about an hour. Because I'm so aware of my time, I felt really guilty because I could have spent that hour doing a million things. From then on, I decided to put my phone away while I was studying. Although the work I'm doing may be difficult or boring, I'm much happier with myself if I focus and get it done instead of procrastinating.

YOUR TURN: Do you have strategies you use to stay focused on your top priorities? If so, what's an example of a strategy you've found helpful? If not, which of Amni's strategies might be useful to you?

Manage Time in Your Online Classes

If your schedule includes online classes, keep in mind that they sometimes present unique time-management challenges. Your traditional courses are scheduled on particular days and times, and you can block off this class time in your schedule. With many online classes, though, the time you spend participating in class is less structured. Most online courses don't require you to attend at any specific time, so deciding when you'll create and respond to online posts and complete other course requirements is up to you. In addition, while some students expect online classes to be easier or less intensive than face-to-face courses, most online classes take as much time as do in-person classes (and sometimes even *more* time). So be sure to schedule enough time to complete your assignments. Try these tips for staying on top of your online coursework.

- ■ **Get comfortable with this class format.** If you're new to online classes, block out time in your schedule to learn how to navigate the online class system. Your instructor and institution can help.

- ■ **Devote time *each week* to work on your assignments.** Be sure that your weekly schedule includes time for studying, reading, and posting work online for your class. Creating a consistent schedule is particularly critical to mastering course material for online classes.

- ■ **Log in to your online class each day.** Even if it's just for five minutes, log in to check for updates from your instructor or posts from other students. That way, you can make sure you're keeping up with assignments and monitoring class discussions.

- ■ **Know your deadlines.** If your instructor gives specific due dates for class assignments, enter them into your schedule for each week of the term.

- ■ **Schedule time for live meetings hosted by your instructor.** Sometimes hosted via tools like Skype or a text chat, live meetings give you opportunities to interact with classmates and instructors in real time.

Consistency Is Key. Online classes are often less structured than face-to-face courses, which means it's up to you to create your own schedule. Your best bet? Keep it consistent: Devote regular time each week to working on your assignments and log in to your courses every day.
Credit line to come.

Overcome Procrastination and Minimize Distractions

Procrastinate: To delay or put off an action that needs to be completed.

If you're like most people, you sometimes put off getting down to work. You check Twitter one more time, send a text—do anything except what you're supposed to be doing. In short, you **procrastinate**. When you procrastinate, you open yourself up to distractions—events or objects in your environment that take your attention away from the task you need to complete.

Procrastination and distractions can undo all the effort you've put into getting organized and taking control of your time. So the next time you find yourself procrastinating or getting distracted, use your critical thinking skills. Ask yourself: "Why am I putting off this task?" or "Why am I not focusing on what I should focus on?" The more you know about what's causing you to fall victim to procrastination or distractions, the more you can work to change your behavior so that you can accomplish your goals.

Beat Procrastination

People procrastinate for various reasons. By understanding the most common root causes, which we'll explore in the section that follows, you can identify when you're falling victim to these causes—and apply the right antidotes.

Low Motivation. If you don't feel motivated to complete a task, you might be tempted to procrastinate. Fight low motivation with these tactics.

CONNECT TO MY EXPERIENCE

Think about a time when you overcame procrastination. Write down why you were procrastinating and what you did to refocus on the task at hand. Identify how you could use this same strategy to combat procrastination in school.

- **Engage in self-reflection.** You may feel unmotivated because you lack a sense of self-efficacy regarding the task at hand, you don't see it as relevant to you, or you have a negative attitude about your studies in general. (See the chapter on motivation, decision making, and personal responsibility.) Try to identify which of these three key ingredients of motivation you're missing. Sometimes simply understanding why you're unmotivated can spur you to take action.

- **Just get started.** If you have reading to do, pick up your textbook and begin. If you have to do research for a paper, log on to the library's Web site, and start searching for articles. In some cases, just telling yourself it's time to work will revive your motivation.

- **Move.** Grab your materials, go somewhere new, and clear your head. Physical motion may be enough to motivate you to focus on the work you need to do.

Perfectionism. Some people avoid starting projects because they want to achieve a perfect result and worry that they won't be able to. If this happens to you, try these strategies to combat perfectionism.

Not-So-Good Housekeeping. Aaron has a test tomorrow, but instead of studying, he has suddenly decided it's time to do laundry. Guess what: He's procrastinating — and he'll have less time to prepare for the test. The lesson? If a task isn't crucial, do it after finishing your *real* priorities. Note to Aaron: Don't worry — that laundry isn't going anywhere. Robyn Breen Shinn/ Getty Images

- **Reframe your expectations.** Give yourself permission to let go of perfectionistic thinking. Instead of telling yourself that everything you work on must be perfect, tell yourself that you'll put your best effort into each project or task.

- **Start small.** Complete some small tasks related to the work you're procrastinating on; then use your success to gain momentum for finishing another set of tasks. Eventually, you'll complete the whole project.

Feeling Overwhelmed.

Feeling Overwhelmed. If you feel overwhelmed by the amount of work facing you, it may be daunting just to get started. Try these tactics to keep moving forward.

- **Be realistic.** Remind yourself that you can't do everything at once and that every journey—however long or short—starts with a single step. Then pick a place to start.

- **Trick yourself.** Tell yourself that you're going to read or write for only ten minutes or that you'll read or write only three pages. Once you get involved in the work, you may look up forty-five minutes later and discover that you're almost finished—and that's a good reason to keep going.

Minimize Distractions

Distractions can be a big challenge for some students, causing them to veer off track. If you intend to study chemistry for two hours but then spend an hour online watching videos of cute cats, you'll lose time you can't get back. To protect yourself against distractions, consider these tips.

- **Find strength in numbers.** With your roommates or family members, agree on a time when everyone focuses on coursework (or schoolwork for your kids) or other quiet tasks. Doing so creates an environment of support and accountability: When everyone around you is studying or working quietly, you'll find it easier to stay focused.

- **Use the "off" switch.** Turn off the television, your phone, and any other devices that create visual or auditory distractions. Log out of Facebook, Twitter, and other social networking sites. Click the setting that turns off that annoying little chime that lets you know you've just received an e-mail. As you plan your study time, allow five minutes each hour to check these devices and respond to messages. That way, you won't feel tempted to do so while you work.

- **Block out other sources of distraction.** For example, close the curtains or pull down the shades in your room so you can't see what's happening outside. If your neighbor is playing loud music, invest in a set of earplugs to block out the noise.

Don't End Up Here! Distractions can gobble up your time. Before you know it, you fall behind in your work. Result? You push off deadlines, disappointing yourself and others counting on you. To avoid ending up in the graveyard of past deadlines, resist any urge to procrastinate. Eliminate distractions. And stick to the schedule you've created. © Drew Dernavich The New Yorker Collection/ The Cartoon Bank

GET IN THE ZONE: IT FEELS GOOD!

Have you ever had the experience of being "in the zone," or fully present while completing a task? If so, you were probably in a mental state of *flow*. You have this experience when you're completely immersed in a task that you consider enjoyable, such as playing a musical instrument, studying, playing sports, praying, or playing video games. Flow involves concentration and reduced self-consciousness. People in a state of flow feel as though they're in control, and they often lose track of time. In his book *Flow: The Psychology of Optimal Experience*, Mihaly Csikszentmihalyi explains that individuals experience flow when they possess the skill needed to complete a task and find the experience challenging and intrinsically rewarding. When you eliminate distractions around you, you can help create the optimal conditions for flow.

A recent study examined college students' experience of flow and the impact on their emotions.

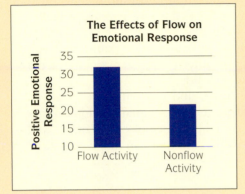

The Effects of Flow on Emotional Response

Students who engaged in a flow activity — including going to class/studying — scored higher on a scale of positive emotional response than did students who engaged in a routine daily task. A higher score indicates more positive feelings.

- Half of the fifty-seven student participants were asked to identify a positive, focused activity they enjoyed (a flow activity) and to engage in that task once during a two-week period.

- The other half of the students were asked to identify an everyday activity (a nonflow activity) and to participate in the task.

- All the students recorded their experience of flow and their emotions before and after the activity.

Interestingly, the two flow activities chosen by the greatest number of students in this research were exercising and going to class/studying. The students who engaged in a flow activity experienced more positive emotions than did students who engaged in everyday activities. The more intense the flow experience, the greater the positive feelings.

THE BOTTOM LINE

You *can* get into a state of flow when you study. To do so, find something in your coursework that interests you, minimize distractions, and completely immerse yourself in that material. Not only will you learn, but you'll also feel good.

REFLECTION QUESTIONS

1. Have you ever experienced flow? If so, what were you doing at the time?
2. What might prevent you from entering a state of flow?
3. What could help you get "in the zone" while you study so you're not tempted to procrastinate?

Mihaly Csikszentmihalyi, *Flow: The Psychology of Optimal Experience* (New York: Harper & Row, 1990). T. P. Rogatko, "The Influence of Flow on Positive Affect in College Students," *Journal of Happiness Studies* 10 (2009): 133–48.

Use Organization and Time Management at Work

The strategies you use to get organized and take control of your time at school are just as essential in your work life. If you manage projects and meet with clients and coworkers every day, you know that things fall apart when they're disorganized and that deadlines are missed when you don't stick to a schedule. Let's consider how you can apply the ideas from this chapter in the workplace.

Get a Job

When you apply for a job, the skills of organization and time management make all the difference. First, you can use these skills to prepare a stellar résumé. Describing your accomplishments will be easier if you've kept track of all the papers and presentations you created in college. For example, if you designed a social media campaign during an internship, keep a copy of the campaign so you can explain in detail what you did.

Second, you'll arrive for interviews on time, and you will have prepared questions for the interviewers and information about your qualifications. Arriving prepared shows that you understand the importance of organization and timeliness—all before you've even said a word. And that can make you stand out in a crowd of job applicants.

Show That You're Dependable

Once you get a job, being organized and effectively managing your time can help you excel in that job—no matter what it is. Let's say you're in auto repair and you tell a customer that her car will be ready by a certain date. You'll be more likely to build customer loyalty if you deliver as promised—which you can do only if you have the necessary tools at your fingertips and if you've scheduled enough time to do the work right. In any job, your boss, customers, and colleagues will appreciate that you're organized and in control of your time. As a result, you'll gain a reputation for getting work done—and done right. Such a reputation could lead to huge opportunities for career advancement.

Make Time for Your Personal Life

When you're organized at work and you control your time, you can boost your productivity on the job, without necessarily having to put in longer hours. In short, you'll work smarter, not harder. As a result, you'll free up more time for your personal life, enabling you to maintain a healthy *work/life balance*. Your job matters, but you also need time for your education, family, friends, health, and fun. Without that balance, you might get so burned out on the job that you have little energy to fulfill your nonwork obligations and goals.

Prioritizing tasks at work helps you complete crucial tasks first. That way, you generate the business results that matter most to your boss and your organization, but work doesn't take over your life. You can also find ways to "unplug" from work outside of your normal job hours. For example, resist the urge to

Organization: The Best Tool. Michael keeps his workspace organized, so he can quickly find the tools he needs to complete jobs for his customers. That makes him more efficient and productive, helping him deliver high-quality work on schedule.
John Lund/Drew Kelly/Getty Images

MANAGING A BUSY WORK SCHEDULE

Photo by Erin L. Maltby

NAME:	**William Hatchet**
PROFESSION:	*New College Student Academic Facilitator*
SCHOOL:	*Augustana College*
DEGREE:	*Bachelor of Arts*
MAJORS:	*Sociology and Africana Studies*

After graduation I moved into my first job as a New College Student Academic Facilitator—I help students navigate college and support programs designed to help them stay in school. I wear several hats in this job and continually balance large projects, meetings across campus, and regular meetings with students. Staying organized and on top of things is critical for me to do my job well.

I figured out quickly that I needed to create a structure to stay organized and manage my busy schedule. I have two main strategies to keep everything straight. First, I use a projects list to keep track of everything I need to get done. As soon as I get a project, I write it down on a list that I carry with me, or I type it into a Word document if I'm at my computer. I add a few details to help me remember everything I need to do for each project. I also use calendars to schedule my time. I have separate work and personal calendars, and I sync them electronically so I always know what I have going on during the week at work and on evenings and weekends away from campus.

The combination of my projects list and my calendars has been working great. Using these tools has really helped relieve my stress. I know that everything I need to do is written down in one of two places. I often carry my iPad with me so I can look things up anytime I need to. These systems also allow me to look ahead, so I can keep track of what I need to work on during any given day and into the future.

YOUR TURN: If you currently have a job, which of the strategies that William describes might help you stay organized at work and manage your time? Have you developed other strategies that work well for you? If so, what are they? If you don't currently have a job, which of William's strategies sound useful for staying organized and managing your time in a job you'd like to get?

> " **Staying organized and on top of things is critical for me to do my job well.**"

respond to work-related e-mails and phone calls at 11:00 p.m., when you should be sleeping. And take advice from Tony Schwartz, a well-known author who writes about balance and work satisfaction: Assess your contribution at work in terms of the *value* you create rather than the amount of time you log in. In other words, focus on doing good work (quality) versus simply measuring the number of hours you work (quantity).[4]

my personal success plan

ORGANIZATION AND TIME MANAGEMENT

Are you inspired to set a new goal aimed at improving your organization and time-management skills? If so, the Personal Success Plan can walk you through the goal-setting process. Read the advice and examples; then sketch out your ideas in the space provided.

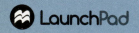 LaunchPad

To access the Personal Success Plan online, go to the LaunchPad for *Connections*.

1 GATHER INFORMATION

Think about your strengths and weaknesses related to organization and time management. What strategies have worked for you in the past? What could you do differently? Revisit your Organization and Time Management score on ACES and review the relevant sections of this chapter for additional ideas.

2 SET A SMART GOAL

Use the information you've gathered to create a SMART goal, making sure to use the SMART goal checklist.

SAMPLE: I'll use my Outlook calendar to plan my time over the next two weeks.

3 MAKE AN ACTION PLAN

Outline the specific steps you'll take to achieve your SMART goal, and note when you'll complete each step.

SAMPLE: Tomorrow night, I'll type my class, study, work, and activity schedules for the next two weeks into my calendar.

4 LIST BARRIERS AND SOLUTIONS

Think about possible barriers to your action steps; then brainstorm solutions for overcoming them.

SAMPLE: Sometimes I forget to check my calendar. To remind me, I'll set the alarm on my phone for 9:00 a.m. and 3:00 p.m. every day. When the alarm goes off, I'll look at the calendar to see if I'm on track.

5 ACT AND EVALUATE OUTCOMES

Now that your plan is in place, take action. Record each action step as you take it. Then evaluate whether you achieved your SMART goal, and make any adjustments needed to get better results in the future.

SAMPLE: I typed my schedules into my calendar as planned. I'm staying on top of my commitments.

6 CONNECT TO CAREER

List the skills you're building as you progress toward your SMART goal. How will you use these skills to land a job and succeed at work?

SAMPLE: I work part-time as a Web designer, and using a calendar will help me meet deadlines and remember client meetings.

1 my information

2 my SMART goal

☐ **S**PECIFIC ☐ **M**EASURABLE ☐ **A**CHIEVABLE ☐ **R**ELEVANT ☐ **T**IME-LIMITED

3 my action plan

4 my barriers/ solutions

5 my actions/ outcomes

6 my career connection

CHAPTER SUMMARY

In this chapter you learned about many important aspects of organization and time management. Revisit the following key points, and reflect on how you can use this information to support your success now and in the future.

- Getting organized helps you quickly and easily find the materials and information you need to carry out the activities required to achieve your goals. To get organized, you need a clean, quiet study space and a system (electronic, paper, or both) for managing and backing up course documents.

- Applying a four-step process can help you manage your time: (1) Track how you're using your time now, (2) identify your priorities, (3) build a schedule that allocates enough time to your top priorities, and (4) use tools to track your progress on your projects so you can hold yourself accountable for meeting your obligations.

- Procrastinating can prevent you from reaching your goals and make you vulnerable to distractions. When you figure out why you're procrastinating, you can address the cause, which may range from low motivation to perfectionism.

- Eliminating distractions (for example, by turning off electronic devices) can help you focus on the work at hand and use your time wisely.

- Getting organized and taking control of your time can help you get a job, excel in that job, and free up time for your personal life so that you maintain a work/life balance.

CHAPTER ACTIVITIES

Journal Entry

MANAGING YOUR TIME

In this chapter we asked you to track your time for one week as a way to think critically about your priorities and time-management skills (see Figure 5.2). Complete this activity and respond to the following questions:

1. How would you rate your ability to manage your time?

2. What do you do well regarding time management? What isn't working so well?

3. What positive changes could you make in the next week to better manage your time?

4. What challenges might you encounter trying to implement these changes? How will you deal with these challenges?

5. Who could offer support, and in what forms?

Adopting a Success Attitude

STANDING UP FOR YOUR PRIORITIES

As you work to clarify your priorities, you'll face some tough choices about how to spend your time, especially when people you care about make requests for (or demands on) your time. In some cases, you'll have to assert yourself and say "no" or offer ideas for arriving at a compromise.

Describe a recent incident in which you should have said "no" to someone who made a request for (or demand on) your time but you said "yes" instead. Which of the following beliefs led you to say "yes"? Check all that apply.

_____ **1.** Saying "no" will hurt and upset them.

_____ **2.** Saying "no" will make them feel rejected.

_____ **3.** If I say "no," they won't like me anymore.

_____ **4.** Others' needs are more important than mine.

_____ **5.** I should always try to please others.

_____ **6.** Saying "no" is rude.

_____ **7.** Saying "no" is unkind and selfish.

To feel better about saying "no," think critically about each belief that you checked off. For each belief, provide a more helpful way of viewing the situation. For example, instead of "Saying 'no' will hurt and upset them," tell yourself, "They might be hurt if I say 'no,' but if they care about me, they'll understand," or "I may hurt someone by turning down their initial request, but maybe I can fulfill the request another time."

Applying Your Skills

PLANNING FOR LARGE CLASS ASSIGNMENTS

If you break down large, complex class assignments into smaller chunks and distribute the workload over the course of a term, they'll seem much more manageable. Review Figure 5.5 and create your own project plan for a big, complicated assignment you'll need to complete this term.

Project:	
Due date:	
Goal:	

Action steps (List all steps)	Estimated time	Deadline	Done

College Success = Career Success

BALANCING WORK AND YOUR PERSONAL LIFE

As you read in this chapter, you can use organization and time-management skills to balance your work and nonwork life so that you can honor your priorities in both.

Do you know someone who has a healthy work/life balance? If so, ask that person for his or her thoughts on these questions:

- How do you balance your work and nonwork priorities? What strategies seem most effective?

- What do you do to stay organized and manage your time in your work and nonwork life?

- What's an example of how being organized and managing your time in your work life helps you manage your nonwork life — and vice versa?

- What are some barriers to juggling multiple responsibilities? How do you deal with those barriers?

Write down what you learned from talking with this person about work/life balance. What strategies could you use now, or in the future if you're not currently working, to balance all of your responsibilities? Do you already use any of the strategies this person has suggested? If so, what are they? And what outcomes have they produced?

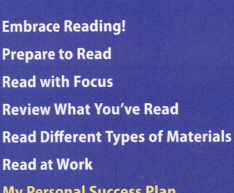
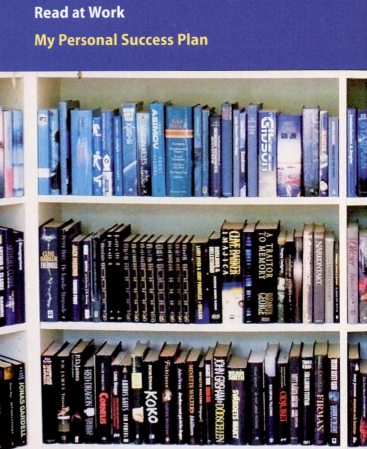

6 Reading for College Success

Embrace Reading!

Prepare to Read

Read with Focus

Review What You've Read

Read Different Types of Materials

Read at Work

My Personal Success Plan

Helena Schaeder Söderberg/Getty Images

What you're doing this very second — reading — is one of the most powerful learning activities you'll do in college. And you'll be doing a lot of it. In fact, reading is the second most frequently used form of communication among college students, after listening.[1]

Do you wonder why your instructors assign so much reading? Consider this: A central reason you're in college is to acquire knowledge. In most of your face-to-face classes, you're in the classroom only a few hours each week, listening to lectures. In online, blended, practical, and discussion-based classes, you spend even less time listening to lectures. By adding reading assignments to the mix, your instructors can cover more material — and that benefits *you* in the long run. So even if you're not a huge fan of reading, try to think of it as a great opportunity to strengthen your learning.

Reading will play a critical role in your work life, too. After all, can you think of a job that requires no reading at all — none? It's not easy to do. Almost every job requires some kind of reading, whether it's e-mails or invoices, medical charts or memos, recipes or research reports. Sure, different jobs may call for different amounts of reading. But it's a safe bet that, to excel in the job of your dreams, you'll have to know how to read, understand what you've read, and integrate the knowledge you've gained from reading into your work.

In this chapter we examine why reading is so important to your college career. We present a three-step process for getting the most from reading: preparing to read, reading with focus, and reviewing what you've read. We also describe strategies for reading effectively in math, science, and online classes, as well as strategies for reading journal articles. In addition, we'll identify resources that can be helpful if you're having difficulty reading. The chapter wraps up with tips on how to apply these concepts and practices on the job.

Reflect

On Your Reading

Take a moment to reflect on your Reading score on ACES. Find your score and add it in the circle to the right.

This score measures your beliefs about how well you read. Do you think it's an accurate snapshot of your current skills in this area? Why or why not?

■ **IF YOU SCORED IN THE HIGH RANGE** and you're confident that this score is accurate, then you can likely count reading among your strengths. This is excellent news. As you know, however, even strengths can be improved. For instance, let's say you've developed some great strategies for reading your history and psychology textbooks, but you find it more challenging to read your biology book. Using the information in this chapter, you can develop new strategies to increase your confidence in reading different types of materials, including your science texts.

■ **IF YOU SCORED IN THE MODERATE OR LOW RANGE,** take steps to improve your reading skills. Explore the ideas and practices in this chapter, and apply them to your course material. When you do, you'll find that you *can* become a more efficient and effective reader. Just give it a try!

MY ACES SCORE

☐ HIGH

☐ MODERATE

☐ LOW

 LaunchPad

To find your **Reading score,** go to the LaunchPad for *Connections.*

Embrace Reading!

In our connected world, most of us spend a great deal of time watching and interacting with screens. We can learn a lot from them, but they're not the only way to learn. Reading is a powerful and necessary skill that you'll be required to master in college, and it will be one of your strongest assets in the workplace. You may even find that you enjoy it! Even better, reading offers unique advantages: It grows your vocabulary, exposes you to new ideas, and may even help you develop a deeper understanding of others.

As you read, you'll uncover theories, discover how things work, gain insights into the past, get immersed in a variety of cultures—and even have fun. Reading is also the gateway to helping you master new skills, such as how to design an experiment, craft a marketing campaign, or write computer code. Depending on your course load, your instructors may ask you to read everything from textbook chapters and novels to scientific articles and transcripts of great speeches.

How you read in college will probably differ from how you've read up to now. College work requires **active reading**, which involves interacting with the content you read, not just gazing at words on the page. You pay close attention. You think about the content carefully. You ask questions about what makes

Active Reading: A reading strategy that involves engaging with the material before, during, and after reading.

FIGURE 6.1 Three Steps to Active Reading

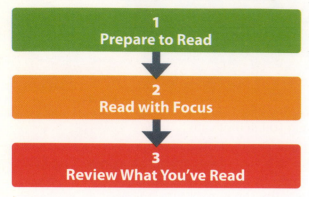

sense and why. These actions help you stay focused, which in turn saves time: You learn and remember more of the material the first time around so you don't have to relearn it later. Active reading has three main steps: preparing to read, reading with focus, and reviewing what you've read (see Figure 6.1). We will explore each of these steps in the following sections.

Before we move on, though, it's important to emphasize the strong connection between reading and your success. Reading is a central life skill: With rare exceptions, successful people use reading skills to gain information and extend their learning. Reading is also a central study skill that sets the stage for the other study skills discussed in this book. As Figure 6.2 shows, reading and attending class kick off your learning experience: When you read and go to class, you take in (or *input*) new information into your brain. You then put *effort* into taking notes and studying, which help you absorb and remember the information. Finally, you demonstrate (or *output*) what you've learned through tests, papers, and classroom presentations.

All of these skills work together. In fact, many of the strategies that help you read successfully—like maintaining a positive attitude, eliminating distractions, and thinking critically about information—can also help you excel at note taking, studying, and writing. When you weave all of these skills together, you maximize your learning—in every course.

FIGURE 6.2 How Academic Skills Connect

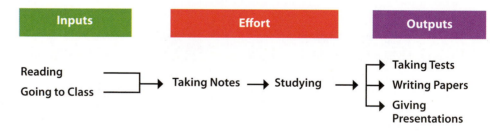

Prepare to Read

Ashley is a competitive runner, and before every race she scouts the course to learn its twists and turns. Ethan is a chef. Before creating a feast, he reviews the recipes involved and gathers all the ingredients and tools he'll need. Both Ashley and Ethan know that preparation is critical for excelling at their work because preparation gives them an advantage: It helps them get ready for what's coming and focus on the task at hand. Reading is also an activity that requires preparation. Try the following tips so that you're ready to read.

Evaluate the Amount of Reading You Have to Do

Figure out how much you have to read and how long it will take you. That way, you can build enough time into your schedule to complete your assignments. Keep in mind that not every reading assignment will take the same amount of time and that each person reads at a different pace. For example, you might read novels in your English literature course relatively quickly, while reading chapters in your algebra book might take longer—or vice versa. And in some classes you may need to read the material more than once to learn it, so you'll have to budget extra time for reading. It can be tricky to estimate these time frames at first, so just do your best. With experience, you'll get better at figuring out how long each assignment will take you.

Preview the Material

Previewing not only gives you a big-picture overview of what you'll be reading but also helps you read more actively. It helps your mind to predict the subject matter and to think about how information you already know relates to what you're about to read.[2] The next time you open up your textbook, take these steps to preview what's coming.

- **Read the preface or introduction.** Review the preface or introduction at the beginning of the book. Authors use these sections to describe the book's chapter structure and goals and to offer tips about how to use the material in each chapter. In the preface of this book, for example, we explain why we've included features such as Voices of Experience and Spotlight on Research in every chapter.

- **Read the table of contents.** At the beginning of any textbook is a table of contents listing the main and supporting headings for each chapter, and often the major features in each chapter. Before you begin an assignment, glance at the contents for the chapter you're about to read.

- **Read the chapter summary.** Many textbooks (including this one) provide chapter summaries, which give an overview of the contents of each chapter and highlight the main ideas. Scan the summary before you read.

- **Look for headings and key terms.** Skim through the chapter, looking at section headings, bold or italicized words, and definitions of key terms in the margins. All of these indicate the important concepts you'll be learning in the chapter.

Get the Lay of the Land. Previewing material you're about to read helps you "get the lay of the land" so that you can predict what's coming and read the material more actively. Byelikova Oksana/Shutterstock

Identify Purposeful Reading Questions

After you preview the material, think of questions you expect to be able to answer once you've finished reading. These are called **purposeful reading questions** because your goal (purpose) in reading the material will be to answer them. Identifying these questions helps you focus your reading on what's most important. Purposeful reading questions vary in complexity; for example, you might want to know the definition of a term (low level of complexity) or the causes of an event (higher level of complexity).

How, precisely, do you go about identifying purposeful reading questions? You've got several options. Sometimes, the material itself provides questions you can use. For example, many textbooks include focus questions at the beginning of each chapter or review questions at the end of each chapter that spotlight which concepts the authors consider most important (see Figure 6.3).

FIGURE 6.3
Creating Purposeful Reading Questions

Purposeful reading questions can come from questions in your reading, such as the outcomes in this textbook excerpt. Or create your own. Here, *leadership* is a key term, so you can ask "How do you define *leadership*?" Text excerpt p. 274, from *Real Communication: An Introduction*, 3e, by Dan O'Hair et al. Copyright © 2015 by Bedford/ St. Martin's. Used by permission.

You can also create your own purposeful reading questions. Keep it simple at first by drafting questions drawn from the chapter's headings and key terms. For instance, if a heading in your calculus book is "Polynomials," you could create the question "What are polynomials?" Then work up to more complex questions, such as, "What are different kinds of polynomials?," "How are polynomial equations solved?," and "How are polynomials used in mathematics and science?" Here are some additional examples of purposeful reading questions you might create in a variety of classes.

- "What were three causes of the War of 1812?" (American history class)

chapter outcomes

After you have finished reading this chapter, you will be able to

- Describe the types of power that effective leaders employ
- Describe how leadership styles should be adapted to the group situation
- Identify the qualities that make leaders effective at enacting change
- Identify how culture affects appropriate leadership behavior
- List the forces that shape a group's decisions
- Explain the six-step group decision process
- List behaviors to improve effective leadership in meetings

What makes a leader? Power? Experience? Decisiveness? In this chapter, we continue our discussion of group communication by examining two additional processes that often emerge in groups: leadership and decision making. These two processes are tightly interrelated: a group's leader affects how the group makes decisions, and the decisions a group makes affect how the leader operates. When leadership and decision making work together in a constructive way, a group stands the best possible chance of achieving its goals. To understand how these processes influence a group's effectiveness, let's begin by taking a closer look at group leadership.

Understanding Group Leadership

It's a word that's constantly tossed about in political campaigns, highlighted on résumés, and used in book titles and biographies. But just what is *leadership*? Scholars have grappled with the task of defining leadership for many years.

Two key terms that show up in many definitions over the years have been *direction* and *influence*. That's because in its most essential form, **leadership** is the ability to direct or influence others' behaviors and thoughts toward a productive end (Nierenberg, 2009). This capacity for influence may stem from a person's power or simply from group members' admiration or respect for the individual. Because influence involves power over others, let's take a look at power—what it is and where it comes from.

- "What's the difference between the unconditioned and the conditioned stimulus in classical conditioning?" (Introduction to Psychology class)
- "How do I diagram the components of a nerve cell and describe the major function of each component?" (Introduction to Biology class)
- "How can I apply the three steps in the active reading strategy?" (this class)

When you create purposeful reading questions, you use your critical thinking skills. You gather information by skimming chapters, summaries, tables of contents, headings, and key terms. You evaluate the information when you figure out what questions to ask. And later, when you read, you apply the new information from the chapter as you answer your own questions.

Use Similar Strategies with All Your Reading Materials

What if you're preparing to read something other than a textbook chapter—something that doesn't have a preface, a table of contents, or boldfaced key terms? You can still use many of the same strategies. For example, you can estimate how much time you'll need to read the material, you can skim the first few paragraphs to get a sense of what the material will cover, and you can scan any headings to get a sense of key points and to create purposeful reading questions. The bottom line? Preparing to read is an effective strategy for all types of reading materials—not just textbooks.

Read with Focus

Once you're prepped and ready to go, take the next step: Complete your reading. Your goal is to absorb, understand, and remember information so you can use what you've learned to write papers, answer test questions, and gain insights into topics covered in your other classes. But you won't be able to remember every word in your reading assignments—no one can. So you need to read with focus: Figure out what information is *most* important, and concentrate on that. To do this, use your critical thinking skills to identify key information and to evaluate the quality of that information. And use your active learning and metacognition skills to select reading strategies that work best for you, depending on your learning preferences and the subjects you're studying. The following tactics can help you focus on the most important information.

Mark Up Your Reading Material

Marking up a text helps you interact with the material you're learning, which in turn helps you understand and remember it. You can mark up reading material in several ways (see Figure 6.4), including annotating the margins of your text, highlighting and underlining key words and phrases, and taking notes.

Annotate. You can *annotate* your reading material by jotting down quick notes, inserting your own examples, drawing symbols ("DEF" might indicate a definition; "EX" might call out an example), and writing quick summaries in your own words—all in the margins of the book or article. Making notes and restating information in your own words requires you to process information

Purposeful Reading Question (PRQ): What's the difference between dreams and sleep thinking?

Dreams and Mental Activity During Sleep

Ex: Being chased through woods

KEY THEME

> A dream is an unfolding sequence of perceptions, thoughts, and emotions that is experienced as a series of actual events during sleep.

☆ *Key Theme!*

KEY QUESTIONS

more great purposeful reading questions!

> How does brain activity change during dreaming sleep, and how are those changes related to dream content?

> What roles do the different stages of sleep play in forming new memories?

> What do people dream about, and why don't we remember many of our dreams?

Dreams have fascinated people since the beginning of time. By adulthood, about 25 percent of a night's sleep, or almost two hours every night, is spent dreaming. So, assuming you live to a ripe old age, you'll devote more than 50,000 hours, or about six years of your life, to dreaming.

Wow. I will spend a ton of time dreaming.

SLEEP THINKING = SLEEP MENTATION

Although dreams may be the most interesting brain productions during sleep, they are not the most common. More prevalent is **sleep thinking,** also called *sleep mentation*. Sleep thinking usually occurs during NREM slow-wave sleep and consists of vague, bland, thoughtlike ruminations about real-life events (McCarley, 2007). Sleep thinking probably contributes to those times when you wake up with a solution to some vexing problem. But at other times, the ruminating thoughts of sleep thinking can interfere with your sleep. For example, on the night before an important exam, anxious students will sometimes toss and turn their way through the night as they mentally review terms and concepts during NREM sleep thinking.

WHEN I HAVE SLEEP THINKING:
– Wake up w/great idea
– Negative: toss and turn w/worry

DEF: SLEEP THINKING

In contrast to sleep thinking, a **dream** is an unfolding sequence of perceptions, thoughts, and emotions during sleep that is experienced as a series of real-life events (Domhoff, 2005). Granted, the storyline and details of those dream events may be illogical, even bizarre. But in the unique mental landscapes of our own internally generated reality, the bizarre and illogical are readily accepted as disbelief is suspended.

DEF: DREAM

Most dreams happen during REM sleep, although dreams also occur during NREM (Domhoff, 2011). When awakened during active REM sleep, people report a dream about 90 percent of the time, even people who claim that they never dream. The dreamer is usually the main participant in these events, and at least one other person is involved in the dream story. But sometimes the dreamer is simply the observer of the unfolding dream story.

So most people do dream.

PRQ: *Dream*   *Sleep Thinking*
Answer   • *Sequence of ideas,*   • *About actual events*
            thoughts, emotions
           • *Seems like real life*   • *General, unclear thoughts*
           • *May be bizarre*   • *Worry or great ideas*
           • *Mostly during REM*   • *Normally during NREM*

FIGURE 6.4   **Marking Your Textbook: A Sample Page**

As you can see from this sample textbook page, you can use a number of techniques to mark your book: making annotations in the margins, highlighting main ideas, and underlining key points. You can also jot down purposeful reading questions and answer them on the page itself (if there's space) or in your notes. Text excerpt p. 147, from *Psychology,* 6e, by Dan and Sandra Hockenbury. Copyright © 2013 by Worth Publishers. Used by permission.

more carefully than if you just highlight or underline (see the next section). Annotating takes some time, but it's worth it—you'll remember the material better later on, and you'll have notes that you can use to study.

Are you reading online? You can still use this approach, but instead of a pen or pencil, use digital tools to mark up the content (see the Read Online Course Materials section later in this chapter).

Highlight and Underline. Highlighting and underlining help you identify main ideas and call out key content such as math formulas, diagrams, and definitions. These popular techniques offer a quick and easy way to spotlight important points and then locate that information later when you're studying. But research shows that when using these techniques, you should proceed with caution: If you highlight or underline mindlessly, then you're not processing the information carefully.[3] Later on, you might find it hard to remember what you've read. In addition, if you highlight or underline too much content, the page will become so busy that your markups will be useless.

To take a more focused approach to using these tools, read each section of the material before you make any marks. Ask yourself: What are this section's main ideas? Then go back to the material and highlight or underline *only* the content that's most important.

Take Notes. You can take notes while you read using a laptop or notebook, and you can return to these notes when it's time to study. If your goal is to read the material just once, take thorough notes (see the note taking chapter for specific methods). Later, as you prepare for a test, you'll study directly from these notes. If you plan to reread the material, try taking broad notes as you read. For example, jot down key words with definitions, record where to find diagrams or charts in the chapter, or write a short summary of the material.

As you read and take notes, look for the answers to your purposeful reading questions, and write them down as you find them. For example, if one of your questions is "What are polynomials?" and you come across the definition of *polynomials* in the chapter, add it to your notes or mark it in your book so that later you can go back and study the definition.

Think Critically about What You Read

College would be simpler if everything you read was trustworthy, but that's not always the case. In fact, one of the best skills you'll develop in college is the ability to *evaluate* the quality, accuracy, and usefulness of information—that is, to think critically about what you're reading.

As you read, form your own conclusions about what you're reading, based on your evaluation of the information. For example, let's say your instructor assigns two readings about wage inequality between men and women. In one of the readings, the author argues that women are paid less because they're more likely to work part-time, take time off to have children, and enter occupations that pay less than more male-dominated ones. In the other reading, the author suggests that the pay gap stems from discriminatory practices in the workplace, such as male managers setting lower salaries for women or selecting other men for promotions. As a critical thinker and an active reader, you can evaluate the soundness of the arguments presented in each reading and the authors' credentials and then formulate your own thoughts about what's causing the gender pay gap.

GAINING CONFIDENCE IN READING

Courtesy of
Jennifer Torres

NAME: **Robert E. Moreno III**

SCHOOLS: *Glendale Community College;
Northern Arizona University*

MAJOR: *Communication Studies*

CAREER GOAL: *Education field*

"One thing I find helpful is to write in the margins of my book and make side notes."

Reading is something I've improved on greatly over the years, especially during my time at Glendale Community College (GCC). As a kid, I loved to read—it was fun. However, when I got to school, it became much more difficult. There was a lot to read! And in class they would make you read out loud. I always worried that my speech impediment would show. It wasn't until I attended GCC that I gained confidence in my reading, found my voice, and started to speak out more.

When I first got to college, I realized two things about reading. First, I'd have to do a lot more reading than I ever did as a kid. And second, I wasn't able to read things as quickly as the other students. However, I've implemented a few techniques to increase my reading speed and my retention of the material. One thing I find helpful is to write in the margins of my book and make side notes. If I don't know a particular word, I look it up so I'll understand what I'm reading. To increase my speed, I learned to first preview the chapter—to quickly look through the layout of the chapter, the headings, the pictures, and get an overall sense of what I'm going to read. Then I go back and fully read the chapter. This might take a little more time initially, but I found it's a great way to understand what I'm reading.

Now when I read out loud, I take my time and control my breathing. This helps me control my stuttering and speak fluently. I've found that reading has helped me become not only a better speaker but also a better writer. And as someone with a speech impediment, I enjoy expressing my thoughts, ideas, and passion in writing for others to read.

YOUR TURN: Have you used any of the reading strategies Robert has used? If so, which ones? What benefits have these strategies provided for you? What challenges?

In addition to evaluation, another important component of critical thinking is application. *Applying* what you read to your own life or to everyday situations can help you learn and remember the material. Take Michelle, who's reading about eye contact and culture in her communications textbook. To connect the material to her own life, she thinks about how disconnected she felt on a recent first date when her date wouldn't look her in the eye, and how welcoming it

feels when Andy, the barista at the coffee shop, looks right at her and smiles. Michelle also thinks about how one of her coworkers seldom makes eye contact with colleagues during meetings. He recently moved to the United States, and Michelle wonders if his behavior during meetings stems from the cultural norms he grew up with. By making these connections, Michelle is processing the material more deeply, a strategy that will help her remember what she learned later in the term.

Clarify Confusing Material

As you read, you'll inevitably run into content—a word, a concept, an example—that you don't understand. Try these techniques to clarify confusing content.

- Carefully reread the material. You might understand it on the second or third try.

- Expand your vocabulary. Look up definitions of unfamiliar words, and use the words in sentences to grasp their meaning.

- Move on. Something you read later in the material might clarify things. Or simply giving yourself a few minutes away from the confusing content might help you see something you missed the first time.

- Ask a classmate or a knowledgeable friend to explain the material.

- Find help online. Reading another author's interpretation of confusing content might help. However, remember that not all Internet sources are trustworthy, so use your critical thinking skills to evaluate what your search engine throws at you.

- Ask your instructor. His or her job is to help you learn, so don't be afraid to ask for clarification when you have questions.

❧ CONNECT
TO MY RESOURCES

List two individuals, departments, or offices at your college that could help you improve your ability to read course materials. How might they help you? For example, can they teach you how to read faster or mark up your texts more effectively?

ASK FOR HELP WITH READING CHALLENGES

Many students find reading to be challenging but are uncomfortable asking for help. Is this true for you? If so, try thinking about your situation this way: Just as athletes, musicians, and business executives work with coaches to improve their performance, you can work with people on campus to improve your reading performance. Knowing when and how to ask for help is a valuable skill that will benefit you now and in the future. So take a moment to consider the following helpful resources.

Staff at the Learning Assistance Center. Most campuses have a tutoring or learning support center that focuses on helping students with reading, studying, and many other skills essential for college success. To find the office on your campus, browse your school Web site or type keywords such as "tutoring" or "academic support" into the site's search function.

Advisers. Advisers are used to working with students who need assistance, and they have likely helped others in your position. Talk with your adviser or someone in the advising office about how to approach reading.

Staff at the Disability Services Office. If you have a diagnosed learning disability or think you might have a reading disability, visit your school's disability services office to find out how the staff there can help.

Boost Your Reading Efficiency

Reading efficiently can help you stay focused on the most important material so that you don't waste time and effort on less relevant content. You can supercharge your reading efficiency by mastering the art of concentration and by increasing your reading speed.

Sharpening your powers of concentration can help you avoid an all-too-common problem: realizing that your mind has wandered and that you have no idea what you just read. Try the following tactics for enhancing your concentration.

- **Set brief reading goals.** Create very short-term, focused reading goals if you're unfocused. Instead of trying to read for ninety minutes, for example, set a goal of reading four pages from your religious studies book and reading your marketing text for fifteen minutes. Dividing your reading into small chunks and switching between topics can help you cover all of your reading assignments without feeling overwhelmed and losing focus.

- **Move around.** If you're bored with your reading and can't concentrate, get up and move. Take a one-minute walk around the stacks in the library, grab thirty seconds of fresh air outside, or throw your book into your bag and head for a different study carrel. Then get back to reading.

- **Remove distractions.** If distractions—noises, people passing by, text message or e-mail pings—are preventing you from concentrating, remove them. For instance, turn off your phone, or close the curtains or blinds so you can't see what's happening outside. See the chapter on organization and time management for more ideas on creating a distraction-free zone.

In addition to sharpening your powers of concentration, increasing the speed at which you read can help you make better, more focused use of your reading time. Reading faster is a skill that you can build with practice. Before you spend any of your money on a speed-reading class, try the following techniques.

- **Read in chunks.** Instead of reading one word at a time, try reading groups of words. (Here's how you could "chunk" the preceding sentence: "Instead of reading—one word at a time—try reading—groups of words.") As you focus on groups of words, your speed will increase. There's no one "right" way to do this; when you read, try different groupings to see what works for you.

- **Use a cue.** Place your fingertip at the middle of the first line of a paragraph. Slowly drag this "cue" down the middle of the paragraph, reading each line as you go. When you use a cue, your eyes follow your finger instead of moving left to right across each line. This forces your mind to read each line in chunks rather than each word individually. This technique may take some practice, but the more you do it, the easier it gets.

- **Skim.** If you have a lot of reading to do and not much time, skim the material. Move your glance quickly across each line or read the first and last sentence of each paragraph. Skimming isn't the most effective strategy for deep understanding of material—you'll likely trade some comprehension for speed—but it's better than not reading at all. Just try not to use this approach unless you're pressed for time.

A Rocket-Assist for Your Reading. Boosting your reading speed lets you get maximum value from your reading time. But you don't necessarily have to take a speed-reading class to master this skill. Instead, you can try some simple but effective tactics.
© CartoonStock

Review What You've Read

After you complete a reading assignment, you might be tempted to say, "Okay, check that off the list!" and continue on with your day. Do your best to resist that impulse: There's still work to be done. By revisiting what you've read, you'll improve your comprehension and recall of the information, and you won't have to relearn the material from scratch as you prepare for exams and assignments. Reciting, summarizing, and reviewing and studying are three potent techniques you can use.

Recite

After you read, take a few minutes to recite the main ideas, key words, and new information you've gained from the reading. When you *recite*, you state the information you've learned out loud (if you're by yourself) or in your head (if you're in the library). Reciting new knowledge helps you remember the information you've learned.

Summarize

Gather the central ideas from a reading, and write them down in your own words, either in your notes or at the end of each section of your textbook. Summaries can take different formats, including bulleted lists and short paragraphs. For example, you might write the following summary for this section of the chapter.

Reading Follow-up
- State the main ideas out loud.
- Write a summary of the key concepts.
- Schedule time to review and study reading notes each week.

Like reciting, summarizing requires you to think carefully about the material you've read, which boosts your comprehension of new concepts.

Review and Study

There are many different ways to review and study the material you've read. If you took notes, look them over between classes. If you wrote summaries, study them while you eat breakfast. Here are some additional ideas.

- After you read a chapter, take ten minutes to discuss the main ideas in it with a study partner.

- Recall the answers to your purposeful reading questions while you drive to school each morning.

- Make up your own test items for each chapter, and share them with members of your study group.

- Share your reading notes with a friend, ask for feedback, and fill in any information missing from your notes.

- Check out the studying and memory chapter of this book, where you'll find a number of additional tips you can use during your review.

A Rave Review. Maura knows that reviewing what she has read can help her remember the key concepts in the material. Here she's flipping through a textbook chapter, reciting to herself the main ideas she just learned. You can use this and other reviewing strategies — just pick the ones that work best for you. Stephen Zeigler/Getty Images

READ FOR FUN AND INTEREST — IT'S GOOD FOR YOU

Did you know that motivation to read is connected to reading improvement? According to a study by Jan Retelsdorf, Olaf Koller, and Jens Moller, students who are internally motivated to read have better outcomes than those who are externally motivated. The researchers followed 1,500 middle school students in Germany for three years. The students told the researchers about their motivation to read and then completed an assessment of their reading ability once a year during the study. The researchers found the following:

- Some students read for enjoyment, meaning they found reading to be a pleasant activity and read in their free time.
- Other students read because they found the subject matter interesting.
- Still other students read for competitive reasons — to become better readers than their peers.

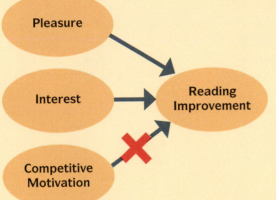

Reading for pleasure and to learn about topics that interest you may help you strengthen your reading skills.

The researchers then compared the students' motivation for reading to their reading performance. Students who read for enjoyment *and* because they were interested in the material displayed the most improvement in reading performance over the three years of the study. Students who read for competitive reasons displayed no improvement in reading performance.

There are two important takeaways from this research. First, you'll have a lot of required reading in college, but if you also find time to read for fun, you might see your overall reading skills improve. Second, try looking for interesting topics in all class readings, even if the class isn't your favorite.

THE BOTTOM LINE

Reading for enjoyment and finding something interesting in all your course materials may help improve your reading performance.

REFLECTION QUESTIONS

1. Recall a time in your life when you read for interest or enjoyment. What benefits might you have gained from that activity?
2. If you don't do much reading for pleasure now, what could you do in the next month to incorporate more of this type of reading into your life?
3. What are two topics you've found interesting in each of your classes this term?

J. Retelsdorf, O. Koller, and J. Moller, "On the Effects of Motivation on Reading Performance and Growth in Secondary School," *Learning and Instruction* 21 (2011): 550–59.

◗ CONNECT
TO MY CLASSES

Have you been doing a lot of reading in your other classes this term? Think about how the ideas in this chapter might help you with that reading. Write down two strategies you can apply immediately to the reading assignments for your other classes.

Read Different Types of Materials

The tips you've learned so far in this chapter can help you with any reading assignment in college. However, there are also more specific tips you can use for particular types of reading materials, such as math and science books, original research articles, and readings for online courses. Give these a try.

Read for Math and Science Classes

Math and science courses aren't identical—for example, chemistry isn't the same as calculus. That said, these courses share enough in common that you can use similar strategies for both science and math reading assignments.

- **Budget your time wisely.** Math and science reading tends to be dense, so schedule enough time to complete it by the due date.

- **Keep up with your work.** Many math and science classes are *linear*: To solve problems in week 2, you have to use what you learned in week 1, and so on. As you read, if you encounter a topic you don't understand, spend enough time on it to grasp it. If you're still struggling with it, get help before your instructor moves too far ahead.

- **Follow the rules.** Math and science have rules that must be followed, so be sure you understand each step of the formula or theorem you're reading about. If you miss a step or break a rule when trying to solve an equation or prove a theorem, you'll be more likely to come up with incorrect answers.

- **Understand symbols and formulas.** If you feel as though you're learning a new language in your math and science classes, that's because in some ways you are. In mathematics and in sciences such as chemistry, engineering, and physics, key information is often expressed in symbols and formulas rather than in words (see Figure 6.5). To understand the material in these classes, pay special attention to these elements—don't skip over them as you read.

- **Study diagrams and models.** While some sciences rely heavily on symbols and formulas, reading material in others—such as biology, anatomy, and geology—includes more text-based descriptions and diagrams and models. Closely examine these visual elements; the information they contain is often just as valuable as the accompanying text.

- **Practice.** Do the exercises in the book, even if your instructor doesn't assign them. Practice helps deepen your understanding of the material.

- **Use flash cards to memorize terms.** You'll encounter many terms in your science courses—for example, the names of organisms in a biology course or the parts of the human body in an anatomy class. Creating flash cards can help you learn and remember these terms. For tips on how to create flash cards, see the memory and studying chapter.

Read Journal Articles

Have you heard of the *New England Journal of Medicine*, *Science*, or *Nature*? These are examples of well-known *journals*—scholarly magazines that publish

FIGURE 6.5 **Reading Science Textbooks**

This page from an allied-health–themed chemistry textbook shows several types of information you might encounter while reading math and science material: abbreviations for dosages, a practice exercise, and a formula for getting the right medicine dosage for people of different weights. Text excerpt p. 23, from *Essentials of General, Organic, and Biochemistry*, 2/e, by Denise Guinn. Copyright © 2014 by W. H. Freeman. Used by permission.

Dosage Calculations

For some medicines prescribed for patients, the dosage must be adjusted according to the patient's weight. This is especially true when administering medicine to children. For example, a dosage of "8.0 mg of tetracycline per kilogram body weight daily" is a dosage based on the weight of the patient. A patient's weight is often given in pounds, yet many drug handbooks give the dosage per kilogram body weight of the patient. Therefore, to calculate the correct amount of medicine to give the patient, you must first convert the patient's weight from pounds into kilograms with an English-metric conversion, using Table 1-3.

It is important to recognize that the dosage is itself a conversion factor between the mass or volume of the medicine and the weight of the patient. Whenever you see the word *per*, it means *in every* and can be expressed as a ratio or fraction where *per* represents a division operation (divided by). For example, 60 miles *per* hour can be written as the ratio 60 mi/1 hr. Similarly, a dosage of 8.0 mg *per* kg body weight can be expressed as the fraction 8.0 mg/1 kg. Hence, dosage *is* a conversion factor:

$$\frac{8 \text{ mg}}{1 \text{ kg}} \quad \text{or} \quad \frac{1 \text{ kg}}{8 \text{ mg}}$$

Dimensional analysis is used to solve dosage calculations by multiplying the patient's weight by the appropriate English-metric conversion factor and then multiplying by the dosage conversion factor, as shown in the following worked exercise.

> Some common abbreviations indicating the frequency with which a medication should be administered include *q.d.* and *b.i.d.*, derived from the Latin meaning administered "daily" and "twice daily," respectively. If the medicine is prescribed for two times daily or four times daily, divide your final answer by two or four to determine how much to give the patient at each administration.

WORKED EXERCISE | Dosage Calculations

1-19 Tetracycline elixir, an antibiotic, is ordered at a dosage of 8.0 mg per kilogram of body weight q.d. for a child weighing 52 lb. How many milligrams of tetracycline elixir should be given to this child daily?

Solution

Step 1: Identify the conversions. Since the dosage is given based on a patient's weight in kilograms, an English-to-metric conversion must be performed. From Table 1-3 this is 1.000 kg = 2.205 lb. The dosage itself is already a conversion factor.

Step 2: Express each conversion as two possible conversion factors. The English-to-metric conversion factors for the patient's weight are

$$\frac{1 \text{ kg}}{2.205 \text{ lb}} \quad \text{or} \quad \frac{2.205 \text{ lb}}{1 \text{ kg}}$$

The dosage *is* a conversion factor between the mass of medicine in milligrams and the weight of the patient in kilograms:

$$\frac{8.0 \text{ mg}}{1 \text{ kg}} \quad \text{or} \quad \frac{1 \text{ kg}}{8.0 \text{ mg}}$$

academic and scientific papers, many of which are written by college professors. In journal articles, professors describe research they're conducting, share new ideas or theories, summarize findings from a broad area of research, or present original works such as poetry or short stories. You've been reading information from journal articles throughout this book: Each Spotlight on Research describes findings that came from a journal article.

**⟩ CONNECT
TO MY CAREER**

What types of materials would you need to read in your dream job (for example, papers, manuals, blog posts)? If you're not sure, ask an instructor or do some research to find out. Then list two techniques from this chapter that you believe could help you read those materials more effectively.

Journal articles are packed with useful information, but they can be more complex than other sources. To read and understand them, you have to know which parts of the article to focus on. Many articles, particularly research articles, have the following sections:

- *Abstract*: a paragraph summarizing the article
- *Introduction*: a review of previous research that supports the study and a description of the research questions, often called *hypotheses*
- *Methods*: a description of what the authors studied and how they studied it
- *Results*: a description of the statistical analysis used to answer the research questions
- *Discussion*: a written summary of the findings or answers to the research questions

You can follow these steps to understand the material in a research article.

1. Read the *abstract* and state the article's main idea in your own words. Once you can do this, you're ready to read the article itself.

2. Read the *introduction*, focusing on the hypotheses at the end of this section. Make sure you know what questions the authors are trying to answer.

3. Read the *discussion*, focusing on the first few paragraphs. The authors will likely state the answers to the research questions in prose form (as opposed to statistical form, which often appears in the results section).

4. Once you understand the research results from the discussion, read the *methods* and *results* sections to see more clearly how the authors came to their conclusions.

Journal articles are written primarily for other college professors, researchers, and experts in the field, so don't worry if you feel confused or overwhelmed at first: you're probably not the only one. Ask for help when you need it. Being able to read and understand even the basic ideas in a journal article is a useful skill, so it's worth investing time now in learning how to do it.

Read Online Course Materials

If you're taking an online class for the first time this term, you may be a bit worried. Does the class have more required reading than your face-to-face classes? Is it a hassle to access the readings online? These are legitimate concerns, but here's good news: You can use a few powerful strategies to handle your online course reading.

- **Be prepared to do more reading.** It's true that online classes require more reading, because you don't spend as much time in class listening to lectures. Now that you know, you can plan in advance how to complete all your reading on time.

- **Create your own schedule.** If your online class doesn't have regular reading assignments or quizzes to help you stay on track, build your own reading schedule—then stick to it.

■ **Make sure you can access online materials.** If you have to access reading materials online, make sure you can do so when the class begins. If you run into any difficulties, ask the instructor for help right away. That way, you'll be confident you can access what you need to complete your assignments.

■ **Learn how to mark up text online.** If you're reading online, learn how to mark up text using the tools available with your program or device. Documents in PDF format, for instance, often allow you to highlight text and make notes in the margins. E-books frequently have the same features (see Figure 6.6). In addition, when you read electronically, you often have access to a search function, which allows you to find something you wrote in a note or to search for a specific term.

■ **Consider printing out materials.** If your reading materials are provided electronically but you prefer to annotate them in paper form, investigate whether you can print them out.

■ **Read and respond to online posts.** You'll often be required to read and respond to other students' online posts in discussion boards for the course. Take time to read and reflect on the posts. You can learn a lot from what others have to say.

FIGURE 5-11 presents an overview of the processes of transcription and translation. In transcription, which in eukaryotes occurs in the nucleus, the gene's base sequence, or code, is copied into a middleman molecule called messenger RNA (mRNA). (Because prokaryotes don't have a nucleus, transcription occurs in the cytoplasm.) This is like copying the information for the chocolate chip cookie recipe out of the cookbook and onto an index card. The mRNA then moves out of the nucleus into the cytoplasm, where translation allows the messages encoded in the mRNA to be used to build proteins.

c lembo   5/29/2015 5:03 PM
Key term! Add messenger RNA (mRNA) to flash cards.

Reply

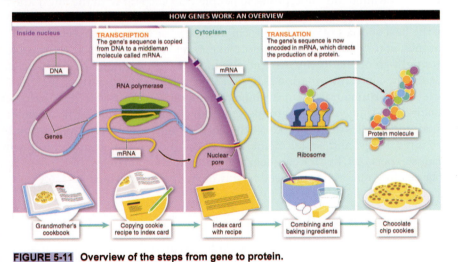

FIGURE 5-11 Overview of the steps from gene to protein.

FIGURE 6.6 **Marking an E-book**

When you're reading online, you can use tools to mark up the material. In this excerpt from a biology textbook, the student has used yellow highlighting to emphasize a key point. She has also included a note reminding herself to add a key term to flash cards she's creating for the chapter.

Read at Work

Almost all jobs require *some* reading, and in many cases, reading is a key part of the job description. (If you want to be a textbook author, you won't get far without reading—trust us!) In fact, reading is so important that "reading comprehension" counts among the core skills needed to perform work in many professions.[4] In this section, we look at ways you can use reading skills on the job. As you work through the section, think about the profession (or professions) that interest you most. Do they involve a lot of reading? Or just a little? What kind of reading? How can you put the reading skills you're learning in this class to good use in your career?

Gather, Analyze, and Apply Information

Reading is a core activity in many jobs because you frequently have to gather, analyze, and apply information to get work done, and for all of those tasks you need strong reading skills. For example, suppose a pharmacist needs to dispense a new drug, but she's uncertain how it will interact with other medications a patient is taking. She has to read about the new medication, analyze whether it can be taken safely with the other medications, and then apply what she learned to this particular patient's situation. In positions like this one (and many others), reading relevant information—and thinking critically about that information—is a crucial part of performing your duties effectively.

Stay Current

Employers want to hire and promote people who keep up with the latest knowledge in their field, and reading can help you do this. Early in your career, identify the best sources of current information in your field. As a psychologist, for example, you might consult a source like *Psychological Bulletin*. As a teacher, you might go online to NASA's Web site to get a new lesson plan. Another way to learn the latest information is to join a professional association, such as the Society for Human Resource Management or the American Psychological Association. Many of these groups send out monthly or quarterly magazines containing articles about trends in the field. Finally, use reliable and reputable Web sites, blogs, and social media to stay up-to-date. For example, following various experts on Twitter can help you find out about articles, blog posts, and other reading materials you need to stay current and informed.

Expand Your Skill Set

You can also use reading to build new skills that are valuable in your career. For example, do you want to learn more about how to use wind turbine technology, design more effective interventions for at-risk youth, or manage social media campaigns for your organization? Do you want to become a whiz at Excel or learn how to create a model of an erupting volcano before teaching a science lesson to your sixth-grade class? Reading can help you get it done. Pick up a book, browse relevant Web sites, or seek out a journal article on your topic of choice.

"What's Shipping Today?"
These order-fulfillment employees use their reading skills to gather, analyze, and apply information that is critical for performing their jobs. Here, they're comparing customer orders and data showing what's in stock in the warehouse. Using this information, they can make sure that enough inventory is available so that customers get the items they want.
Paul Bradbury/Getty Images

READING TO SUCCEED AT WORK

Courtesy of
Albert Galvin

NAME:	**Al Galvin**
PROFESSION:	*Recreation Specialist II*
SCHOOL:	*Kansas State University*
DEGREE:	*Bachelor of Science in Agriculture*
MAJOR:	*Parks and Resource Management*

As a Recreation Specialist II, it's my responsibility to manage the allocation and programming for 147 sports fields in Clark County. I spend about 80 percent of my time on the computer, so I do a lot of my reading online. Many times I'm talking on the phone, looking on my computer at field schedules and availability, and looking up information about the organization or person I'm speaking to. Reading about them helps me better qualify the person/organization in order to better help them. I research these organizations — which include sports leagues, teams, and concessionaires — online. I see what people say about them and follow up with their backgrounds a bit. I also end up reading all sorts of things for the different groups that want to use our facilities. In addition to reading e-mails, I have to research by-laws, regulations, or policies from different groups who want to use the fields. I'm reading all the time.

Recently we had a situation where some groups claimed to be nonprofits, but I wasn't sure they really qualified. Nonprofits get priority when it comes to using the fields, and they pay reduced fees to do so. Figuring out which organizations were nonprofit turned out to be a massive project. We conducted an internal audit of our organizations and the required paperwork they give us. We researched every organization's nonprofit status on the IRS Web site. Some of them had been revoked and we needed to know why. I ended up reading through hundreds of pages of IRS information about how this whole thing works. Without myself and a few others really reading about regulations and policies, we would have had numerous organizations who weren't following our own policies. Without reading, I wouldn't have found the information I needed to do my job effectively.

YOUR TURN: Do you currently have a job? If so, what kinds of reading are most useful for excelling in your job? If you're not currently employed but want to pursue a particular career, what kinds of materials will you likely need to read in order to do your job well?

> " **Without reading, I wouldn't have found the information I needed to do my job effectively.**"

my personal success plan

READING

Are you inspired to set a new goal aimed at improving your reading skills? If so, the Personal Success Plan can walk you through the goal-setting process. Read the advice and examples; then sketch out your ideas in the space provided.

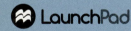

To access the Personal Success Plan online, go to the LaunchPad for *Connections*.

1 GATHER INFORMATION

Think about your strengths and weaknesses related to reading. What reading strategies have worked for you in the past? What could you do differently? Revisit your Reading score on ACES and review the relevant sections of this chapter for additional ideas.

2 SET A SMART GOAL

Use the information you've gathered to create a SMART goal, making sure to use the SMART goal checklist.

SAMPLE: I'll create purposeful reading questions before I read the next chapter in my economics book.

3 MAKE AN ACTION PLAN

Outline the specific steps you'll take to achieve your SMART goal, and note when you'll complete each step.

SAMPLE: Tomorrow night, I'll turn each bullet point from the chapter summary into a purposeful reading question.

4 LIST BARRIERS AND SOLUTIONS

Think about possible barriers to your action steps; then brainstorm solutions for overcoming them.

SAMPLE: I've never done this before, so I might have a hard time writing questions. If so, I'll ask my study partner Ethan to take a look at my questions before class on Friday.

5 ACT AND EVALUATE OUTCOMES

Now that your plan is in place, take action. Record each action step as you take it. Then evaluate whether you achieved your SMART goal, and make any adjustments needed to get better results in the future.

SAMPLE: My purposeful reading questions were mainly about definitions, which limited how much I learned from the chapter. Next time, I'll try writing more analytical questions.

6 CONNECT TO CAREER

List the skills you're building as you progress toward your SMART goal. How will you use these skills to land a job and succeed at work?

SAMPLE: Using purposeful reading questions helped me read with focus. I'd like to become a financial analyst, and I'll need that type of focus while I read annual reports and profit and loss statements.

1 my information

2 my SMART goal

☐ **S**PECIFIC   ☐ **M**EASURABLE   ☐ **A**CHIEVABLE   ☐ **R**ELEVANT   ☐ **T**IME-LIMITED

3 my action plan

4 my barriers/ solutions

5 my actions/ outcomes

6 my career connection

CHAPTER SUMMARY

This chapter explored a wide range of concepts and strategies for getting the most from your college reading. Revisit the following key points, and reflect on how you can use this information to support your success now and in the future.

- Along with attending class, note taking, studying, test taking, and writing and presenting, reading is a critical academic skill. Reading and attending class set the stage for excelling at other study skills, so reading is foundational to your college success.

- To understand, remember, and apply what you've learned from reading class materials, you need to take a three-step active reading approach: (1) prepare to read, (2) read with focus, and (3) review what you've read.

- Strategies for preparing to read include evaluating how long your reading will take; previewing your textbook preface, table of contents, and key terms; and developing purposeful reading questions — questions that you want to be able to answer once you've finished the reading.

- Strategies for reading with focus include marking up your reading materials, thinking critically about what you're reading, clarifying material you don't understand, and boosting your reading efficiency by sharpening your concentration and increasing your reading speed.

- Strategies for reviewing what you've read include reciting key concepts in your own words, summarizing them in a bulleted list or paragraph, and reviewing and studying your notes.

- If you find reading to be challenging, you can contact the learning assistance center, an adviser, or staff at the disability services office for help.

- In addition to using the other strategies mentioned in the chapter, you'll want to master strategies for reading specific types of materials, such as math and science textbooks, journal articles, and readings assigned in your online classes.

- The critical thinking skills you use to handle your college reading — including gathering, analyzing, and applying information — will prove just as valuable in your work life. By knowing how to get the most from your reading, you can excel at your job, stay up-to-date with knowledge in your field, and build new skills.

CHAPTER ACTIVITIES

Journal Entry

READING IN THE INFORMATION AGE

We live in the Information Age, a time characterized by the publication, consumption, and manipulation of ever-greater amounts of information using computers and technology. In your journal, respond to the following questions:

1. How has the increased use of digital tools (such as laptop and tablet computers, the Internet, e-readers, and smartphones) affected your reading? For example, do you read more or less than you used to? Why? Has what you read changed? If so, how? Do you find it easier or harder than before to understand and remember what you read?

2. If you grew up with digital tools and technologies and therefore can't answer the previous questions from a personal perspective, try answering them from a societal perspective. For example, how do you think technology has changed the way people read?

3. What are the possible benefits of reading in the Information Age? The possible challenges? How might these benefits and challenges affect your college experience?

Adopting a Success Attitude

DISCOVERING ENJOYMENT IN READING

Reading for pleasure has numerous benefits: It can build your knowledge, improve your vocabulary, boost your reading speed, enhance your creativity and imagination, and encourage attentiveness and focus. Moreover, reading for pleasure can relieve stress and promote positive emotions.

Choose four literary genres from the following list. For each genre you choose, identify a book that you might like to read. (Search online or go to a bookstore to get ideas.) Provide the full title of the book, the author's name, a brief description of the book (two to three sentences), and the reason it interests you.

Literary Genres

classic literature	horror	autobiography/biography
fantasy/adventure	mystery	nonfiction (factual information)
historical fiction	romance	poetry
crime/detective	humor	
science fiction	suspense/thriller	

Now set a goal for your reading. When will you read the titles you've listed?

Applying Your Skills

LEARNING TO READ WITH A PURPOSE

Preparing to read is a critical step in the active reading process, and previewing your reading is one method you can use to prepare. Previewing gives you a sense of what you'll be reading, prepares you to absorb new information, and helps you read with focus.

Preview one of the chapters in this textbook that you haven't read yet. Read the title, the chapter outline, and the first few paragraphs of the chapter (the introduction). Then look for the main headings and any boldfaced terms and read the chapter summary. Finally, write down five purposeful reading questions — ones you expect to be able to answer, or would like to answer, after you've read the full chapter. If you have trouble developing such questions, look at the examples in the Prepare to Read section of this chapter or try crafting Who?, What?, When?, Where?, How?, and Why? questions.

When you read the chapter later in the term, see if you can answer the purposeful reading questions you've developed.

College Success = Career Success

EXPANDING YOUR PROFESSIONAL VOCABULARY

Identify a professional journal or magazine related to your current career (if you're working), a future career (if you have one in mind), or a career that you're curious about (if you're undecided). (If you aren't sure what journals or magazines relate to your career, do a Google search, ask an instructor in the appropriate department, contact a librarian at your college, or ask someone working in this field.) Select an article from the publication, and use the tips you learned in this chapter to preview and read the article.

Write down five words from this article that are new to you or that seem important in the career you've identified. Next to each word, write down the definition. If the definition doesn't appear in the article, look the word up in a dictionary. Hold on to these words and definitions — if they're related to your current or future career, you can bet you'll see them again!

7 Taking Effective Notes

Supercharge Your Note Taking with a Four-Step Strategy

Experiment with Note-Taking Methods

Note-Taking Tips for Math, Science, and Online Classes

Apply Note Taking at Work

My Personal Success Plan

Asia Images Group/Getty Images

Let's be honest: Note taking isn't the most exciting topic to study. In fact, you probably groaned at the thought of reading a whole chapter about taking notes. Now that we've got this out in the open, how can you approach this chapter with a positive attitude? Try to change your thinking about note taking.

At its heart, note taking is much more than writing or typing words: It's a way to record, organize, and manage information so that you can *learn* from and *use* it. To be a good note-taker, you need to recognize which information is most important, figure out how to record the information so it's clear, and use your notes to study. When you build these skills — as you'll do by using the strategies in this chapter — you'll better understand what you're learning and, as a result, perform better on exams and homework assignments. In short, note taking is a survival skill for college.

Note taking can also help you learn and manage information at work. For example, suppose you're meeting with team members to kick off a new project. During the meeting you take notes about your role in moving the project forward and how you'll interact with others on the team once the project is launched. Or let's say you work for an advertising agency. You're in charge of designing an ad campaign for a new client, so you call the client to talk about that company's product and its goals for the campaign. You take notes during the phone conversation. Later, when you start thinking in more depth about how to tackle the project, you use your notes to generate ideas.

In this chapter we present a four-step strategy for taking notes: (1) prepare to take notes; (2) actively listen, watch, read, and participate when you read or attend a lecture; (3) record information; and (4) review your notes. We then examine four note-taking methods: outlining, the Cornell system, mapping, and charting. Next, we explore specific strategies for taking notes in math, science, and online courses. Finally, we show how note taking can help you excel at your job.

Reflect

On Your Note Taking

Reflect

Take a moment to reflect on your Note Taking score on ACES. Find your score and add it in the circle to the right.

This score measures your beliefs about how well you take notes. Do you think it's an accurate snapshot of your current skills in this area? Why or why not?

☐ **HIGH**

☐ **MODERATE**

☐ **LOW**

LaunchPad

To find your **Note Taking score,** go to the LaunchPad for *Connections.*

■ **IF YOU SCORED IN THE HIGH RANGE** and you have a strong track record of effective note taking, then this is likely one of your strengths. Excellent! Now think about how you can enhance this strength. For instance, you might learn a new strategy in this chapter that helps you maintain focus during lectures. Or you might find a way to restructure your notes so they're easier to follow when you study for exams. The more strategies you have, the better you'll get at taking notes.

■ **IF YOU SCORED IN THE MODERATE OR LOW RANGE,** you've got the perfect opportunity: Use the strategies in this chapter to strengthen your note-taking skills. Sample some of the different techniques presented, and figure out which ones help you most effectively record the information you need. Take control of your learning!

Supercharge Your Note Taking with a Four-Step Strategy

Note taking plays a key role in academic success.[1] When you combine it with other important study skills and activities—reading, going to class, studying, taking exams, and writing and speaking—note taking helps you absorb, think about, remember, and use new information you're learning in your courses. For instance, when you take notes in class or while reading an assigned textbook chapter, you can use those notes later to study for an exam or to deliver a presentation in class.

There is no "right" format for taking notes; you can choose from a variety of methods, depending on what works best for you. But no matter which method (or methods) you choose, you'll get the most learning power from your notes if you approach note taking strategically. We recommend a four-step strategy: You start with preparation; you actively listen, watch, read, and participate; you record the information you're learning; and you review your notes (see Figure 7.1).

Let's take a closer look at each step.

FIGURE 7.1 Four Steps to Effective Note Taking

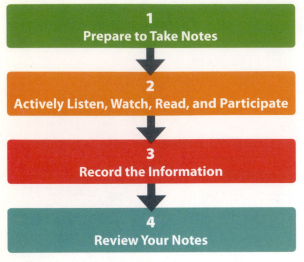

1
Prepare to Take Notes

2
Actively Listen, Watch, Read, and Participate

3
Record the Information

4
Review Your Notes

Step 1: Prepare to Take Notes

When you *prepare* to take notes, you'll find it much easier to focus on the most important information once you actually *take* notes—for instance, when you're listening to a lecture, reading an assignment, or watching a video. Because preparation helps you focus, it boosts the quality and usefulness of your notes. Use these tactics to prepare successfully.

- **Gather the materials you'll need to take notes.** For example, find your textbook and the previous notes you took for that class or project. Decide ahead of time whether to handwrite your notes or type them on a laptop or tablet (see the Spotlight on Research). If you choose to write by hand, make sure to have a notebook, pens, and a highlighter handy. If you're trying out a new note-taking app, which you can find with a quick Internet search, get comfortable with it before using it in class.

- **Create a system to label, organize, and store your notes.** That way, you can easily find and review your notes later when you want to use them to study for an upcoming exam or to complete a homework assignment. The chapter on organization and time management contains ideas for creating a system for labeling, organizing, and storing your notes.

- **Preview key concepts.** If you're preparing to take notes during a lecture, review the course syllabus and complete any required reading before class. If you're preparing to take notes while reading, use the previewing strategies described in the reading chapter, such as reviewing textbook

Don't Leave Prep to the Last Minute. Don't wait until the last second to prepare to take notes. Instead, take time to get organized and gather any materials you'll need ahead of time. Will you be taking notes at a lecture? If so, arrive a few minutes early, get focused, and review your notes from the previous class. © Dale May/Corbis

chapter summaries, headings, and definitions to get a sense of the major ideas in the reading material.

- **Follow your schedule.** If you're attending lecture, arrive a few minutes early to review your notes from the previous class. If you plan to take notes while reading, follow your study schedule and begin work at the time you had planned.

- **Review your instructor's PowerPoint slides and bring them to class.** If an instructor provides slides in advance, you can start to familiarize yourself with the key concepts that will be covered in class. That way, you won't have to write or type what's already on the slides during lecture. Instead, you can focus on the instructor's verbal explanation and take notes that expand on the information in the slides, either on the slide printout itself or in a separate document. In fact, taking your own notes instead of relying solely on your instructor's slides has huge benefits: You think more about the information you're learning, so you stand a better chance of understanding, remembering, and applying it.

- **Bring unanswered questions to class.** If you have unresolved questions about your reading assignments, bring them to class. Your instructor may provide the information you're looking for—or you can ask the questions in class to get the answers you need.

- **Stay positive.** Remind yourself that note taking helps you maximize your learning.

Step 2: Actively Listen, Watch, Read, and Participate

To take good notes, you'll need to focus on the information you're receiving, whether it comes to you during a lecture, from something you're reading or discussing, or even from a video you watch for class. Focusing helps you identify the most important information in what you're hearing or seeing so that you can capture it accurately for later review and use.

To sharpen your focus on the key information, *engage* with that information by actively listening, watching, reading, and participating (depending on the note-taking situation). These techniques can help.

- **Eliminate distractions.** Even when you're trying hard to pay attention, it can be tempting to grab your phone and text friends or reply to e-mails. When you give in to distractions, though, you miss chunks of information you're supposed to absorb and record. So, take steps to eliminate distractions—for example, turn off your phone when you need to focus. The organization and time management chapter offers additional ideas for creating a distraction-free zone.

- **Empower yourself to concentrate.** If you're taking notes in class, sit in the front; you'll find it easier to hear your instructor and participate in class discussion. Plus, when your instructor is looking you in the eye, you'll be less likely to daydream, fiddle with your phone, or doze off. If you're taking notes while reading, find a quiet location in which to work.

- **Look for written cues to important concepts in your reading.** When you take notes while reading, look for section headings as well as boldfaced terms. These signal important concepts in the material. (See the reading chapter for more information.)

- **Listen for verbal cues from your instructors about what's important.** In class, instructors' speech patterns can signal that certain information is especially crucial—for example, raising or lowering their voice when emphasizing points, or slowing down and repeating key concepts. Instructors might also use certain words and phrases alerting you to important material: "The main advantage . . . ," "Some of the challenges . . . ," "What we can conclude from this . . . ," "A key component . . . ," and (a student favorite) "People, this will be on the test."

- **Watch for nonverbal cues.** Pay attention to your instructors' gestures and movements during class. Some instructors step out from behind the lectern, stop moving, point to a PowerPoint slide, or make direct eye contact when emphasizing an important point. We know of one instructor who rang a cowbell each time he introduced an important concept. (Most instructors are probably subtler than this!)

- **Participate in class.** Get involved in what you're learning in class. If your instructor encourages discussion, become an active participant: Contribute your thoughts about the topic of the day; ask questions about topics you're curious about; and volunteer responses to your instructor's questions. Participating in class can be intimidating—particularly if you're uncomfortable speaking in front of others, the class is large, or you find the topic of discussion confusing—but give it your best shot. By participating actively, you can clarify confusing concepts, gain additional insights into what you're learning, and stay focused on the material. And all of this helps you take better notes.

Attention, Please! In real life, instructors seldom have audiences this attentive—watching their every move and writing down their every word. But imagine how good instructors would feel if audiences were this engaged. With that in mind, show courtesy to your instructors when you attend lectures. For instance, listen attentively and resist any urge to fiddle with your phone.
© CartoonStock

CONNECT
TO MY EXPERIENCE

Think back to a time when you actively participated in class— for example, when you asked a great question, answered a question, or got your fellow classmates involved in a discussion. Briefly explain how it felt to contribute. Were you nervous? Excited? How do you plan to participate in your current classes?

Step 3: Record Information

When it's time to record information you hear or read, do it quickly, accurately, and in a way that makes sense to you. Later in the chapter, you'll learn four specific methods for recording information, but these general strategies can also help.

- **Label your notes.** At the top of the page, include a label with the course title, lecture topic, date, and a page number. If you handwrite your notes, use only one side of the page, and start notes for each lecture or reading assignment on a new piece of paper. If you type your notes, create a new document or move to a new page for each lecture or reading assignment.

- **Resist the urge to write down *everything*.** Your instructors will talk faster than you can write, and not everything said in class or printed in a book is critical information. Instead, record only the main points and the most important details, using the active learning techniques you just read about.

- **Learn to paraphrase.** Recording information *verbatim* (word-for-word) is important with chemical or mathematical formulas, definitions, dates, names, and diagrams because later you might need to reproduce these exactly on tests, in lab reports, or in papers. Often, though, it's best to **paraphrase** information by restating it in your own words.[2] For example, when you take notes as you read, if you just copy the words on the page into a notebook, you're not interacting with the material. When you paraphrase, on the other hand, you have to think about what you're reading, and then translate your understanding into your own words. Because you're interacting with the information, you're more likely to understand and remember it. Paraphrasing is also useful in class when you need to summarize the main points of a lecture or record key ideas from a PowerPoint slide. Table 7.1 shows an example of paraphrasing.

Paraphrase: To restate information in your own words.

TABLE 7.1 Example of Paraphrased Content

Original content	Paraphrased content
"The first human beings to arrive in the Western Hemisphere emigrated from Asia. They brought with them hunting skills, weapon- and tool-making techniques, and other forms of human knowledge developed millennia earlier in Africa, Europe, and Asia. These first Americans hunted large mammals, such as the mammoths they had learned in Europe and Asia to kill, butcher, and process for food, clothing, and building materials. Most likely, these first Americans wandered into the Western Hemisphere more or less accidentally in pursuit of prey."	• First people in Western Hemisphere came from Asia • Thousands of years of knowledge and expertise: hunting, tools, weapons • Hunted mammoths — source of food, clothing, shelter • Probably accidental migration, searching for food

Source: James L. Roark et al., *The American Promise: A History of the United States,* 6th ed. (Boston: Bedford/St. Martin's, 2015), p. 4.

TAKING NOTES?
GRAB A PEN AND PAPER

With the popularity of laptops and tablets, more and more college students are coming to class with a computer. Typing notes is convenient, and often neater and faster than writing. But a question arises: When it comes to learning information for tests, is one method more effective than the other? Researchers Pam Mueller and Daniel Oppenheimer set out to investigate.

In the first of three studies, the researchers asked sixty-seven students to watch brief, recorded lectures and take notes using either a laptop or pad and paper. Students were asked to use their normal note-taking procedure from lecture classes — either typing or writing. After the note-taking activity, participants spent about thirty minutes doing other things and then were tested using two types of questions: fill-in-the-blank questions that required them to recall facts from the lecture, and essay questions that required them to apply the ideas from the lecture. Several interesting findings emerged.

	Handwritten notes	**Typed notes**
Recall test performance	+ (Performed well)	+ (Performed well)
Application test performance	+ (Performed well)	− (Performed less well)
Quantity of notes	− (Recorded less information)	+ (Recorded more information)
Quality of notes	+ (Took higher-quality notes)	− (Took lower-quality notes)

In this study, students who handwrote their notes performed better on application tests and took higher-quality notes than did students who typed their notes.

- Both groups performed equally well on the recall test (fill-in-the-blank questions).
- Students who handwrote their notes did much better on the application test (essay questions).
- Students who typed their notes recorded more information from the lecture — normally a good thing — but much of it was word-for-word. As you just read, paraphrasing is often the best way to learn and remember.

THE BOTTOM LINE

If possible, try writing your notes by hand. Doing so can help you apply the information you learn and take higher-quality notes than typing because you're more likely to paraphrase than to record information word-for-word.

REFLECTION QUESTIONS

1. Do you handwrite or type your notes? Why have you selected this method?
2. If you type notes, do you record information word-for-word or put ideas into your own words?
3. If you prefer to type your notes, will you try handwriting your notes now that you've learned about this study? Why or why not?

P. A. Mueller and D. M. Oppenheimer, "The Pen Is Mightier Than the Keyboard: Advantages of Longhand over Laptop Note Taking," *Psychological Science* 25 (2014): 1159–68.

- **Use symbols and abbreviations to save time.** You can create your own shorthand using symbols and abbreviations that work for you. For example, you might use an asterisk (*) to flag important information and the approximately symbol ($\approx$) to indicate approximate numbers. (See Figure 7.3 and Figure 7.4 for more examples of useful symbols and abbreviations.)

- **Use metacognition to recognize when you don't understand information.** If you realize you have no idea what your instructor is saying or notice that you don't understand a sentence you just read, you're using metacognition. When you recognize that you're confused, you have information you can act on: Write down your questions and get clarification as soon as you can. You might use a star, an exclamation point, or a question mark to indicate the confusing material or leave space to later jot down notes when you get answers to your questions. Taking action to clarify concepts will get you the answers you need—*before* you see the material on a test.

- **Ask questions.** If your instructor allows questions during class (and most do!), raise your hand when you don't understand material. Asking questions shows your instructor that you're engaged in class and care about what you're learning. If the instructor prefers to answer questions after class or during office hours, speak with him or her at the designated time and place.

- **If you have a disability, make use of accommodations.** Depending on the type of disability you have, you may be able to audio- or video-record lectures or have another person take notes for you.

Ask Questions to Create Top-Notch Notes. As you're taking notes, notice when you don't understand something. If you're in class, ask questions to clear up any misunderstanding. That way, you'll be sure that you recorded information accurately — and you can study from your top-notch notes later on. Claudia Paulussen/Shutterstock

Step 4: Review Your Notes

After you take notes, review them. Are they accurate? Complete? Do you have unanswered questions? If the information in your notes looks wrong or you don't understand it, your notes won't help you learn the material and use it to answer test questions or do class projects. Use these tips for reviewing your notes.

- **Review your notes when ideas are fresh in your mind.** After you've taken notes, spend a few minutes skimming them to check that the information still makes sense. If you find things that are questionable, mark them so you know to come back and clarify them. Try to review your notes within a day to fill in missing information; otherwise, you might come back to the material a few days later and have no idea what your notes mean.

- **Compare your notes with other students' notes.** See whether you're recording the same information and capturing the same level of detail as your classmates, and take the opportunity to clarify any concepts you found confusing.

- **Talk with your instructor.** Visit your instructor during office hours, and ask for feedback on the quality of your notes. If you have questions or don't fully grasp the material, ask for help.

❯ CONNECT TO MY RESOURCES

Which of your friends or classmates are great note-takers? What systems are they using? Ask two of them to show you how they take notes. Write down three things you learn from them or ideas you'd like to try.

- **Practice paraphrasing.** If you wrote something down word-for-word in your notes, try paraphrasing this content. Paraphrasing will help you understand the ideas more fully.

- **Compare your notes to the study guide.** If your instructor provides a study guide, compare your notes to the material it contains. Are the main ideas from your notes similar to those of the study guide? If not, add any missing content to your notes.

- **Clarify and reorganize your notes.** If your handwritten notes are hard to read, type them out. If your typewritten notes are confusing, retype them in a clearer form in a new document. Reorganize the content of your notes to clarify the connections between ideas. If your notes are incomplete, fill in the gaps. According to research, meaningful time spent reviewing and rewriting your notes more clearly may help you get higher scores on exams.[3]

Experiment with Note-Taking Methods

There is no single "best" note-taking method: Different methods work well for different people in different courses. In this section we describe four popular methods. As you read about each one, think about the note-taking methods you've used in the past. Which ones worked well for you? Which ones didn't? Keep in mind that note taking is a survival skill. As you gain experience and score more successes, your note-taking skill will improve, and your sense of self-efficacy will grow stronger.

Outlining

Creating an outline is a common, formalized way of taking notes (see Figure 7.2). Outlining helps you organize the material as you record your notes, making it easier to search for and review key information when you study. It works particularly well when instructors use a similar approach in their PowerPoint slides, but outlining can be used in any note-taking situation—inside and outside of class. You've probably used outlines to write papers; you can use the same format when taking notes.

- **First level.** Use uppercase Roman numerals (such as I, II, III) to represent the main ideas from a lecture or reading. You may be able to identify these before you read by previewing the chapter, or before class by reviewing lecture slides posted by your instructor.

- **Second level.** Use uppercase letters (such as A, B, C) to record the key points that support the first-level headings.

- **Third level.** Use Arabic numerals (such as 1, 2, 3) to record facts, details, or examples that support and illustrate the ideas in the second-level headings.

- **Additional levels.** You can add additional levels by indenting further and using alternating numbers and letters at each level.

- **Bullet points.** If you find letters and numerals too formal, use different levels of bullet points instead.

FIGURE 7.2 Taking Notes in Outline Format

First-Year Experience 101—September 23—Page 1

I.   Motivation
    A. Affects how much homework I get done
    B. 3 key components influence my motivation
II. Self-efficacy
    A. Definition: Belief that I can perform the actions needed to reach a goal
    B. Can I be effective?
    C. Stronger self-efficacy means more likely to manage setbacks
    D. 4 factors strengthen self-efficacy—from Albert Bandura
        1. Having success
        2. Observing successful others (modeling)
        3. Getting support/encouragement from others
        4. Using a little bit of stress as a motivator
III. Relevance
    A. Relevance: Achieving a goal will make a positive difference
    B. More relevance means increased motivation
    C. 5 strategies to make things more relevant
        1. Pick out a topic of interest in every class
        2. Connect course content to long-term goals
        3. Focus on transferable skills I can get from each class
        4. Keep it practical: Keep GPA up to keep scholarships
        5. Remember that I love to learn—each class is an opportunity
IV. Attitude
    A. Good attitude makes me resilient, allows me to enjoy success and
        learn from mistakes
    B. Positive attitude will help me be more motivated, energized, focused
    C. 3 ways to maintain a positive attitude
        1. Find something positive in my work—even something small
        2. Take one class in my major each term if possible
        3. Use positive self-talk; use reframing to change negative to positive

OUTLINING AND OTHER NOTE-TAKING STRATEGIES

NAME: **Nicole S. Williams**

SCHOOL: *Indiana University–Purdue University Fort Wayne*

MAJOR: *Business Management*

CAREER GOAL: *Financial Adviser or Accountant*

"**I've found the outlining technique to be a very effective note-taking strategy.**"

I've found the outlining technique to be a very effective note-taking strategy for me. I always use bullet points, main points, and subpoints. I came across this strategy in high school. My high school teacher really didn't write many notes on the board. She talked most of the time. So, when she did write on the board, I knew the information was important, and I chose it as the main point in my outline. Then I usually added the things she said afterward as my subpoints. I've been using this technique ever since.

Outlining is clear and flows nicely for me. I'm an organized person, so I need my notes organized and in order so I can make sense of them. This strategy helped me in many courses, especially those in big lecture halls, such as psychology and anthropology.

I'm always ready to take notes. I always read assignments and books with a pencil in my hand so I can write down information. Also, I listen closely to speakers in class, because they don't always write down the key points. As a matter of fact, most of the important concepts are verbally stated, so you have to be an active listener.

I also review my notes for clarity, although I admit that I don't review as much as I should or would like to. But with a test coming around — say that my test is next week — I'll usually try to review my notes for at least an hour, then take an hour break, and then go back and review them again. I try to do this for the whole week until the test comes up. Then, if I have questions about my notes, I'll go to professors at least three days before the test. That's how I usually review.

YOUR TURN: Have you used outlining to take notes? If so, what benefits has this method offered you? What challenges has it presented? If you haven't used outlining, what's the reason?

Cornell System

The **Cornell system** organizes each page of your notes into sections: Your initial notes go on the right, key points go in a cue column on the left, and a summary section goes at the bottom of the page (see Figure 7.3). This system helps you study because after attending class or reading, you return to your notes to expand on the material you just learned. To create notes using the Cornell system, follow these steps.

1. **Divide the page.** Draw a horizontal line about two inches from the bottom of the page. The space below the line is the *summary section*. Next, draw a vertical line about two and a half inches from the left side of the page, meeting the horizontal line across the bottom. The area on the left is the *cue column*. The area on the right is the *notes* section, where you'll write notes during class or while reading.

2. **Take notes.** Record information in the notes section in any form you like, such as an outline, paragraphs, or bullet points. Don't try to write down everything from the instructor's lecture or your reading material. Instead, focus on key concepts, supporting details, dates, formulas, and examples. Leave space between each idea in your notes. You can add information here later, or just use the space to keep your notes clean and easy to read.

3. **Write cues.** Once you finish taking notes, add cues to the cue column. Cues can be main ideas, key words, formulas, questions, diagrams, or examples that correspond to the notes you've already taken, or answers to any purposeful reading questions you've developed. (See the reading chapter.) Line up your cues with the corresponding content in the notes section. When it's time to study your notes, use the cues to find information quickly or to create flash cards, with the cue on one side and the content from your notes on the other.

4. **Summarize.** After you've created your cues, write a brief summary at the bottom of the page that restates the main ideas from your notes. To summarize, you have to understand the material, so writing the summary proves that you've grasped what you've read or heard. When it's time to study, use the summary as a quick review of the ideas from that page of notes.

Cornell System: Method of note taking that organizes each page of content into sections: initial notes on the right, key points in a cue column on the left, and a summary section at the bottom of the page.

❝ CONNECT TO MY CAREER
Note-taking skills come in very handy at work. If you're currently employed, write down two strategies you're already using to take notes successfully on the job. If you're not employed, write a short paragraph about how note taking could help you excel in a career you're considering.

Find Your Personal Style. Your personal note-taking style, that is. When you experiment with different methods of recording information, including the Cornell system, you're sure to find one (or more) methods that are just the right fit. **Credit line to come**

FIGURE 7.3 Taking Notes Using the Cornell System

First-Year Experience 101, Sept. 23, Page 1

★ Get motivated = succeed in college

Motivation — connected to my study and homework completion
- 3 key components of motivation

Bandura = psychologist = self-efficacy

Self-efficacy — belief that I can perform actions needed to meet goal
- Albert Bandura: 4 things build self-efficacy

Me = Strong self-efficacy for speaking in class, weak self-efficacy for writing papers.
Visit writing center??

- Experiencing success
- Observing successful others (models)
- Getting support/encouragement from others
- Using a little stress to motivate (but not too much)

Relevance = the "R" in SMART!

Relevance — if things are important to me, I'm more likely to be motivated
- Find a topic of interest in each class
- Connect coursework to long-term goals
- What transferable skills can I get in each class?
- Practical things are more relevant
- Remember that I love to learn

Positive attitude = powerful motivator

Attitude — having a positive attitude can help me stay motivated
- Benefits: being resilient, enjoying success, learning from mistakes

"I've studied hard, so I'm confident I'll do well on this test."

- Always look for the positive
- Take a class in my major each term, if possible
- Positive self-talk and reframing are tools I can use

Summary:
A person's level of motivation can affect his or her success in college. Motivation includes three key components: self-efficacy (belief in one's ability to perform certain actions), relevance, and a positive attitude. Students can use a variety of strategies to strengthen self-efficacy, make tasks relevant, and stay positive.

Mapping

A *map* is a graphical depiction of course material. It includes *nodes* and *branches* that show the connections among concepts. Detailed maps also incorporate symbols and other markings that further describe the content (see Figure 7.4). Maps are particularly useful if you're a Visual learner. Some students sketch their maps before class with main ideas from a textbook chapter and then fill in content while listening to the lecture. For others, maps work best as study tools. The key to effective mapping is to create a consistent system and focus on key words rather than trying to cram in too much detail. With practice, you can learn how to use nodes, branches, and symbols to organize material and make course concepts come alive.

- **Nodes.** Nodes represent the main topics and key ideas from the lecture or reading assignment. Create a system of nodes that works for you, either with one main node (topic) in the center of the page or several large nodes on each page. When you create one central node, you can add smaller nodes to represent concepts that support the center node's main topic. For instance, in Figure 7.4 "Motivation" is the central node, and "Self-Efficacy," "Relevance," and "Attitude" are smaller nodes with supporting concepts.

- **Branches.** Branches represent supporting details, such as examples, formulas, and dates. Branches might be smaller circles, squares, or simply

FIGURE 7.4 **Sample Notes Map**

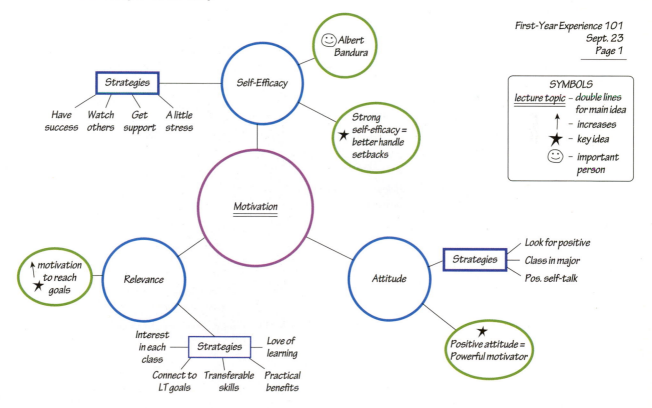

a straight line pointing to information. Their shape and location show how the details connect to specific nodes and how different pieces of supporting information relate to one another. For instance, in Figure 7.4 the rectangular branches indicate strategies that can help strengthen each component of motivation.

- **Symbols.** You can use symbols such as stars or exclamation points to emphasize important concepts in your map. For example, a number inside a box might represent an important date; a smiley face might indicate an important person (see Figure 7.4). You can also use different kinds of lines to reflect the nature of connections among details or associations between nodes and branches.

Charting

A chart is a series of rows and columns designed to organize main ideas, key concepts, and supporting details. Charts allow you to record information in a way that's easy to study from later. Consider the sample chart from a first-year

FIGURE 7.5 Using Charts to Take Notes

Motivation Comparison Chart, First-Year Experience 101 Sept. 23 page 1

Topic	Features	Strategies
Self-efficacy	• Related to my belief that I can perform the actions needed to meet a goal • Strong sense of self-efficacy means I'm more likely to manage setbacks effectively	• Experience success • Watch successful others • Get support/encouragement • Have just a little stress as a motivator
Relevance	• When I believe that achieving a goal will make a positive difference • Helps motivate me to reach for goals	• Pick a topic of interest in each class • Connect class to long-term goals • Build transferable skills in all classes • Keep things practical • Focus on love of learning
Attitude	• Benefits include becoming resilient, enjoying successes, and learning from mistakes • Motivation and positive attitude are connected	• Always look for the positive • Take a class in my major each term, if possible • Use positive self-talk and reframing

experience class, shown in Figure 7.5. The main topic is found in the left-hand column, and the other two columns highlight defining features and strategies related to the main topic. Charts work particularly well in classes where your instructor always presents course content in the same way. You can sketch out a rough draft of the chart before you go to class and then fill it in during the lecture.

Note-Taking Tips for Math, Science, and Online Classes

The basics of note taking apply in most learning situations: You need to prepare, focus, record, and review information, whether you're taking computer science or composition. But science, math, and online classes have unique characteristics, so additional, specialized strategies can come in handy. In science and math classes, for example, you'll come across a lot of formulas, diagrams, and equations. You'll need to record these quickly if you're in lecture, and record them accurately both in class and while reading. And online classes don't have traditional lectures at all, so you'll take notes on other types of information. By adjusting your strategies to account for these differences, you can record the information you need efficiently and effectively.

Taking Notes in Math and Science Classes

Whether you take one math or science class or ten over your college career, try these strategies for taking good notes.

- **Be ready to record formulas and equations.** Formulas and equations are sentences written in mathematical notation. When you write down a formula or an equation, carefully record and label each of the components or steps in the process. Where appropriate, also note how the formula or equation is used.

- **Leave space in your notes.** Leave enough room in your notes to draw diagrams, write formulas and equations, and copy down problems. Also leave space to record each step as you solve problems and to show your work (see steps 1–4 in Figure 7.6).

- **Use good scientific laboratory practice.** If you think you've made a mistake in a formula, an equation, or a diagram, don't erase or scratch out everything you've written. Instead, draw one or two lines through the part containing the mistake. These lines will help you trace your thinking later and find errors that need fixing. To create a clean version, rewrite the material on a new page of notes.

- **Keep writing if you get off track.** If you fall behind the lecture when writing down a problem or a diagram, mark where you got off track and

CONNECT TO MY CLASSES

Identify your most challenging class. Which of the note-taking methods described in this chapter would work best for you in that class? Jot down two reasons you think this method would be a good fit for that course.

FIGURE 7.6 Sample Page of Math Notes

Math and science notes include lots of diagrams and problems. Give yourself plenty of space to write things out and show your work, and if you make a mistake, neatly cross it out. Carefully written notes can be useful when you run into problems and need to ask for help — others can see what you've done and help you identify the correct answers.

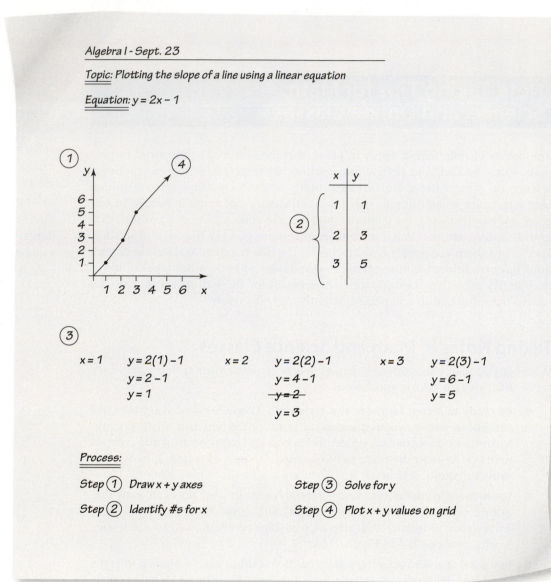

keep writing down what your instructor is saying. You want to record as much of the information as possible — you can always go back later to fill in what you missed.

■ **Learn the shorthand.** In your math or science classes, learn the shorthand for those fields. For instance, if you know that Hz = hertz and d = distance in physics, or that BTU = British thermal unit in chemistry, you'll take notes faster and better understand what the information means.

- **Ask for help when you need it.** If you don't understand a concept, talk with a tutor or your instructor to get clarity. Because math and science classes tend to be linear (meaning information builds from class to class), you need to clear up any confusion immediately to stay on track. Moreover, forming a good relationship with your instructors will help you succeed in these classes.[4]

Taking Notes in Online Classes

The note-taking strategies you use for traditional classes are the same for online classes and *hybrid* classes (a blend of face-to-face and online). But online classes don't meet as regularly as face-to-face classes, so students sometimes fall behind and cut out time to take notes. To avoid this scenario, make sure you spend as much time taking notes in your online class as you do in your other classes. For example:

- When you watch videos or listen to audio recordings of lectures, take notes.
- When you read online, take notes.
- When someone makes an important point on the class's discussion board, take notes.

And don't forget to manage your time. When your instructors post recorded lectures online, resist the impulse to spend less time (or no time) taking notes, on the assumption that you can always go back and view the lectures again. You can—but it's more efficient to view lectures just once and take good notes rather than having to watch them several times because your notes are incomplete.

Write While You Watch. Marina is taking notes while watching a lecture her instructor has posted online. This is a smart move: If she didn't take notes, she might have to watch the video several times to grasp the content, and she'd have no recorded information to use while studying for exams. © Greg Vote/CORBIS

Apply Note Taking at Work

By now, we hope you've started thinking critically about how to use note taking to master what you're learning in school. We also hope you're considering how the ideas in this chapter might help you in your career—whether it's one you have now or one you might pursue in the future. In this section we explore in more depth how note taking can help you excel at work.

Demonstrate Accuracy and Attention to Detail

Paying attention to details and accurately recording information—two hallmarks of good note taking—are just as important in the workplace as they are in college. How an employee captures detailed information can make or break an organization or a business—and can even have life-and-death implications. Think about it: If a nurse writes down incorrect details about a patient's drug allergies, that patient could become very ill or could even die if someone prescribes the wrong drug. If a baker mistakenly writes down that a bride wants a chocolate wedding cake instead of vanilla, that unhappy bride could write a negative online review of the bakery—driving potential new customers away. For almost all employees, the ability to capture information accurately is a key job requirement.

Transform Information

Have you ever explained something computer-related to a relative who has no experience with technology? Have you ever studied with a friend and found yourself explaining a complex idea in a way that made the concept more understandable—for your friend *and* yourself? In scenarios like these, you're *transforming* technical or complicated information; in other words, you're restating it in a way that others can understand. You practice this skill every time you paraphrase while taking notes.

Transforming information is particularly useful in *STEM* fields (science, technology, engineering, and math), but it's also useful in sales, education, and many other careers. The more comfortable you feel with absorbing information and restating it in an accessible way, the more effectively you can communicate this information to others in the workplace.

Use the Information You Record

At its heart, note taking involves accurately recording, organizing, and managing information so you can learn from and *use* it. In the work world, you might use information captured in notes to create slide presentations, press releases, research reports, infographics (which present ideas and data in a visual format), ad campaigns, business plans, and other documents. Whenever you record, organize, and manage information through note taking, you get a chance to communicate what you've learned in a clear, understandable, and creative way.

Good Notes, Good Care.
Emily works for a primary care physician. When patients arrive, she interviews them, records their blood pressure and weight, and writes notes about their health concerns, medications, and tests they need to schedule. By taking detailed, accurate notes, she helps the doctor provide the right care for patients.
ERproductions Ltd./Getty Images

TAKING NOTES ON THE JOB

Courtesy of
Robert L.
Hawkins

NAME: **Rob Hawkins**

PROFESSION: *Police Lieutenant / U.S. Army Sergeant First Class, Retired*

SCHOOL: *American Military University*

DEGREES: *Associate of Arts; Bachelor of Arts*

MAJORS: *Personnel Administration; Criminal Justice*

Accurately taking notes and recording information is critical to effective police work. Understanding crime scenes, finding and arresting suspects, writing reports, and getting convictions all require good notes. When I get a call and start to gather information, one of the first things I do is to create a map of the situation. Each node of the map is a different person involved in the case, and I use branches to indicate the relationships among these individuals. I write down information near each node, including what the person observed or what he or she told me. I also put stars next to critical pieces of information and cross things out when I can eliminate a suspect or determine that certain information doesn't apply. These maps are very useful when I write up case reports — I can look at the maps and understand each situation better. Sometimes maps help me make connections between pieces of information or think of other questions to ask an individual. They stimulate my thinking on the case.

Maps are useful in all kinds of situations, not just during an investigation. I used the same system in the military to create operations orders. Also, when I was training an Afghan battalion commander during my last deployment, I used maps to help him create an organization and structure for the five hundred men he was leading.

YOUR TURN: If you currently have a job and use note taking in your work, explain how you use it and how it helps you. If you don't currently have a job, identify a job that interests you, and brainstorm how note taking might help you in that job.

> " **Understanding crime scenes, finding and arresting suspects, writing reports, and getting convictions all require good notes.**"

my personal success plan

NOTE TAKING

Are you inspired to set a new goal aimed at improving your note-taking skills? If so, the Personal Success Plan can walk you through the goal-setting process. Read the advice and examples; then sketch out your ideas in the space provided.

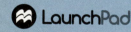

To access the Personal Success Plan online, go to the LaunchPad for *Connections*.

1 GATHER INFORMATION

Think about your strengths and weaknesses related to taking notes. What strategies have worked for you in the past? What could you do differently? Revisit your Note Taking score on ACES and review the relevant sections of this chapter for additional ideas.

2 SET A SMART GOAL

Use the information you've gathered to create a SMART goal, making sure to use the SMART goal checklist.

SAMPLE: I'll use the Cornell system to take notes for the next two weeks.

3 MAKE AN ACTION PLAN

Outline the specific steps you'll take to achieve your SMART goal, and note when you'll complete each step.

SAMPLE: By Wednesday, I'll format twenty pages of notes using the Cornell system. I'll use these pages to take notes in class for the next two weeks.

4 LIST BARRIERS AND SOLUTIONS

Think about possible barriers to your action steps; then brainstorm solutions for overcoming them.

SAMPLE: If I have any trouble getting used to the Cornell system, I'll remind myself that it takes practice to get comfortable with a new note-taking method.

5 ACT AND EVALUATE OUTCOMES

Now that your plan is in place, take action. Record each action step as you take it. Then evaluate whether you achieved your SMART goal, and make any adjustments needed to get better results in the future.

SAMPLE: I used different formats (outlines, paragraphs, bullet points) to record information on my Cornell pages. That ended up being confusing, so I'll use a more consistent format from now on.

6 CONNECT TO CAREER

List the skills you're building as you progress toward your SMART goal. How will you use these skills to land a job and succeed at work?

SAMPLE: I want to become a nurse practitioner, so I'll need to collect information from patients about their health concerns and present it in reports to health care providers. Using the Cornell system will help me do that effectively.

1 my information

2 my SMART goal

☐ **S**PECIFIC ☐ **M**EASURABLE ☐ **A**CHIEVABLE ☐ **R**ELEVANT ☐ **T**IME-LIMITED

3 my action plan

4 my barriers/ solutions

5 my actions/ outcomes

6 my career connection

CHAPTER SUMMARY

This chapter described the skills needed to take good notes in all types of classes, introduced four note-taking methods, and explored how note taking can help you excel at work. Revisit the following key points, and reflect on how you can use this information to support your success now and in the future.

- To take good notes, you need to follow a four-step process: prepare to take notes; actively listen, watch, read, and participate to focus on the information you're hearing or reading; record information; and review your notes.

- You can use a number of methods to take notes. This chapter describes four such methods: outlining, the Cornell system, mapping, and charting.

- Outlining is a structured way to take notes that involves recording information at different levels using letters and numerals or bullet points.

- In the Cornell system, you record notes, cues, and summaries on a single page. You first make notes and then go back to write cues and summaries that will be useful for studying.

- Mapping presents information visually. Nodes, branches, and symbols help you organize and depict relationships among ideas.

- Charts organize a large amount of information in a series of rows and columns.

- To take good notes in math and science classes, you need to be especially thorough in noting formulas, equations, and diagrams. Learning math and science shorthand (such as abbreviations) will help you take notes quickly and accurately.

- When taking notes for online classes, keep up with class material, schedule enough time for note taking, and take notes on all the information you're exposed to (such as recorded lectures, videos, and discussion board posts).

- At work, taking good notes can help you demonstrate accuracy and attention to detail, transform information so it's easy for others to understand, and use information to develop a wide range of documents and presentations and to complete important projects.

CHAPTER ACTIVITIES

Journal Entry

ASSESSING YOUR NOTE-TAKING STRATEGY

Up to now, how have you approached note taking? Describe the steps you follow to take notes and the method(s) you use. Now that you've read this chapter and understand the four-step note-taking strategy and the four methods discussed, what (if anything) was missing in your previous note-taking strategy and the methods you used? Will you adopt a different strategy for taking notes in the future? Try different methods? Explain your decision.

Adopting a Success Attitude

BUILDING CONFIDENCE IN IDENTIFYING KEY POINTS

It takes time to build strong note-taking skills. This activity focuses on building your confidence in one component of note taking: identifying key points of a message.

First, in a notebook, create three headings across the top of a page: "Advertiser," "Product," and "Key Selling Points" (see the example). Under the headings, add numbers 1 through 10. Now watch a series of television commercials. For each commercial, write down the name of the advertiser, the product, and the key points the ad is making to interest you in the product. For example, the advertiser may be an insurance company that's trying to sell car insurance, and the key selling points are the company's low-cost premiums and fast processing of claims. If you're watching TV with other people, ask them to help. Have fun with it!

Advertiser	Product	Key Selling Points
1.		
2.		
3.		
Etc.		

Applying Your Skills

IMPROVING YOUR NOTE-TAKING SKILLS

Select a note-taking method described in this chapter (outlining, the Cornell system, mapping, or charting) that you haven't used before but would like to try. During the next week, use this method in a specific class to take notes during lecture, for reading assignments, or both. After each note-taking session, review your work within twenty-four hours and respond to the following questions:

- What are the main ideas of the lecture or reading you took notes on? What material was unclear? What questions do you have? (Talk with your instructor to clarify any confusing concepts.)

- Overall, what did you like about this note-taking method? What challenges did you encounter?

- Will you continue to use this method? Why or why not? If not, what other method will you try instead?

College Success = Career Success

TAKING EFFECTIVE NOTES AT WORK

At work, taking good notes enables you to record instructions, deadlines, action items, ideas, and questions. In long meetings, note taking can help you stay alert, focused, and actively engaged. It can also communicate your interest in and commitment to your work, as well as your desire to succeed.

For this activity, pretend that your boss has sent you to a professional conference. She wants you to attend a presentation at the conference, give her a one-paragraph summary of the main ideas, and report what you learn to your colleagues at the next staff meeting. To do this exercise, follow these steps:

1. Go to the TED Talk Web site (www.ted.com/talks) and watch a video on a topic that interests you or is related to your future career. TED Talks are "ideas worth spreading"—short presentations designed to share information and opinions and to inspire viewers.

2. As you watch the TED Talk, pretend you're at the conference, sitting in the audience. Take notes that capture the speaker's main ideas, and write down any questions or ideas you have about the topic. (If you were at an actual conference, you'd have an opportunity to ask the speaker questions or share your own ideas.)

3. After watching the TED Talk, write a one-paragraph summary of the talk. Consider having someone review your notes and summary paragraph to give you feedback on whether you've captured the main ideas. (Note: This person doesn't need to have watched the TED Talk. If you took good notes, the information you've recorded will be clear.)

4. Now pretend that you're back at work and that you have to report to your colleagues on what you learned from the talk. With a partner or a small group (in or outside of class), briefly describe the TED Talk, highlight the speaker's main points, and share your questions and observations.

8 Memory and Studying

Learn How Your Memory Works

Study Basics: Set Yourself Up for Success

Do-It-Yourself Studying: Create Your Own Study Tools

Study for Your Math, Science, and Online Classes

Use Memory and Studying at Work

My Personal Success Plan

Picture a student sitting in the library, eyes half open, staring blankly as he slowly turns pages of handwritten notes. He seems to be studying, but his mind isn't focused, and he's just going through the motions. You probably wouldn't be surprised if this student looked up twenty minutes later, only to realize he had no better grasp of the information in his notes than when he started. When you don't pay attention to and think actively about what you're learning, it's hard to remember that information and use it to answer test questions, contribute to discussions, or complete projects. Information doesn't magically end up in your brain. That's why you need study strategies that help you remember — strategies you'll learn in this chapter.

There's no question that studying effectively and remembering what you study help you excel in college, but guess what: These skills are also important in the workplace. Today, jobs change rapidly, and the most successful people know how to learn and remember new information and then use it at work. Think about your instructors: They know their fields of study so well that they can share their knowledge in their job — teaching — without having to read straight from a book or their notes. They also use their knowledge to excel at other types of work, such as conducting research or publishing articles.

No matter what career you end up pursuing, knowing how to absorb and retain new information will come in handy. For instance, if you're in information technology (IT), you might study software specifications so that you can integrate a new application into your company's IT system. Or if you're in marketing, you might study regional demographics to determine where your company should launch its next product. Knowing how to study and remember information helps you learn continuously — and that's exactly what employers want.

With these points in mind, we start this chapter with memory basics, including how people take in information, create memories, and forget. Then we consider strategies that help you stay focused and productive while you're studying and help you remember what you learn. Finally, we offer ideas for how you can use these strategies on the job.

Reflect

Reflect

On Your Memory and Studying

Take a moment to reflect on your Memory and Studying score on ACES. Find your score and add it in the circle to the right.

This score measures your beliefs about how well you study and remember information. Do you think it's an accurate snapshot of your current skills in this area? Why or why not?

☐ **HIGH**

☐ **MODERATE**

☐ **LOW**

LaunchPad

To find your **Memory and Studying score,** go to the LaunchPad for *Connections.*

■ **IF YOU SCORED IN THE HIGH RANGE** and you're confident that this score is accurate, then memory and studying may be strengths for you. That's great news. Remember, though, that even strengths can be improved. For instance, maybe you routinely create flash cards and practice test questions — tools that help you study and remember information. If you learn how to create other kinds of do-it-yourself study tools, too, you'll be in a much better position to switch tools as needed to suit the subject matter or the settings in which you're studying.

■ **IF YOU SCORED IN THE MODERATE OR LOW RANGE,** take action. This chapter — in fact, your entire college experience — gives you a powerful opportunity to build your memory and study skills. You can strengthen these skills with time and practice, and this chapter is filled with ideas to help you do so.

Learn How Your Memory Works

Think of memory and studying as partners who walk hand in hand. After all, if you can't remember the information you're studying, you won't learn it. As a result, you won't be able to use it later to get work done for class. To understand how memory works, and why it sometimes fails, it helps to think about how your brain takes in the information coming from your textbooks and instructors — and then turns that information into memories. Memory involves three processes:

1. **Encoding,** or taking in information and changing it into signals in our brain
2. *Storing* the information in our memory
3. *Retrieving* the information when we want to remember it

To get a basic sense of how memory works, consider what happens when you run out of milk. You open the door of the fridge, and you see a milk carton on the shelf. You pick it up and realize it's almost empty. This information from

Encoding: Taking in information and changing it into signals in our brain.

your senses of sight and touch is *encoded* into your brain as an idea: You need to pick up milk on the way home. You repeat this thought several times as you head to class ("Don't forget to buy milk"), and this repetition *stores* the idea in your memory. Later, on your way home, you *retrieve* your memory about the milk and stop at the store to pick up a carton.

How You Remember

Making memories is incredibly complex, and scientists have many theories about exactly what occurs and why. According to one common model, which we'll focus on here, there are three stages of memory: sensory memory, short-term/working memory, and long-term memory.[1] The processes of encoding, storage, and retrieval connect these three stages together. In the following section, we'll look at how this relationship works—and how it helps us remember what we learn.

Sensory Memory:
Process that uses information from the senses to begin creating memories.

Sensory Memory. In the first stage, **sensory memory**, you take in information through your five senses and form fleeting memories based on those experiences. In college, for example, information can come in through your ears (when you listen to lectures) and your eyes (when you read textbooks). In some classes you might also use touch as you perform experiments or use equipment. A few lucky students, like those of you taking culinary classes, will also get to smell and taste in class. As you absorb information through your senses, you form sensory memories of these experiences.

But sensory memories last only a split second. Our senses are constantly bombarded with information, and our brains can't take in everything.[2] It's only when we pay attention to information that it is *encoded* and moves to the next stage of memory: short-term/working memory (see Figure 8.1).

Short-Term Memory:
Memory that stores a small number of items for a short period of time.

Short-Term/Working Memory. Our **short-term memory** is quite limited in how much information it can hold and for how long it can hold it. Research shows that most people can hold about four to seven things in their short-term

FIGURE 8.1 **The Basics of Memory**

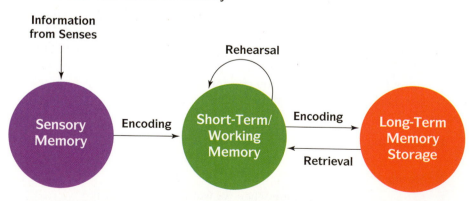

Source: Adapted from David G. Myers and C. Nathan DeWall, *Psychology in Everyday Life*, 3rd ed. (New York: Worth Publishers, 2014), p. 194.

memory at once, and that information lasts for only twenty to thirty seconds.[3] Have you met someone new, only to forget his or her name when you start chatting? Blame your short-term memory.

To make information "stick," you need to put effort into remembering the information. For example, when you are first introduced to another student, you might repeat (or *rehearse*) his name in your head five times as soon as you hear it. In addition, you might make a mental note to ask him if he wants to be your study partner for the next exam. When you put this kind of effort into remembering someone's name, you're engaging your **working memory**—the part of your short-term memory that actively processes memories and information. Thinking about, applying, rehearsing, and connecting new information to your existing memories are all ways to use your working memory, and they help your brain encode the information and move it to the next stage: long-term memory.

Working Memory: The part of short-term memory that actively processes memories and information.

Long-Term Memory.

Unlike sensory or short-term memory, the storage capacity of your **long-term memory** seems limitless, and memories here can last forever (although they don't always).[4] This is where you *store* the record of your life, such as your earliest childhood memories, your tenth birthday party, and your wedding day. Long-term memory is where you keep the facts, ideas, procedures, and skills you learn in college, such as the circumstances that led to the American Revolution and the process of cell division. It's also the place from which you *retrieve* your memories when you need them—for instance, when you're taking a history or biology quiz or when you run into a new acquaintance and greet him by name.

Long-Term Memory: Memory that stores a potentially limitless amount of information for a long period of time.

Putting It All Together.

How do the three stages of memory work together? To understand this, it's helpful to compare them to the process of creating a spreadsheet. Suppose you're trying to save money to pay next term's tuition, so you decide to create a spreadsheet showing how much you spent last month. You take the following steps.

- First, you gather information about your income and expenses, such as paycheck stubs and credit card statements. When you see the information in front of you, you create a *sensory memory* of the facts and figures.

- Next, you create a spreadsheet file on your computer and enter your expenses into it. The process of typing numbers is similar to your memory's *encoding* process—it's how information gets into the file. As you're typing, you realize that you haven't saved the spreadsheet on your computer. The unsaved spreadsheet is like your *short-term/working memory*: Until you make the effort to save it, you could lose the information if you had a power outage or your hard drive crashed.

- Finally, you save the spreadsheet file, which is like *storing* information in your *long-term memory*. Later, you open the file and *retrieve* the data.

Of course, your brain is much more complex than any computer program. For example, a computer shouldn't forget unless there's a mechanical failure, but a human brain can forget with normal age wear and tear. Still, this analogy gives you the basic idea of how the memory processes and stages work together.

Why You Forget

We've seen how memory works, but what happens when it *doesn't* work? Why do we forget? Forgetting occurs when there's a breakdown in one of the memory processes. Imagine that you meet a new acquaintance named Julio, but when you run into him a week later, you can't remember his name. What happened? There are several possibilities. If you didn't hear his name when he first told you, then that information never made it into your sensory memory. Or you might have heard his name, but it slipped away because you didn't pay enough attention to keep it in your working memory. This represents an *encoding failure*: The information got lost or wasn't in your mind long enough to move to your long-term memory.[5] The other possibility, and certainly the more frustrating one, is that you did create a long-term memory for Julio's name but you still can't remember it. This is a *retrieval failure*.[6]

To further understand forgetting, let's revisit the budget spreadsheet analogy. Imagine two different scenarios.

Scenario 1: When you finish working on the spreadsheet, you don't give it a meaningful file name. Instead, you call it "Document 1." You don't pay attention to where you save it on your computer. And finally, you don't open the file for nine months. When you finally want to look at the spreadsheet, you'll probably have a hard time finding it.

Scenario 2: This time, you look closely at the computer screen as you name the file "Monthly Budget." You save the file in your "Finances" folder. Then you access the file weekly for nine months, adding new expense and cost data at the end of each week. You'll probably find it much easier to locate, open, and use the file in this scenario than in scenario 1. Why? Because you paid attention when you named the file, you saved it in an accessible folder, and you worked with it repeatedly. By doing this, you used all the memory processes. You took in the information using your senses, and you worked with and retrieved the information many times, which helped the memory stick.

When you learn material for your classes, the ability to encode, store, and retrieve information is crucial. Think about it this way: Scenario 1 is similar to reading a textbook chapter only once and then trying to remember information from the chapter while you're taking a test a few weeks later. If you don't put effort into studying the chapter, you won't create strong memories of what you read, and you'll have trouble remembering the information when you need it. By contrast, actively thinking about the new information, making meaningful memories of the information, and repeatedly accessing the information by studying and reviewing it will move that information from your sensory memory to your short-term/working memory, and from there to your long-term memory. In this way, you'll remember what you've learned, both at test time and far into the future.

Memory Mastery. If you find yourself remembering what you've learned in class, don't be surprised—or scared. Congratulate yourself: You've mastered major memory skills. For example, you've transformed short-term memories into long-term memories by actively reviewing information. Now you can retrieve what you've learned when you need it! © CartoonStock

"Want to hear something scary? This is the third time this week I've gotten off the bus and still remember what I learned."

Study Basics: Set Yourself Up for Success

Now that you understand how memory works, let's shift our focus to study strategies that help you remember and use your newfound knowledge. But first, ask yourself how you feel about studying. Do you dread it? Find it boring? Feel anxious about it?

If you have negative views of studying, try changing how you think about it. Instead of seeing studying as a task that you have to do, consider it an *opportunity* for you to build valuable skills and work toward your goals. For example, suppose you want to become the first person in your family to get a college degree, or you want to get a certificate because you'd like to make a career change. Each hour of studying gets you one step closer to achieving your long-term goal.

This doesn't mean that studying will always be easy. If your friends, family members, or coworkers are out having fun while you're home reviewing notes the night before a test, you might be tempted to say, "Maybe I can finish this later . . ." no matter how motivated you are to do well. And sometimes you might have so many obligations competing for your attention that you let studying take a backseat to other commitments. But as challenging as situations like these can be, they're opportunities to show that you can be *persistent*, that you'll keep trying and keep doing the work needed to achieve your goals. Persistence also helps when you encounter the inevitable setbacks. For instance, if a study strategy doesn't produce the result you want on the first attempt, you can try it again. If it still doesn't work, you can experiment with other strategies until you find one that does work.

In this section we describe tried-and-true study strategies for mastering course material. As you consider them, keep in mind that memory and studying are closely intertwined with the vital skills we discuss in other chapters, such as reading, note taking, and test taking. For example, to study effectively, you need the notes you took on your reading assignments and lectures. In addition, the information you learn by studying helps you answer exam questions and complete class projects. Studying is, without a doubt, a key component of academic success.

With this in mind, check out the following study strategies to see which ones appeal to you most.

Space Out Your Study Time

What's the most productive way to learn new material? Space out your studying across multiple days and study in small blocks of time.[7] For example, if you have ninety minutes to study before work each morning, try spending thirty minutes each on psychology, math, and biology. Then do the same thing the next day and the day after that. Why is this strategy effective? Think back to the budget spreadsheet example earlier in the chapter: The more you work with the material, the more you remember about it. By contrast, trying to "cram" large amounts of information into your brain all at once (especially late at night) leads to poor performance on tests.[8]

⟩ CONNECT TO MY CLASSES

How do you usually study for your classes? Do you break up your studying into small chunks of time spread across multiple days? Do you study for fewer but larger blocks of time? Describe which scheduling tactics have worked best for you, and why.

Maximize Study Opportunities

To make the most of study opportunities identify brief periods of time that are going to waste and turn them into mini study sessions. For instance, if you have thirty minutes between classes, use some of that time to review your chemistry notes. If you have a fifteen-minute break at work, use it to look over flash cards you created for a class. Small bits of time here and there add up, and if you're a busy student on the go, taking full advantage of these moments is crucial. And thanks to mobile technology, studying anywhere is easier than ever. You can put your notes on your smartphone or tablet, and quickly review them while you're waiting in the doctor's office or commuting on the bus.

Minimize Distractions

As useful as technology is as a study aid, take care that it doesn't become a distraction. If you text while you're reading notes on your phone or you glance up from your notebook each time you get a new e-mail, you'll have trouble creating long-term memories of the information you're trying to study. Although multitasking may seem like a good idea, your mind isn't truly capable of focusing on more than one thing at a time, so distractions prevent you from giving your full attention to the material you're trying to learn.[9] For tips on how to eliminate distractions while you're studying, see the organization and time management chapter.

No Grumpy Cats Allowed. When you're studying, it's easy to let distractions creep in — like surfing online to see how Grumpy Cat's Las Vegas book signing went. (Yes, she really had a book signing!) But distractions can impair your concentration and prevent you from remembering information. So catch up on Grumpy Cat's latest antics — but only *after* you've finished studying. Rex Features via AP Images

Join a Study Group

Have you ever heard the saying "There's strength in numbers"? When it's time to study, working with other students can help you learn and improve your performance on tests.[10] There are several types of study groups. Many schools offer **Supplemental Instruction** for especially difficult classes, which consists of study groups led by students who did well in those classes in the past. Your instructors might also set up study groups for their classes to encourage students to work together. Alternatively, you can create your own study group with classmates who want to support one another and work together. If you set up a study group yourself, create an agenda to help the group focus on particular topics at each meeting. Without some kind of direction, group members may end up wasting valuable study time.

Before attending a group meeting, spend time studying on your own, and identify specific questions you'd like help with. For instance, if you're struggling to understand the ins-and-outs of interest groups in your American Government class, ask the study group leader or your study partners for help. And be prepared to teach others in the group about topics you understand well. One of the most powerful ways to truly understand material (not just memorize it) is to teach it to someone else. A study group gives you that opportunity.

Strength in Numbers. Joining a study group is a great way to master material. Group members can help one another grasp difficult course content. And when you explain a topic to other members, you deepen your understanding of that topic. That deeper understanding will pay off during tests.
Stephen Simpson/Getty Images

Make Connections

You can make lasting memories of new information by linking what you're studying to your life, to a familiar situation, or to memories you already have. For instance, Cecily is studying for a midterm exam in Introduction to Biology, and she needs to remember the main parts of an animal cell. As she studies, she sees that one part of the cell, the Golgi apparatus, is made up of flat, oblong shapes that are connected and stacked on top of each other. Their function is to process carbohydrates and proteins and sort them for transportation throughout the body. To Cecily, the Golgi apparatus looks a lot like stacked pancakes. She thinks about her favorite breakfast: pancakes and bacon, which provide the body with carbohydrates and protein. Now that she's made an association between that breakfast and the Golgi apparatus, it will be easier to remember what she learned when she takes the midterm.

When you make connections and apply information to other situations, you're using a powerful process called elaborative rehearsal. In **elaborative rehearsal**, you associate the meaning of new information with other information already stored in your memory, making it easier to recall the new information later. As an added bonus, making connections requires critical thinking—a vital skill that helps you evaluate, learn, and use new information at school and at work.

Supplemental Instruction: A student-led study program for especially difficult classes.

Elaborative Rehearsal: The process of making connections between new ideas and other information already stored in your memory.

Do-It-Yourself Studying: Create Your Own Study Tools

Mastering the basic study strategies described in the previous section is a great first step. As a next step, we focus on how to create your own study tools—an approach that helps you learn *and* gives you flexibility in how you study. You've spent hours sitting in class or responding to posts online, reading your text-books, and taking countless pages of notes. When you create your own study tools, you bring all these efforts together to learn on a deeper level, strengthening your comprehension. Creating study tools is like using your working memory to encode information into your long-term memory: You *actively* process course material to make new memories, which you can use later on tests and projects. So take a look at the tools described in this section, and find the ones that interest you most.

Write Flash Cards

If you want a study system you can take anywhere, try creating flash cards. You can make these from paper note cards or even use a flash card app on your computer or phone (see Figure 8.2). Flash cards are a blank slate—you can put anything you want on them. For instance, you can put key words on one side of the card and definitions on the other, or write historical events on one side and the dates when they occurred on the reverse side. You can also use them to quiz yourself on broad concepts, themes, or theories.

How do flash cards help you remember? For some people, the act of writing helps the concepts stick. In addition, as you flip through the flash cards over and over, you use **rote rehearsal**; in other words, you memorize specific information or facts by studying the information repeatedly. This approach is valuable when you need to remember specific facts, such as the parts of the human body or mathematical formulas. In general, flash cards are less useful when you need to demonstrate comprehension of more complex information, such as how the Ottoman Empire changed from the thirteenth to seventeenth centu-

Rote Rehearsal:
Memorization of specific information or facts by studying the information repeatedly.

FIGURE 8.2 Electronic Flash Cards

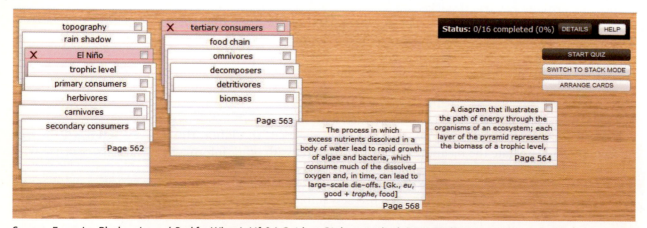

Source: From Jay Phelan, *LaunchPad for What Is Life? A Guide to Biology*, 2nd ed. (New York: W. H. Freeman, 2013).

USING STUDY TOOLS TO SUCCEED

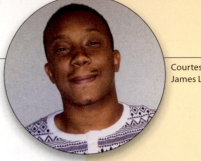

Courtesy of
James Lawrence

NAME: **James Lawrence**

SCHOOL: *Mississippi Gulf Coast Community College*

MAJOR: *Psychology*

CAREER GOAL: *Clinical Psychologist*

When I first started junior college, I was nervous about my classes and really didn't know what to expect from my professors. I had heard that college was harder than high school and required more studying — something my mama called "burning the midnight oil." I honestly didn't know how to study because in high school I never had to. I just went to class, listened to the teacher's lecture, completed my worksheets, and passed the test.

It was the second week of classes when the difference between high school and college really sank in. I realized that there were no more worksheets and that just attending class wasn't going to allow me to succeed. Most of my classes included four exams — each covering material from up to six chapters — and I needed to do more than just memorize the material in all those chapters. I panicked, then made friends in each of my classes. We formed study groups, and in those groups I picked up some new strategies for learning. Some students in the group used flash cards to help them study, and others would review their notes repeatedly or make their own test questions to practice understanding the material.

Making flash cards worked best for me because it made me act on the material rather than just reading it over and over. I had to identify and write a concept on one side of the card and write the explanation on the other side. Having to write the material down was a concrete way for me to interact with the content. Then I could quiz myself using the cards no matter where I was on campus. You have to think of your brain as a muscle — if you don't challenge it, it will become weaker!

YOUR TURN: **Have you ever created flash cards? If so, how well did this study tool work for you? What were the advantages? The challenges?**

"You have to think of your brain as a muscle — if you don't challenge it, it will become weaker!"

ries. So, for a well-rounded study strategy, use flash cards in addition to other techniques in this chapter.

As you use your flash cards to study, keep these tips in mind.

- Shuffle the cards regularly and review them multiple times. Recognizing the content one time won't help you master it.
- Go through the cards twice a day for the entire week before an exam.
- If you find yourself flipping through the cards mindlessly, set them aside for a few minutes and come back to them when you can stay focused.

Create Review Sheets

As you record information from lectures and reading assignments, you'll find yourself building up mounds of pages and stacks of bulging notebooks. To manage all this information, try creating a review sheet by condensing pages of detailed notes into a one-page document. When you condense material, you include only the information you really need—such as the main ideas from your notes, annotations you made while reading a textbook chapter, problems from your math class, or dates from your history class. Give yourself some flexibility, though: If one page is too limiting, create a separate review sheet for each chapter that will be covered on a test. You can also share and compare your review sheets with classmates, and each person can offer ideas for improving them and filling in gaps.

Use Purposeful Reading Questions

If you've created and answered purposeful reading questions while taking notes on a textbook chapter or other reading assignment (see the reading chapter), you have a ready-made study tool. Review the questions in your notes, cover up the answers, and answer the questions out loud to yourself or with a study partner. Or combine your purposeful reading questions with other study tools. You might make flash cards with a question on one side and the answer on the other. If you like the Cornell notes system, write your questions in the cue column on the left and your answers in the notes section on the right; then use the summary section at the bottom to restate in your own words the key ideas you want to remember (see Figure 8.3).

FIGURE 8.3 Using Purposeful Reading Questions and Cornell Notes to Study

Introduction to Nursing

Purposeful reading questions:
What are the three levels of preventive care? What is an example of each level?

1. Primary prevention: prevent healthy individuals from acquiring illness
   Example: educate people on use of sunscreen
2. Secondary prevention: illness/disease has occurred, but person wants to slow its progress
   Example: individual visits dermatologist regularly and has suspicious growths removed
3. Tertiary prevention: treat illness/disease to limit impact
   Example: treat individual with skin cancer

Summary:
Preventive care has three levels: primary (preventing healthy people from getting sick), secondary (slowing progress of disease), and tertiary (limiting disease's impact through proper treatment).

ANSWER PRACTICE QUESTIONS — IT WORKS!

At the end of each chapter, many textbooks provide study or practice questions (which you can use as purposeful reading questions). Two Dutch researchers examined the impact of these questions on students' performance in a psychology class. The researchers gave 201 students more than five hundred questions to help them plan their study time and prepare for an exam at the end of the class. These were short-answer essay questions, designed to help students focus on the main topics from their reading — for example, "What are the basic components of the central nervous system?" and "What causes Down syndrome?" At the end of the class, the researchers examined the relationship between the number of study questions the students answered and how they performed on the final exam. They found the following:

- Only 51 percent of the students passed the exam.
- The students who passed answered an average of 81 percent of the five hundred study questions before taking the exam.
- The students who failed answered an average of 41 percent of the study questions before taking the exam.

The researchers also asked the students how the questions were helpful. The students said that the study questions helped them plan their studying, better understand the course material, and prepare for the exam.

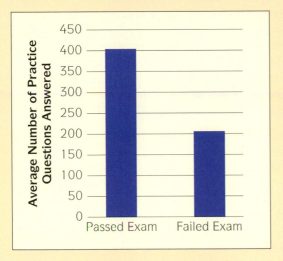

Students who passed the exam answered almost twice as many practice questions as those who failed the exam.

THE BOTTOM LINE

Answering more practice questions before taking an exam can help you pass the exam.

REFLECTION QUESTIONS

1. **How often do you use the practice questions included in your textbooks to study for tests? Have you found these practice questions helpful?**
2. **Have you ever created your own study questions? If so, how did they work for you?**
3. **Will you use practice questions to study for tests in the future? Why or why not?**

P. Wilhelm and J. M. Pieters, "Fostering Effective Studying and Study Planning with Study Questions," *Assessment and Evaluation in Higher Education* 32 (2007): 373–82.

Create Practice Tests

Creating your own practice test is a powerful way to prepare for an exam. When you write your own test questions, you think about the exam topics in detail—and that can help you deepen your understanding of the material and commit it to memory. To create a practice test, first figure out the most important information you'll need to know for the exam. Use your critical thinking skills to evaluate all the information from class lectures and reading assignments, and decide which information matters most. To do this, review your notes from class, your textbook, and notes you took while reading. And don't forget to look over any purposeful reading questions you created—these are a great place to start.

Once you've identified the key topics, create questions that focus on these areas. You might create matching questions for dates and events in history class, essay questions for economics class, multiple-choice questions for accounting or biology, and practice problems for chemistry or math. Create answers for each question. Finally, trade test questions with classmates and challenge one another to answer them. As you answer more and more questions correctly, you'll build up your confidence in the material.

Draw a Mental Picture

Another way to use your working and long-term memory is to *visualize*, or create a mental picture, of the material you're studying. Start by looking at the image you want to re-create in your mind. It might be a figure from your chemistry text showing the molecular formula for benzene, or the parts of a blueprint for your construction course. Cover up the original image and try to picture what it looks like in your mind. Then look back at the actual image: How well does your mental picture match the image? Repeat this activity until the image in your mind matches the image you see on the page.

Use Mnemonics

Mnemonic: A learning strategy that helps you memorize specific material.

If you want to memorize specific material you can create a **mnemonic** (pronounced "neh mon ik"), which is a trick or strategy to remember information. For example, the rhyme "Thirty days hath September, April, June, and November . . ." is a mnemonic for remembering the number of days in each month. Mnemonics help you remember specific information you need to recall for an exam or to solve a problem. Creating a mnemonic requires critical thinking, as well as some creativity. Try the following popular mnemonic strategies.

Acronyms. Make an *acronym*, a word created from the first letter of each word you want to remember. For example, the acronym HOMES can help you remember the five Great Lakes (Huron, Ontario, Michigan, Erie, Superior). In your Introduction to Psychology class, the acronym OCEAN can help you remember the five major personality traits (openness, conscientiousness, extraversion, agreeableness, neuroticism). In this class, the acronym SMART can help you remember the steps of the goal-setting process (specific, measurable, achievable, relevant, and time-limited).

Associations. Create associations between new information and things you already know. Let's say you want to memorize a list of Greek gods for your art history course. You start with Zeus, king of the gods, whom you associate with your uncle, who happens to be a large and powerful man. Zeus's wife, Hera, you associate with your aunt Helen. (Both names start with *H*, which is easy for you to remember.) Next you associate Ares, the son of Zeus and Hera, with your cousin. You might take the association even further and imagine how all of these gods would interact at your family reunion. As you create these associations, you're practicing elaborative rehearsal and building long-term memories of this new information.

Method of Loci. Associate words you need to remember with locations that are familiar to you. For instance, suppose you're trying to remember the sequence of early U.S. presidents. You could associate each president with the sequence of actions you perform while getting from your apartment to school. You wake up and say good morning to George Washington (the first president), whom you imagine sitting on your dresser. Next you see John Adams (the second president) at the breakfast table. Then you greet Thomas Jefferson (the third president) as you leave your apartment. Finally, you see James Madison (the fourth president) at the end of your driveway. The memory links you choose don't have to make sense. In fact, it's better if they're funny, outrageous, or off-the-wall: They'll capture your attention, making them easier to remember.

Acrostics. An acrostic is a phrase or sentence in which the first letter of every word corresponds to a list of words you want to remember. Acrostics are especially useful when you want to memorize words in a particular order. Some common acrostics are "Every Good Boy Does Fine" (E, G, B, D, F) for lines on the treble clef, or "Kids Prefer Cheese Over Fried Green Spinach" (kingdom, phylum, class, order, family, genus, species) for the order of taxonomy in biology. Can you think of what the acrostic "My Very Energetic Mother Just Served Us Nachos" represents? Here's a hint: We all live on "E."

Hungry for Acrostics? Acrostics are potent memory boosters. For example, the acrostic "Kids Prefer Cheese Over Fried Green Spinach" can help you remember the order of taxonomy in your biology class (kingdom, phylum, class, order, family, genus, species). You can make up acrostics yourself to remember information, especially terms that go in a specific order. *Left:* Isuaneye/Shutterstock *Right:* littleny/Shutterstock

Study for Your Math, Science, and Online Classes

Math and science classes differ in some important ways from classes in other disciplines; for example, they emphasize solving problems. And online classes differ from traditional face-to-face classes; for instance, in online classes you can usually watch lectures or respond to discussion posts whenever you want. To learn and remember information effectively, adapt your study strategies and tools to the unique characteristics of these classes.

Math and Science Classes

Many of the study strategies you've already learned in this chapter can be used in all your courses, but several additional suggestions will be particularly helpful in your math and science classes.

- **Get plenty of practice solving problems.** Complete all the problems in your textbook, even if your instructor doesn't assign them, and do any problems provided by your instructor. If a study guide or a tutor gives you additional problems, solve those too. Many Web sites also offer practice math, physics, or chemistry problems. Your textbook may even come with access to such online practice problems (see Figure 8.4).

FIGURE 8.4
Solving Practice Problems

Completing plenty of practice problems, like the ones shown here, is a great way to study for math and science classes. So try your hand at all the problems provided in your textbook — even those your instructor hasn't assigned — and check out Web sites offering practice problems. From COMAP, *LaunchPad for For All Practical Purposes: Mathematical Literacy in Today's World* 9th ed. (New York: W. H. Freeman, 2015).

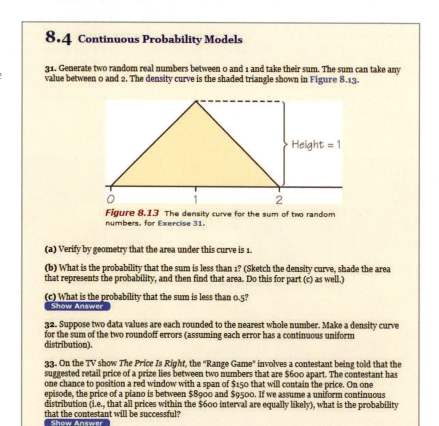

8.4 Continuous Probability Models

31. Generate two random real numbers between 0 and 1 and take their sum. The sum can take any value between 0 and 2. The density curve is the shaded triangle shown in Figure 8.13.

Height = 1

Figure 8.13 The density curve for the sum of two random numbers, for **Exercise 31**.

(a) Verify by geometry that the area under this curve is 1.

(b) What is the probability that the sum is less than 1? (Sketch the density curve, shade the area that represents the probability, and then find that area. Do this for part (c) as well.)

(c) What is the probability that the sum is less than 0.5?
Show Answer

32. Suppose two data values are each rounded to the nearest whole number. Make a density curve for the sum of the two roundoff errors (assuming each error has a continuous uniform distribution).

33. On the TV show *The Price Is Right*, the "Range Game" involves a contestant being told that the suggested retail price of a prize lies between two numbers that are $600 apart. The contestant has one chance to position a red window with a span of $150 that will contain the price. On one episode, the price of a piano is between $8900 and $9500. If we assume a uniform continuous distribution (i.e., that all prices within the $600 interval are equally likely), what is the probability that the contestant will be successful?
Show Answer

- **Check your answers when solving problems.** Do your answers make sense? Are they what you expected? For example, if you're calculating the amount of force acting on a moving object, it wouldn't make sense to have a negative value as an answer. Testing yourself in this way can help you determine how well you understand the formula or equation featured in the problem. In addition, evaluate whether you're making similar or repeated mistakes when you solve problems so that you have time to correct these mistakes before an exam.

- **Write down units when solving problems.** As you work on a problem, make sure you're using the correct units of measure. If your solution is supposed to be in hertz (Hz) and instead it's in seconds, you know you've made a mistake. By making this a habit, you can catch a lot of simple mistakes.

- **Create lists of theorems, formulas, symbols, and vocabulary.** Review these lists during your study time.

- **Explore Khan Academy (www.khanacademy.org).** This free, online resource provides brief lectures and demonstrations of many math and science concepts.

> **CONNECT TO MY RESOURCES**
>
> Your adviser, instructors, and the staff at the tutoring center are just a few of the many people on campus who can help you strengthen your study skills. Write down the office location, phone number, contact person, and Web site for two study resources on campus. How will you use these resources?

Online Classes

Whether you're studying for online classes or traditional face-to-face courses, most of the same techniques can help you master material in both environments. The following tips, though, are particularly useful in studying for online courses.

- **Study all class materials.** In an online class, you may have to watch recorded instructor lectures or online videos. Add the notes you take during these lectures or videos to your study materials for the class.

- **Set up an online study group.** Create an online discussion group with your classmates to share information or practice questions. Your online course-management system might offer videoconferencing so you can hold a virtual study group.

- **Explore online study resources at your school.** Your school may have online tutors, extra recordings of lectures, or other resources specifically designed for students taking online classes. Investigate your options.

The Virtues of Virtual Study Sroups. Are you taking an online class? If so, join an online study group. You can share insights and swap practice problems with other students. And if your course-management system offers videoconferencing, give it a try. Videoconference participants can see one another, making it even easier to communicate. Andrey Popov/ Shutterstock

Use Memory and Studying at Work

The ability to study and remember information is just as valuable *outside* the classroom as it is *inside* the classroom: Employers want to hire and promote people who keep learning and growing, and mastering memory and study strategies can help you do exactly that.

Become a Subject Matter Expert

When you're motivated to learn and study, you'll continue to build knowledge about your chosen field. You may even become a *subject matter expert*: someone who constantly learns new information to build a deep understanding of his or her field, whether it's banking regulations, solar panel design, or software development. Being an expert is a big advantage in the workplace, as employers value go-to individuals who have the knowledge and skills the organization needs to succeed.

Expert Communicator. When you excel at learning and remembering information, you can become a subject matter expert. Being an expert makes you valuable in the workplace, especially when you communicate your knowledge to others. Here, Jessica Collison, flight director for the Mars Rover *Spirit*, shares her expertise at a press conference. © Newscom

Communicate Using Elaborative Rehearsal

As you saw earlier, elaborative rehearsal involves making connections between new information and things you already know. Elaborative rehearsal helps you not only learn and remember information but also explain complex ideas to other people, such as customers and colleagues. Suppose that you're a computer systems analyst and you need to explain the concept of computer bandwidth to a client, including how small and large bandwidth differ. You explain that small bandwidth is like a garden hose (it has low data flow) and that large bandwidth is like a fire hose (it has large data flow). You're connecting a new concept, computer bandwidth, with something most people know about: the difference between garden and fire hoses. As a result, the client "gets" the concept because you've communicated it effectively.

Use Your Memory to Build Personal Connections

Have you ever walked into a coffee shop where the barista knows your regular order? Has a supervisor in another department ever called you by name? If so, you know that it creates a feeling of personal connection when people remember details about you. You can use your memory to build such connections yourself. Remembering details about others shows that you're interested in their lives and helps to forge positive relationships. It's rewarding on a personal level to make connections in a work setting, but these connections can also have business-related benefits: The people you connect with may be the source of your next sale, or they might help you network to get a promotion.

Be a Lifelong Learner

One of the best benefits of memory and study strategies is that you can use them to become a *lifelong learner*. Lifelong learners—who keep building their knowledge and skills long after graduation—tend to be curious about the world around them, apply study skills when they encounter something they don't

LIFELONG LEARNING

Courtesy of Deborah L. Bobbio

NAME: **Deborah Bobbio**

PROFESSION: *Software Engineer*

SCHOOL: *Miami Dade College*

DEGREES: *Associate in Arts; Associate in Science; Bachelor of Science*

MAJORS: *Computer Art Animation; Computer Engineering Technology; Electronics Engineering Technology*

During college I focused mostly on the hardware side of computers and engineering. When I got my first job out of college, it was as a software engineer, which is a field I had little experience with before my senior year. Fortunately my employer didn't expect me to be an expert right away—I developed my skills during the first few months on the job. I was very preoccupied with being able to keep up, but I was also excited to learn about something I didn't have much experience with. I knew that, for me to be successful, I had to keep studying and learning.

My employer put me on a big project right away, so I started looking for free online classes and reading up on the programming language I needed. I also learned that it's okay to ask for help. When I got stuck with something, I would do some research or talk with a fellow developer. Taking small breaks was extremely important; it helped me focus so I wouldn't just stare at the information and then forget what I learned.

Just like in school, at work there are deadlines, projects, and problems to solve—some of which are easier than others. As with homework, I've learned that it's all about practice. The more work I do, the more I learn. No one will expect you to be an expert right out of school, but if your employers see you utilizing all your resources to get the job done, they'll recognize it. I'm motivated to keep learning, and this job has given me the incredible opportunity to do that.

YOUR TURN: If you currently have a job, how do you learn and remember the information you need to perform your job? If you're not employed but are interested in a particular job or career, what kind of information will you need to master to excel in that role? How will you master it?

> " For me to be successful, I had to keep studying and learning."

know, and look for new skills to develop. Lifelong learning keeps your brain active, makes life more interesting, and has benefits for your career: It helps you develop your skills, making you more valuable to your organization and more marketable if you decide to look for a new job or ask for a raise.

my personal success plan

MEMORY AND STUDYING

Are you inspired to set a new goal aimed at improving your memory and study skills? If so, the Personal Success Plan can walk you through the goal-setting process. Read the advice and examples; then sketch out your ideas in the space provided.

 LaunchPad

To access the Personal Success Plan online, go to the LaunchPad for *Connections*.

1 GATHER INFORMATION

Think about your strengths and weaknesses related to remembering and studying. What strategies and tools have worked for you in the past? What could you do differently? Revisit your Memory and Studying score on ACES and review the relevant sections of this chapter for additional ideas.

2 SET A SMART GOAL

Use the information you've gathered to create a SMART goal, making sure to use the SMART goal checklist.

SAMPLE: I'll create a set of flash cards for each of my classes and study each set for ten minutes a day, between classes.

3 MAKE AN ACTION PLAN

Outline the specific steps you'll take to achieve your SMART goal, and note when you'll complete each step.

SAMPLE: I'll use the first twenty minutes of my next study session to create flash cards.

4 LIST BARRIERS AND SOLUTIONS

Think about possible barriers to your action steps; then brainstorm solutions for overcoming them.

SAMPLE: If I forget to review my flash cards between classes, I'll set a reminder on my phone to help me remember.

5 ACT AND EVALUATE OUTCOMES

Now that your plan is in place, take action. Record each action step as you take it. Then evaluate whether you achieved your SMART goal, and make any adjustments needed to get better results in the future.

SAMPLE: I made so many flash cards that I didn't have time to review all of them between classes. I'll pare them down to just the most important information.

6 CONNECT TO CAREER

List the skills you're building as you progress toward your SMART goal. How will you use these skills to land a job and succeed at work?

SAMPLE: My ability to remember specific pieces of information will help me if I become a tax accountant. I'll be able to understand and apply the many changes in tax law that occur each year.

1 my information
_____
_____
_____
_____

2 my SMART goal
_____
_____
_____

☐ **S**PECIFIC   ☐ **M**EASURABLE   ☐ **A**CHIEVABLE   ☐ **R**ELEVANT   ☐ **T**IME-LIMITED

3 my action plan
_____
_____
_____
_____
_____

4 my barriers/ solutions
_____
_____
_____
_____

5 my actions/ outcomes
_____
_____
_____
_____

6 my career connection
_____
_____
_____
_____

CHAPTER SUMMARY

In this chapter we looked at how memory works and explored strategies and tools you can use to study. Revisit the following key points, and reflect on how you can use this information to support your success now and in the future.

- Memory involves three processes: encoding, storing, and retrieving information. Creating a memory begins with taking in information through your five senses (sensory memory). Information resides briefly in your short-term memory, and you can use your working memory to move it into your long-term memory.

- Forgetting occurs when there is a failure to encode or retrieve information.

- Basic study strategies include building many small amounts of study time into your schedule, finding opportunities to study throughout the day, minimizing distractions, joining a study group, and making connections between concepts you're learning and information you already know.

- You can also build your own memory and studying tools, including flash cards, review sheets, purposeful reading questions, practice tests, mental pictures, and mnemonics. Creating your own study tools requires you to engage more deeply with the course content, so you strengthen your comprehension of the material and your ability to remember it.

- Completing as many practice problems as possible, checking your answers, using correct units of measure, making lists of formulas and terms, and using online resources can help you study for math and science classes.

- Good study strategies for online classes include studying all course materials, accessing online resources, and creating virtual study groups.

- You can excel in your job and advance your career by using memory and study strategies and tools to become a subject matter expert and a lifelong learner, as well as to communicate information and build personal connections at work.

CHAPTER ACTIVITIES

Journal Entry

ACTIVATING YOUR MEMORY

Describe a time when you successfully remembered items in a list or specific pieces of information (for example, certain dates from history, all the bones in the human hand, or a favorite family recipe). What memory strategies or tools helped you remember this information?

Now describe an experience in which you forgot a key piece of information. What do you think happened? Was it an encoding error (meaning the information never made it into your short-term memory)? Was it a retrieval failure (meaning you had stored the information in your long-term memory, but you couldn't remember it when you needed to)? What strategies described in this chapter could have helped you encode or retrieve this material?

Adopting a Success Attitude

FINDING MOTIVATION TO STUDY

Motivation is a study aid: It can help you stay focused and accomplish tasks efficiently and effectively. Your attitude can affect your level of motivation: When you feel negatively about a class, a test, or studying in general, you risk setting yourself up for failure. Select one class that you find particularly challenging; then respond to the following questions to adopt a more positive attitude toward studying for that class.

1. What long-term goals do you want to achieve by attending college? How will studying for this class help you achieve your goals?

2. What is one positive statement you can tell yourself over and over (a mantra) to get through this class?

3. What are some specific good things that will come from studying for this class? For example, what knowledge, abilities, attitudes, relationships, or study skills will you build as a result? How will these good things be useful in future classes or in your career?

4. In what ways are you in control over how and when you study for this class? What are the benefits of having this control?

5. What negative thoughts or beliefs do you have about studying for this class? Play devil's advocate and challenge each thought or belief.

Applying Your Skills

USING MNEMONICS TO ENHANCE MEMORY

When you use mnemonics to remember new information, you take personal responsibility for your learning by improving your chances of moving information from your short-term memory into your long-term memory.

Choose a class in which you need to remember a string of words or ideas for an upcoming exam. Then complete the following steps to create your own acrostic (a type of mnemonic). We've provided an example to get you started.

1. Select a list of words or ideas you need to remember. Write these words in a column (vertically) and underline or highlight the first letter in each word.

2. Identify words that begin with each of the underlined or highlighted letters.

3. Put the words together to create a short phrase or a sentence. This is your acrostic.

4. Use your acrostic, and then assess how well it worked. Did it help you remember the information? If not, you may need to change the words in step 2 to create something more fun, interesting, or memorable.

Example: Remembering Piaget's four stages of cognitive development in children.

Step 1	Step 2	Step 3
Sensory Motor Stage	Six	Six Penguins Cooked Falafel
Pre-operational Stage	Penguins	
Concrete Operational Stage	Cooked	
Formal Operational Stage	Falafel	

College Success = Career Success

FORMING STUDY GROUPS

Study groups have an important place in college and at work. In college, members of study groups offer each other moral support and share ideas. At work, colleagues may form groups to study for a licensing exam, learn about a new product, design a marketing campaign, or prepare for a big meeting or presentation. Forming a study group at school can help you build teamwork skills — skills that many potential employers value.

With these advantages in mind, build a plan for forming a college study group by answering the following questions:

1. For which class(es) will you form a study group?

2. Who will you ask to be in your study group? Why?

3. How many people will be in your group?

4. How often will the group meet? Where? For how long?

5. If the study group is for an online class, how will the group differ from a study group created for a face-to-face class? How will you communicate with group members?

6. Who will be in charge of creating the agenda for each study group session?

7. How will you study as a group? What strategies from this chapter will you use? Why?

Now that you have a plan, don't wait — start building your study group today so that you can begin meeting this term!

9 Performing Well on Exams

Prepare for Tests

Manage Test Anxiety

Learn Test-Taking Strategies

Follow Up after Tests

Use Test-Taking Skills at Work

My Personal Success Plan

When you hear the word *test* or the word *exam*, what comes to mind? Do you picture yourself guzzling coffee as you cram late into the night? Do you envision your palms getting sweaty and your heart starting to pound as test time creeps closer? Do you worry that failing an exam could negatively impact your future? If you answered "yes" to these questions, you're not alone: For many students, tests have tremendous power and meaning. That makes sense: Doing well on tests helps you get good grades, which in turn helps you keep your financial aid, stay in college, and ultimately get the job of your dreams.

Before you start hyperventilating, though, let's put exams in their proper perspective. Yes, doing well on them matters, but exams are *not* measures of your worth as a human being. They're *not* broad indicators of your intelligence. They don't even completely measure your knowledge of a given topic. A single exam will *not* dictate the future direction of your life, and often it won't make or break your grade for a course.

Rather, an exam is a snapshot of your ability to answer a specific set of questions on a given topic. It's an opportunity to demonstrate (to yourself and your instructor) that you've studied and that you can apply your new knowledge to the questions posed on the test. As such, tests let you "show what you know."

When you do well on a test, you demonstrate that you understand complex information — a skill that's important not only for school but also for any career you pursue. In your work life, you'll encounter projects, presentations, and other situations in which you need to demonstrate your knowledge. You may even have to take exams to become certified or licensed for specific careers or as part of continuing education requirements. By building your test-taking skills now, you'll be ready to dazzle later, whenever you need to show mastery of material.

This chapter starts off with strategies you can use to prepare for exams. Next we discuss test anxiety and how to manage it. You'll discover tactics for approaching the types of exams you'll encounter in college and for reflecting on your performance once the exam is over. Finally, the chapter wraps up with ways to use your test-taking skills at work.

Reflect

On Your Test Taking

Take a moment to reflect on your Test Taking score on ACES. Find your score and add it in the circle to the right.

This score measures your beliefs about how well you take tests. Do you think it's an accurate snapshot of your understanding? Why or why not?

■ **IF YOU SCORED IN THE HIGH RANGE,** this is great news; you're likely a strong test taker. But you can still build on this talent. For instance, if it's harder for you to take essay tests than multiple-choice tests, you can use the strategies you find in this chapter to make essay tests more manageable. As you read, jot down tactics you'll try out to improve your performance on exams. By doing so, you'll also strengthen skills in self-management, preparation, and persistence — all of which will come in handy long after you graduate.

■ **IF YOU SCORED IN THE MODERATE OR LOW RANGE,** remind yourself that tests can intimidate even the most prepared student, and you're probably facing many of the same challenges as your classmates. Like all the other success skills in this book, performing well on exams is a skill you can build in college. Read on to find out how.

MY ACES SCORE

☐ **HIGH**

☐ **MODERATE**

☐ **LOW**

 LaunchPad

To find your **Test Taking score,** go to the LaunchPad for *Connections.*

Prepare for Tests

According to an old saying, "Success is 90 percent preparation and 10 percent perspiration." The idea that preparation leads to success isn't a new concept— throughout the book we've stressed that investing time up front helps you learn and retain more information—but it's equally relevant in this chapter. Why? Because taking the time to prepare is one of the most *crucial* parts of taking tests successfully.

You can use many test preparation strategies to set yourself on the right path; in fact, some of them may already sound very familiar. Let's explore them in more depth.

Build a Sensible Study Schedule

The road to successful test taking begins on the first day of class, when you receive your syllabus and start creating your personal study schedule. The chapter on organization and time management is packed with strategies you can use to create and follow a schedule for studying for each exam. For example, if you space out your studying over time, rather than cram it all into the day

CONNECT TO MY EXPERIENCE

Think about a time when you studied effectively for a test and earned a good grade. Write down everything you did to study, and put a star next to the things you'd like to do to prepare for your next exam. Also, write down any new strategies you'll try next time, including how you'll adjust your schedule if needed.

before the test, you'll retain more information[1] and feel less stressed when exam time approaches. Build a sensible schedule that gives you plenty of time to prepare, to learn, and to remember (see Figure 9.1).

Use Your Study Skills

All the other study skills described in this book—including reading, note taking, strengthening your memory, and studying—can also help you prepare for tests and exams. As an example, the memory and studying chapter includes a number of strategies you can use to prepare for tests of all kinds. Flash cards can help you get ready for true/false and matching questions and for classes where you need to memorize formulas. Review sheets work well to prepare you for essay questions, and completing practice problems can prepare you for math and science exams. If you've created your own practice tests, take them again the day before an exam. And by all means, contact your study group members and review the information together before the test—they'll provide support and encouragement, and they're a great source of information if you have questions.

Know the Exam Format

Knowing the exam format is critical to getting ready for a test. It also takes some of the anxiety out of the test-taking experience. Early in the term, find out what kinds of questions your instructors will include on their exams. Some instructors put this information in the syllabus; in other classes, you may have to ask. In addition, figure out whether the exams are **cumulative** (covering all the material you've learned so far in the course) or whether they include only new material you've learned since the previous test. This information will affect how you prepare.

Cumulative Exams: Exams that cover everything you've learned in the course up to that point in the term.

Review Previous Exams

If your instructors provide their previous exams as a study aid, use them to get some practice and familiarize yourself with the types of questions you'll see on tests. Your instructors may make these tests available online, in a study guide, or in their offices. If your instructors don't mention previous exams, ask them if these exams are available—the worst they can say is "no." Also, even if an instructor doesn't let students review previous exams, he or she may review test material during the class period before the exam or host a study session. Take advantage of all of these opportunities.

Talk with Your Instructor

Your instructors want to help you succeed—that's why they teach—so visit them during their office hours if you have questions or concerns about exams. Sometimes students feel intimidated by in-person visits, but office hours are designed so that students can meet and talk with instructors and learn one-on-one. A subject matter expert will be sitting in the room with you, ready to clarify questions and provide advice—what a great opportunity!

FIGURE 9.1 **A Sensible Study Schedule**

Instead of cramming right before Thursday morning's algebra exam, this student has blocked out study time in advance and planned thirty minutes of review the night before the test (see blue highlights). Note, too, that she'll practice yoga the morning of the test to calm her nerves and that she goes to bed at a reasonable hour and always eats breakfast. This careful preparation will boost her chances of doing well on the exam.

	Monday	Tuesday	Wednesday	Thursday	Friday
7:00 am :30	BREAKFAST	BREAKFAST	BREAKFAST	BREAKFAST	BREAKFAST
8:00 am :30	BIO 101	YOGA	BIO 101	YOGA	BIO LAB
9:00 am :30	STUDY FYE 1 HR. BIO 1 HR.	ALGEBRA II	STUDY ECON	ALGEBRA II EXAM	BIO LAB
10:00 am :30	STUDY FYE 1 HR. BIO 1 HR.	FREE TIME	STUDY ALGEBRA	FREE TIME	WORK
11:00 am :30	FYE	LUNCH	FYE	LUNCH	WORK
12:00 pm :30	LUNCH	WORK	LUNCH	RESEARCH FOR HISTORY PAPER	WORK
1:00 pm :30	ECONOMICS	WORK	ECONOMICS	RESEARCH FOR HISTORY PAPER	WORK
2:00 pm :30	BIO STUDY TEAM MTG.	STUDY BIO	STUDY FYE 1 HR. HISTORY 1 HR. 30 MIN.	RESEARCH FOR HISTORY PAPER	WORK
3:00 pm :30	BIO STUDY TEAM MTG.	STUDY ALGEBRA	STUDY FYE 1 HR. HISTORY 1 HR. 30 MIN.	FAMILY TIME	WORK
4:00 pm :30	FREE TIME	STUDY ALGEBRA	STUDY FYE 1 HR. HISTORY 1 HR. 30 MIN.	FAMILY TIME	WORK
5:00 pm :30	FREE TIME	DINNER	DINNER	DINNER	DINNER
6:00 pm :30	SOFTBALL PRACTICE	STUDY ECON	SOFTBALL PRACTICE	HISTORY	STUDY ECON
7:00 pm :30	DINNER	STUDY ECON	WORK	HISTORY	FREE TIME
8:00 pm :30	FAMILY TIME	FAMILY TIME	WORK	HISTORY	FREE TIME
9:00 pm :30	STUDY HISTORY	BED	EXAM REVIEW	FREE TIME: CELEBRATE EXAM!	FREE TIME
10:00 pm :30	STUDY ALGEBRA	BED	BED	BED	BED
11:00 pm :30	BED	BED	BED	BED	BED

♦ **CONNECT**
TO MY RESOURCES

Many resources on campus (like study groups and instructors) and off campus (like family members to watch your children while you study) can help you prepare effectively for exams. Write down three resources you'll use to help you prepare for tests this term.

To get the most from these visits, prepare a list of questions beforehand. For example, you might ask, "What will the exam format be?," "How much time will we have to complete the exam?," or "How would you recommend preparing for the test?"

Most instructors' office hours are first come, first served, so consider making an appointment before you go. Also, if you can't make it to office hours, don't give up: Ask your instructor if he or she is willing to meet with you before or after class so you can get the answers you need.

If you're taking an online class, you may not be able to visit your instructor in person, but you can still find ways to communicate. Some professors hold "virtual" office hours, during which they're available to chat or answer questions online. Alternatively, use e-mail or contact your instructor to schedule a phone call.

Stay Healthy

The week leading up to an exam can be stressful, and you may find yourself skimping on sleep, devouring junk food instead of taking time to prepare meals, and cramming for the test rather than hitting the gym. These behaviors may be understandable, but they can backfire and sap your energy. As a result, when test day comes, you may deliver a less-than-stellar performance.

Resist any urge to change your routine right before a test. Instead, make a plan to stay healthy. Try to stick to your normal exercise, dietary, and sleep routines—going into a test well rested is vital to performing your best. Also, give yourself a wake-up insurance policy: If your exam is first thing in the morning, set your regular alarm plus a second alarm as backup.

Manage Test Anxiety

Test Anxiety:
Nervousness or worry about performance on an exam.

If you experience some level of **test anxiety** (nervousness or worry) before or during an exam, guess what? You're normal. Research has found that between 25 percent and 40 percent of students have experienced test anxiety.[2] In fact, a mild level of test anxiety is actually a *good* thing: It helps you stay attentive and focused while you prepare for and take the test. Intense test anxiety, though, can cause damaging, obsessive thoughts of failure ("I'm going to bomb this test"; "I know I'll fail this class"). It can also spawn feelings of doom and dread following the test ("I just know I gave the wrong answer on question 9"). If you have intense test anxiety, you might experience physical reactions such as sweating, nausea, shortness of breath, or headaches. Your mind might even "go blank" during the exam.

The good news is that you *can* manage test anxiety and its negative effects—both before and during exams. To do so, try these tactics.

- **Breathing.** Breathe in to the count of three ("one, two, three") and breathe out in reverse ("three, two, one"). Repeat this pattern several times. Note how calm you feel as you exhale.

- **Muscle relaxation.** Choose a muscle group, tense those muscles for a count of ten, and then relax them. For example, curl your toes tightly

Your Happy Place? If you have test anxiety, visualizing a place that relaxes you, and imagining yourself in that place, can help calm your nerves. You can visit this place anytime you want — when you're studying hard for an exam and starting to feel anxious, or even during the test if your stomach suddenly twists into knots. S-F/ Shutterstock

and then relax. Repeat or move on to another muscle group, such as your lower leg muscles and then upper leg muscles.

- **Preparation.** If you feel especially anxious about tests when you're not sufficiently prepared, add more time to your study schedule. Take practice tests to get comfortable with the test format.

- **Reframing.** Reframe any negative thoughts about failing the test as positive thoughts. For example, if you're thinking, "I'm going to freeze up," write that down; then rewrite it as "I've worked hard, and this test will let me demonstrate my knowledge." (See Table 9.1 for more reframing examples and the Spotlight on Research for more on the power of positive thought.) Put your positive statements in a prominent place you can see every day, and repeat them to yourself whenever you think about your next exam.

- **Visualization.** Envision a place that relaxes you—a beach, a meadow, a forest—and visualize yourself in it. "Visit" this place in your mind to relax before or during an exam.

TABLE 9.1 **Reframing Negative Messages**

Negative thought	Positive reframe
I'm going to forget everything I've studied.	I'm well-prepared and I know the material.
I'm terrible at taking tests.	I'm getting better at taking tests.
If I fail, I'll get kicked out of college.	It's only one test, not my whole college career.
I'm not smart enough.	I *am* smart enough and I belong here.

Courtesy of
Stephanie
Young

PREPARING FOR TESTS AND OVERCOMING TEST ANXIETY

NAME:	**Stephanie Young**
SCHOOL:	*Oklahoma City Community College*
MAJOR:	*Diversified Studies*
CAREER GOAL:	*Dental Hygienist*

> "I calm myself down by breathing easily and slowly."

When I was taking college algebra, I learned that I need to breathe. I would hold my breath through a portion of my tests because I had test anxiety, and one night I just told myself I have to get over this — it's not going to work. Now, before an exam I make sure to set aside ten minutes just to look over my notes, to assure myself that what I've been studying isn't anything to be afraid of. During this time, I calm myself down by breathing easily and slowly. I also run a lot, and I feel calmer when I run. I try to stay positive, because I know I'm not going to do well if I tell myself I'm not going to do well.

When I first started school, I would cram before tests, and it wouldn't work. Cramming made my anxiety issues worse. I would also feel really burnt out, and then I wouldn't do well. Now, I break up my studying. If there are ten things I have to learn for a test, I'll focus on two things each day. Also, I'll rewrite my notes and read over them throughout the day. If I can tell my husband how something works, then I feel comfortable about it, and I move on. I'm a mom and I have a four-year-old who needs my attention, too, so it works for me to study in small amounts.

I have a study buddy, and that makes preparing for tests a lot easier. I also use the biology lab at school. The lab assistants there are students, too, and are really knowledgeable. It's reassuring to know that they're learning what I'm learning and that I can move on like them. They'll sit and tutor you, too, if you need a tutor. It's hands-on in the biology center, and I really like that. Mingling with other students in the lab helps because sometimes what they're learning is being taught in a different way.

YOUR TURN: If you experience test anxiety, have you used any of the strategies for managing it that Stephanie describes? If so, which ones? How have they worked for you? What (if any) other strategies have you found helpful?

- **Worry time.** This strange-sounding technique has helped many people manage anxiety: Plan twenty minutes each day for worrying about an upcoming test. During this "worry time," focus as hard as you can on your worries. Set the timer on your phone, and at the end of the twenty minutes, stop worrying and go on with your day. If you feel anxious at other times during the day, put those thoughts and feelings aside until your next scheduled worry time.

- ■ **Worry journal.** Record all your worries in a journal. Write down what you're afraid of, along with the emotions and physical sensations you're experiencing. Then close your journal to symbolize that you're setting aside your worries for the rest of the day. Or when you're done writing, rip the page out of your journal, crumple it up, and "throw away" your worries.

- ■ **Campus resources.** Talk with a counselor about test anxiety or any other issues affecting your ability to succeed in school. If you experience test anxiety because you have difficulty understanding course material, work with a tutor to establish a regular study schedule and boost your confidence.

Learn Test-Taking Strategies

When test day rolls around, you can go into the exam knowing that you've spent time preparing, and now it's time to perform. Most of your success depends on the hard work and learning you've done before the test, but during the test you can use the strategies in this section to maximize the benefits of this preparation.

Start Smart

It's "go" time: The exam is in your hands (or on your screen). Get a solid start by taking these steps.

- ■ **Write your name or student ID.** Depending on your instructor's instructions, put your name or student ID number on the test documents. These documents might include the test questions, an electronic answer sheet, or a booklet where you'll write essay responses.

- ■ **Read the directions.** Instructors design their tests in different ways, so carefully read the test instructions before answering any questions. For example, some instructors discourage guessing by giving *negative* points for an incorrect answer and *zero* points if you leave the answer blank. Others ask you to choose more than one answer to a question. Find out what the rules are before you start.

- ■ **Preview questions and budget your time.** Quickly review the types of questions on the test and the points assigned to each. For instance, a 50-point test may have ten multiple-choice questions worth 1 point each and two essay questions worth 20 points each. Knowing this helps you budget your time and might reduce feelings of anxiety.[3] For example, if you have fifty minutes to complete the 50-point test, spend no more than one minute on each multiple-choice question and about twenty minutes on each essay question. If you spend four to five minutes on one low-value multiple-choice question, you'll have less time for the high-value essay questions. Also, use all the time provided. If you finish early, take advantage of the remaining time to check your answers.

◖ CONNECT TO MY CAREER

Do you have a job now, or have you had one in the past? If so, write down a time when you experienced anxiety on the job. How did you manage those feelings? How might you manage similar feelings if they occur again? Select two strategies from this chapter, and explain how they could help you.

THE POWER OF POSITIVE THOUGHT: IT CAN HELP WITH TEST ANXIETY

Not surprisingly, people who suffer from test anxiety tend to get lower scores on exams than those who don't experience test anxiety.[4] And they often experience negative feelings and expect to perform poorly. But there is good news: According to one study, you can combat these effects by harnessing the power of positive thought.

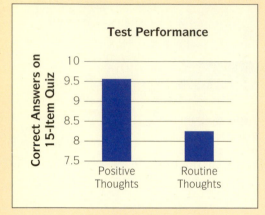

The group of students who had strong positive thoughts performed better on the quiz than the group of students who had routine thoughts.

In a study by Donna Nelson and Ashley Knight, researchers asked 118 students to engage in a brief writing task and then take a quiz. Students in one group were asked to write about a recent successful experience, focusing on a time when they overcame a challenge and felt good about themselves. Students in another group wrote about what they did in a typical morning. Students then answered questions about their feelings, how they manage stress, and any anxiety they felt about the upcoming quiz. Then they took the quiz. Students in the positive-thoughts group:

- Had more positive feelings, a more optimistic attitude, and less test anxiety than students in the routine-thoughts group
- Had greater confidence in their stress-management skills than students in the routine-thoughts group
- Performed better on the quiz than students in the routine-thoughts group

THE BOTTOM LINE

Simply remembering successes and thinking positive thoughts can help you reduce anxiety and perform better on exams.

REFLECTION QUESTIONS

1. Have you experienced test anxiety in the past?
2. If you have experienced test anxiety before, how do you think your attitude affected your performance?
3. If you experience test anxiety now (or if you ever do in the future), what strategies will you use to manage it?

D. W. Nelson and A. E. Knight, "The Power of Positive Recollections: Reducing Test Anxiety and Enhancing College Student Efficacy and Performance," *Journal of Applied Social Psychology* 40 (2010): 732–45.

- **Start with easy questions.** Tackle the questions you know the answers to first. If you're especially well prepared for an essay question, start with that. If you can easily answer fifteen true/false items, begin with those. Responding to questions that are easy for you can help you gain confidence. Be sure, though, to keep in mind the overall points; leave enough time to answer the high-value questions, whether they're hard or easy.

- **Manage any test anxiety.** If you tense up as you start the test, use the relaxation techniques described earlier. In particular, remind yourself that you're prepared, and it's time to show what you know.

Answer Multiple-Choice Questions

Exams during your first term and those in larger classes will likely contain multiple-choice questions. To answer them, you have to accurately recall information, evaluate multiple options, and eliminate poor choices. Try these strategies to improve your performance on multiple-choice questions.

- **Read the directions carefully.** Often, you'll be prompted to pick the single best answer for a multiple-choice question, but occasionally you may have to select more than one response. In addition, sometimes a multiple-choice question will ask you to identify which of the options is *incorrect*. Finally, check whether your instructor gives negative points for incorrect answers.

- **Answer the question in your mind *before* reading the answer choices.** Before you look at the response options, answer the question in your mind if you can. Then look through the options for a choice that matches your answer. If you find one, you can be relatively confident it's correct.

- **Mark any questions you skip.** If you don't know the answer to a question and want to come back to it, clearly mark the question you skip so you can easily find it later. If you're using an electronic scoring form, leave that response blank and return to it later.

- **Cross out all wrong answers.** As you read through each answer option, eliminate all choices that you know are incorrect. Crossing out wrong answers will help you focus on the options you're seriously considering.

- **Read all the options.** Before marking your response, read all the answer options carefully. Instructors may use tricky language to make sure that you're paying attention and that you really know the material. They may also include several items with similar wording.

- **Look for mismatches in how the question and the answer options are worded.** Response options that don't match the question in some way may be incorrect. For instance, if the question contains a singular noun, options that are plural nouns are likely incorrect. Or if the question names a category and one of the answer responses contains something that doesn't fit in that category, that

"We prefer to call this test 'multiple choice,' not 'multiple guess.'"

Choose; Don't Guess. Try answering each multiple-choice question in your mind before looking at the answer options. That way, you're thinking rather than guessing — and you can *choose* the correct response. © CartoonStock

response is likely wrong. As an example, the following question asks about organs.

> Which organs can be susceptible to cancer? Check all that apply.
>
> _____ A. Lung
>
> _____ B. Brain
>
> _____ C. Uterus
>
> _____ D. Foot

Answer D (foot) is not an organ, so it is incorrect.

- **Look for clues in other questions.** From time to time, you'll find the answer to one question in the wording of another question.

- **Look for conditional and unconditional language.** Answers that use conditional language (such as *frequently*, *mostly*, and *typically*) tend to be correct. Answers with unconditional language (such as *always*, *forever*, *totally*, *never*, and *only*) are often wrong.

- **Consider "all of the above."** If at least two of the answer options are correct, then "all of the above" or "all of the choices" is often your best response.

- **Look for the longest answer option.** All things being equal, if you don't know the answer to the question, then choose the longest answer option. Test question writers tend to make the correct responses longer than the others.

Answer Matching Questions

Matching questions require you to connect test items in one list with the correct answer in a second list (see Figure 9.2). These questions allow instructors to cover a great deal of information in a single test question. One challenge of these questions is that if you get one pair wrong, it keeps you from getting another right. Try some of these ideas to answer matching questions.

- **Read the directions or question prompt very carefully.** Be sure you know exactly what the question is asking you to match.

- **Read through all the options.** Take time to read all the items in both lists. Getting familiar with both lists will ensure that you know everything the question covers.

FIGURE 9.2 **Sample Matching Question**

Match the therapy theory with the correct theorist.

1. Gestalt	a. Perls
2. Person-centered	b. Skinner
3. Cognitive	c. Freud
4. Behavioral	d. Beck
5. Psychoanalysis	e. Rogers

- **Start at the top of one list.** Matching questions are most commonly presented as two columns. Start with the first item in one of the columns, and search through the other column to find the correct answer. After you find the answer, move on to the second item in the column. If you don't find the correct answer, skip it and move to the next item, and so on.

- **Answer questions you know first.** First make any matches you're confident are correct. Skip over the ones you're not sure about.

- **Match all the items.** Matching questions usually have the same number of items in each column. Make sure you match all the items.

- **Draw a line between items.** If you're taking a written test rather than an online test (and you have a pencil that you can erase), draw a line between answers in the two columns. This approach allows you to see which items you've matched and which options remain. It also prompts you to match all the items.

- **Quickly double-check your answers.** After you've matched all the items, briefly review your answers to make sure you've used all the items and you haven't duplicated any answers.

CONNECT TO MY CLASSES

So far, which of your college classes has had the most challenging tests? What has made those tests so difficult for you? Write down two strategies that could help you overcome these challenges.

Answer Fill-in-the-Blank Questions

Fill-in-the-blank questions can be more challenging than multiple-choice questions because you don't have several responses to choose from. Instead, you have to produce the answer yourself. The following strategies can help.

- **Think about the key concepts, dates, and main topics of the class.** These are often the answers to fill-in-the-blank questions. For example, suppose a major topic covered in your U.S. history class is the Civil War. On a test, you see the question "On November 19, 1863, President Abraham Lincoln gave an address dedicating the Soldiers' National Cemetery in Gettysburg, the site of a significant battle in the [blank]." The answer that goes in the blank would be "Civil War."

- **Write something.** Unless there is a penalty for guessing, write something in each blank provided in the question.

- **Check grammatical fit.** For example, if the blank in the sentence requires a noun, make sure your answer is a noun. If the blank requires the past-tense form of a verb, be sure your answer takes that form.

- **Check your work.** After you've filled in all the blanks in a sentence, reread the sentence to make sure your responses make sense and are grammatically correct.

Answer True/False Questions

True/false questions can be challenging to answer, particularly when they're long and include language that seems designed to trip you up. On the positive side, you always have a 50 percent chance of being correct. Consider these strategies for answering true/false questions.

- **Look for conditional and unconditional language.** As with multiple-choice questions, conditional terms (including *sometimes*, *often*, *generally*, *seldom*, or *some*) suggest that the statement is probably true. Uncondi-

Tools for tackling tough test questions. A potent set of strategies can help you tackle difficult test questions. For instance, with a true/false question, unconditional language (such as *all* and *only*) often indicates a false statement. For fill-in-the-blank questions, your answers should be in the correct grammatical form — for example, use a noun if the blank calls for a noun. Lisa F. Young/Shutterstock

tional language (such as *all*, *only*, *invariably*, or *entirely*) often indicates a false statement.

- **Choose "false" if any part of the answer option is incorrect.** For example, the statement "The noble gases include helium, neon, argon, krypton, xenon, radon, and hydrogen" is false because hydrogen is not a noble gas.

- **Rewrite double negatives.** If a statement includes double negatives, cross them out and reread the item to determine if it is true or false. Take the sentence "The sun will never not rise in the east." If you cross out "never" and "not," you get "The sun will rise in the east," which is true.

- **Guess "true."** If you have no idea whether the item is true or false (and your instructor doesn't deduct points for guesses), then select "true" as your response. As instructors, we can tell you that it's easier to write test items that are true than those that are false.

Answer Essay Questions

You'll often encounter essay questions on college tests, particularly in upper-level and smaller courses with fewer students (and thus fewer essays for instructors to read). Most essay questions require you to describe topics in detail, make arguments, or analyze information. For these questions, you need to use your critical thinking skills. In fact, your answers may need to show a mix of the levels of learning represented in Bloom's taxonomy (see the critical thinking chapter), which range from knowledge, comprehension, and application to analysis, synthesis, and evaluation. Here are some suggestions for answering essay questions effectively.

"Will Mr. 'No Comment' please remain after class."

"No Comment"? No Dice. Answering essay test questions takes careful thought about what the question is asking for. You won't get away with just jotting down careless or silly responses. Instead, you need to review the question's wording, and use critical thinking to generate a strong answer. © CartoonStock

- **Read the question carefully.** Essay questions often include one or more of the following terms: *define, summarize, apply, explain, compare/contrast, critique, illustrate, justify, outline, describe, review*. Circle these terms in the question, and make sure you're answering the question that's being asked. For example, if a question asks you to compare and contrast two theories and your response merely defines them, you're not answering the question.

- **Budget your time.** If you have thirty minutes and three essays to write, give yourself ten minutes for each.

- **Organize your response.** Before you start writing, briefly outline your response. Decide on a main point and supporting details for each paragraph in your essay. Use your outline to ensure you're answering the question completely. Also, leave space at the end of your answer in case you have time to return to the essay and want to add a few more supporting details.

- **Write neatly.** If you have poor handwriting, take time to write legibly so that your instructor can read your response.

- **Proofread.** If possible, leave yourself time to proofread each essay so that you can fix any problems with grammar and spelling, flow of ideas, and accuracy of content. Draw a line through any problem areas, and neatly write your revision above the crossed-out material.

Take Math and Science Tests

In your math and science classes, test questions often are about solving problems—for example, showing a proof, solving for a variable in an equation, or drawing the electron configuration of a copper atom. Consider these strategies when you answer problem-solving questions.

- **Show your work.** Write out each step of your answer. This will help you double-check your work and show your instructor how you arrived at your answer.

- **Check for basic errors.** Review your work to catch and fix simple mistakes, such as mixing up positive and negative signs, rounding a number incorrectly, or calculating operations out of order.

- **Tackle hard problems last.** If you encounter a difficult problem, skip it and do the easier ones first. Return to the hard one later.

- **Answer all the questions.** Write down something for each question. Even if you can't solve an entire problem, you might get partial credit for the work you do show.

- **Make your answers legible.** Make sure any diagrams and proofs you write are clear and neat. Sloppy or unreadable work will hurt your grade.

Take Tests Online

During your college experience, you'll probably take at least a few exams online (see Figure 9.3). Even traditional classes that meet face-to-face may have online tests. Use the following strategies to take online exams successfully.

FIGURE 9.3 **Sample Online Test Question**

To prepare for an online test, practice *taking* an online test. This question comes from LearningCurve, an online self-assessment system that may be available with this textbook. Questions like these will help you get comfortable with course material and an online testing environment.

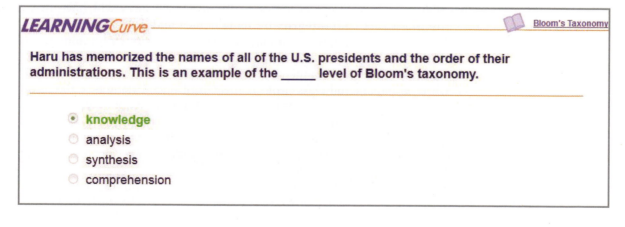

- **Use your notes sparingly.** Most of your online tests will be open book/open note but they'll also be time-limited. During an open book/open note test, you can use the book and your notes as a resource. However, you won't have time to look up the answer to every question. Study as you would for any other type of test, and use your notes and book to verify answers for just a few questions.

- **Check your browser.** Make sure that your computer's browser works with the test-taking platform. Your instructor may recommend a specific browser, or you may need to check the login procedure to confirm you can access the test-taking system.

- **Test your Internet connection.** Before starting the exam, check that you have a secure, stable Internet connection. If you lose your Internet connection during the test, don't close the browser. Instead, reestablish the connection and try to continue. A broken connection or closed browser may cause the system to mistakenly conclude that you've finished taking the test. If this occurs, contact your instructor immediately and explain the situation.

- **Reserve a quiet space.** Find a quiet, distraction-free space to complete the exam. If necessary, make arrangements ahead of time with roommates or family members.

- **Don't start until you're ready.** Most online exams are *forced completion*, meaning that once you start, you can't stop and return later to finish. Wait until you're ready; then begin.

- **Enable pop-ups.** Sometimes questions appear as pop-ups, so before you start, make sure your browser will allow pop-ups during the exam. Use the browser's Help feature to find out how to disable the pop-up blocker.

- **Record your answers.** If your instructor allows it, write down your answers as you complete the exam. Record the question number and your response to multiple-choice, true/false, matching, and fill-in-the-blank questions. For essay questions, copy and paste your answers into a Word document. That way, if your answers somehow get lost, you can use your saved responses to re-create them.

Take Tests with Integrity

Integrity: Being honest and displaying behavior that is consistent with one's values.

Throughout your college career, you and your classmates will have many opportunities to act with **integrity** by being honest and demonstrating behavior that reflects your values. You'll take personal responsibility for and ownership of your education, which you likely value highly. For example, you'll spend time studying when you'd rather do something more fun, and you'll do your own work on papers and class projects instead of plagiarizing (see the information literacy and communication chapter). Taking tests is another critical opportunity to act with integrity—again, by doing your own work rather than cheating. When it comes to test taking, cheating can involve anything from peeking over a neighbor's shoulder and copying down her answers to looking at a copy of a stolen exam.

Students decide to cheat for a variety of reasons: They're overwhelmed by college demands, they don't have enough time to prepare effectively, they're not

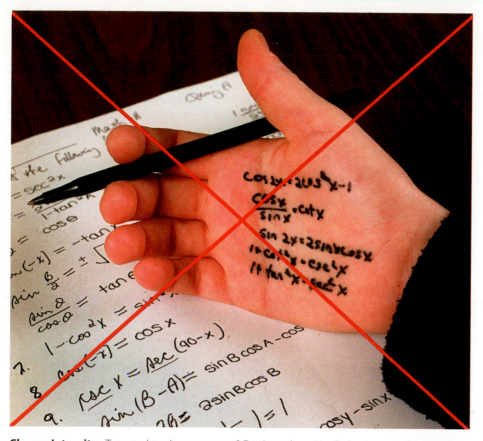

Choose Integrity. Tempted to cheat on a test? Don't go there. You'll cheat yourself out of an opportunity to learn, and if you get caught, you could be expelled from school. Are those risks really worth the possibility of scoring a few extra points on an exam? © Spencer Ainsley/The Image Works

sure how to study for tests, or they simply don't want to put in the effort to succeed. But cheating comes with some high costs. For one thing, if you cheat, you're cheating *yourself* out of the opportunity to learn—so you're wasting your tuition money. You're also being unfair to all the students who put in the effort to learn the material. And if you decide to cheat and you get caught, you may fail the exam, fail the entire course and have to repeat it, and have a written record of the event permanently attached to your student file. You might have to go in front of a student panel at the college, or you could even be expelled. These risks just aren't worth the possibility of scoring a few more points on an exam by cheating.

Also take care to avoid any *appearance* of cheating during exams. For instance, if you're taking a closed-book exam, pulling out your phone or rummaging in your bag for gum, an extra pen, or scratch paper is asking for trouble. If you need to do any of these things, let your instructor know. If you have study materials with you, put these in your bag before you enter the classroom, and turn off your phone. If your instructor *believes* you've cheated, even if you haven't, you may be severely penalized. Don't put yourself in a position to be questioned.

Follow Up after Tests

Have you ever taken a test, walked out of the classroom, and then never thought about the experience again? As tempting as that might be—particularly right after the test ends—once you've completed a test, you have a valuable opportunity to follow up by thinking critically about your approach and using your insights to make improvements in the future.

Evaluate Your Approach: Did Your Prep Work Pay Off?

Right after you take a test, reflect on the experience and how prepared you felt. It might take some time before you receive your exam results, but immediate self-reflection can help you get a sense of your performance. To prompt that reflection, ask yourself:

- Was the test harder or easier than I expected?
- Did the test cover the material I studied?
- Did I spend enough time studying?
- Did I effectively eliminate distractions and stay focused while I was studying?
- Which of my study and preparation strategies helped me the most with this test?
- Which of my study and preparation strategies helped me the least with this test?
- What new types of strategies would I like to try when I prepare for my next test?

You can use your responses to these questions to determine your next steps. If you're confident you did well on the test, reflect on what led to this success, and resolve to take a similar approach for the next test or for tests in other classes. For instance, if studying in a distraction-free zone was an effective strategy, then plan to continue this practice during future test prep. If you feel you didn't do as well as you hoped, identify the reasons, and take steps to do better next time—for example, by changing up your study strategies and trying something new.

Get Hard Evidence

In addition to self-reflection, after-test follow-up involves finding out your results on the exam. In most classes, instructors hand back graded exams so you can see how you did on each question. If tests aren't handed back, visit your instructor during office hours, and ask if you can look at your exam to get insights on how to improve your performance on future tests. And be sure to discuss your performance and test-taking strategies with your instructors. After all, they use exams to determine if you're learning course material. By talking with them, you show that you're interested in the material and that you want to understand what your instructor is assessing.

Tap into Your Instructor's Insights. If your instructors hand back graded exams, look over your results to see how you did on each question. Talk with your instructors about your performance and the test-taking strategies you used. They can offer helpful ideas for preparing more effectively for exams and tackling different types of test questions. Blend Images/Hill Street Studios/Getty Images

Learn from Your Mistakes

What if your exam grade is less than you hoped for or expected? First, realize that at some point this happens to everyone. Take a few deep breaths, and acknowledge that it's perfectly natural to feel disappointed or upset. Next, remind yourself that a test evaluates your performance on one set of questions, on a specific day. One poor test result doesn't reflect your overall ability to succeed in college. By identifying what led to the disappointing results, you can figure out how to do better next time.

If you feel you did everything right and still had a poor outcome, seek out resources on campus. Explain to your instructor how you prepared for the exam, and get his or her feedback on what you might do differently next time. Work with a tutor or a study group to learn other test-preparation strategies. And definitely make use of the Personal Success Plan—for example, you can write a positive goal focused on improving your test results the next time around.

Use Test-Taking Skills at Work

If you think that test taking has nothing to do with the work world, think again. The skills needed to excel on tests in college courses are just as valuable in any job or career you pursue. As in college, effective test taking lets you "show what you know" at work.

Answer Questions Confidently

In any job you'll need to respond to questions from your supervisor and coworkers, and possibly customers and suppliers. Of course, these people won't ask you multiple-choice, fill-in-the-blank, or true/false questions or demand that you write an essay. But the preparation and thinking skills needed to respond effectively to their questions are the same skills you use to answer questions correctly on college tests.

For example, suppose your boss asks you to evaluate proposals from five marketing agencies that want to handle the advertising campaign for your company's new product. You'll need to recall detailed information about the product, evaluate the different options presented by the agencies, and eliminate poor choices (such as agencies that charge high fees). These are the same skills you use to respond to multiple-choice questions on exams.

Or let's say a patient asks about the side effects of his medication or a coworker wants to know which part to replace to fix a wind turbine's gearbox. To answer these questions, you "fill in the blank" by providing a precise, accurate response. If you're in human resources, a coworker might ask you about the health care options in your company's benefits plan. You'll need the same critical thinking skills—in this case, comparing and contrasting several options—that you draw on when taking essay tests.

The test-taking abilities you're developing can help you respond to all types of questions in the workplace—which, in turn, can help you do everything from demonstrating product knowledge, to boosting sales, to building relationships.

Take Exams for Work

Besides helping you answer questions at work, test-taking skills can be useful for taking work-related exams. These skills can help you pass licensure or certification exams required to enter professions ranging from landscaping, paralegal work, and real estate to counseling and graphic design. In some careers, employees also have to take annual performance assessments to show whether they're functioning at the required level in their job.

In addition, many professions require individuals to earn continuing education credits, which provide evidence of ongoing learning and professional development. Large organizations might also provide educational opportunities such as online tutorials, which often conclude with tests to show what you've learned from the training. For example, suppose you're a new manager, and you take an online course on how to create a budget. After finishing the tutorial, you complete a test that checks your knowledge. The results include feedback on course content you need to review to address any weak areas—information you can use to get the most out of your learning experience.

Licensed to Serve. Are you interested in a career that requires you to pass a licensure or certification exam? If so, the test-taking skills you build in college can help you pass that exam, demonstrating that you have the expertise needed to effectively serve your clients or customers. © Jose Luis Pelaez, Inc./Corbis

TAKING TESTS ON THE JOB

Courtesy of
Amy Hildreth

NAME:	**Amy Hildreth**
PROFESSION:	*Registered Nurse*
SCHOOL:	*Des Moines Area Community College*
DEGREE:	*Associate Degree in Nursing*
MAJOR:	*Nursing*

I went back to school when I was thirty-four to become a registered nurse. In nursing school you're evaluated on written exams and skills. The written exams may have several correct answers, but you have to learn how to choose the best answer. Also, you need to be able to perform skills/scenarios in front of instructors. It was a tough curriculum — each term our class size got smaller and smaller — but I learned how to prepare for exams so I could make it through.

This regular evaluation of my skills and knowledge continued even after I graduated from the nursing program. After graduation you have to sit for a national licensing exam with the board of nursing in order to demonstrate competency as a registered nurse. To prepare for this exam, I enrolled in a week-long review class and purchased books and CDs with hundreds of practice questions so I could test myself. Those practice questions were a huge help.

After I passed the board of nursing exam, I had more testing to complete. Before I could start my first job as an RN, I had to perform math calculations for drug conversions and IV pumps and take a pretest to assess my basic nursing knowledge. Also, now that I'm an RN, there are continuing education and recertification requirements. We have practice skills and scenarios we have to attend yearly, and there are multiple tests and worksheets to complete for the unit I work in. There are also continuing education requirements to renew my license, and I'm working on becoming certified in my nursing specialty (critical care), which is similar to preparing for my licensure exam. I'll go to a study course and take practice tests in order to get ready.

Knowing how to prepare for exams has been critical to my success — both inside and outside of school. Figuring out how to prepare for exams in college helped me become an RN, and now these same skills are helping me move forward in my career.

YOUR TURN: Are you interested in pursuing a job that will require you to pass certification or licensure exams? If so, which preparation strategies described by Amy sound most useful to you? If you've already passed such exams, what strategies helped you most? If you've had difficulty passing these exams, what might you do differently in the future?

> " Knowing how to prepare for exams has been critical to my success — both inside and outside of school."

my personal success plan

Are you inspired to set a new goal aimed at improving your test-taking skills? If so, the Personal Success Plan can walk you through the goal-setting process. Read the advice and examples; then sketch out your ideas in the space provided.

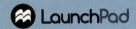

To access the Personal Success Plan online, go to the LaunchPad for *Connections*.

1 GATHER INFORMATION

Think about your strengths and weaknesses related to taking exams. What strategies have worked for you in the past? What could you do differently? Revisit your Test Taking score on ACES and review the relevant sections of this chapter for additional ideas.

2 SET A SMART GOAL

Use the information you've gathered to create a SMART goal, making sure to use the SMART goal checklist.

SAMPLE: To reduce my test anxiety, I'll practice breathing techniques and visualization for ten minutes each night.

3 MAKE AN ACTION PLAN

Outline the specific steps you'll take to achieve your SMART goal, and note when you'll complete each step.

SAMPLE: Starting tonight, I'll use breathing techniques for various amounts of time and visualize different kinds of images until I find the right combination.

4 LIST BARRIERS AND SOLUTIONS

Think about possible barriers to your action steps; then brainstorm solutions for overcoming them.

SAMPLE: Muscle relaxation didn't work for me before. If these new techniques don't work, I'll visit the counseling center to get more help with relaxation skills.

5 ACT AND EVALUATE OUTCOMES

Now that your plan is in place, take action. Record each action step as you take it. Then evaluate whether you achieved your SMART goal, and make any adjustments needed to get better results in the future.

SAMPLE: The visualization/breathing combination worked great. When I tense up, I picture a waterfall, breathe deeply, and start to relax.

6 CONNECT TO CAREER

List the skills you're building as you progress toward your SMART goal. How will you use these skills to land a job and succeed at work?

SAMPLE: I'm learning to relax in difficult situations, so things will go more smoothly when it's time for me to interview for a job or give a big presentation.

1 my information

_____
_____
_____
_____

2 my SMART goal

_____
_____
_____
_____

☐ **S**PECIFIC ☐ **M**EASURABLE ☐ **A**CHIEVABLE ☐ **R**ELEVANT ☐ **T**IME-LIMITED

3 my action plan

_____
_____
_____
_____

4 my barriers/ solutions

_____
_____
_____
_____

5 my actions/ outcomes

_____
_____
_____
_____

6 my career connection

_____
_____
_____
_____

CHAPTER SUMMARY

In this chapter we explored a range of ideas for succeeding on your college exams. Revisit the following key points, and reflect on how you can use this information to support your success now and in the future.

- Each exam you take is a snapshot of your ability to answer a specific set of questions on a particular day. Performance on any one exam will not make or break your college career.

- Key strategies for preparing for tests include building a study schedule, using study strategies, learning the exam format, reviewing previous exams, talking with your instructor about how best to prepare, and sticking to your regular routines to stay healthy.

- Moderate worry about a test can improve your performance, but intense test anxiety can lead to lower test scores. Strategies for managing intense test anxiety include breathing exercises and muscle relaxation, preparation, reframing negative thoughts into positive ones, visualizing a relaxing place, scheduling worry time, and using a worry journal. Most campuses have additional resources for managing anxiety.

- When exam time arrives, it's important to first read the instructions and determine the points for each section, and then budget your time. Answering the easier questions and the highest-value questions first is a good strategy.

- You can use a wide variety of strategies to take tests with multiple-choice, matching, fill-in-the-blank, true/false, and essay questions. You can also use specific strategies to prepare for problem-solving tests in math and science and for tests administered online.

- Deciding not to cheat on tests reflects integrity. But you also need to avoid behaviors that give the appearance of cheating, such as looking at your phone while taking a test.

- After taking an exam, you can assess the effectiveness of your approach to preparing for and taking the test. Then you can use your evaluation to apply successful strategies to other exams or to improve your approach so that you get better results in the future.

- The test-taking skills you develop in college can help you enter and advance in a job or career, by enabling you to answer questions from others in the workplace and to complete licensure or certification exams and continuing education credits.

Journal Entry

EVALUATING YOUR APPROACH TO EXAMS

Reflect on your previous approach to taking exams by responding to the following questions:

- In the past, how did you typically prepare for exams? What test-taking strategies did you use?
- Have you ever experienced test anxiety? If so, what do you think caused it?
- How did you follow up after a positive test-taking experience? How did you follow up after a negative test-taking experience?

Now that you've read this chapter, consider whether you need to overhaul your test-taking approach. In the future, what (if anything) will you do differently to prepare for tests, manage any test anxiety, take tests, and follow up after the test?

Adopting a Success Attitude

REFRAMING NEGATIVE SELF-TALK ABOUT EXAMS

Have you ever said anything negative to yourself before taking an exam? Thoughts are powerful — they can influence how you perform. To positively affect your performance, let's practice reframing negative thoughts about exams into thoughts that reflect optimism, hope, personal responsibility, and empowerment.

Read the negative thought on the left, and then create a more positive thought on the right, using the categories to guide you. The next time a negative thought about an exam creeps into your mind, see if you can reframe it as a positive thought.

Negative thought

Pessimistic
"I don't think I'll do well on this exam."

Blame
"The instructor created an impossible exam!"

Inability
"I'll never be able to memorize all this material!"

Victim
"I don't think the instructor likes me; he'll probably give me a lower grade than everyone else."

Hopeless
"I'm never going to pass this exam! Why even study?"

Crisis
"My life will be ruined if I flunk this test!"

Positive thought

Optimistic
Example: "This exam will be challenging, but I'll study and do my best."

Ownership
_____

Empowerment
_____

Master of my destiny
_____

Hopeful
_____

Opportunity
_____

Applying Your Skills

ANTICIPATING ESSAY QUESTIONS

In college your instructors will probably tell you if an exam will include essay questions, but they likely won't give you the exact questions in advance. So you'll need to anticipate the types of essay questions you'll see on the test. Let's practice.

Pretend you'll be taking an essay exam on this chapter. Review the chapter and your notes, looking for important concepts that could be turned into essay questions. Then create one essay question using each of the following verbs: *describe*, *summarize*, *explain*, *compare/contrast*, *critique*, and *outline*. To get you started, here's an example: "*Explain* how the test-preparation and test-taking skills presented in this chapter can be used in the workplace." Finally, test yourself on chapter concepts by answering two of the questions you created.

College Success = Career Success

EVALUATING YOUR PERFORMANCE

This chapter described the importance of analyzing what went right and what went wrong after taking a test. At work, regularly evaluating your performance helps you identify strengths and weaknesses, set goals, make adjustments, and, ultimately, become a more effective, efficient, and valuable employee. In fact, you may be asked to provide a self-evaluation in a performance review or discuss your approach to self-evaluation in a job interview.

To practice self-evaluation, number your paper from 1–10 and provide a self-rating for each item using the following scale:

Never	Infrequently	Sometimes	Frequently	Always
0	1	2	3	4

_____ **1.** Attends class (in person or online)

_____ **2.** Demonstrates positive attitude

_____ **3.** Participates in class discussions

_____ **4.** Completes assigned readings

_____ **5.** Asks for help when necessary

_____ **6.** Sticks to a study schedule

_____ **7.** Is open to instructor feedback

_____ **8.** Checks spelling on written assignments

_____ **9.** Turns in homework on time

_____ **10.** Takes the lead in small group discussions

Choose two behaviors you rated lower than the others, and describe the steps you'll take to increase your ratings in the next two weeks. Turn in this self-evaluation to your "supervisor" (your instructor) for feedback.

10 Information Literacy and Communication

Develop Information Literacy

Find the Information You Need

Evaluate the Information You've Found

Communicate Information through Writing

Avoid Plagiarism

Present in Class with Confidence

Use Information Literacy and Communication Skills at Work

My Personal Success Plan

When you start working on class assignments, is the information you need already in your head? When you sit down to write, do the words flow easily onto the page? When you deliver a presentation, do you calmly stroll up to the front of the room and then wow the crowd? These scenarios might happen occasionally (and isn't it great when they do!). For most people, though, finding information and communicating it through writing and speaking are often difficult. Maybe you have trouble locating useful sources for a paper and clarifying your thoughts in writing, or you suffer from "stage fright" when giving presentations. If so, here's good news: Although finding information and communicating it through writing and speaking take work, you can build these skills. Here's even better news: College is the perfect place to do it.

As a college student, you'll use these skills all the time. For example, you'll probably have to write papers with references to outside sources and give class presentations. You'll also use these skills in your job. Police officers, for instance, need to write reports and speak with authority during traffic stops and daily briefings. Civil engineers must record the results of structural tests or explain the design needs of a new bridge. Logistics managers for consumer-products companies have to know which products customers have ordered and which products are available, and then get customers those products on time. Many careers involve large amounts of information gathering, writing, and speaking (for example, criminal attorney, sales representative, or reporter). But to excel in almost every job, you'll need to communicate effectively through one or both of these means.

The ability to find, evaluate, and communicate information is called *information literacy*. In this chapter we start by focusing on the first two components of information literacy: locating information and evaluating its quality. Then we move to its third component: communicating that information through writing and speaking. We explain how to navigate the writing process, avoid plagiarism, and give strong class presentations. Finally, we consider how you can use all these skills in your career. These concepts are closely linked to critical thinking, so throughout this chapter we note how you can use your higher-level thinking skills to track down information and communicate your ideas.

Reflect

On Your Information Literacy and Communication Skills

Reflect

Take a moment to reflect on your Information Literacy and Communication score on ACES. Find your score and add it in the circle to the right.

This score measures your beliefs about how well you can find and communicate information. Do you think it's an accurate snapshot of your current skills in this area? Why or why not?

■ **IF YOU SCORED IN THE HIGH RANGE** and you're confident that this score is accurate, you may excel at finding and communicating information effectively. This is great news, but don't stop there: Use the information you find throughout this chapter to become an even stronger researcher and communicator. For example, learn how to track down new, reliable sources of information for research papers; take steps to sharpen your writing skills; or try out new tips for delivering a persuasive presentation.

■ **IF YOU SCORED IN THE MODERATE OR LOW RANGE**, seize the day! Use the strategies from this chapter and this course to grow as a researcher, writer, and speaker. With time, practice, and a positive attitude, you can build your skills and develop confidence in each of these three areas.

☐ **HIGH**

☐ **MODERATE**

☐ **LOW**

LaunchPad

To find your **Information Literacy and Communication score**, go to the LaunchPad for *Connections*.

Develop Information Literacy

Meet Destiny, who is several weeks into her first term of college. She has two weeks to write a short paper for her political science class, and the paper must reference five academic sources. She isn't sure where to start, so she Googles "dictatorship." Instantly, she has pages and pages of information at her fingertips. As the options fill her screen, Destiny's confidence grows—she's well on her way to getting this paper done! She copies paragraphs from the first five Web sites that show up in her search results and pastes them into her paper. Since she knows that copying someone else's work is cheating, she rewrites the paragraphs in her own words. She includes references to the sites where she got her information, as well as a few images to jazz things up. She feels good when she hands the paper in, but later she receives the bad news: She got a D. Confused and upset about what happened, she asks herself: What did I do wrong?

To answer this question, Destiny needs to understand **information literacy**. Information literacy includes a number of elements, but we'll focus on three of the most essential: finding information, evaluating its quality, and effectively communicating it to others (see Figure 10.1).

Information Literacy: Finding information, evaluating its quality, and effectively communicating it to others.

FIGURE 10.1 Key Elements of Information Literacy

Destiny had trouble with all three elements. First, she didn't locate the type of information the assignment required (academic sources). Instead, she used the first sources that showed up in her Internet search, without considering whether they were appropriate for an academic paper. Second, she used the information without checking whether it was reliable. Third, the patchwork of paragraphs she stitched together from five different Web sites and then rephrased didn't communicate a clear, smoothly flowing message.

Destiny wasn't information literate, so she made some serious mistakes in her paper. But you don't have to go down the same road. Let's look closely at each element of information literacy, beginning with the first: where to find information.

Find the Information You Need

To write a paper or create a presentation, you need to track down information. Where should you start? Try the library. Although the Internet may make libraries seem outdated, they're hugely valuable: Not only do they contain countless resources, including many electronic ones, but they also have staff who can answer questions and help you find what you need. If you haven't gone to the campus library yet, add a visit to your to-do list this term.

Keep in mind that you don't have to be *in* the library to take advantage of its resources. Whether you're sitting in the library itself, at your desk, or at your kitchen table, you can access the library's Web site. From there, you can explore a wealth of physical and electronic resources you'll need to write papers and complete assignments, including the following:

Cite: To give another author credit when you include his or her ideas in your paper or project.

- **Books.** Books provide more depth and detail than many other information sources. Prominent book authors are usually experts in their subject matter, and they add credibility to your writing when you acknowledge, or **cite**, their ideas in a paper. Use the library Web site's search tool to look for books by topic, title, or author. If the library doesn't have a book you need, check whether an electronic version is available or whether you can borrow the book from another library.

- **Journal articles.** Instructors and other experts often publish research findings, theories, and literature reviews in professional journals. Journal articles are typically *peer-reviewed*, meaning that other experts review, comment on, and approve the articles before they're published. Peer review is part of the scientific process, and it helps to ensure that the journal's information is useful and trustworthy. Journals are a good source for facts and other information you need. However, you might find it more difficult to read articles than books because articles are generally written for other professionals in the field.

- **Newspapers and magazines.** Information in newspapers and magazines is often timely because these periodicals are published more frequently than books or journals. Look to newspapers and magazines for descriptions of recent events or in-depth reporting. These articles have less technical detail than what you'll find in journal articles, but they're easier to read.

- **Encyclopedias, archives, and historical documents.** Encyclopedias provide broad overviews of many topics and are a good starting place for gathering basic information. Archives and historical documents can also be valuable sources of information. For instance, to write her paper on dictatorships, Destiny might have quoted from or described part of the Declaration of Independence.

- **Databases.** Using databases on your library's Web site, you can find collections of journal articles, magazine and newspaper articles, videos, government reports, and images on specific topics. If Destiny had started with databases rather than with Google, she could have found articles about dictatorships from highly respected sources such as the *Journal of International Affairs* and the *Economist*. Many libraries organize their databases by field, so you can search by specific topics of interest.

- **Course reserves.** Some instructors create a set of physical or electronic readings for a course that students can access through the library's Web site. When your instructor puts extra time into making these materials available, you know that he or she considers the information important, so be sure to take advantage of them.

↳ CONNECT TO MY CAREER

To learn more about a career that interests you, find and read one article in a peer-reviewed journal or professional magazine related to this career. (For example, a geology major might read the *Journal of Geophysical Research*.) What was most intriguing about the article you chose?

Information Treasure Trove. Libraries are great places to find the information you need to write a paper or craft a presentation. Not only are they packed with books, journals, magazines, newspapers, and online tools for tracking down an array of sources, but they also have librarians who are trained to help you find information. So visit your library today.
iStock/© Rayman/Getty Images

Evaluate the Information You've Found

Once you've found information, you need to evaluate its quality. Evaluation is a key component of critical thinking because it requires higher-level thinking skills. To prompt reflection and analysis, ask yourself questions such as "Can I trust what I'm reading right now?"

In some ways, evaluating the quality of the information you find is like examining the quality of ingredients when you're baking. Just as you wouldn't put a rotten apple into a pie, you don't want to include weak or questionable information in your papers. Recognizing bad information isn't as easy as picking out a rotten apple, but the strategies in this section can help.

Basic Quality

Ask some simple questions about the basic quality of the information. When looking at a book, check the name of the publisher. Have you heard of the company? Does the publisher have a well-developed Web site? With the rise of self-publishing, anyone can write and print a book.

If you're examining a journal article in the library, see if it includes a list of professionals who edit and review articles for the journal. If you've found an article through your library's Web site or another online database, do a quick search to make sure the journal is peer-reviewed.

When you're evaluating Web sites, trustworthy sources will clearly state who maintains the site and will often be linked to other well-known, respected sites. Sites ending in *.edu* or *.org* may be more appropriate for research purposes than *.com* sites.

Author Credibility

To determine an author's credibility, investigate the answers to these questions: Do you recognize the author's name? Has your instructor referred to the author in class, or does the author's name appear in your textbook? What can you find out about the author's background and credentials? Is he or she an expert on the topic? As you read the source, ask yourself how well the author has covered the topic. Does he or she seem well informed?

Objectivity

Quality sources maintain objectivity by presenting all sides of an issue. If the author has a particular bias, he or she should make that known. For instance, politically conservative or liberal writers should be up-front about their views. A bias doesn't mean that the author's writing is flawed or useless, but you do need to be aware of it and consider how well the author has supported his or her views. If the author merely states a biased view without backing it up, you probably shouldn't include this information in your paper or presentation.

"I just read an online article that says you should never believe anything you read online."

Online Articles: Trustworthy — or Not? It's important to think critically about any information you read, but it's especially important to evaluate information published online. Why? Because anyone can post anything they want — without undergoing a peer-review process. So put extra care into assessing an online article's trustworthiness. © Cartoonstock

Currency

Check the publication date of books and journals. How current is the information you're evaluating? How current does it need to be? A description of the Internet written in the mid-1990s might be a great resource for a project on the history of the Internet, but not for a project focused on today's Internet-related issues. Also check the dates of the citations in articles or books. If the dates of the citations are close to the article's or book's date of publication, the authors were using current information. With Web sites, look for the dates when articles were posted and for references to more recent events so that you can see whether the content is refreshed regularly. However, don't assume that older content is worthless; a thirty-year-old book for a geology class might still be a good source if it's an important work in the field.

Wikipedia

Using information from Wikipedia in papers and presentations is a controversial topic on college campuses.[1] Information on Wikipedia might be inaccurate or purposefully misleading because anyone can edit content on the site. The people making revisions may or may not be experts on the content they're altering. With peer-reviewed journal articles or edited textbooks, on the other hand, people who are experts on the subject matter have read and reviewed the information. Peer review doesn't guarantee complete accuracy, but it does make the information more trustworthy than content in Wikipedia articles.

Before you use Wikipedia, follow two rules of thumb. First, investigate the wealth of electronic resources available through your library. Second, ask your instructors for their thoughts about the site. Some may tell you to avoid Wikipedia altogether. Others may say that you can use it as a starting point for research on a topic, but only if you confirm the information through other sources.

Communicate Information through Writing

As you've likely seen for yourself, almost every college course includes some type of writing assignment, from essay questions and research papers to creative writing and lab reports. *Why* do instructors assign so much writing? It's not to torture you—remember, they have to read all the papers they assign! Rather, writing assignments help instructors answer two important questions: (1) Do my students understand the key concepts we're covering in class? and (2) Can they think critically about the material? You use all aspects of critical thinking—gathering, evaluating, and applying information, as well as reviewing outcomes—when you write in college. The strategies in this section can help you apply those skills to your writing assignments.

Prepare to Write

Preparing effectively for your writing assignment will help you stay on track later when you write the first draft and make revisions. As you read this section on preparation, think back to Destiny's experience. If you had fourteen days to write a paper on dictatorships, how would *you* prepare?

Clarify Your Purpose. When you understand *why* you're writing—your purpose—you can more easily organize the information and ideas in your written piece and focus on the points you want to convey. Consider these different purposes for writing:

- **To inform.** One reason for writing is to inform the reader about a particular topic. Most of your papers in college will serve this purpose, including research reports, annotated bibliographies, review papers, and lab reports.

- **To persuade.** In persuasive writing, you might start by conveying information about a topic and then seek to persuade your reader to view the topic in a particular way. Editorial assignments in a journalism class, policy papers in a government course, or advertising plans in a marketing course fit into this category.

- **To express or entertain.** In expressive writing or writing for entertainment, you convey your thoughts and ideas or tell stories to enlighten an audience. Examples include writing poems or short stories for a literature course, plays for a theater course, and song lyrics for a music course.

Make a Plan. Writing assignments often take longer than you expect, so schedule plenty of time to complete them. Plan out each part of the process: preparing, writing your first draft, revising, and polishing. As an example, see Figure 10.2, which is a schedule for a short research paper (about two to five pages). Not only does it build in time to write the first draft, but it also includes seven and a half hours of preparation (reading, researching, and outlining) and then four and a half hours of revising and polishing. While not everyone spends the same amounts of time on each part of the process, significant chunks of time are usually required for each step. Building a plan helps you manage and get the most from that time.

The Magic of Writing. Anything you write has a purpose, such as informing, persuading, or entertaining. When J. K. Rowling wrote the Harry Potter series, she set out to entertain her readers. And entertain she did—so much so that people waited in line until midnight to get the next volumes in the series. Some fans, like this one, even dressed up as characters from the books. Lisa Maree Williams/ Stringer/Getty Images

FIGURE 10.2 Sample Plan for Each Step in the Paper-Writing Process

Monday, 6:00–8:00 p.m.	**Read/Research:** Find two journal articles and two book chapters. Read and take notes from one journal article.
Tuesday, 9:00–10:00 a.m.	**Read/Research:** Read and take notes from second article.
Wednesday, 1:00–4:00 p.m.	**Read/Research:** Read and take notes from both book chapters. Find additional articles or chapters if necessary.
Saturday, 9:00–10:30 a.m.	**Outline:** Write an outline for the paper.
Sunday, 9:00–11:00 a.m.	**Write draft 1:** Use outline to write first draft.
Tuesday, 8:00–9:30 a.m.	**Revise to create draft 2:** Review and edit draft 1.
Wednesday, 1:00–3:00 p.m.	**Revise to create draft 3:** Review and edit draft 2. Ask a friend to read and provide feedback.
Thursday, 6:00–7:00 p.m.	**Polish:** Use feedback to make last edits and polish draft 3 (final draft) several days before it's due. Schedule time over weekend to celebrate hard work!
Monday, 8:00 a.m.	**Hand in final draft**

Choose a Topic. For some writing assignments, your instructor will give you a topic. For others, you can choose a topic. If you can choose your own topic and need inspiration, think about what you've found interesting in class, ask your instructor for ideas from previous terms, or talk with your classmates about how they chose a topic. You can also explore different ideas for paper topics by rereading your textbook and looking for the articles and books it cites, or by reviewing suggested readings listed in your course syllabus. Picking an interesting topic will help you stay motivated during the writing process.

Conduct Research. Researching your topic gives you a chance to put your information literacy skills to work by finding information and evaluating it. You can conduct research for all types of projects, although informative writing often requires more research than persuasive, expressive, or entertaining writing.

When you're researching, tap into the wide range of sources described earlier in this chapter, and use your critical thinking skills. Remember to evaluate what you're reading by asking yourself:

- Does the author's argument make sense?
- Is it credible?
- Are there alternative arguments worth considering?

When you evaluate information you've found through research, you point out problems with an argument or provide alternative arguments. Then, when you write your paper, you can include your questions and evaluation in the draft.

For example, let's say you're writing a short paper on drowning deaths for a public health class. You've found an article whose author claims that eating ice cream causes drowning. The author backs up this claim with numbers showing that ice-cream consumption and drowning rates increase together. If you neglected to use your critical thinking skills, you might say, "Makes sense—people eat ice cream, get cramps, and drown." But if you had your critical thinking hat on, you would be open to alternative explanations, such as this one: Both swimming (and hence drowning) and eating ice cream increase during the warmer summer months. So, although it may appear that one event causes the other, something else—the warm weather—is actually causing both events to increase. The point? Don't unthinkingly accept the viewpoints you come across in your research. Rather, think critically before you take what you read as fact.

Create an Outline. An outline helps you organize your ideas before you start writing. You can use it to sketch out the structure of your entire paper and ensure that you have all the required components of the assignment, such as an introduction, citations (if required), main and supporting ideas, and a conclusion. The sample outline in Figure 10.3 has two levels of headings, but you can add as many headings and as much detail as you want. You can also include examples or quotations that you plan to use in your paper—or you can keep it simple and leave such details for the writing step. For more on the benefits of outlining, see the Spotlight on Research.

FIGURE 10.3
Sample Outline

Title: The Value of Writing SMART Goals
I.   Introduction
     A. Personal example of setting goals
     B. Outcome of goal setting
II. Value of Goal Setting
     A. Research by Smith and Smith (2012) documenting
         the positive effect of goal setting
     B. Goal setting leads to intentional actions
III. SMART Goals
     A. Specific
     B. Measurable
     C. Achievable
     D. Relevant
     E. Time-limited
     F. Research by Jones and Marquez (2012)
         demonstrating positive effects of SMART goals
IV. Conclusion

CREATE AN OUTLINE TO IMPROVE YOUR WRITING

Can creating an outline improve the quality of your written work? According to an experiment conducted by researcher Ronald Kellogg, the answer is "yes!" In his study, college students read arguments for and against outfitting city buses with equipment to serve individuals with disabilities. Then they wrote a paper in which they expressed support for the idea. Some students were instructed to create an outline first, while others were told to just start writing. Researchers then examined the length of the paper, the time spent writing, the writing speed, and the writing quality.

What did they discover? Students who created an outline before writing

	Outline	No outline
Length of paper	+ (longer)	− (shorter)
Writing time	+ (more)	− (less)
Writing speed	+ (faster)	− (slower)
Overall quality	+ (higher)	− (lower)

Creating an outline has a positive impact on writing.

- Wrote longer papers than those who didn't create an outline (an average of 139 more words).
- Spent more time writing (about seven minutes longer).
- Wrote faster (11.3 compared to 8.5 words per minute).
- Produced papers that were rated as higher quality by two judges.

THE BOTTOM LINE

Creating an outline can result in greater productivity during the writing process and a higher-quality paper — and, therefore, improved performance in college.

REFLECTION QUESTIONS

1. How often do you create an outline before writing a paper or other assignment?
2. If you've never created an outline, will you do so in the future? Why or why not?
3. After reading about this study, what would you tell a friend about the value of outlining?

R. T. Kellogg, "Attentional Overload and Writing Performance: Effects of Rough Draft and Outline Strategies," *Journal of Experimental Psychology: Learning, Memory, and Cognition* 14 (1988): 355–65.

Writer's Block? Just Start! You've done your research and created an outline for your paper. Now it's time to write your first draft, but that blank page is terrifying. What do you do? The best way to get started is to just begin writing. Once you get a few words down, the rest will flow more easily.
Jenny Sturm/Shutterstock

Thesis: The main idea or argument of a paper or an essay.

Write Your First Draft

Once you've taken time to prepare, you're ready to write your first draft. For some students, all the preparation makes this part easy. For others, writing a draft can be intimidating or overwhelming. If you find it challenging to get started, think of writing like rolling a boulder down a hill: The hardest part is the first push to get the massive object moving. Once you put those first few words on paper, the rest of the process comes more easily. As you sit down to write, use the techniques in this section to craft a strong draft.

Develop a Thesis Statement. A **thesis** statement is the main idea or argument you want to convey, and it sets the stage for your entire paper. You can create your thesis at various points in the writing process. You might draft it during your research to organize your thoughts, and include it in your outline to provide clarity to that document. Or you might choose to write a thesis statement once your research and outline are done.

How you word your thesis depends on your writing purpose. For example, if you write a thesis statement about SMART goals, it might vary according to purpose.

- **To inform:** Learn how to set and achieve your goals using SMART criteria.
- **To persuade:** You should try SMART goals to improve your note-taking skills.
- **To express:** This is how I used a SMART goal to improve my note-taking skills and succeed in college.

Craft an Engaging Introduction. Grab your reader's attention right from the start by creating a compelling introduction to your paper. Imagine, for example, that you're writing an essay on hunger. A perfectly serviceable—but dull—introductory sentence might read: "Hunger is a serious problem in the United States." Compare that statement with this one: "One out of the next six people you meet will go to bed hungry tonight." Wouldn't that second sentence make you want to keep reading much more than the first?

Think Critically. You'll have the opportunity to demonstrate your critical thinking skills many times as you write your draft. Here are just a few examples of how you can incorporate critical thinking into the writing process.

- **Provide evidence.** Incorporate citations and ideas from your sources into your draft. A paper on poverty that simply says "poverty is bad" shows you haven't really thought about your topic. But if you include statistics on the number of children in poverty who go to school hungry each day, you'll demonstrate that you found and applied evidence. Just be sure to credit others when you use their ideas to support your point.
- **Interpret information and draw conclusions.** As you write, interpret and draw conclusions from the information you're working with, and incorporate these into your paper. For instance, suppose that a key source for your paper is an article about how national economies have become increasingly interconnected. You could think up three of your own

examples showing the impact of globalization and work these into your draft. Then, at the end of the paper, you could identify what you see as the positive or negative effects of globalization.

- **Compare and contrast.** If appropriate for the writing assignment, describe similarities and differences between topics. For instance, for a political science class, you might compare and contrast the reasons the United States entered the wars in Iraq and Afghanistan.

- **Generate new ideas.** For some writing, you'll have an opportunity to generate original ideas—for example, in forms such as poetry, essays, or short stories in an English class, or by brainstorming new ways to use an existing product or tool in a design or engineering class.

Structure Your Paragraphs Carefully. When you're writing, pay attention to how you structure each paragraph. The most common approach is to start with the main idea and then follow it with supporting ideas, examples, facts, or details. Focus on only one main idea in each paragraph; start a new paragraph as soon as you begin writing about another main idea.

Add a Conclusion. End your draft with a conclusion that pulls your thoughts together. A strong conclusion restates your thesis, revisits the major findings or recommendations of your paper, or summarizes your argument. To come full circle, you might even connect the concluding paragraph to the catchy introduction you created at the start of your paper.

Revise and Polish Your Paper

Once you've written a first draft of your paper, it's time to revise and polish it. Consider these ideas for editing and finalizing your work.

- **Include transitions.** Transitions connect your paragraphs and smooth the flow of ideas throughout your entire work. (For instance, the first sentence under the heading "Revise and Polish Your Paper" serves as a transition from the preceding section.) If your paper sounds choppy, adding transitions between paragraphs can help.

- **Use a formatting and style guide.** The MLA (Modern Language Association) and APA (American Psychological Association) have established guidelines for formatting papers and citing sources. These style guides will help you with some of the "nuts and bolts" of writing a paper—such as the format to use for the title page, line spacing, margins, paragraph indents, headings, page numbers, and citation style. Including citations is especially important for avoiding *plagiarism*, which occurs when you use someone else's work and call it your own (more on this later in the chapter). Ask your instructor or check your syllabus to determine which style guide you should use.

- **Read your paper out loud.** You can identify language that sounds awkward and then revise as needed to make your writing more fluid.

- **Have someone else read your paper.** Ask a friend or classmate to give you honest feedback. Someday you can return the favor.

- **Use campus resources.** Use any resources your school offers to help with writing. Make an appointment at the writing center, work with a tutor, or ask your instructor to review a draft of your writing.

CONNECT TO MY CLASSES

You'll use your critical thinking skills in every writing assignment in college. Select an upcoming assignment in this or another class, and write three or four sentences describing how you'll demonstrate critical thinking as you complete that assignment.

GETTING FEEDBACK ON YOUR WRITING

NAME: **Ashley J. Willey**

SCHOOLS: *Highland Community College; University of Nebraska*

MAJOR: *Advertising and Public Relations*

CAREER GOAL: *Copy Writing*

> **"I enjoy being critiqued by as many people as possible, and I find it helpful to gain multiple perspectives."**

I've learned that the best way to become a good writer is to read good books. These books inspire me to try to emulate as many styles as possible until my own style shines through. I find myself playing around with different narration styles that I would typically never have used. I'm also blessed to have had a very good English professor, who taught me how to appreciate the knowledge I've gained and encouraged me to use methods of revision that have been amazing learning tools for me.

One of the best things I've done as a writer is to attend creative writing workshops. I enjoy being critiqued by as many people as possible, and I find it helpful to gain multiple perspectives. It's important to go to your professors for their opinion, and not only to other students. Your professors are professionals who can provide you with the most experienced, educated opinion. I follow their advice to the best of my ability, until I get feedback that my work is creating the impression that I was aiming for. This allows me to learn from my mistakes and perfect my craft.

I'm comfortable building professional relationships with my professors and going to them after hours for advice. I'm not ashamed to ask for help, because I know that my professors are there for me. Many students fail to take advantage of the many resources available in the college setting because they're closed off and are so focused on their goals that they miss out on opportunities. I'm getting my degree not for me but, ultimately, for my daughter. In order to go to college, I first had to obtain my GED without the help of my daughter's father, who was not supportive of my obtaining my education. I began community college as a single mother and am now attending the University of Nebraska. I want to set the bar as high as I possibly can for my daughter.

YOUR TURN: Have you used any of the approaches that Ashley describes for improving your writing? If so, which ones? How useful have these approaches been? Have you found any other approaches helpful?

- **Polish and proofread.** Once you've revised your draft several times to address macro-level issues of structure, flow, and clarity, give your written piece a final polish. Then step away from your paper and take a break, returning with fresh eyes to revisit and proofread it carefully. Fix any spelling, grammar, and punctuation errors, and make sure it reads just as you want it to.

Write in Online Classes

You can use the strategies we've just explored to write papers in both face-to-face and online classes. However, some additional techniques can be especially helpful for writing online. Online classes are more likely to include writing assignments such as blog posts or written comments on other students' posts. Your posts and comments will be graded, so you want to make sure they're high quality. To do so, try these tips.

- Write in complete sentences. Shorthand and slang are fine for Facebook and Twitter, but use more formal and thoughtful language when writing for your online classes.

- Writing posts in online classes can feel conversational—there is a back-and-forth exchange of information—but remember that in online conversations you don't have nonverbal cues and tone to provide context, so the tone you had in mind doesn't always come through. As you type posts for online classes, read them out loud and listen to how they sound. Could readers interpret your tone in a more negative way than you intended? If so, rephrase your comments so that they're more positive and constructive.

- Pay attention to your emotions and how quickly you respond in these classes. If you're having a heated discussion on a controversial topic, consider writing out your post on a piece of paper and coming back to it twenty minutes later to make sure it conveys your message appropriately.

Avoid Plagiarism

Cheating and plagiarism are very serious issues in college, and research suggests that rates of these forms of academic misconduct are increasing.[2] In the chapter on taking exams, we explore how to approach test taking with integrity by answering questions yourself and being careful not to cheat. When it comes to writing, honest students take care to avoid **plagiarism**. Plagiarism occurs when one person uses another person's words or ideas and presents them as his or her own. In some cases, plagiarism is intentional. When a student takes a paper off the Internet, puts his or her own name on it, and turns it in, that's a clear case of plagiarism. When a student knowingly copies information into a paper without putting it in quotation marks and citing the original author of the information, that's also intentional plagiarism.

CONNECT TO MY RESOURCES
Your campus probably has a wide variety of resources that can help you improve your writing. Find and write down the name, location, and hours of a writing resource at your campus.

Plagiarism: When one person presents another person's words or ideas as his or her own.

CONNECT TO MY CLASSES

Plagiarism can have serious consequences. Examine the syllabi for your courses. Find and write down the consequences of plagiarism as listed on one of your course syllabi. List any additional consequences you can think of that aren't shown on the syllabus you've selected.

But plagiarism isn't always intentional. Let's say a student copies a sentence from a source and puts it in his paper, planning to go back later to credit the author, but then forgets. Is this plagiarism? At many schools the answer would be "yes"; often, instructors don't distinguish between intentional and unintentional plagiarism. If you do get caught plagiarizing, whether you meant to plagiarize or not, you may have to rewrite your paper. Even worse, you might automatically fail the course, have to meet with the dean of your college, or even be expelled.

We assume that since you're in college, you value your education and will honor your values by not plagiarizing intentionally. But what's your best defense against accidental plagiarism? Develop good research and writing habits: Find out how your instructors want you to use citations in your paper; use a style guide; and apply the following strategies.

- **Take notes in your own words.** When reading books, articles, or original documents, avoid copying large sections of material. Instead, paraphrase these sources (see the chapter on note taking) by taking notes in your own words, and then use these notes to write your paper. Give credit to the original author by citing the source where you got the information.

- **Use quotation marks for direct quotations.** If you use someone else's exact words, which you should do only in moderation, always use quotation marks and cite the source from which you took the quotation.

- **Keep track of where your information comes from.** You might use one color of ink to copy a sentence from a book and a different color for your own words. Be consistent so that you always know which notes and ideas are yours and which are others'.

- **When in doubt, give credit.** If you aren't sure whether you need to cite a source, err on the side of caution and include the citation to the original work.

- **At the end of your paper, include a bibliography or reference list.** This list shows that you've done research and that you're giving appropriate credit for the ideas in your paper.

- **Seek guidance.** If you have any concerns, ask your instructor or someone from the campus writing center to review your paper before it's due and give you some guidance on avoiding unintentional plagiarism.

Present in Class with Confidence

Speaking in front of a group—for a solo class presentation, for example, or as part of a team project—is a skill that colleges consider part of a well-rounded education and that employers value.[3] Just as writing a paper does, authoring and delivering a speech demonstrates your understanding of course content and also shows off your critical thinking skills: To speak intelligently about a topic, you have to gather information about it, evaluate that information, use it in your presentation, and then afterward review the outcomes of your talk—all key components of critical thinking.

As valuable a skill as public speaking is, however, for many people it's utterly terrifying. What can you do if the thought of standing in front of the class gives you stomach butterflies and sweaty palms? You can practice and build your skills to increase your confidence. It won't happen overnight, but any student can become a successful public speaker.

Know Your Purpose — and Your Audience

To begin, give yourself plenty of time to plan your presentation. Use that time to figure out the purpose of the presentation and the major points you want to make. For example, if you have to demonstrate a medical procedure in your nursing class, you may design your presentation to *inform* your audience about how to perform the procedure. If you're going to show a new smartphone application you developed in your mobile computing class, your purpose may be to *persuade* classmates that the app is worthwhile. You might even perform a one-act play to *entertain* classmates in your drama course.

To plan your presentation properly, you also need to consider your audience. Ask yourself:

- **How many people will be there?** If you're presenting to a small group (fewer than thirty people), you can move around the room and involve your audience. You can pose questions, have listeners complete tasks and report back to the larger group, or even stimulate discussion among audience members. With larger groups, this interactive style is more difficult, so you may decide to spend your time addressing the audience as a whole.

- **How much do they know about your topic?** If your topic is new to the audience, share what you've learned while researching your presentation. If your topic is covered in the textbook, your listeners probably know the basics, so use your presentation to provide new information or discuss the topic in more depth.

- **How can you capture the audience's interest?** Brainstorm ideas for grabbing your audience's attention at the start of your presentation—for example, by developing a funny (and tasteful) anecdote or joke, a personal story, or an example that will engage the audience while also setting the stage for your topic.

Craft Your Presentation

Many of the same strategies you use to write papers can also help you create presentations. Like written work, most presentations have a thesis statement, an intriguing introduction, a well-structured

Delivering a Slam-Dunk Talk. Top-notch speakers know their audience. Here, the coach of the Los Angeles Lakers is surrounded by reporters, but he knows they're only part of his audience. The other part is made up of people who read articles in which he's quoted, listen to his comments on the radio, or watch video of him on news outlets. Is he nervous? Probably a little.
© USA Today Sports

multipart argument, and a clear conclusion. As with papers, you'll develop several drafts of your presentation as you work to create the finished product.

Presentations usually use more visual aids than written pieces do, so consider what types of visuals will strengthen your message. You can use slides containing text and images (PowerPoint and Prezi are popular slide-creation tools) or physical objects that demonstrate a process (such as taking blood pressure) or clarify a key concept (such as how electrons move during a chemical reaction). As you weigh your options, pay attention to the visuals your instructors use in class, and consider your own preferences. What types of visuals capture *your* attention the most? Whatever visuals you decide to include, keep in mind that such aids work best when they convey main ideas and aren't overly complex (see Figure 10.4).

Practice Your Presentation

Fear of speaking in public is very common,[4] and practicing your presentation is the best way to become more comfortable, confident, and calm. Once you've crafted your presentation, rehearse it several times to polish the following elements of your talk:

- **Time.** Work to stay within the time limit. If you have twenty minutes to speak, for example, try keeping your talk between fifteen and seventeen minutes as you practice. That way, you'll know that your presentation isn't too short or too long, and you'll have a few minutes left for questions from your audience.

- **Voice volume.** Make sure you're speaking loudly enough. If you'll be using a microphone to give your presentation, practice talking at the same volume you'd use when sitting next to another person. If you won't have a microphone, practice speaking loudly enough so that people at the back of the room can hear you. And vary the volume and pace of your

FIGURE 10.4 **Lecture Slides: Cluttered and Clean**

A text-heavy slide (left) is more effective when it's been pared down, broken into bullets, and jazzed up with an image (right). Sergey Nivens/Shutterstock

Introduction to Human Resource Management

The first step for HR professionals is to hire new employees. After new employees are hired, the second step is to onboard these individuals. Onboarding is the process of orienting individuals to the policies and culture of the organization. After that, HR professionals are responsible for overseeing the training and development of these individuals. Another task for the HR professional is administering the pay and benefits systems as well as developing new policies and procedures related to working at the organization.

Introduction to Human Resource Management

- Essential HR functions
  - Hiring new employees
  - Onboarding new employees
  - Training and development
  - Performance management
  - Administering pay and benefits
  - Developing policies and procedures

voice to keep everyone energized—speaking in a monotone is a surefire way to put your audience to sleep.

- **Body language.** Practice showing confidence and authority through your posture and other body language. Stand up straight, make eye contact, and imagine conversing with your audience—glancing only briefly at your notes or slides if needed. Also practice using hand gestures to emphasize points, and avoid nervous gestures that will distract your audience (like tugging at your hair or wringing your hands).

To practice your presentation, consider asking trusted friends, colleagues, or classmates to watch you. They can provide feedback on how you can improve. Or record your practice sessions on your smartphone or computer and critique your own performance. It may be hard to hear critical feedback or watch yourself on video, but these techniques will help you strengthen your presentation—and boost your confidence.

Deliver a Great Presentation

When the big day arrives, you can do several things to present successfully.

- **Look the part.** Even if your appearance isn't factored into your official grade for the presentation, your instructor and audience will notice what you're wearing. So, approach class presentations as you would a job interview. Ditch the shorts and flip-flops in favor of business casual or nicer clothes. Professional apparel gives you an air of credibility and conveys to your audience that you take the assignment seriously.

- **Arrive early.** By arriving early, you'll have time to get set up and organize your presentation, notes, and any materials you plan to use.

- **Breathe and visualize.** Take deep breaths and visualize yourself being successful. Settling your nerves in advance will help you deliver a smooth presentation.

Stage-Fright Antidote. Would you give a toast at your best friend's wedding without rehearsing it beforehand? Probably not. So why would you give a class presentation without practicing it first? Rehearsing can give you the confidence you need to fight stage fright. That way, you can focus on delivering your message. Lucy Clark/Shutterstock

Harness the Power of Technology: Present Online

Increasingly, online classes require students to prepare presentations and deliver them using technology tools such as videoconferencing. Many of the strategies for giving successful presentations also apply to online presentations, but you may have to master some new technology skills to make your presentation a success—for example, adding narration to a slide presentation or setting up conferencing tools such as Skype or WebEx on your laptop. If you have concerns about using any required technology to deliver your online presentation, ask your instructor for help. And be sure to schedule some extra time during the preparation phase to try out any technology and make sure it's running smoothly.

Use Information Literacy and Communication Skills at Work

The information literacy and communication skills you build in college will be valuable assets after you graduate. Not only will you use them during the job-application process, but they're also important for accomplishing tasks and sharing your ideas with others once you're on the job.

Sell Yourself to Potential Employers

No matter what your occupation, being able to write and speaking intelligently about your own skills and experiences can help you "sell" yourself to potential employers. You'll likely need to write a résumé and a cover letter as part of the job-application process and to go on interviews. If you have weak writing and speaking skills, you'll find it hard to convince potential employers that you're the ideal candidate. In addition, many organizations ask employees to complete an annual self-evaluation, which often involves writing and presenting a summary of your accomplishments. You'll need information literacy skills in order to pull together, evaluate, and present that information.

Work with Information Effectively

Information literacy and communication skills can help you work with information effectively once you're on the job. In fact, in a recent survey employers listed oral communication, writing, and information literacy as three of the top six skills colleges should emphasize for new graduates.[5] Look at Table 10.1 for ideas about how people in various occupations might use the skills in this chapter. Then ask yourself: "How will I use them in *my* desired field?"

Communicate Your Great Ideas

Your experiences on the job can inspire you to develop big, creative ideas—for example, plans for new products that will boost sales or new processes that will increase efficiency. To showcase your creativity or share your ideas, you need to communicate them verbally or in writing. For example, if you're a software developer, you might give a presentation about how your new app will revolu-

TABLE 10.1   Using Information Literacy and Communication Skills in Different Careers

Career	Example
Nonprofit campaign manager	Research past campaigns, identify best practices used by successful campaigns, and communicate ideas for a new campaign to the project team.
Computer systems administrator	Find and evaluate software options in response to a new security threat. Write a report describing the benefits and drawbacks of each option.
Soil conservationist	Collect soil samples, analyze them, and write a report documenting your findings.
Radiologic technologist	Stay up-to-date on scanning procedures, explain them to patients, and direct patients' actions during scans.

MANAGING AND COMMUNICATING INFORMATION

NAME:	**Matt Mahler**
PROFESSION:	*Production Supervisor*
SCHOOL:	*Southern New Hampshire University*
DEGREE:	*Associate of Arts*
MAJOR:	*General Studies*

Courtesy of Matthew Mahler

Writing and communicating were among my strongest areas in college, and I continue to use these skills on the job. Before my recent promotion to Production Supervisor, I served as the Interim Production Manager at the bread factory where I work. Obtaining ingredient information, determining its quality, and creating a way to manage and then communicate that information were all skills I used to do my job.

Before I took this position, people had to guess how many ingredients to order each week, and this caused us to fall short a lot. The ordering process was also problematic, as orders were written on a form and faxed to the supplier. To improve the quality of information we were working with, I started using Excel to track our daily ingredient usage to be more precise in weekly ingredient ordering. I also changed the ordering procedure: I e-mailed our order, which eliminated the problem of lost or unreadable faxes and created a record of our weekly orders.

Closely monitoring ingredient usage also helped me communicate more effectively with the mixers. I could see when there was an overscaling of ingredients, and I had tangible data to show the mixers while I coached them. Being able to quantify the ingredients that were being overscaled into dollar amounts gave the mixers a clear picture of what was happening and how important it was to avoid waste.

Overall, managing information and then clearly communicating information to my production team and supplier helped improve the efficiency of the factory and cut our mistakes down to nearly zero.

YOUR TURN: If you're currently employed, what kinds of information do you need to find, and in what ways do you communicate that information? If you're not employed but have a particular career in mind, how will knowing how to find and communicate information help you excel in that career?

> " Clearly communicating information . . . helped improve the efficiency of the factory and cut our mistakes down to nearly zero."

tionize social networking. As an astronomer, you might write a scientific paper to detail your discovery of a distant galaxy. When you know how to express your ideas effectively, you can make a meaningful contribution to your company or organization, your community, your customers—and even your own professional development.

my personal success plan

INFORMATION LITERACY AND COMMUNICATION

Are you inspired to set a new goal aimed at improving your information literacy and communication skills? If so, the Personal Success Plan can walk you through the goal-setting process. Read the advice and examples; then sketch out your ideas in the space provided.

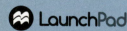 LaunchPad

To access the Personal Success Plan online, go to the LaunchPad for *Connections*.

1 GATHER INFORMATION

Think about your strengths and weaknesses related to information literacy and communication. What strategies have worked for you in the past? What could you do differently? Revisit your Information Literacy and Communication score on ACES and review the relevant sections of this chapter for additional ideas.

2 SET A SMART GOAL

Use the information you've gathered to create a SMART goal, making sure to use the SMART goal checklist.

SAMPLE: I'll create an outline for my economics paper that's due next week.

3 MAKE AN ACTION PLAN

Outline the specific steps you'll take to achieve your SMART goal, and note when you'll complete each step.

SAMPLE: I'll spend one hour this Sunday night writing my outline.

4 LIST BARRIERS AND SOLUTIONS

Think about possible barriers to your action steps; then brainstorm solutions for overcoming them.

SAMPLE: Outlines have always been hard for me. If I get stuck, I'll take my outline to the writing center on Monday and get feedback.

5 ACT AND EVALUATE OUTCOMES

Now that your plan is in place, take action. Record each action step as you take it. Then evaluate whether you achieved your SMART goal, and make any adjustments needed to get better results in the future.

SAMPLE: For this big paper I didn't leave enough time to develop my outline, so for my next assignment I'll build more time into that phase of the writing process.

6 CONNECT TO CAREER

List the skills you're building as you progress toward your SMART goal. How will you use these skills to land a job and succeed at work?

SAMPLE: Using outlines will help me organize my writing. When I become a public relations specialist, I'll use them to write effective press releases.

my personal success plan

1 my information

2 my SMART goal

☐ **S**PECIFIC   ☐ **M**EASURABLE   ☐ **A**CHIEVABLE   ☐ **R**ELEVANT   ☐ **T**IME-LIMITED

3 my action plan

4 my barriers/solutions

5 my actions/outcomes

6 my career connection

CHAPTER SUMMARY

In this chapter you learned about information literacy and communication skills. Revisit the following key points, and reflect on how you can use this information to support your success now and in the future.

- Information literacy is the ability to find, evaluate, and communicate information through writing or speaking.

- Information sources include books, journal articles, newspapers, magazines, encyclopedias, databases, and course reserves.

- Critically evaluating the quality of information involves considering whether your source is credible, objective, and current.

- Preparing to write includes clarifying your purpose, scheduling time for each step in the writing process, selecting a topic that interests you, using your information literacy skills to read and research, and creating an outline.

- A well-written piece has a clear thesis, an engaging introduction, focused paragraphs with smooth transitions, and a strong conclusion. It also meets requirements for proper formatting and citations and is polished and free from grammatical errors.

- Writing in college requires you to demonstrate your critical thinking skills by, for example, providing evidence, interpreting information, drawing conclusions, comparing and contrasting, and generating new ideas.

- In your online classes, you can communicate effectively by keeping your blog posts professional and providing constructive comments on discussion boards.

- Plagiarism occurs when one person takes credit for another person's words or ideas, accidentally or deliberately. By citing sources and developing good research and writing habits, you can avoid plagiarism.

- Creating a strong classroom presentation involves planning what you want to say, crafting the content, practicing thoroughly, and taking steps to prepare yourself the day of the presentation. In online classes, it also involves using technology tools such as videoconferencing.

- Information literacy and communication skills can help you excel in your career by enabling you to "sell" yourself during the job-application process, work with information effectively on the job, and communicate your ideas.

CHAPTER ACTIVITIES

Journal Entry

SPEAKING IN PUBLIC

Describe an experience in which you spoke in public. It might have been a persuasive speech you delivered to classmates, a sales pitch to customers, a pep talk to the soccer team, or a proposal to the city council. How did this experience affect your feelings about public speaking? What strengths do you have as a public speaker? What are your opportunities for growth as a public speaker? How can you use your college experience to enhance your public-speaking skills?

Adopting a Success Attitude

OVERCOMING WRITER'S BLOCK

For some people, negative thinking and self-doubt can create a mental block, making it difficult to even begin writing an assigned paper. If this happens to you, try using freewriting to break through this writer's block. With freewriting, you write as much as you can about a specific topic for a set period of time without any constraints. Let's give it a try.

Sit down at a computer and type your topic at the top of the page (or write it on a piece of paper). You may want to choose a topic that relates to a writing assignment for another class. Set a timer for ten minutes, and then type or write whatever comes to mind about this topic — thoughts, feelings, beliefs, questions, arguments, experiences, and so on. Don't worry about organization, grammar, punctuation, or spelling. Type or write as fast as you can, and don't stop until the timer goes off. When it does, congratulate yourself — you've overcome writer's block! Now review what you wrote. Did you generate any new ideas that might help you with your writing assignment? If not, it's okay — you may need to try freewriting a few more times to start seeing results. Don't give up on this technique after only one try!

Applying Your Skills

FINDING INFORMATION AND CITING SOURCES

For many college writing assignments, you'll need to find information in various sources and accurately cite those sources. This activity gives you practice developing these skills.

1. Identify a topic you find interesting or even controversial. For help, type "controversial essay topics" into your Web browser.

2. Locate four sources of information related to your topic. For example, sources may include books, magazine or newspaper articles, research articles from scholarly journals, and Web documents or reports.

3. Provide citations for the information sources you found. Depending on your instructor's preference, use either MLA (Modern Language Association) or APA (American Psychological Association) style to cite each source. If you need help in citing a particular type of source, consult one of the many free online tutorials or contact your school's library or writing center.

For example, let's say you chose the topic "Should Performance-Enhancing Drugs Be Accepted in Sports?" You identify as useful resources the book *Steroids: A New Look at Performance-Enhancing Drugs* by Rob Beamish and the newspaper article "There Are No Sound Moral Arguments against Performance-Enhancing Drugs" by Chuck Klosterman. Your instructor requires APA style for citations, so you cite these sources as follows:

Beamish, R. (2011). *Steroids: A new look at performance-enhancing drugs*. Santa Barbara, CA: Praeger.

Klosterman, C. (2013, August 30). There are no sound moral arguments against performance-enhancing drugs. *The New York Times*. Retrieved from http://www.nytimes.com

College Success = Career Success

PROVIDING INSTRUCTIONS EFFECTIVELY

Presentation skills can be quite valuable in the workplace, and one way you can use these skills is to train others. For example, your boss may ask you to explain to new employees how to complete a multistep task. If you break down a complicated task into small, specific steps, you'll find it easier to explain the task to others.

To practice this skill, follow these steps.

1. Find a partner, and gather two sheets of paper and a pencil.

2. Without showing your partner what you're doing, draw something simple on one piece of paper, such as two lines or an abstract shape.

3. Without showing your partner your drawing, give him or her instructions for how to draw your design on the other piece of paper. Be specific about where to begin ("Hold the piece of paper horizontally, and begin two-thirds of the way down the left-hand side of the page . . ."), and specify how long and how big to make each shape or line.

4. If your partner can't understand your instructions, ask him or her to erase part of the drawing. Then give your partner alternative instructions.

5. Once your partner is finished, compare his or her drawing against your original drawing. How well do they match?

Reflect on this activity. What did you learn from this process about giving instructions and communicating effectively?

11 Connecting with Others

Enhance Your Communication Skills

Build Emotional Intelligence

Resolve Conflict

Grow and Sustain Healthy Relationships

Embrace Diversity

Connect with Others at Work

My Personal Success Plan

Hector Mandel/Getty Images

magine how you would respond to the following scenarios:

- While your significant other is talking, your mind starts to drift. Suddenly your loved one snaps, "You never listen to me!" and stomps out.
- You review your psychology syllabus on the first day of class, and you see that there will be a group assignment. You don't know anyone else in the class.
- In a job interview, the interviewer explains that the company wants to hire employees who respect people's differences and treat each other fairly. She asks you to give examples of how well you work with people from diverse backgrounds.

If you can easily imagine an effective way to respond to each of these scenarios, you may have a natural ability to connect with other people — and to maintain those connections. And if you had difficulty responding to these scenarios? You can learn how to build and strengthen connections, even in challenging or emotionally charged situations. In fact, no matter how confident you are in your abilities, there is always room for growth, and it's worth investing the time to strengthen your skills.

Why is connecting with others so important? Because healthy connections form the foundation of a successful, satisfying life, both while you're in school and after you graduate. For example, the connection skills we explore in this chapter may help you communicate more effectively, understand and manage emotions, and resolve conflicts productively. In addition, you can use these skills to build and sustain healthy, positive relationships with a diverse array of people — from group members and instructors in college, to supervisors, colleagues, and customers in the workplace.

With that in mind, this chapter begins with a look at two vital aspects of effective communication: listening actively and speaking effectively. We then explore how to strengthen your *emotional intelligence* (including how to recognize, understand, and manage emotions in yourself and others) and manage conflict. Next, we examine how connecting with others can enhance your existing relationships, help you build new ones, and strengthen your relationships with people from different backgrounds. Finally, we consider the benefits of transferring these skills to the workplace.

Hector Mandel/
Getty Images

Reflect

On Your Connections with Others

Reflect

Take a moment to reflect on your Connecting with Others score on ACES. Find your score and add it in the circle to the right.

This score measures your beliefs about how well you connect with others. Do you think it's an accurate snapshot of your current skills in this area? Why or why not?

■ **IF YOU SCORED IN THE HIGH RANGE** and you're confident that this score is accurate, you may be great at making connections. Still, consider how you can strengthen this skill. For example, you can probably think of at least one interpersonal interaction — a job interview, a disagreement with a classmate, an argument with a loved one — that you could have handled more effectively if you had better understood and managed the emotions that arose during that interaction. As you read this chapter, you'll learn new techniques you can use to build on your current connection skills.

■ **IF YOU SCORED IN THE MODERATE OR LOW RANGE**, take action: This chapter is filled with tips and strategies you can use to connect more effectively with others. Use these approaches to boost your confidence and build rewarding relationships with the people in your life!

MY ACES SCORE

☐ **HIGH**

☐ **MODERATE**

☐ **LOW**

 LaunchPad

To find your **Connecting with Others score**, go to the LaunchPad for *Connections*.

Enhance Your Communication Skills

Communication is at the heart of connecting with others. When we communicate, we engage in a back-and-forth exchange that helps us learn information and build relationships with the people around us. In college you'll communicate with a wide variety of people, in many different situations. Some of the most important conversations will be one-on-one: For example, you might clarify concepts with an instructor, discuss project plans with a classmate, or exchange first-year survival tactics with a friend. Communication experts call this active exchange of information between two people (and sometimes more) **interpersonal communication**.

Interpersonal communication is a two-way street where each person takes turns speaking and receiving. When you're the speaker, your goal is to convey your message clearly to the person on the receiving end. When you're the receiver, your goal is to listen actively to the speaker's message and to provide short responses called *feedback* that show you've heard and understood the message — or to ask for clarification if you haven't. (See Figure 11.1.) The roles of speaker and receiver may quickly reverse if the receiver has something more substantial to contribute to the conversation.

Interpersonal Communication: An active exchange of information between two or more people.

FIGURE 11.1
Interpersonal Communication

Ideally, a speaker conveys a clear message to the receiver. The receiver hears the complete message, overcoming any barriers; interprets it accurately; and then gives the speaker feedback. The receiver may also contribute substantial content to the conversation, thus becoming the speaker. Szefei/Shutterstock

In this section we focus on your role as the receiver of information, including how to listen and how to respond when barriers to a conversation prevent you from hearing or understanding the full message. Then we touch on ways you can communicate your message effectively when you're the speaker—a topic we continue to explore throughout the chapter.

Become a Better Listener

Strange as it may seem, one of the best ways to become a good communicator isn't to speak—it's to listen. As we discuss in the chapter on note taking, during *active listening* you pay close attention to a speaker and focus on his or her message so that you can take accurate, useful notes. In interpersonal communication, active listening demonstrates your respect for others and helps you grasp their meaning when they speak. Active listening involves communicating nonverbally and providing verbal feedback.

Nonverbal Communication. Your body language says a lot about how well you're listening to another person, and the following techniques can help you stay engaged and attentive.

- **Make eye contact.** Maintain an appropriate amount of eye contact with the person who's talking. Preferred levels of eye contact vary according to culture or context, but most Americans prefer eye contact of moderate intensity—enough to show interest, but not so much that the person feels that you're staring.

- **Maintain open body posture.** Convey attentiveness by using an *open posture*—face the speaker, sit up straight, relax your shoulders, and keep

CONNECT TO MY CAREER

Ask a friend or relative to pretend to interview you for your dream job. Shake hands with the "interviewer." As you answer his or her questions, be mindful of your eye contact, body posture, and body movement. Afterward, ask for feedback on the messages you conveyed nonverbally.

your arms at your sides or folded in your lap. Avoid any temptation to cross your arms because this *closed posture* may convey irritation, anger, discomfort, or disagreement with the speaker or his or her message.

- **Watch your body movement.** Lean slightly toward the speaker to show that you're ready to listen or want to hear more. Nod occasionally to encourage the person to continue, or to convey your understanding of (or agreement with) what he or she is saying.

- **Stay focused.** Maintain your focus on what the other person is saying; for instance, try not to glance at your phone or give in to other distractions.

Provide Feedback. In addition to nonverbal communication, you can show that you're listening to someone and that you understand his or her message by providing verbal feedback.[1] Here are several ways to provide feedback effectively.

- **Give brief encouragement.** When used occasionally, brief responses such as "yes," "uh-huh," and "okay" indicate that you're paying attention to the message. (Although when used too frequently, they may give the impression that you want the speaker to hurry up and stop talking.)

- **Paraphrase.** If you summarize or *paraphrase* what the speaker said by restating it in your own words, you can check your understanding of the message ("So, what I hear you saying is . . .").

- **Manage barriers.** Interpersonal communication isn't perfect, and sometimes barriers—everything from noise to confusion to distractions—can cause communication to break down. To overcome barriers, address them tactfully by asking a follow-up question, providing information, or sharing your own insights (see Table 11.1). You may also contribute to the conversation by helping manage the other person's emotions and defuse heated situations using *emotional intelligence*, which we'll explore later in the chapter.

TABLE 11.1　**Using Feedback to Manage Communication Barriers**

Communication barrier	Examples of possible feedback
You couldn't hear what the speaker said because of a loud noise.	"Sorry, but I couldn't hear what you said. Can you explain again?"
You didn't understand what the speaker said.	"I'm not sure I get what you're saying. Can you clarify what you mean?"
You zoned out for a minute and lost track of the conversation.	"I apologize. I lost focus for a second. Could you repeat what you just said?"
The speaker seems distracted.	"I may be wrong, but you seem a bit distracted. Do you want to pick this up later, when things have calmed down?"
The speaker is telling you one thing, but his or her expression and body language convey something else.	"I know you're telling me that everything's fine, but you look sad."

"I'm Listening." When you're listening to someone else, your body posture, verbal responses, and other cues communicate how well you're receiving the speaker's message. Look at these two people: Are they listening to each other? Is their conversation going smoothly? What clues indicate how effectively they're communicating?
© Linda Winski/PhotoEdit, Inc.

Become a Better Speaker

Feedback shows that you're listening to a conversation, but what do you do when you want to communicate something more substantial—to become the speaker yourself? Throughout the rest of this chapter we'll look at specific techniques that will help you express your message thoughtfully, effectively, and honestly—during both pleasant and not-so-pleasant conversations. We begin by discussing emotional intelligence, which you can use to speak with others openly and sensitively.

Build Emotional Intelligence

Emotional Intelligence: The ability to recognize, understand, and manage your own and others' emotions.

Emotional intelligence—the ability to recognize, understand, and manage your own and others' emotions—is a critical part of communicating and connecting effectively with others (see Figure 11.2).[2] It can also help you learn about yourself and better manage how you respond to others. Thus emotional intelligence is both *inter*personal (between people) and *intra*personal (within ourselves).

To see how emotional intelligence works, let's say your friend Gustavo just broke up with his significant other. He's weeping as he tells you about the breakup, so you *recognize* that he's sad, and you might seek to *understand* the reason for his sadness by saying, "Did you think things were going better than they really were?" You might then try to help Gustavo *manage* his sadness by offering a sensitive response: "I'm so sorry, Gustavo. That must be hard. Is there anything I can do to help?"

And during conversations, recognizing, understanding, and managing your *own* emotions can also help you communicate more effectively. For example, suppose a coworker tells you excitedly that she just received the employee of the month award. You always arrive for work early and talk enthusiastically with customers, so you feel strongly that you deserve the award more than your coworker, who spends all day on her phone and takes too many breaks. You recognize that you feel unappreciated, and thanks to this understanding, you can rein in your emotional reaction and respond appropriately. Instead of shouting, "You don't deserve that award!" you can manage your emotions and politely congratulate your coworker. Later, you can look up the criteria for the award and schedule a meeting with your boss to discuss his perceptions of your work performance.

Let's take a closer look at how you can handle situations like these in healthy ways by mastering the three key elements of emotional intelligence.

FIGURE 11.2 **Components of Emotional Intelligence**

Source: Synthesized from the work of Mayer and Salovey (2008; 1997).

Recognize Emotions

The first step in exercising emotional intelligence is recognizing emotions—identifying what you or another person is feeling and labeling it.[3] Is it sadness? Excitement? Anger? Embarrassment? Joy?

Your Emotions. To better recognize your own emotions, there are a number of strategies you can try, including the following:

- Find and use words that designate emotions. Google "feeling word list," and select specific words that describe how you feel. Avoid generic words such as *happy*, *sad*, *mad*, and *glad*—instead choose words that depict the intensity of your emotions. For example, if you're unhappy, would you describe yourself as *slightly disappointed* or *completely devastated*?

- Consider how your body is reacting physically to an emotion. Is your heart pounding? Are you sinking in your chair? Are you becoming hot? Clenching your teeth? Getting teary-eyed? Physical responses can provide clues to our feelings.

In some cases, you might have various conflicting feelings about the same situation, and that's okay—feelings are complicated. However, denying feelings (especially negative ones) can cause problems. For example, if you're stressed out and you don't recognize it, you can't manage the stress. As a result, you might develop headaches, high blood pressure, or ulcers; feel overwhelmed or unmotivated at school or work; or start experiencing conflict in your personal relationships. Recognizing that you feel stressed is the first step to doing something *about* that stress.

Others' Emotions. There are also strategies you can use to recognize emotions in other people. For example:

- Ask the person what he or she is feeling.

- Pay attention to what others tell you. Notice when someone says he or she is feeling "excited," "thankful," "sad," or "frazzled."

- Notice what the person's body language seems to be saying. If a friend says he's "fine" but he's wringing his hands, you might conclude that he's actually feeling nervous or worried.

CONNECT TO MY EXPERIENCE

Select a strong feeling you've had today (good or bad) and rate the intensity of this feeling on a scale of 1 (low intensity) to 10 (high intensity). As you reflect on this feeling, record your reactions. What thoughts or words do you associate with this emotion? What physical reactions?

Name That Emotion. When you're trying to recognize the emotions that another person is feeling, look at their gestures, facial expressions, and other clues. What emotion do you think the people in the photo on the left are experiencing? What about the person on the right? What cues led you to arrive at your interpretations? *Left:* © DreamPictures/Blend Images/Corbis *Right:* wavebreakmedia/Shutterstock

Paralinguistics:
Changes in the voice
(such as volume or pitch)
that convey emotion.

- Pay attention to **paralinguistics**—changes in the voice that convey emotion. When people are angry or anxious, for example, their throat muscles may tense up, giving their voice a higher pitch. If they're excited, their voice might get louder.

Understand Emotions

Once you've recognized your own emotions or those of another person, the next step is to understand why these feelings are occurring. Then you can manage the emotions effectively.

Your Emotions. When it comes to understanding your own emotions, let's start with an example: Suppose you just got your paper back in English class, saw that you got a D, and reacted by feeling angry. To better understand yourself, ask "Why do I feel this way? What's making me angry?" Maybe you think you're angry at your instructor because you believe you deserved a B, and the grade you got makes you wonder whether your instructor respects you. As you reflect more deeply, though, you may realize what's actually happening: You're really angry at *yourself* for not putting more effort into your work.

Understanding where your feeling of anger comes from can help you think before you act. That way, you can manage the emotion and respond constructively to the situation. For instance, if you conclude that you're angry at yourself for not putting more effort into your work, you'll probably adopt more effective strategies the next time you write a paper for class—rather than storming into your instructor's office and demanding to know why she doesn't respect you.

Empathy: The ability
to understand another
person's emotions.

Others' Emotions. When you understand another person's emotions, you have **empathy** for that person, even if you haven't had the same experience that triggered that person's emotion. For example, suppose your coworker Rashida tells you she just completed her first marathon. You hate running and have never completed a marathon. But by imagining yourself in her shoes or recalling an experience you've had that gave you a similar sense of accomplishment, you can feel some of the same pride and excitement that Rashida is feeling. And that empathy can help you respond appropriately, with feedback such as "That's great news, Rashida! You must feel fantastic about achieving your goal!"

Manage Emotions

In the personal and financial health chapter, we explore how to manage stress, depression, and anxiety so that they don't affect your academic performance. In this section we focus on managing the emotions you might have toward a speaker, as well as the emotions of those around you.

Your Emotions. How can you manage your own strong emotions? As an example, let's take another look at anger. If you find yourself getting angry with someone because of something he or she said, what can you do? Once you *recognize* your anger and *understand* where it comes from, you can manage it using a number of techniques.

- Take a deep breath and count to ten.
- Use empathy to put yourself in the other person's shoes, or ask the other person questions to try to understand his or her perspective.
- Calmly let the person know you're reacting intensely to what he or she is saying.
- Take a brisk five-minute walk to blow off steam.

These tactics can help dial down the intensity of your emotion, enabling you to think more clearly and respond more appropriately to the situation.

Others' Emotions. When you see other people experiencing strong emotions, you can help them manage these feelings in a sensitive and respectful way. Your goal is not to change or control what they feel but to provide empathy and, if appropriate, to help them work through their feelings or connect them with professional resources. The following strategies may be useful.

- Let them know you recognize that they may be having a hard time.
- Invite them to share their feelings with you, and listen to them actively.
- Put yourself in their shoes and provide a compassionate response.
- If you've had a similar feeling or experience, share it and let them know what helped you through it.
- Instill hope that their situation can change.
- Offer assistance and connect them to appropriate campus or community resources if needed.

Managing emotions is a key step toward resolving interpersonal conflicts and restoring healthy connections between yourself and others—a topic we'll turn to now.

CONNECT TO MY RESOURCES

Let's say that your classmate, who is going through a difficult breakup, has been feeling sad and lonely. Research and record the resources that are available on your campus to help this student. How might you suggest in a sensitive way that this person contact these resources?

Boiling Mad? If you don't effectively manage your emotions (especially negative ones), they can boil over—triggering unproductive responses that just worsen the situation that initially upset you. Are you "boiling mad" about something someone said? If so, adopt the emotion-management strategies that work best for you—even if it's just taking a quick walk to let off steam. KC Slagle/Shutterstock

Resolve Conflict

Conflict arises when two or more people disagree. Disagreeing with a friend about which movie to see, disputing your grade on a pop quiz, receiving a customer complaint—these and many other types of disagreement can lead to conflict, which makes it an inevitable—and normal—part of life. But not all conflict is the same. In cases where the disagreement is minor, for example, the incident may end with a quick compromise. In cases where you feel that compromising would go against your values, on the other hand, the conflict may be harder to resolve.

Conflict can be scary, and we all deal with it in different ways. Some people deny there's a problem or give in to the other person to maintain harmony. On the opposite end of the spectrum are those who fight ferociously for what they believe in or compete to "win" every time. But the ideal outcome of any conflict is a resolution that's agreeable to everyone involved. Such resolutions often require collaboration among the parties.

As we saw earlier, communicating effectively and honing your emotional intelligence can help you work through difficult situations. But you can also use assertiveness and "I" statements.

Assertiveness — or Aggression?
Assertive behaviors help you express your thoughts and feelings and pose questions in respectful ways. Assertiveness works far better than aggression in interpersonal conflict because it invites honest conversation rather than triggering defensiveness. Considering the aggressive stance these two men have adopted, do you think they'll resolve their conflict productively? *Koji Aoki/Aflo/Getty Images*

Be Assertive

Being *assertive* means stating your thoughts, feelings, and opinions and advocating for yourself without disrespecting others or their views. Although being assertive can be daunting, it's good for your mental health and your relationships.[4] For example, by letting an instructor know you need help in his or her class, you can gain access to resources that will help you succeed. By asking your boss for clarification on a work assignment, you can complete the assignment more effectively. By telling your romantic partner you want more intimacy, you can start a conversation in which you both brainstorm ways to feel more connected.

Assertiveness differs from *passivity*, in which people keep their thoughts and feelings to themselves to "avoid causing trouble." Some situations call for passivity. For example, at the funeral of someone you thought was dishonest, it would be inappropriate to express your opinions about that person. However, your ideas, opinions, feelings, and needs matter. If you don't speak up for yourself in situations where doing so is appropriate, your needs may go unmet.

Assertiveness also differs from *aggression*, which involves humiliating, criticizing, blaming, attacking, or threatening others. Aggressive communicators provoke feelings of fear or dislike. By contrast, assertive communicators are respectful. They take responsibility for getting their needs met, address issues as they arise, and speak openly and honestly.

To be an assertive communicator, you must first value yourself and know and respect your own feelings and opinions. Not everyone will like what you have to say, but by being honest, you'll likely earn their respect. Consider these assertiveness strategies.

- Before making a request, know what you want to ask for.
- Show confidence in your feelings and opinions by making eye contact with others and demonstrating confident nonverbal behavior, such as an open posture.
- Speak clearly and concisely. Emphasize the key points you're communicating.
- If you're making a statement, end it with a downward inflection in your voice. Ending with an upward inflection will make your statement sound like a question, signaling uncertainty.
- If you didn't do anything wrong, don't apologize.
- Remind yourself that you have the right to say "no" and to change your mind.
- Take the strongest stance on issues that matter most to you. For less significant issues, practice the vital art of knowing when to let it go.

Use "I" Statements

Statements beginning with "I" show that you're taking ownership of your thoughts and feelings—such as "I felt hurt when you didn't respond to my text" or "I think I'm confused by your behavior." By using "I" statements, you express your thoughts and feelings clearly, honestly, and constructively[5] and create a respectful environment in which you can explain how something the other person said or did has affected you. During disagreements or conflicts, "I" statements give the receiver the chance to respond or clear up any misunderstanding and give the speaker a chance to request the receiver's help in finding a solution.

For example, suppose Petra, your housemate, keeps leaving dirty dishes in the sink before heading off to work. You're angry, and your first impulse is to say, "You're such a slob" or "You're the most inconsiderate person I know."

"So Much for Crashing on the Couch." You just got home after a tough day at school and work. You go to crash on the couch—and find yet another pile of laundry left by your housemate. You're furious. What "I" statements could you make to productively express your feelings about the situation and arrive at a solution that works for both of you? Africa Studio/Shutterstock

Such blaming or judging statements tend to make others defensive.[6] Instead, you might say calmly: "I get frustrated when you leave dirty dishes in the sink because I feel like I have to spend extra time scraping them off, and it's harder for me to get to school on time. I'd like to talk about this so we can find a solution." By sharing your feelings, Petra has a chance to reflect on her behavior and how it affects you. She may feel motivated to start rinsing the dishes herself, but if not, you might respectfully suggest a solution: "Perhaps we could each be responsible for washing our own dishes. What if we agree to do this at least four times a week?"

Use All Your Skills to Resolve Conflicts

Together, being assertive, using "I" statements, and drawing on the other skills you've learned about in this chapter (active listening, providing feedback, exercising emotional intelligence) can help you resolve conflicts. The following process, which incorporates each of these skills, shows you how.

1. **Identify the problem.** Use active listening to pinpoint the nature of the conflict. Then assertively state your perspective of it ("It seems to me that we disagree about who should do which parts of this project"). If several people are involved in the conflict, let all the participants provide their own perspective on what the problem is. Convey your understanding of their perspective by providing feedback.

2. **Understand your emotions.** Identify the feelings you're experiencing. If they're intensely negative, use your emotional intelligence to understand and manage them. Then provide an "I" statement to communicate your feelings ("I'm feeling frustrated by our inability to create a clear plan for this project, because without a plan we could do sloppy work and miss the deadline").

3. **Understand others' emotions.** Empathize with others or ask questions to better understand the feelings of those who disagree with you ("What's causing you to feel upset by what I'm proposing?").

4. **Investigate others' viewpoints.** Ask questions to better understand others' perspectives ("How did you arrive at your thoughts about who should do the various parts of the project?").

5. **Find common ground.** Identify points of agreement ("I know we all want to submit a well-done project on time").

6. **Stay positive.** Frame the conflict as a problem that needs to be solved—not an indication of poor character or incompetence on the part of those who disagree with you ("Let's fix this situation together" versus "What's wrong with you people?").

7. **Involve others in creating the solution.** Ask everyone involved in the conflict to brainstorm possible solutions. List the potential solutions and talk about each one, with the goal of identifying one that everyone can accept and support.

8. **Compromise if necessary.** If it's impossible to arrive at a solution that pleases everyone, see which participants are willing to compromise for the sake of moving forward. Implement the compromise, and thank them for helping the group make progress.

Grow and Sustain Healthy Relationships

All the connection skills we've discussed so far—effective communication, emotional intelligence, conflict resolution—have an overarching purpose: helping you build and sustain healthy relationships while you're in college. These relationships are important because to succeed in school, you need a strong *social support network*—a group of people who encourage you when things get tough and join in celebrating your accomplishments. This network can include people outside of school, as well as classmates, faculty members, members of study groups, and people you meet in campus clubs, professional organizations, or even online. In this section we look at how to connect with the important members of your social support network.

Connect with Classmates

Getting to know your classmates can help you build a network of people who—whether they become good friends or just study partners—can keep you motivated and connect you to information and other resources you need to succeed in class.

To forge connections in face-to-face classes, notice which students seem motivated to learn. Strike up a conversation with these students before or after class, and ask if they might be interested in organizing a study group.

If you're taking an online class, look for opportunities to get to know your classmates. For example, some online classes may require students to introduce themselves in a discussion forum and respond to one another's introductory posts. And online classes often provide separate discussion forums in which students can get to know each other and share resources related to the class, the college, or other common interests.

Connect with Instructors

When you feel connected to your instructors, you'll feel more comfortable asking them for help. And when they know you, they'll be more likely to give you career advice, point you to internship or job opportunities, and write you letters of recommendation. So try chatting with your instructors before class, after class, or during their office hours—although take care to maintain an appropriate degree of professionalism in these conversations. Telling an instructor you saw a great concert last night is fine. Describing how wild and crazy you got at the concert, on the other hand, is not.

Getting to Know You. . . . Meeting classmates is a great way to start building a network of people who can support you and connect you to the resources you need to succeed in school. So take every opportunity strike up conversations with fellow students. Who knows? Some may become lifelong friends. John Giustina/Getty Images

**CONNECT
TO MY CLASSES**

Which of your current instructors seem most approachable? Why? For those who don't seem approachable, forge a connection by visiting them during their office hours or contacting them by e-mail. Then write a short paragraph about your experience, including how it affected your impressions of these instructors.

And keep in mind that you communicate with your instructors not only with conversation but also with your nonverbal behavior. In a face-to-face class, getting to class on time, sitting near the front of the room, making eye contact, shutting off your phone (no texting), and taking notes shows your respect for your instructors and your interest in the class material. And in an online course, your instructor will assess other aspects of your communication, including the quality and frequency of your discussion board posts and your e-mail etiquette. Be sure to follow the guidelines in the following box when crafting e-mails to your instructors.

HOW TO COMMUNICATE WITH YOUR INSTRUCTOR VIA E-MAIL

1. Use the subject line to indicate the content and purpose of your e-mail ("Question about deadline extension for English literature paper").

2. Address your instructor formally by his or her appropriate title — for example, "Dear Dr. Jones. . . ."

3. If you don't know the instructor personally, explain who you are. For example, "I am a student in your 8:00 a.m. English literature class."

4. Be courteous in your tone, even if you're stating a complaint.

5. Use complete sentences, proper sentence structure, and correct spelling and grammar. Proofread your message and use the spell checker before you hit "Send."

6. Keep your message brief and to the point. If something requires a long explanation, set up an in-person meeting.

7. Never use all capital letters in an e-mail. That's considered shouting.

8. Review your e-mail to make sure you've included all relevant details and any required attachments.

Connect with Your Campus Community

Connecting with the larger campus community is another great way to meet people and build relationships. Your school may have a number of student-led clubs and organizations to fit your interests, values, and affiliations — everything from a Ballroom Dance Club and a Campus Vegetarian Society to a Korean American Student Association and an Accounting Club. Additionally, you may want to get involved in student government to develop leadership skills or join other student organizations that provide services to the local community, such as Big Brothers Big Sisters. Your college may even offer classes that combine classroom instruction with volunteer experience in the community, called **service learning**. With so many opportunities, your options for meeting and connecting with other people are endless!

Service Learning:
Classes that combine classroom instruction with volunteer experience in the community.

spotlight on **research**

THE VALUE OF GETTING INVOLVED ON CAMPUS

You may be thinking, "Joining a campus club sounds fun, but I need to focus on getting good grades." Absolutely, you need to fulfill your obligations, but research shows that getting involved on campus has benefits. Let's look at one study.

Researchers at a large state college tracked the extracurricular activities of almost 15,000 first-year students to determine how active involvement on campus related to their grades and how long they stayed in college. The students were divided into two groups: those who participated in extracurricular activities (student clubs, student government, orientation) at least once during their college career and those who never participated in any extracurricular activities. Of those who participated, 64 percent were involved in one activity, 24.8 percent in two activities, and 11.2 percent in three to eight activities. The researchers discovered some interesting facts.

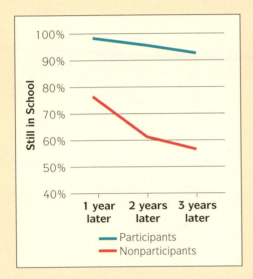

In this study, students who participated in campus activities remained in school at higher rates after one, two, and three years than students who didn't participate in campus activities.

■ Students who participated in campus activities achieved higher cumulative GPAs than those who didn't.

■ Students who participated in campus activities remained in college at higher rates than those who didn't.

Why might this be so? Other research provides some clues. First, getting involved on campus can make college more fun and interesting, thus motivating students to invest more time and energy into their studies.[7] Second, participation in campus activities can help students connect with others on campus, increase their social support network, and develop confidence and social skills—which in turn may make it easier to ask for help from instructors, advisers, or other college resources.[8] Finally, feeling like a valued member of the campus community may instill a sense of pride and belonging that further serve as motivation.

THE BOTTOM LINE

Participation in campus activities is associated with academic success and staying in school—just two of the many benefits of getting involved.

REFLECTION QUESTIONS

1. Do you currently participate in any campus activities or organizations? Why or why not?
2. How could joining a campus organization help you succeed academically?
3. How could joining a campus organization be good for your career?

J. Wang and J. Shiveley, *The Impact of Extracurricular Activity on Student Academic Performance* (Sacramento: California State University, Sacramento, Office of Institutional Research, 2009).

Connect with Others Online

Joining online communities and networks that fit your interests and needs can also help you build relationships.[9] For example, through social media sites such as Facebook and Twitter and professional networking sites such as LinkedIn, you can meet others and stay connected through activities like wall posting, picture sharing, and instant messaging. If you want to meet people who share your interests, you can join an online discussion forum. If you want to make changes in your life, such as losing weight or stopping drinking, you can join an online support group.

But use caution in your interactions with online communities. In particular, reflect on what you're posting. Five years from now, would you be embarrassed by the photo of yourself you just shared? If a potential employer saw the image, could it jeopardize your chances of getting your dream job? (Yes, some recruiters will search your name on the Web.) And think critically about others' posts, including their trustworthiness: Is the information accurate? Is its source reliable and respectable? Finally, if you arrange a face-to-face meeting with someone you met online, practice personal safety: Let someone else know about the meeting, get together in a public place, and consider bringing a friend along with you.

Stay Connected with Friends and Family

It takes time and effort to maintain relationships, but even as a busy college student you can use active listening, emotional intelligence, and assertiveness skills to show the people in your life *off* campus just how special they are. Here are a few strategies for preserving meaningful relationships with friends and family while in college.

- Stay connected with your loved ones through e-mail, texting, Facebook, phone calls, or face-to-face visits.
- Actively listen to any concerns or fears they might have for you.
- Share your hopes and dreams with them.
- Let them know how they can support you emotionally while you're in school.
- Invite them to campus or show them your online coursespace so that they feel they're part of your college experience.
- Communicate your needs assertively. Don't assume they can read your mind.
- Develop empathy—try to understand what it's like for them to spend less time with you.
- Let minor disagreements go.
- If tensions build, address the issue in a calm, respectful way using "I" statements.
- Try to negotiate mutually beneficial solutions to any conflicts that arise.

MAINTAINING RELATIONSHIPS

NAME:	**Samuel Caleb Stumberg**
SCHOOL:	*Montana State University, Billings*
MAJOR:	*History Education*
CAREER GOAL:	*Teaching*

Courtesy of
Samuel Caleb
Stumberg

Working part-time, going to college full-time, and maintaining a social life is anything but easy. Balancing my relationships, work, and school is what has helped me get through the tough times. Family and friends are extremely important; they provide support, love, and joy. However, maintaining relationships and doing well in school require good communication skills and the ability to make time for others.

I try to make as much time for my friends and family as I can. I like to get coffee with my friends in between classes or go on runs with them. Playing games is always fun — anything that can bring people together. I live far away from my family, so it's difficult to stay in touch with them. I try to call them once a week, for an hour or so, to catch up.

Maintaining relationships isn't all fun and games, though. Recently, some problems arose with my roommates. We said things that we didn't mean, and it seemed like our friendships would end. One of our main problems was that we weren't all in the same room; we were relying on texting for most of our communication. Texting is a terrible form of communication because you can't see the other person or communicate emotion.

Eventually, we were able to resolve our problem. We dropped the fighting and started to speak more assertively. We found that it was better to be respectful to the people with whom you're discussing an issue. Use your words wisely and aim your criticisms at the topic, not the person. When we started communicating like adults, we realized how childish our disagreement was. We apologized to one another, and things were settled. I learned that if you want to maintain friendships, sometimes you have to bite your tongue.

YOUR TURN: Have you ever had a disagreement with important people in your life, as Caleb did with his roommates? If so, what did you learn from this experience? What approaches seemed most (or least) useful for managing the disagreement and maintaining the relationship? Do you agree with Caleb that texting is a poor form of communication? Have you used it successfully?

> " **Balancing my relationships, work, and school is what has helped me get through the tough times.** "

Embrace Diversity

In school and at work, you'll have many opportunities to build relationships with a diverse array of people, many of them different from you in any number of ways. Some of these differences might be visible, such as gender, skin color, age, and physical ability. Other differences may not be immediately apparent, such as income, religious affiliation, ethnicity, and sexual orientation.

The term **diversity** refers to characteristics or attributes that make us different from one another and that can be the basis for membership in a group. Differences make us unique, and they make the world a more vibrant and interesting place. Imagine how boring life would be if everyone was exactly the same!

In this section we explore many types of diversity you'll encounter in life. We also consider the importance of respecting others' experiences and appreciating what makes them who they are. Finally, we look at how thinking critically about your own actions and attitudes can help you build strong relationships with people of all kinds.

Diversity:
Characteristics or attributes that make us different from one another and that can be the basis for membership in a group.

Recognize Differences

If you were asked to describe yourself, what would you say? Would you talk about physical characteristics, such as your hair color or height? Would you mention your age, where you grew up, or your life goals?

When we describe ourselves, we can draw from many characteristics—physical appearance, personality traits, interests, family background, values, skills, and many more. All of us are *multidimensional*—we're defined by many different aspects of our identity. As you think about the diversity you see on your campus, at work, and in your personal life, reflect on the characteristics that make us unique and shape our experiences. Just some of the many characteristics are listed in Table 11.2.

Respect Differences

When you meet students and instructors in your classes, colleagues at work, or people in your personal life, they bring with them diverse experiences, backgrounds, beliefs, and opinions. You can build relationships with and learn from them by practicing *tolerance*: acknowledging, valuing, and respecting what makes them different from you and from one another. When you're tolerant, you may not always agree with someone, but you try to understand his or her perspective by showing empathy and "agreeing to disagree." Being tolerant means treating people with dignity and respect, accepting that not everyone thinks or acts like you, and recognizing that diversity adds richness and color to life.

Unfortunately, some people look down on or even mistreat those who are different from them. Such reactions can occur if a person has inaccurate beliefs about a particular group or has had a negative experience with a member of a group and then generalizes that experience to the larger group ("I don't trust teenagers because a teenager vandalized my car last year"). Lack of exposure to a particular group can also cause such reactions because people can be suspi-

TABLE 11.2 Common Elements of Diversity

Element	Description	Did you know?
Race	A way to classify people into groups according to physical characteristics such as skin color, hair color, facial features, and body build.	Guessing someone's race based on physical features is risky because appearances may be deceiving. Further, many people are multiracial, which may not be clear from physical appearance alone.
Ethnicity	A way to identify a group of people with a common ancestral heritage and, often, a shared history and culture (language, traditions, food, clothing styles, values, beliefs, art, literature).	In the United States, people who identify as Hispanic or Latino (from places such as Mexico, Puerto Rico, and Cuba) are the largest and fastest-growing ethnic group.[10]
Gender	Refers to characteristics that a society or culture defines as masculine or feminine. Gender is different than *sex*, which refers to biological rather than cultural differences.[11]	Gender can also refer to one's own experience of being a man or a woman (gender identity), how a person presents him- or herself to the world (gender expression), or expectations others have for an individual based on their perception of the person's gender (gender roles).[12]
Sexual orientation	Refers to an enduring pattern of attraction to others, such as persons of the opposite sex (heterosexuality), the same sex (homosexuality), or both sexes (bisexuality).[13]	You may never know someone's sexual orientation unless the person tells you. If someone shares his or her sexual orientation with you, don't assume that it's been shared with everyone else.
Mental and physical ability	Refers to a person's ability to perform one or more major life activities, such as caring for oneself, walking, speaking, breathing, and thinking.	Mental or physical impairments, or disabilities, can limit someone's ability to perform major life activities. Sometimes it's clear that someone has a disability (such as when a person uses a wheelchair). Other times, the disability isn't so visible (such as when a person has dyslexia).
Religion	An organized system of spiritual beliefs, traditions, and practices agreed upon by a group of individuals.	Many colleges offer classes on world religions. These classes can be a great way to learn more about different belief systems.
Socioeconomic status	Refers to social standing or prestige based on income, occupation, or education.[14]	Visible status symbols, such as the way a person dresses, don't always accurately reveal socioeconomic status. Some wealthy people spend modestly, for instance, while some people in financial straits spend lavishly to build their image.
Age	Indicates how old a person is, which determines the social, political, economic, and technological events the individual is exposed to in his or her lifetime.	Terms such as *Baby Boomers* (born 1946–1964), *Generation X* (born early 1960s to early 1980s), and *Millennials* (born early 1980s to early 2000s) are used to classify people who were born during different time periods.

Diversity's Power. Why should you embrace diversity and treat others who are different from you with respect and appreciation? By doing so, you can learn a lot and forge mutually beneficial connections. Those connections make life far richer — and more interesting — than it would be if you associated only with people who are exactly like you. © Tim Pannell/Corbis

cious of what's unfamiliar. These reactions play a part in *stereotyping*, or assigning real, imagined, or exaggerated characteristics (negative or positive) to all members of a particular group — for example, "All American tourists are rude" or "Everyone from the East Coast is well educated."

Treating people less favorably based on their membership in a particular group is called **discrimination**. For example, it's considered discrimination if a manager avoids hiring well-qualified job candidates because of their age (*ageism*), race (*racism*), gender, religion, or sexual orientation. Colleges and workplaces have established policies against all forms of discrimination, so report any incidents of discrimination you witness. Doing so will help make these environments safe places for diverse ideas, interests, beliefs, opinions, and lifestyles. If you've ever experienced discrimination, you know firsthand how important it is to combat it.

Discrimination:
Treating people less favorably because of their membership in a particular group.

Think Critically about Differences

Thinking critically about yourself and others is vital to building relationships with people who are different from you. It can help you appreciate their perspectives, empathize with them, and develop new viewpoints. Let diversity enrich your relationships by using these strategies.

- **Know yourself.** Consider the components of your own identity. What makes you visibly different from other students? What differences would people learn about only by getting to know you? How have these differences influenced the person you are today?

- **Know your biases.** Ask yourself whether you feel uncomfortable talking or working with any groups of people. If so, what might have caused this discomfort? How might your own background and life experiences have influenced these feelings?

- **Gain information.** Learn more about people who are different from you, including how their group has been treated throughout history. For example, take a class such as Men and Masculinity or Comparative Religions. Attend public events offered by your school, such as a Martin Luther King Jr. celebration. Learn how to create a safe space for lesbian, gay, bisexual, transgender, queer, and questioning (LGBTQQ) individuals by attending a Safe Zone Training Program.

- **Seek personal contact.** The more you interact with people who have different backgrounds, the more comfortable you'll feel. Talk together about the same things you would discuss with other friends. Explore what you have in common. Discover how you differ, and identify what's interesting or valuable about those differences.

- **Be open to feedback.** As you interact more with people who are different from you, you may unintentionally offend them through word or action. If this happens, use active listening to understand their viewpoint, and remain open to their feedback. Apologize, and thank them for the opportunity to learn from the experience.

- **Advocate.** Use your assertiveness skills to stand up for others whom you see being treated unfairly because of something that makes them different. Let people know that you don't want to hear offensive language, jokes, stereotypical remarks, or insults directed toward a particular group of people, including any groups you're a member of. Report illegal discrimination, hate crimes, and other abuse to authorities.

Forge Positive Connections. Spending quality time with people who have different experiences than you is a great way to get to know them and appreciate their unique perspectives and backgrounds. © Jim Marshall/ The Image Works

Connect with Others at Work

Connecting with others not only benefits you in college but is also crucial to career success. When you know how to build and maintain healthy, positive relationships with other people in a work setting, you're more likely to get the job of your dreams—and then excel at it once you're hired.

Impress an Interviewer or Employer

Try these tips for making a good impression when you're looking for a job and once you've joined an organization's ranks.

- **Ace the interview.** Arrive early for a job interview, make good eye contact, and use a firm handshake to communicate your interest, enthusiasm, and respect. In addition, listen actively to the interviewer, ask relevant questions, and clearly state your skills and career goals.

  - **Maintain professionalism through social media.** Be aware that potential employers may review your posts on social media to assess your professionalism, integrity, and ethics, so make sure they'll like what they see if they access your profile.

  - **Leverage your existing relationships.** Relationships you've already built can help you get a job. For instance, a classmate might know of a job opening that interests you. Or your instructors may give you letters of recommendation to share with interviewers.

  - **Further your career.** Once you have a job, use your connection skills to advance in your career. For example, to negotiate a raise with your boss, use assertiveness to explain what value you bring to the organization and why you deserve a pay increase. Or clearly describe your career goals, including a promotion you're eyeing, and ask for "stretch assignments"—challenging work that lets you build the skills needed for the higher-level role you want.

The Workplace Connection. Connecting with others at work can help you collaborate productively with your colleagues, boss, and employees (if you're a manager). Result? Workers deliver their best performance on the job. Productive connections at your job can also help you advance your career and forge enduring friendships. Chicasso/ Getty Images

Work Effectively with Colleagues

In a work setting, differences in personality, goals, work styles, and ability can spark disagreements. Supervisors know that conflict can erode productivity, so they expect coworkers to get along. The skills laid out in this chapter can help you manage these conflicts. Here are some suggestions.

- **Bridge cultural gaps.** Your colleagues or clients may come from many places around the globe. Learn about their homeland and customs, such as holidays and cuisine. If you sense that you may have offended someone unintentionally, apologize and ask for feedback on your behavior. Use this feedback to improve. And if someone unintentionally offends you, use "I" statements to gently enlighten him or her.

- **Offer feedback sensitively.** At some point in your career, you may be asked to supervise someone or manage a project. In this role you'll need to give others feedback so that they can improve their performance. To provide such feedback, let them know what they're doing well before offering

BUILDING RELATIONSHIPS

NAME:	**Carlos Robles**
PROFESSION:	*Research Assistant*
SCHOOL:	*Loyola University Chicago*
DEGREES:	*Associate of Arts; Bachelor of Science*
MAJORS:	*Secondary Education; Spanish*

Building interpersonal relationships has been critical in helping me to grow as a professional. One of the reasons I was able to get my first job was because of relationships I had built in college. I learned of the job opening through a classmate, and several of my professors had worked there, so they provided strong recommendations that helped me get the job.

Building interpersonal relationships has also helped me further my education. When I decided to go back to college to work on my master's degree in public policy, I called upon professors from my undergraduate years and asked them to write me letters of recommendation. I also relied on my professors and the executive director at a former job to help me explore career options and where to go for grad school. These connections have been instrumental in helping with my career search.

Now that I'm in grad school I continue to build meaningful working relationships that might help me in the future. Right now I work at the National Center for Institutional Diversity doing research on how to increase access to higher education. In my job, I develop programs that bring prominent speakers to campus to talk about educational equality. Not only am I learning from these amazing professionals, I'm also building relationships with very well-known speakers who might be great connections later in my career.

YOUR TURN: If you're employed, did you leverage relationships to learn about your current job opportunity and to get the job? If so, how? If you're currently seeking a particular job, how might your existing relationships help you?

> " **Building interpersonal relationships has been critical in helping me to grow as a professional.** "

criticism. And frame your feedback in terms of behavior they can change ("I need you to arrive at meetings on time") versus a character attack ("You don't care about this project"). Offer support and suggestions for how they can make the desired change in behavior.

- **Avoid gossip.** It's fun to talk and laugh with people at work, but try to steer clear of office gossip. Gossip erodes morale and can get you in trouble. So talk about entertaining topics with your coworkers, but don't repeat confidential news or make fun of others behind their back.

my personal success plan

Are you inspired to set a new goal related to connecting with others? If so, the Personal Success Plan can walk you through the goal-setting process. Read the advice and examples; then sketch out your ideas in the space provided.

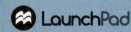

To access the Personal Success Plan online, go to the LaunchPad for *Connections*.

1 GATHER INFORMATION

Think about your strengths and weaknesses in connecting with others. What strategies have worked for you in the past? What could you do differently? Revisit your Connecting with Others score on ACES and review the relevant sections of this chapter for additional ideas.

2 SET A SMART GOAL

Use the information you've gathered to create a SMART goal, making sure to use the SMART goal checklist.

SAMPLE: Starting next Monday, I'll use "I" statements whenever a disagreement arises between me and someone else.

3 MAKE AN ACTION PLAN

Outline the specific steps you'll take to achieve your SMART goal, and note when you'll complete each step.

SAMPLE: During all my interactions with others next week, I'll notice if I'm using blaming or accusatory language and will reframe my comments as "I" statements.

4 LIST BARRIERS AND SOLUTIONS

Think about possible barriers to your action steps; then brainstorm solutions for overcoming them.

SAMPLE: If I get so upset during a disagreement that it's hard to transform blaming language into "I" statements, I'll count to ten and try again.

5 ACT AND EVALUATE OUTCOMES

Now that your plan is in place, take action. Record each action step as you take it. Then evaluate whether you achieved your SMART goal, and make any adjustments needed to get better results in the future.

SAMPLE: Counting to ten didn't help me reduce my frustration as much as I had hoped. The next time my emotions get away from me, I'll try taking a short, brisk walk instead.

6 CONNECT TO CAREER

List the skills you're building as you progress toward your SMART goal. How will you use these skills to land a job and succeed at work?

SAMPLE: In any career I pursue, learning how to manage conflict effectively will help me work well with others and stay productive on the job.

my personal success plan

1 my information

2 my SMART goal

☐ SPECIFIC ☐ MEASURABLE ☐ ACHIEVABLE ☐ RELEVANT ☐ TIME-LIMITED

3 my action plan

4 my barriers/ solutions

5 my actions/ outcomes

6 my career connection

CHAPTER SUMMARY

This chapter introduced you to fundamental skills for connecting with others in college, work, and life. Revisit the following key points, and reflect on how you can use this information to support your success now and in the future.

- In interpersonal communication, ideally a speaker conveys a clear message to the receiver. The receiver hears the complete message, overcoming any barriers; interprets it accurately; and then gives the speaker feedback. The receiver may also contribute more substantial content to the conversation, thus becoming the speaker.

- The three steps to exercising emotional intelligence are recognizing, understanding, and then managing your own and others' emotions.

- Assertive communication can help you constructively resolve conflicts by sharing your thoughts, feelings, and needs in an honest, respectful way.

- Using "I" statements can also help you resolve conflicts effectively. By showing that you're taking responsibility for your feelings and reactions, you're less likely to trigger defensiveness in the other person.

- Communication skills, emotional intelligence, and the ability to constructively work through conflicts with others can help you build and sustain positive, healthy relationships.

- Knowing how to interact effectively with people from diverse backgrounds is valuable in college and the workplace because it helps you change and grow.

- Knowing how to connect with others can help you impress interviewers, advance in your career once you get a job, and interact effectively with colleagues.

CHAPTER ACTIVITIES

Journal Entry

ENHANCING EXISTING RELATIONSHIPS

Identify two personal relationships that are important to you, such as your relationship with your parents, children, significant other, sibling, or best friend. For each relationship, reflect on the following questions:

- How do you see this relationship changing while you're in college?

- What are your hopes for this relationship? What are your concerns?

- What specific actions will you take to maintain this relationship while you're in college?

- How might this person support you in achieving your academic goals?

Adopting a Success Attitude

BUILDING EMOTIONAL INTELLIGENCE

Everyone is entitled to feelings — good, bad, or ugly. When we have negative feelings, it's important to recognize them, try to understand them, and respond to them in healthy ways. This exercise will help you reflect on negative feelings you've had and how you reacted. If you find that your reaction had negative consequences, you can think about how you'll handle things differently in the future.

From the following list of feeling words, choose five emotions that you experienced in the last week. Then, on a separate piece of paper, respond to the questions below for each emotion you've identified. An example is provided.

Feeling Words

irritated	aggressive	resentful	provoked	disappointed	helpless
embarrassed	shy	distrustful	pessimistic	discouraged	lonely
sorrowful	crushed	offended	anxious	preoccupied	fearful

What emotion did you experience?	Embarrassed
What caused this emotion?	I responded incorrectly to a question in class.
How did you respond?	I left class early and skipped the next class.
What was the consequence?	I missed a quiz and was given 0 points.
If appropriate, provide an alternate response	If this happens again, I'll tell myself it's okay to be wrong and will remain in class to seek the right answers.

Applying Your Skills

COMMUNICATING ASSERTIVELY

Respond to the following scenarios by using an "I" statement to convey your feelings, the situation's impact on you, and your interest in arriving at a solution to the problem.

1. You're working on a group project for class. You show up at the second group meeting with your part of the project complete. No one else has done any work yet. You feel angry and disappointed.

   "I" message: _____

2. You like to bring your lunch to work, but the office refrigerator is disgusting! It's full of forgotten leftovers and rotten fruit. You decide to say something to your coworkers.

   "I" message: _____

3. You have a big test tomorrow and need to study. No one else in the house seems to care. The television is blaring, the phone keeps ringing, someone's blasting a stereo, and the dog is scratching at the door to go outside.

   "I" message: _____

College Success = Career Success

WRITING PROFESSIONAL E-MAILS

Effective e-mail communication is important in both college and the workplace. The best e-mails are brief and focused and have an informative subject line that helps the receiver quickly determine your e-mail's purpose and whether your message needs immediate attention. Rewrite the following e-mail messages to ensure that they convey the most important information. If necessary, edit to make the tone more professional, the subject line more informative, and the message more efficient.

To: Instructor
From: Student
Re: Class

How's it going? I'm thinking I'm going to be late to class tomorrow night. We have a sales meeting at work tomorrow at 3 p.m. which will probably go until 4 p.m. My boss is a talker, so maybe even later. Since my car died, I've been taking the bus. I'll have to look at the schedule to tell you when I'll be able to get to class. Maybe around 4:45 or 5:00 if I don't miss the bus. Be sure to let me know if you talk about anything important before I arrive. See you then!

To: Boss
From: Employee
Re: Important—Impending Vacation

I remember you saying we should check with you to schedule our vacation. I am thinking about going somewhere warm this year—maybe Florida or Arizona. If I went to Florida, I might drive. If I went to Arizona, I might fly there. Either way, I would like to go sometime in the next six months—maybe in late February when it is still cold. Maybe I could take the last week of February? If not, the second to last week of February would be good too. Let me know what you think so I can begin to plan my vacation. Thanks!

12 Personal and Financial Health

Stress Less, Feel Better

Physical and Mental Health

Sexual Health

Financial Health

Personal and Financial Health at Work

My Personal Success Plan

C lose your eyes, and create a mental image of what stress feels like to you. Perhaps you're picturing a 20-pound weight in your backpack, and you can almost feel it pulling on your shoulder straps. Maybe you're imagining an itchy sweater that's three sizes too small, a metal vise squeezing your head, or a dark storm cloud following you around, ready to dump rain on you at any moment. Is your image as awful as any of these? Not as bad? Worse?

Now think about the relationship between feelings of stress and your personal and financial health. If you're like many people, there's a clear connection between how stressed you are and how good you feel — and even between how stressed you are and how well you manage your money. For example, if you're anxious about presenting in class, your blood pressure might rise and you might lose sleep. And high stress levels might prompt you to engage in a little "retail therapy" and splurge on things you don't need (or can't afford) in an effort to distract yourself from your troubles.

Conversely, your personal and financial health choices can affect how stressed you feel. For instance, if you don't get enough sleep, eat nothing but French fries every day, and never exercise, you'll probably experience stress in the form of exhaustion and anxiety. If you don't manage your money carefully, you may run out of funds for everyday expenses, further ratcheting up your stress levels.

The good news about this connection is that if you make the right decisions about your personal and financial health, you can control your stress levels — and this chapter shows you how. First, we examine stress in more detail. Then we explore key aspects of your physical well-being and mental health and consider ways to manage both. Next, we present strategies for maintaining sexual health and explore how to enhance your financial health through budgeting, understanding financial aid, and managing credit. Finally, we look at how strengthening your personal and financial health can benefit you in the workplace.

Reflect

On Your Personal and Financial Health

Take a moment to reflect on your Personal and Financial Health score on ACES. Find your score and add it in the circle to the right.

This score measures your beliefs about how healthy you are physically, mentally, and financially. Do you think it's an accurate snapshot of how you feel in this area? Why or why not?

■ **IF YOU SCORED IN THE HIGH RANGE** and believe this score is accurate, then staying healthy and financially stable may be one of your strengths. Excellent! But remember: You can always work to improve strengths. For instance, if you're already getting enough exercise, explore how you could also improve your diet. Or if you've built an effective budget, identify ways you could reduce your spending to free up funds for tuition and other important expenses.

■ **IF YOU SCORED IN THE MODERATE OR LOW RANGE**, use the suggestions in this chapter to better manage your health and to stay on track financially. Once you identify and implement strategies that work for you, you'll feel better physically and mentally, as well as more fiscally secure.

MY ACES SCORE

☐ **HIGH**

☐ **MODERATE**

☐ **LOW**

LaunchPad

To find your **Personal and Financial Health score**, go to the LaunchPad for *Connections*.

Stress Less, Feel Better

Why is stress such a major factor in our lives? To answer this question, let's explore how stress works and how it affects us. When you feel stress, your body releases stress hormones, such as cortisol and adrenaline.[1] Such hormones can speed up your heart rate and breathing. In addition, your muscles tense up, and your body readies itself for a fight-or-flight response—a primitive reaction in which you either combat the danger facing you or run away from it.

The fight-or-flight response was useful long ago in our evolutionary history. If a lion chased you, a surge of adrenaline would give you the strength to whack the animal over the head with a club or run away. Either move could boost your chances of survival. Today, many of us don't regularly face the kinds of perils that call for a fight-or-flight response. However, if we keep *experiencing* that response, we get bombarded with the resulting physical changes, which can lead to health problems such as anxiety, ulcers, fatigue, weight gain, and depression.[2]

How can you avoid these problems? Start by understanding your own personal stressors, which are events and situations that tend to freak you out. To get a better sense of your stressors, look at the list of some common college

FIGURE 12.1 **Common College Stressors**

___ Starting/Restarting College

___ Significant Change in Income

___ Disruption to Sleeping Pattern

___ Illness

___ Major Paper/Assignment/Exam

___ Start/End of a Dating Relationship

___ Problems with Family Members

___ Choosing a Major

___ Job Change

___ Making a Presentation in Class

___ Balancing School, Work, and Family

___ Other Stressors: _____

stressors in Figure 12.1 and check off any items you experienced during the last year. Note that any event that intensifies your emotions and physical reactions—whether distressing or joyous—can be a stressor. For example, you can feel stress when you end a relationship or when you start a new one.

The good news is that you *can* manage stressors, and the most potent strategies for doing so involve keeping your mind and body healthy and your finances under control. First, let's turn to two vital components of personal health: your physical and mental well-being.

Physical and Mental Health

Feeling unwell—physically or mentally—can hurt your academic performance by making it hard to go to class, pay attention, study, and get your assignments done. So try to do whatever you can to maintain your well-being—including eating right, staying active, and getting enough sleep—and you'll be way ahead of the game. Let's explore strategies for staying healthy and feeling good.

Eat Right

Have you ever come home after a stressful day and gobbled up a pint of ice cream or a giant bag of potato chips—only to realize that you felt just as stressed, and maybe a bit ill, once all the goodies were gone? Guess what: What and how much you eat has a big impact on your health (in the short *and* long term), your energy level, and even your mood.

That said, always eating healthy isn't easy in college. If you're juggling family responsibilities, a job, and coursework, you're probably on the go from morning until night. Finding time to prepare nutritious meals may seem impossible. And if you live on campus, you may have access to dining halls and food trucks that offer an array of fast foods with high amounts of fat, salt, and sugar.

Let's consider some ideas for navigating these environments and discuss the consequences of eating too much—or too little.

Learn about Healthy Eating. When you make healthy dietary choices, you give your body the sustenance and energy it needs for you to function effectively at school. To learn about healthy eating, visit the U.S. Department of Agriculture's MyPlate program at www.choosemyplate.gov. An updated version of the food pyramid, MyPlate offers guidelines on issues such as what proportions of the different food groups should be included in every meal and how to eat healthy on a budget. There's even MyPlate On Campus, which spotlights strategies students can use to adopt a healthy lifestyle.

In addition to MyPlate, take advantage of other information sources to learn about healthy eating. For instance, read the nutrition facts on foods you buy. On campus, ask dining services for information about the calories, fat, sodium, and sugar in the meal choices. The more information you have, the better choices you can make about which foods to pick and which to skip.

So Many Choices. . . .
You're at a buffet, ready to load your tray. You have countless options—so how can you pick the healthiest? Ask about the calories, fat, sodium, and sugar in the meal choices. And check out the USDA's MyPlate program to find out what portion of each food group should go on your plate. Mario Savoia/ Shutterstock

Master Healthy-Eating Tactics. The following strategies may seem obvious, but they deliver a powerful, healthy-eating punch.

- Start your day with a light, nutritious breakfast, such as fruit and yogurt, instead of calorie-laden breads and meats. This kind of breakfast energizes you, kick-starts your metabolism, and helps you concentrate.

- Keep healthy snacks in handy places, such as your backpack, car, and refrigerator or pantry at home.

- Eat more fruits and vegetables. If you change from fewer than three servings a day to more than five servings, you can cut your risk of heart disease by 17 percent![3]

- Stay away from processed foods and beverages. They have a lot of preservatives, sugar, and fat.

- Avoid supersized meals. Instead, take a smaller plate and say "no" when someone offers a larger portion. These easy steps will reduce your calorie intake.[4]

- Carry a water bottle with you, and keep drinking and refilling it. You'll stay hydrated—essential for feeling well both physically and mentally.

Get Help for Eating Disorders. People often use healthy eating strategies as part of a plan to lose weight or maintain a certain weight. Managing your weight can be a good thing if you do so in a balanced, careful way. But if weight loss becomes your main focus in life and you start to engage in dangerous eating behaviors, you risk serious health problems. Severely restricting food intake and having an irrational fear of gaining weight are symptoms of *anorexia nervosa*. Engaging in binge eating followed by intentional purging (vomiting), obsessively overexercising, and abusing diuretics are symptoms of *bulimia nervosa*. These disorders can make you seriously ill—and even kill you.[5] If you show symptoms of these disorders, or you know someone who does, support is available: seek help now at your campus's health and counseling centers.

The Five-Minute Workout. You don't have to be an elite long-distance runner to get the much-touted benefits of this form of exercise. In a 2014 study published in the *Journal of the American College of Cardiology*, researchers concluded that running just five minutes each day can add years to your life.[8] That's a lot of bang for your jogging buck! Cultura Edwin/Getty Images

Stay Active

Get more exercise! We've all heard this before, and there's a good reason why: Exercise helps build muscle strength and improves cardiovascular fitness. It's also a great way to manage the stress of being a college student.[6]

Every week, try to get at least 150 minutes of moderate exercise or 75 minutes of vigorous exercise.[7] If you have difficulty following an exercise routine or if you hate gyms, build an exercise schedule that works for you. For instance, break the 150 minutes into 30 minutes of exercise, five days a week. Or do a 45-minute workout two days a week and squeeze in several 10- to 15-minute walks to get the additional hour.

You can also take advantage of everyday tasks and events to get more exercise.

- If you have a car, park some distance away from class, your job, or the grocery store, and walk to your destination.
- Take stairs instead of elevators.
- During study breaks, take a walk around the library or do jumping jacks in your room.
- Sign up for a fitness class at the recreation center.
- Ask a friend to work out with you. Having company can keep you motivated.
- Join an intramural sports team.

Don't Skimp on the Z's

CONNECT TO MY CLASSES

Have you set up a sleep schedule that supports your course schedule? For example, do you go to bed earlier the night before your early-morning classes? Write down the ideal sleep schedule for your current classes. Compare this to your current sleep schedule. What's one change you can make to better align these schedules?

Do you often stay up until 1:00 a.m. playing video games, scrolling through your Facebook news feed, or texting friends? Do you frequently stay up late studying or doing laundry after putting your kids to bed? Getting enough sleep affects our ability to function each day;[9] when we're overtired, dealing with stress is much more difficult. If you usually get less than seven to eight hours of good-quality sleep each night, you're probably exhausted. To get enough Z's and feel your best each day, try these strategies.

- Avoid late-night cramming. Organize your time so that you can get a full night's sleep before exams and can finish assignments on time.
- Stay away from caffeinated or energy drinks in the late afternoon or evening.
- Get enough exercise, particularly earlier in the day.
- Don't nap during the day; napping only makes it harder to fall asleep once you're in bed for the night.
- Establish a regular sleep schedule—then stick with it.
- If you have trouble falling asleep, try relaxation techniques such as deep breathing, tensing and releasing muscles throughout your body, or envisioning peaceful scenes.

STAYING HEALTHY AND COPING WITH STRESS

Courtesy of Mathew W. Schneider

NAME: **Mathew Schneider**

SCHOOL: *University of Texas at Arlington*

MAJOR: *Biology*

CAREER GOAL: *Physician Assistant*

In my second year of college, I was struggling to balance my schoolwork, family life, and work. I also felt alone at school—I'm forty-three years old and almost retired from the military, so I felt different from this young crowd I now call my classmates. This was stressful. When I'm stressed, I find it difficult to accomplish things, I feel irritable, and I lose my appetite. Sleep becomes a huge issue for me; at night I'll just toss and turn and get rings under my eyes from not sleeping.

This semester, I was determined to change my sleep habits. In my Human Physiology class, I learned that sedentary activities, such as just going to class and studying, reduce energy levels and metabolism rates. When I found this out, I developed a goal of living healthier. This is an ongoing battle, but I've found that exercise helps me sleep better. It has also built up my energy level and helped me cut back from a pot of coffee a day to two cups (never after 6:00 p.m.). I've gone from restless sleep, which gave me no energy for the day, to quality sleep after exercise, which helped me feel fully functional and energized. Exercise has made a world of difference to me this semester.

In order to get control of my stress, it has also helped to get support. My wife has been supportive when I feel stressed out. When my stress is school-related, my classmates, study groups, and student organizations have been the most comforting. I created a support group where I made friends and improved my grades. This tool helps me handle even my hardest and most stressful classes. I'm well known in the biology department as the study-group king, and I've found that so many others have been helped by this group as well.

YOUR TURN: To what degree do you identify with Mathew's experiences with exercise and with getting support for managing stress? For example, what role does exercise play in your life as a college student? Whom do you turn to for moral support when you're feeling overwhelmed?

> " **Exercise has made a world of difference to me this semester.** "

287

HEALTHY BEHAVIOR IS GOOD FOR YOUR GRADES

Do you get eight hours of good-quality slumber every night? Are you an "early to bed, early to rise" person? Do you have breakfast every day? If your answer to these questions is "no," then your health — and your academic performance — could be suffering, according to findings from a study of almost two hundred first-year college students. The researchers asked the students about their health-related behaviors during the first semester of college and then obtained their grade point average at the end of the term. When the researchers analyzed the data, they identified several significant relationships between health behaviors and grades. Higher grades were associated with

- Going to bed earlier and getting up earlier during the week and on the weekend
- Regularly eating breakfast

The researchers also discovered that the students who slept more on the weekends than they did during the week had lower grades. This finding suggests that using weekends to catch up on missed sleep is no substitute for being well rested all week long.

Behavior	Impact on GPA
Sleeping well during the week and on the weekend	+ (positive)
Eating breakfast	+ (positive)
Catching up on sleep during the weekend	− (negative)

Your sleeping and eating habits are connected to your grades.

THE BOTTOM LINE

Getting enough sleep and eating breakfast every day are linked to better grades in college.

REFLECTION QUESTIONS

1. How are your sleeping and eating habits affecting your academic performance?
2. What is one change you could make right now to improve your sleeping habits?
3. What is one change you could make right now to improve your eating habits?

M. T. Trockel, M. D. Barnes, and D. L. Egget, "Health-Related Variables and Academic Performance among First-Year College Students: Implications for Sleep and Other Behaviors," *Journal of American College Health* 49 (2000): 125–31.

Take Care of Your Mental Health

Taking care of your mental health is just as important as nurturing your physical health. If you're feeling down or worried, just going to class or reading a textbook chapter might seem as impossible as climbing Mount Everest. Depression, anxiety, eating disorders, substance abuse, and other mental-health issues are all too common among college students.[10] The good news, however, is that you *can* get better if you experience these challenges and there are people who can help.

In this section we look at anxiety and depression, two of the most common mental-health problems affecting college students.

Anxiety. If you experience excessive worry, dread, or fear, you may have anxiety. For some people anxiety is a general, all-encompassing sensation. For others it's more specific; for instance, they might feel anxious in social settings or while taking tests. Anxiety can also express itself as panic attacks, during which your heart starts racing in your chest for no apparent reason, you can't catch your breath, and you feel as though you're having a heart attack. If you suffer from anxiety that's far beyond everyday worry, reach out for help. The counseling center, an adviser, a clergy member, or another person you trust can connect you with the resources you need, on or off campus.

Depression. Depression is common among college students, particularly since adjusting to college can result in feelings of loneliness, loss of previous friendships, or discomfort in being in a new environment. Left untreated, depression can affect your appetite, causing you to lose or gain weight; keep you awake at night or make it hard to get out of bed in the morning; and leave you feeling listless, with little interest in activities you used to enjoy.

❥ CONNECT TO MY RESOURCES

Many campuses have mental-health services, such as counseling centers, that can help students manage a wide range of challenges. Even if your school doesn't have a fully staffed counseling center, it can still refer you to the appropriate health care professionals. Find out what mental-health services are available on campus, and record their contact information.

Comfort Dogs. If you're like most college students, final exam time can intensify your anxiety to panic levels, so you need to take extra-good care of yourself. Students at the University of California at Riverside have an unusual resource available to them: specially trained "comfort dogs" brought by their owners to help students manage exam-week anxiety. © Spencer Grant/PhotoEdit, Inc.

Depression can range from very mild (feeling down a couple of days a month) to severe (feeling suicidal). If you experience symptoms of depression that last for more than two weeks or that make it hard for you to get through the day, or if you have experienced depression in the past and experience its symptoms again—including thoughts of hurting yourself—get help immediately. To manage feelings of depression, reach out to others who can help you: a therapist, clergy, friends, family. You *don't* have to go it alone.

Don't Abuse Alcohol and Drugs

Alcohol and drug abuse are serious health problems on many college campuses. Why do students use drugs and alcohol? Some do so because they think it will help them manage stress. Others think that it's an expected part of being a college student and that "everyone's doing it." (Actually, many college students *overestimate* the amount of binge drinking that goes on at their school, so the assumption that "everyone's doing it" is wrong.[11])

At worst, abusing alcohol and drugs can lead to addiction and cause health problems (such as liver damage) and death from overdose. At best, it costs you money you could spend on other, more useful things. The healthy choice? Avoid illegal substances altogether; if you choose to use legal substances, adopt an "everything in moderation" mind-set. In addition, follow these rules to protect your physical safety—as well as your reputation.

- When you go out with friends, designate a responsible member of the group to stay sober and make sure that everyone gets home safely at the end of the night.
- Remember why you're in college and your goals for the future. You'll be less likely to let your partying get out of hand.
- Don't post photos online of yourself drinking or taking drugs. Potential employers may find them—and pass you over for a job.
- If your use of alcohol or drugs prevents you from attending or doing well in your classes, if you feel that you can't control it, or if important people in your life express concerns about it, you may have an addiction problem. Seek out confidential help at the counseling center.

Sexual Health

For students who choose to be sexually active, practicing safe sex helps minimize stress and promotes overall health. Reducing your risk of sexually transmitted infections and using effective birth control if you're not ready to start a family are two important ways to take control of your sex life and adopt healthy sexual behavior.

Avoid Sexually Transmitted Infections

There are many types of **sexually transmitted infections (STIs)**—illnesses spread through the exchange of bodily fluids during sexual activity. If you're sexually active, how do you stay safe? Start by educating yourself. Table 12.1

Sexually Transmitted Infections (STIs): Illnesses, some treatable and some incurable, that are spread through the exchange of bodily fluids during sexual activity.

shows the frequency, symptoms, and treatment methods for six common STIs. As you can see, some STIs are curable; others aren't. Then take steps to reduce your risk. For example:

- Have sex with only one partner at a time—a person you know well.
- Always use condoms.
- Get tested for STIs regularly, even if you don't have any symptoms. You can pass on an STI to someone else without even knowing you have one.
- Have your partner get tested regularly.

Issues of sexual health are very personal, but if you have any questions or concerns about STIs, talk with someone you trust who can advise and support you—for example, a counselor, a clergy member, your physician, or a mentor. This person can connect you with the information you need to stay safe and healthy.

TABLE 12.1   Common STIs in the United States

STI	Number of new cases per year in the United States	Symptoms	Treatment
Human papillomavirus (HPV)	14 million	There are many types of HPV. Men and women can experience warts in the genital area. HPV can also lead to cervical and other cancers.	No cure. Treatments exist for illnesses caused by HPV.
Chlamydia	2.5 million +	Many people have no symptoms. Women can have vaginal discharge. Men can experience discharge from their penis or pain when urinating.	Curable. Treated with antibiotics.
Gonorrhea	800,000 +	Men may have a burning sensation when urinating or a yellowish, white, or greenish discharge from their penis. Women may have pain or discharge, but most have no symptoms.	Curable. Treated with antibiotics, but some drug-resistant strains are developing.
Genital herpes	750,000 +	One or more blisters near the genitals. Commonly mistaken for a skin infection.	No cure. Outbreaks are treated to shorten duration.
Syphilis	55,000 +	Sore on the skin or genitals is the first sign. Left untreated, rashes and sores then appear on other parts of the body.	Curable. Treated with antibiotics.
HIV/AIDS	45,000 + (HIV)	Few or no symptoms early. Later, men and women may have weight loss, fatigue, cough, fever, or white spots on the tongue or throat.	No cure. Medications help people live with the disease.

Source: Centers for Disease Control and Prevention, http://www.cdc.gov/std/healthcomm/fact_sheets.htm.

Practice Birth Control

If you're a woman having sex with a man and you don't want to start a family now, practicing birth control can give you peace of mind and prevent the stress that can come with an unplanned pregnancy. If you're a man having sex with a woman, using a birth control method designed for men is a good idea, especially if you're not certain that your partner is using birth control. There are many birth control options. Some require prescriptions; others are sold over the counter; still others involve behavior choices. Most don't protect against STIs.

Physicians on campus or at community health centers can prescribe some of these options and share information about each method's risks and benefits, which can help you choose the options right for you.

- Birth control pill: a pill a woman takes orally at the same time each day.
- Patch: a skin patch a woman wears. She applies a new patch each week for three weeks and wears no patch during the fourth week, when she should get her menstrual period.
- Intrauterine device (IUD): a small device inserted in a woman's uterus by a health care provider. Some IUDs can be used for up to ten years.
- Vaginal ring: a small ring inserted in a woman's vagina for three weeks and removed during the fourth week, when she should get her menstrual period.
- The shot: an injection of pregnancy-preventing hormones that lasts for three months.
- Condoms: sheaths that are worn over the penis or inserted into the vagina.
- Abstinence: choosing not to engage in sexual intercourse.[12]

Financial Health

If you're like most students, one big reason you're in college is to graduate, get a job, and make enough money to pay your bills and plan for the future. When you earn a college degree, you make a tremendous investment in yourself and your future financial health. As Figure 12.2 shows, people with an associate's degree earn, on average, $124 more per week than those with only a high school diploma, and those with a bachelor's degree earn $433 more per week. That translates into roughly $6,400 to $22,500 of additional income each year for the rest of your life, depending on the degree you get. Imagine what you and your family could do with that added income! Plus, as Figure 12.2 also shows, people with a degree are less likely to be unemployed.

As important as it is to your financial future to get a degree, you will likely face at least a few financial challenges while you work toward your goals. In fact, in a recent survey, seven out of ten Americans identified money as a significant stressor in their lives.[13] As a college student, you may be worrying right now about how you'll pay next term's tuition, pay for child care next week, or whittle down your student loan and credit card debt. But if these and other

FIGURE 12.2 Earnings and Unemployment Rates by Educational Attainment

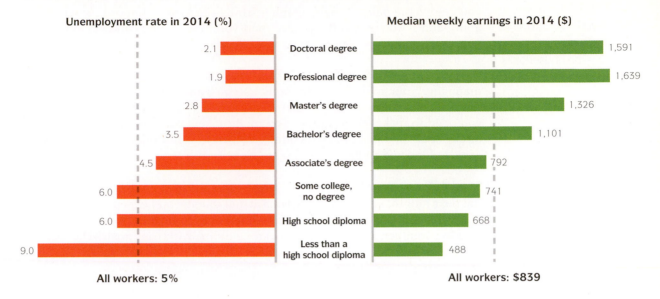

Note: Data are for persons age twenty-five and over. Earnings are for full-time wage and salary workers. Source: Current Population Survey, U.S. Bureau of Labor Statistics, U.S. Department of Labor, http://www.bls.gov/emp/ep_chart_001.htm.

financial worries keep you up at night, you *can* take steps to take control of your finances—starting with creating a budget.

Create a Budget

A **budget** is a critical survival tool for your financial health. It is your financial plan: It documents your income and expenses over specific time periods (such as a week, month, or year). Creating and sticking to a budget lets you take control of your money, live within your means, and achieve your financial goals. To create a budget, follow these steps.

Budget: A plan that documents income and expenses for a specific period of time.

Step 1: Gather Information. For one month, collect your bank statements, loan and scholarship information, pay stubs, and any regular bills. Track *all* of your spending over the course of the month, and keep all of your receipts in one place, such as a desk drawer. If you spend $2 on a cup of coffee and don't get a receipt, jot down "$2 coffee" and the date on a piece of paper and save it. You'll need all this information to build your budget.

Step 2: Record Your Income and Expenses. Using a form or spreadsheet like the one in Figure 12.3, enter into the "Last Month" column all the income and expense information you gathered for the previous month (in step 1). Then subtract your total expenses from your total income to obtain your balance for the past month. If your income was greater than your expenses (a financially

CONNECT TO MY EXPERIENCES

When you were growing up, how did your family manage the household's income? Was there a budget for monthly income and expenses? If so, how useful was the budget? If not, what were the consequences? Write one page about what your early experiences taught you about budgeting.

healthy situation), your balance will be positive. If you spent more than you made (a financially unhealthy situation), your balance will be negative. Once you see where your money's coming from—and more important, where it's going and if you're spending more than you make—you can decide whether you need to manage your money more effectively.

Step 3: Use Your Insights to Make Changes. If you discover that you aren't managing your money as effectively as you'd like (perhaps you're spending more than you bring in), you can create a new budget reflecting the changes you need to make. For example, you might take a part-time job to earn more, or cut back on unnecessary spending. Return to your budget, and record your expected income and expenses in the "Next Month" column.

Step 4: Track Your Results and Refine Your Budget Further. At the end of the next month, see how closely your actual income and expenses match what you budgeted for the month. Use any differences to further tweak your budget to bring your actual earning and spending in line with your goals. The sections that follow provide ideas you can try.

FIGURE 12.3 Recording Your Income and Expenses

Budget Worksheet		
Income	Last Month	Next Month
Scholarships		
Work		
Support from family		
Loans		
Savings		
Other:		
Total Income		
Expenses		
Tuition		
Books/supplies		
Housing		
Utilities		
Electricity		
Internet		
Cable		
Food		
Meal plan		
Groceries		
Dining out		
Phone		
Car payment		
Child care		
Debt payments		
Entertainment		
Other		
Total Expenses		
Total Income:		
– Total Expenses:		
Balance:		

Reduce Your Spending

If you usually spend more than you make or you just want to save some money, try reducing your spending. You may find some easy ways to do this. For example, if Callista wants to cut her spending by $100 a month, she can brew her own coffee each morning instead of buying coffee on the road, and she can eliminate one night out each week. Other solutions may require more sacrifice. If Callista's goal is to graduate with less than $5,000 in debt, she may have to take fewer classes per term so that she can work more hours and pay more tuition up-front.

To make it easier to reduce your spending, distinguish between your must-haves (needs) and nice-to-haves (wants). For instance, Jerome *needs* a car to get from work to class, but he *wants* to keep his new SUV, which comes with a monthly payment he can barely afford. As tempting as it is to keep that SUV, Jerome could boost his financial health by trading it in for a car that doesn't break his budget.

Being honest with yourself about your needs and wants and cutting your expenses can be hard, but here are some ideas that can help.

- If you live on campus, change to a less expensive meal plan. If you live off campus, shop smart by using coupons and buying products on sale.
- Drop your cable plan.
- Find a cheaper Internet service.
- Explore housing options. Is it cheaper to live on campus? Would you save money by selling your house and renting? Can you find a roommate to share expenses?

Are You a Super Couponer? You don't have to be an extreme couponer to rein in your spending on groceries and other necessities. You can make a number of everyday, relatively moderate changes. Once added up, these changes can help you reduce your expenses and bring your budget in line with your income. **Kansas City Star/Getty Images**

- Cancel your gym membership and use campus facilities or exercise outdoors.
- Go an extra two weeks between haircuts.
- Explore options at your school for taking more classes each term. Full-time students can often take one or two more classes each term without paying more, which adds up to substantial savings. But take care that you don't get overloaded: Talk with your adviser and family about how to make this work.

Get a Job to Boost Your Income

Working is a fact of life for most college students. According to the National Center for Education Statistics, four out of ten full-time students and seven out of ten part-time students work while attending college.[14] Working has important advantages. You make money, gain valuable experience, build your skills, apply what you're learning in class to the real world, and build your résumé.

However, there are potential risks associated with working, and it's good to be mindful of these as you schedule your time. Students who work more than fifteen hours a week and those who work off campus are more likely to have lower grades and leave school before graduating.[15] If you have a stressful job and work long hours, you might also have trouble putting enough time into your studies.

If you're balancing work and school effectively now, continue taking good care of yourself so that you don't get overwhelmed. If doing both is becoming problematic, consider taking fewer classes or getting more financial aid. You can talk about possible solutions with an adviser, your family, and your school's financial aid office.

Navigate Financial Aid

It's no secret that college is expensive and that financial aid is a lifesaver for students who couldn't otherwise afford to go. According to the U.S. Department of Education, about two-thirds of all undergraduate students receive financial aid,[16] in forms such as public or private loans, grants, scholarships, or work-study programs.

Many sources of aid are available, but learning about and applying for aid can be stressful. A good place to start is with the basics: how to apply for aid, what types of aid exist, and how to keep your aid once you receive it.

FAFSA. If you're currently receiving financial aid, then you've already completed a form called the Free Application for Federal Student Aid (FAFSA). If you haven't yet applied for financial aid, start with the FAFSA. This tool assesses your (or your family's) financial situation and calculates how much the federal government believes you can afford to pay for college—which determines how much aid you qualify for. To learn more about the FAFSA, go to www.fafsa .ed.gov or visit your college's financial aid office.

Grants. One common type of financial aid is a *grant*, which is money provided by the government or your college that you're not expected to repay. The federal government gives grants based on financial need (such as Pell Grants) as well

Dialogue for Dollars. Navigating the complex world of financial aid is challenging. So talk with someone in your college's financial aid office — and find out what types of aid are available, how to apply for aid, and how to keep it. One meeting with a financial aid officer could make a world of difference for your academic and financial future. Hero Images/Getty Images

as military service (such as Iraq and Afghanistan Service Grants). Your state government might provide grants to in-state residents who earned a strong high school GPA or those who graduated in the top half of their class and attend a two- or four-year college in the state. Your college may also provide grants based on financial need or past accomplishments.

Scholarships. As with grants, you don't have to repay scholarships. Scholarships come from different sources and are awarded for different reasons, such as financial need, talents or accomplishments, membership in a cultural or religious group, or a student's area of study (for example, education or health science). Your high school or college may award scholarships, or you can earn them through your community, private organizations or businesses, and sometimes even your employer. Web-based services can help you find scholarships, but be sure to start with secure sites that don't charge a fee.

Student Loans. Many students take out a loan to help pay for college. However, if you borrow large amounts and choose a low-paying career or don't ever graduate, you could have trouble paying what you owe. So before you sign up for a loan, understand the pros and cons of borrowing that money. Research the different types of loans available to you, and talk with your adviser to make sure you're taking all the courses required for graduation. Spending an extra year, or even an extra term, in college may mean more loans. Visit the career center to learn how much you can expect to earn if you graduate with your intended degree. Will your future income be enough that you can repay your loans and still afford to eat? And remember: Whenever you borrow money, you

❚ CONNECT TO MY RESOURCES

If you've taken out student loans, it's not too early to craft a strategy for repaying them. Visit the financial aid office and ask about (1) your expected total debt upon graduation, (2) the average debt of graduates at your school and the percentage of students who can't repay their loans, and (3) options for reducing your loans.

have to pay interest on the loan. Often, the faster you pay off the loan, the less interest you'll end up paying in the long run, which can save you big bucks.

Here are some common loans available to students.

- **Direct subsidized loans.** The federal government provides these loans. They usually have a lower interest rate than other types of loans, and interest doesn't *accrue* (get added to the loan) while you're in school. Students qualify for these loans based on financial need.

- **Direct unsubsidized loans.** These government-provided loans tend to have higher interest rates than subsidized loans, and interest accrues while you're in school. All college students are eligible for unsubsidized loans, regardless of financial need.

- **Direct PLUS loans.** PLUS is a federal loan program that lets parents borrow money for the college expenses of a dependent student. PLUS loans have a higher interest rate and charge more fees than other federal loans.

- **Private loans.** These loans are issued by institutions such as banks, credit unions, or colleges. Compared to federal loans, they often have higher interest rates and fewer repayment options.

Work-Study Programs. If you receive a work-study award, you can apply for an on-campus job that's been set aside for someone with financial need. Positions fill up quickly, and placement isn't guaranteed, so talk with someone in the financial aid office if you want to explore what's available. Sure, the work-study job you get may not be perfect or exciting—you may find yourself making copies or delivering mail. Still, every job offers learning opportunities, and some work-study jobs can even give you experience in your field of study. For instance, if you want to be a journalist, a work-study job that involves helping your journalism professor write a book could teach you a lot about your dream profession.

Keeping Your Financial Aid. After all the time and energy you put into applying for and securing financial aid, take the following steps to keep it—or even increase it.

- **Fulfill requirements.** Understand and fulfill all the requirements for keeping your financial aid. For example, if your GPA falls below a certain level or if you drop a class and become a part-time student (which colleges and funding sources define differently), you may lose your aid.

- **If your financial situation changes, see if you qualify for more aid.** For instance, if you or a primary wage earner in your family loses a job, talk with your school's financial aid office about what has changed and how that affects your aid eligibility.

- **Keep looking for aid.** You may qualify for different scholarships as you progress through college. For instance, a donor may have established a scholarship for junior and senior engineering students who want to go into public service. Regularly research emerging opportunities like these.

- **Apply for financial aid each year.** Be sure to complete the FAFSA and any other required applications on time so that you can keep your aid every year.

⟨ CONNECT TO MY CAREER

Are you currently working? If so, you can build valuable skills, even if your current job isn't in your future career field. List three skills you'll need in your future career, or a career that interests you, that you can develop in your current job. How will you build these skills?

Control Your Credit Cards — So They Don't Control You

When you buy something with a credit card, you're taking out a short-term loan from the credit card company and promising that you'll pay for the purchase later. Like student loans, credit cards come with interest rates. You have to pay that interest if you don't pay off your credit card balance in full every month. But credit card interest rates can be shockingly high—as much as 20 percent or more.

To grasp how this high level of interest can affect your financial health, meet Jason. He has a $3,000 balance on his credit card, which charges 18 percent interest. If he makes only the minimum payment of $75 each month (and doesn't spend any more on the card), he'll end up paying a total of $6,923.08 over more than eighteen years!

If you have a credit card, look at one of your statements. Credit card companies are required to tell you how much you'll pay in the long run if you make only the minimum monthly payment on your balance. Once you start racking up big credit card debt, it's very hard to whittle it back down, so keep that number in the forefront of your mind. It could motivate you to whip out that "plastic" less often—and maybe even cut up your card and throw it away.

If you're going to use credit cards, try these tactics for keeping your debt under control.

- Use only one card. If you have several cards, pay off and close all of them except one.

- Pay off the entire amount every month—on time.

- Consider getting a debit card. This functions like a credit card when you make purchases, but it's tied to your checking account and withdraws money that you already have.

- Check your credit report for errors. Each year, you can get a free copy of your credit report from each of the three credit-reporting agencies (Equifax, TransUnion, and Experian). To get your reports, go to www.annualcreditreport.com.

Combat Credit-Card Debt. If you don't pay your credit card balance in full every month, the interest can start piling up. The accumulating interest makes it increasingly difficult to pay off the balance, and ultimately you can get buried under a mound of debt. High credit card balances can also hurt your credit score, making it hard for you to take out loans in the future. © Cartoonstock

Personal and Financial Health at Work

Behaviors that nurture your personal and financial health at school will help you do the same at work. And employers want healthy, financially stable employees, who tend to be the happiest and most productive.[17] When you're healthy and financially secure, you'll also enjoy your job more. Consider these ideas for securing your health at work—and reaping the rewards.

Boost Your Productivity

Eating healthy and managing stress (including financial pressures) can boost your productivity at work. After all, when you feel well and in control, you can get more done. Here are some simple but powerful ideas.

Escape the Sedentary Work Life. Sitting at a desk all day can lead to back and neck problems, as well as stress and anxiety from lack of exercise. Gary's fighting back by treadmilling at a stand-up desk. What are some other ways to get up and get moving during the workday? AP Photo/Michael Conroy

- **Brown-bag it.** Packing your lunch gives you complete control over your diet—and it's a lot cheaper than buying food at work.

- **Get moving.** If you have a sedentary job, make an effort to move around. Take the stairs rather than the elevator, or park your car far from the front door. Go for short, brisk walks during work breaks. If your job involves a lot of repetitive motion, such as operating a piece of equipment over and over in the same way, occasionally flex your muscles and stretch to avoid getting tendinitis or repetitive-movement injuries.

- **Take breaks.** It's hard to stay productive at work without taking short breaks. Spend a few minutes throughout the day relaxing and taking deep breaths. Step outside for some fresh air. Or chat with a coworker for a few minutes while you're refilling your mug at the water cooler.

- **Manage your mental health.** If you're in a job that generates a great deal of emotional stress (such as social work or law enforcement), that stress can erode your productivity if you don't take steps to manage it. Take extra care to manage your mental health—for example, talk with a therapist, practice relaxation techniques, or spend quality time with people who love and support you.

- **Use your company's wellness plan.** Many companies offer a wellness plan as part of their employee-benefits package. Wellness plans can include a variety of services, such as help with quitting smoking or a discounted gym membership. If you take advantage of these options, you might even get a break on your health insurance premiums.

Manage Work Budgets

The budgeting skills you use to manage your own financial health can also keep your company "healthy." For instance, suppose you own a small business. If you find creative ways to cut travel costs, you might free up funds you can channel into your marketing budget—and boost sales as a result.

Or let's say you're a manager responsible for tracking your group's revenue and expenses. If your organization wants to boost profitability, you might scour your departmental budget, looking for places where your team can cut spending or increase revenue. And if you're not a manager? You can still help brainstorm ideas for enhancing revenue and reducing costs—something every organization appreciates.

MANAGING STRESS

Courtesy of Nadine Hernandez

NAME:	**Nadine Hernandez**
PROFESSION:	*Program Specialist*
SCHOOL:	*Rio Hondo College*
DEGREE:	*Associate of Arts*
MAJOR:	*General Studies*

It's taken me many years, but I've figured out how to manage stress, and I am much more successful today because I've learned that I have to take care of myself first. I was the first in my family to go to college, and during the many years I spent working on my A.A. degree, I had the thought in my head that "people like me don't go to college." As a first-generation college student and single mother, I had no educational support from an adult, like a role model or mentor. I also had child-care issues, and I worried about my daughter's and my younger sister's and brothers' well-being — and this was in addition to dealing with family finances and balancing part-time work, school, and parenting. All of these things were incredibly stressful and made it challenging to stay in school. One day I decided to go to the counseling center on campus, where I learned ways to manage the anxieties and fears I was experiencing.

I now work as an EOPS (Extended Opportunities Programs and Services) Program Specialist, where I get to work with educationally and economically disadvantaged students by supporting them with guidance from start to finish through the community college process. I also plan and conduct workshops for economically and educationally disadvantaged single mothers who live below the poverty line and are going to college. I teach my students the same stress-management skills that I continue to use today: Take care of yourself first, prioritize your tasks, eat healthy, and get rest and regular exercise. I also encourage students to use the counseling center if they need more help. Using stress-management techniques has been a crucial part of my success, and I enjoy helping others use these tools to succeed.

YOUR TURN: If you're currently working and have experienced stress on the job, have you used any of the stress-management techniques Nadine found useful? If so, which ones? What, if any, additional strategies have you found helpful? If you're not currently working but have a career in mind, what might be the most difficult stressors associated with that career? How will you manage them?

> " Using stress-management techniques has been a crucial part of my success."

my personal success plan

PERSONAL AND FINANCIAL HEALTH

Are you inspired to set a new goal aimed at improving your personal or financial health? If so, the Personal Success Plan can walk you through the goal-setting process. Read the advice and examples; then sketch out your ideas in the space provided.

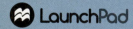 LaunchPad

To access the Personal Success Plan online, go to the LaunchPad for *Connections*.

1 GATHER INFORMATION

Think about your strengths and weaknesses related to personal and financial health. What health- and money-management strategies have worked for you in the past? What could you do differently? Revisit your Personal and Financial Health score on ACES and review the relevant sections of this chapter for additional ideas.

2 SET A SMART GOAL

Use the information you've gathered to create a SMART goal, making sure to use the SMART goal checklist.

SAMPLE: Starting next week, I'll increase the amount of time I exercise from one hour to two and a half hours each week.

3 MAKE AN ACTION PLAN

Outline the specific steps you'll take to achieve your SMART goal, and note when you'll complete each step.

SAMPLE: Tomorrow I'll find out where the on-campus gym is located and go check it out.

4 LIST BARRIERS AND SOLUTIONS

Think about possible barriers to your action steps; then brainstorm solutions for overcoming them.

SAMPLE: I know gyms are often crowded, so I'll find out which time slots are least busy at the on-campus gym and schedule my exercise time for those slots.

5 ACT AND EVALUATE OUTCOMES

Now that your plan is in place, take action. Record each action step as you take it. Then evaluate whether you achieved your SMART goal, and make any adjustments needed to get better results in the future.

SAMPLE: I wasn't able to find enough non-busy time slots at the gym to increase my exercising to two and a half hours per week. So I'll add a few twenty-minute jogs around my neighborhood to fill in the gap.

6 CONNECT TO CAREER

List the skills you're building as you progress toward your SMART goal. How will you use these skills to land a job and succeed at work?

SAMPLE: Working out is great for stress management. Getting the recommended amount of exercise each day will help me manage stress when I start a new job after college.

my personal success plan

1 my information

2 my SMART goal

☐ SPECIFIC ☐ MEASURABLE ☐ ACHIEVABLE ☐ RELEVANT ☐ TIME-LIMITED

3 my action plan

4 my barriers/ solutions

5 my actions/ outcomes

6 my career connection

12

chapter review

In this chapter we examined many strategies for nurturing your personal and financial health. Revisit the following key points, and reflect on how you can use this information to support your success now and in the future.

- Safeguarding your personal and financial health can help you manage stress. Constant severe stress can lead to physical, emotional, and mental-health problems.

- Your personal health includes your physical well-being and your mental health. Eating a healthy diet, staying active, and getting enough sleep can all enhance your physical well-being and mental health, enabling you to stay sharp in class and get the most value from your studies.

- Anxiety and depression are two common mental-health problems for college students. Knowing what your resources are and asking for help can be critical for managing these conditions.

- Sexual health is another key aspect of personal health. If you're sexually active, understanding and protecting yourself against sexually transmitted infections (STIs) through safe sexual practices, and practicing effective birth control if you're not planning to start a family yet, are critical.

- Managing your finances effectively can also help you mitigate stress and reach your goals. Creating a budget, and then refining it as needed, can help you manage your money effectively.

- Tactics for reducing spending include distinguishing between your needs and wants and, if need be, sacrificing your wants in order to get your spending under control.

- Tactics for increasing income include finding a job and getting financial aid.

- Understanding your credit card interest rate and paying down balances are keys to managing credit.

- The same behaviors that nurture your health in school can help you maximize your productivity and job satisfaction at work.

CHAPTER ACTIVITIES

Journal Entry

INOCULATING YOURSELF AGAINST STRESS

When you're physically and mentally fit, you prevent (or *inoculate* yourself against) stress. Stress inoculation includes paying attention to your physical health (nutrition, exercise, sleep) and mental health (social support, seeking help). List what you do now to take care of your physical health. What, if anything, would you like to do in the next two weeks in addition to the items on your list? Why? Now list what you do to take care of your mental health. What, if anything, would you like to do in the next two weeks in addition to the items on your list? Why?

Adopting a Success Attitude

COPING WITH STRESS USING HUMOR

The phrase "laughter is the best medicine" is especially true when it comes to relieving stress. Laughing relaxes tense muscles; reduces blood pressure and heart rate; exercises the muscles in your face, diaphragm, and abdomen; boosts your immune system; and triggers your body to release pain-fighting hormones. In fact, after you've had a big laugh, you could be free of muscle tension for as long as forty-five minutes. Plus, laughter boosts your mental health by distracting you from stress.

With these advantages in mind, do the following:

1. Find a funny cartoon, joke, quotation, or picture, and put it somewhere you can easily see it when you need a good chuckle.

2. Describe the item, where you placed it, and how often you glanced at it.

3. Explain what kinds of events made you want a laugh break. Then describe what impact, if any, these laugh breaks had on your stress levels.

4. Consider finding additional funny items and sharing them with others, or even creating a scrapbook or Pinterest board of things that make you laugh.

Applying Your Skills

USING YOUR FINANCIAL RESOURCES

As you just read, many types of scholarships are available to help you pay for college. Take the following steps to learn about your scholarship options.

1. Choose two of the following sources of information to search for scholarships you could apply for if you meet the qualifications.

    _____ Meet with a financial aid adviser or career counselor at your college.

    _____ Search your college's financial aid Web site.

    _____ Use the U.S. Department of Labor's free online scholarship search tool at http://www.careerinfonet.org/scholarshipsearch.

    _____ Contact your employer to see if they offer any financial assistance.

    _____ Go to the library and search for books on college scholarships.

    _____ Identify state-specific scholarships. Go to your state's Web site (for example, www.texas.gov) and search for "college scholarships."

    _____ Inquire about scholarships through your membership in local religious, cultural, or community organizations.

    _____ Contact professional associations related to your field of interest and investigate any scholarship opportunities.

    _____ Learn more about Reserve Officers' Training Corps (ROTC) scholarships through the Army, Air Force, Navy, or Marines (www.rotc.com).

2. Review the scholarship opportunities that you found. Choose one scholarship that you'd like to apply for.

3. Write down the title of the scholarship, the application criteria, and the application instructions. Then apply!

College Success = Career Success

MANAGING STRESS AT WORK

Managing stress at work is similar to managing stress in college. In fact, if you practice these strategies now, they'll be easier to perform in a work environment.

Describe a situation that's causing you stress. Then examine the chart below, which presents four ways to deal with a stressful situation. Two ways involve changing the situation, and two ways involve changing your reaction to the situation.

Read through each box and select "yes," "no," or "unsure" as you determine if this is a strategy you can use to deal with your stressful situation. After completing the chart, write down what you think is the most useful strategy in this situation. Then implement it. What challenges, if any, did you encounter as you implemented this strategy? How did you manage those challenges? What results did you get by implementing this strategy? On a job interview, if you were asked to describe how you handle stressful situations, what would you say?

Change the situation		Change your reaction to the situation	
Strategy 1: Avoid the stress	**Strategy 2: Alter the stressor**	**Strategy 3: Adapt to the stressor**	**Strategy 4: Accept the stressor**
Can you say "no"? *Yes No Unsure*	Can you ask for help? *Yes No Unsure*	Can you think more positively about the situation (find a silver lining)? *Yes No Unsure*	Can you give yourself an incentive to complete the task? *Yes No Unsure*
Can you alter your behavior to avoid the stress? *Yes No Unsure*	Can you schedule your time differently to reduce the stress? *Yes No Unsure*	Can you adjust your standards and not seek perfection? *Yes No Unsure*	Can you accept that some things are beyond your control? *Yes No Unsure*
Can you pare down your to-do list? *Yes No Unsure*	Can you delegate some tasks to others? *Yes No Unsure*	Can you recognize and reduce self-defeating thoughts you're having ("should," "must")? *Yes No Unsure*	Can you see how you would do things differently next time? *Yes No Unsure*
Can you avoid or limit your time with the person causing the stress? *Yes No Unsure*	Can you communicate your feelings and concerns to the person causing the stress? *Yes No Unsure*	Can you understand the perspective of the person causing the stress? *Yes No Unsure*	Can you let go of anger and resentment toward the person causing the stress, and move on? *Yes No Unsure*

13 Academic and Career Planning

Consider Your Interests, Values, and Skills

Develop an Academic Plan

Investigate Career Options

Academic and Career Planning Milestones

Keep Developing Your Career — Even While You Work!

My Personal Success Plan

Think of people you know who have completed college and have entered the work world. If you asked them to describe their academic and career experiences, you'd probably hear a variety of responses. One person might say, "I always wanted to go into teaching, so it was easy to decide on my degree, major, and classes." Someone else might say, "I thought I wanted be an anthropologist, but when I took some computer science courses and loved them, I changed my mind." Another person may say, "I studied to get a job as an accountant, but after working in that field for a while, I wanted to try something new. I'm on my third career!"

As these responses suggest, everyone's academic and career experiences are different. You can think of going through college and then entering the work world as a *general* path: You start school, choose an area of academic study, complete your degree or certificate, graduate, and then find a job. For some people, this process may be straightforward and easy. But many people find twists and turns along the way. Why? As you travel this path, you constantly learn about yourself—your dreams, your values, your interests—and you continually build new skills. You explore and experiment with different areas of study and with ideas about what careers might interest you. Along the way, you grow and change. Consequently, your plans may change. In the end, your academic and career paths will be unique to you.

This chapter helps you start your journey by providing the information you need in order to think critically about your options and make decisions that are right for you. The chapter will help you whether you've already chosen your major, classes, and career, or whether you're unsure about one or more of these decisions. First, we explore how knowing your interests, values, and skills can help you start building academic and career plans. We then focus on the key components of academic planning, how to conduct career research, and important milestones in the academic and career development processes. Finally, we look at ways to keep developing your career, even after you've entered the work world.

Willie B. Thomas/
Getty Images

Reflect

On Your Academic and Career Planning

MY ACES SCORE

☐ **HIGH**

☐ **MODERATE**

☐ **LOW**

 LaunchPad

To find your **Academic and Career Planning score**, go to the LaunchPad for *Connections*.

Take a moment to reflect on your Academic and Career Planning score on ACES. Find your score and add it in the circle to the right.

This score measures your beliefs about how familiar you are with academic and career planning and how confident you are that you can create good plans. Do you think it's an accurate snapshot of your understanding? Why or why not?

■ **IF YOU SCORED IN THE HIGH RANGE** and you believe this score is accurate, you may be very knowledgeable about crafting academic and career plans and confident in your ability to do so. However, plans can change, and strengthening your planning skills can help you feel confident that you're continuing to make the best decisions for you. As you read this chapter, keep an open mind and use the new information you learn to solidify your plans.

■ **IF YOU SCORED IN THE MODERATE OR LOW RANGE**, don't be discouraged. Many students question their ability to navigate the hundreds of courses their school offers, and many are anxious and unsure about choosing a major and a career. You'll have plenty of chances to strengthen your planning skills in this class, as you learn about degree options, course requirements, career possibilities, and ways to use insights about yourself to make these important decisions.

Consider Your Interests, Values, and Skills

Your academic and career choices will be as individual as you are, so the best way to start planning for these two important aspects of your life is to know yourself. And that means thinking critically as you gather and interpret information about your own interests, values, and skills—and then use the resulting insights about yourself to start building future plans.

Explore Your Interests

As we discuss in the chapter on building a foundation for success, your interests are your personal preferences—for example, what you like to do in your free time, what course subjects you enjoy, how you like to work, and with whom. These preferences can shed light on what kinds of courses and careers you might find most satisfying. If you don't have a clear idea of your interests or you want to learn even more about yourself, the strategies in this section can help.

Take an Interest Inventory. One way to investigate your interests is to take an *interest inventory*, which is a survey of your preferences. A useful and free inventory is the O*NET Interest Profiler, which you can access at www.mynextmove .org/explore/ip or by searching online using the phrase "my next move interest profiler." Completing this inventory may take 10–15 minutes but it's worth it—your results will help you think about jobs or professions that may appeal to you. Plus, the inventory can help you with academic planning by giving you insight into what kinds of courses and majors you'd find most intriguing. Complete this inventory now, and then we'll discuss how to interpret your results.

Understand Holland's Interest Types. Once you have the results of your interest inventory, the next step is to look at what they mean. The inventory is based on the work of John Holland, a renowned career psychologist who developed a system that describes people and work environments using six categories: Realistic, Investigative, Artistic, Social, Enterprising, and Conventional.[1]

- **Realistic (R).** People with Realistic interests enjoy working with their hands, working outside, using tools, installing and repairing things, or working with animals, and they enjoy studies that give them these opportunities. They're drawn to occupations in such fields as construction, veterinary and earth sciences, landscaping, and other work that's done primarily outdoors or in physically demanding environments—for example, forestry, physical education, athletics, personal training, and recreation or wildlife management.

- **Investigative (I).** People with Investigative interests like analyzing and solving problems and enjoy science, technical, or medicine-oriented courses. They find satisfaction in almost all areas of science and may work as university professors, doctors, and engineers or do research and development work in most industries.

- **Artistic (A).** People with Artistic interests are creative, intuitive, sensitive, and expressive. They prefer working with ideas and expressing their ideas through writing, sculpting, dancing, painting, acting, or musical performance. Some gravitate toward art-related studies and work as art instructors, as dance therapists, or in the fashion industry. Others write for newspapers or magazines or work as freelance writers.

- **Social (S).** People with strong Social interests enjoy helping, coaching, teaching, or counseling others. They may be drawn to studies and careers related to teaching, child and elder care, or community leadership and social justice. They may become psychologists, physical therapists, social workers, or occupational therapists.

- **Enterprising (E).** People with strong Enterprising interests like to influence, lead, persuade, and manage others. They may enjoy business studies and gravitate toward careers that emphasize fundraising, human resources, law, or management.

- **Conventional (C).** People with Conventional interests usually prefer structure in their school and work environments. They tend to be detail oriented, enjoy working with numbers or data, and are precise in their work. They frequently find satisfaction in the banking and finance industries, the computer sciences, or organizational departments such as payroll and purchasing.

**♦ CONNECT
TO MY EXPERIENCE**

Think about a job, an extracurricular activity, or a volunteer experience you had in the past. What Holland interest area best describes that experience? Write down which aspects of that experience you enjoyed the most and the least, and explain why. Use these insights to brainstorm the kinds of jobs you want to pursue (or avoid) in the future.

Social Interest in Action? Holly, a speech therapist, shows Vincent how to count with his fingers. She loves her work. Her interests probably fall under Holland's Social type, characterized by a desire to help, teach, and coach others. This interest may have strongly influenced her academic choices, including her degree, major, and classes. © Christina Kennedy/ PhotoEdit, Inc.

As you consider the results of your inventory, keep in mind that it's perfectly normal to have interests in more than one of these areas. If your interests span two or three categories, the key is to consider which studies and occupations would let you combine your varied interest types. For example, in school, choosing more than one major might let you explore several academic interests, such as business and recreation. In the work world, being an art gallery director might let you express both your Artistic and Enterprising interests, and working as an outdoor adventure counselor might satisfy your Social and Realistic interests. Later in this chapter, we'll look more closely at how to use knowledge of your interests to explore possible careers.

Explore Your Values

Your values are what you consider important — really important (see the chapter on building a foundation for success). They stem from your experiences with your family, your community, or your faith. Because you're in college, your academic values probably include getting a good education; if you're the first in your family to go to college, they may also include making your family proud.

In addition to academic values, you also have **work values**. These are the aspects of your work or your work environment that you consider important. To learn more about your work values, examine the items on the list below and ask yourself: How important are each of these values to me?[2]

Work Values: The aspects of your work or your work environment that you consider important.

- **Achievement:** using your abilities and gaining a feeling of accomplishment
- **Independence:** trying out your own ideas, making your own decisions, and working without supervision
- **Recognition:** having opportunities to advance in your career, direct the work of others, and be recognized for your accomplishments

Amazing Maze. Two artists created this labyrinth made out of books. What work values do you think they hold dear: Recognition? Independence? Achievement? If you're not sure, imagine yourself as an artist. If you're artistic already, what work values would *you* most like to express in your career? What kinds of jobs would best enable you to express those values? Peter Macdiarmid/ Getty Images

- 🟩 **Relationships:** getting along with coworkers, doing things for other people, and not having to do things that violate your ideals
- 🟩 **Support:** receiving helpful supervision, being treated fairly by your organization, and getting appropriate training
- 🟩 **Working conditions:** being busy all the time, receiving appropriate pay, feeling secure in your job, and constantly doing different activities

Understanding your work values—and their relative strength—can help you identify careers, and academic programs related to those careers, you might find satisfying. It can also help you make trade-offs. For example, if you become an elementary school teacher, you may have relatively little opportunity for advancement, and you probably won't get rich. But you'll go to work each day knowing you're helping others learn. Depending on your work values, this trade-off might be worthwhile—or it might not. Also note that some careers reinforce certain values and not others, depending on the setting or specialty. In the law profession, for instance, corporate lawyers typically earn a lot more money than public defenders do. If the law appeals to many of your work values but one of your strongest values is financial security, you might aim for a career in corporate law.

As you consider your work values, keep two things in mind: First, if you don't have much work experience, you may not have a clear picture of your work values just yet. That's okay: Your values will come into sharper focus as you get experience. Second, work values can change. For instance, someone who's raising a family may consider job security a critical work value. Once his children are grown, however, job security may not be as important, and perhaps he'll place more value on work that lets him feel that he's contributing to society. The upshot? Understanding your work values is an ongoing process, not a one-time event.

Explore Your Skills

As a college student, you probably excel at, and enjoy using, certain academic skills more than other skills. For instance, maybe you take detailed, accurate notes and ace most tests, but you find it more challenging (and terrifying) to make class presentations. The same is true about the work world. Take Janelle, a computer programmer. Her work involves writing computer code, reading project specifications, using logic and reasoning to solve problems, understanding her clients' and supervisors' needs, and managing her time so her projects stay on schedule. She loves writing code, but she dreads meeting with clients. By understanding her skills, she can look for a programming job that emphasizes what she's good at and what she enjoys—a position that focuses more on writing code than on tending to client relationships.

When it comes to work skills, here's another important point: Some are specific and are needed in only a few careers—such as writing computer code. Others are transferable and are used in many different careers—such as solving problems with logic and reasoning, listening to others, and managing your time. Your transferable skills let you cast your "career net" more widely, opening up a wider range of occupations that you could succeed in.

But you don't have to limit your options to work experiences that call for *only* your best skills. You can also seek out experiences that will let you develop new skills or strengthen your current skills. For instance, suppose you'd like to enhance your leadership skills. You could identify volunteer opportunities, leadership positions in campus clubs and organizations, part-time work, and training opportunities at your employer (if you're currently working) that would help you become a more confident leader. You might even establish a goal to develop this skill over the next few months, which you can document in your Personal Success Plan.

Technical + Transferable Talents. The U.S. Forest Service Fire Guard School trains wildfire fighters. Students learn not only highly technical skills but also transferable skills, which employers value in a variety of work settings. For instance, students learn how to work seamlessly with others to take quick, effective action to address problems. © Aaron Schmidt/Tandem Stock

HOPE AND ENGAGEMENT PROMOTE ACADEMIC SUCCESS AND CAREER DEVELOPMENT

According to a study presented in the chapter on building a foundation for success, students who have high levels of hope stay in school and graduate at a higher rate than those with less hope. But hope is also related to other important components of academic and career success, as revealed by a recent research collaboration between Penn State and the University of British Columbia.

Researchers measured a number of items: levels of hope, student engagement on campus (such as active and collaborative learning and student-faculty interactions), grade point average (GPA), and *vocational identity*, which is a person's understanding of his or her career goals, interests, and strengths. They discovered the following relationships.

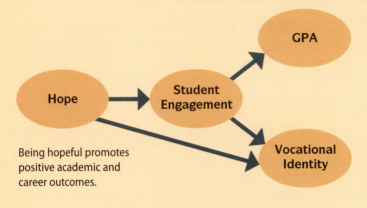

Being hopeful promotes positive academic and career outcomes.

- Students with higher levels of hope were more engaged, and students with high engagement scores achieved higher GPAs.

- Students who had high levels of hope and who were engaged on campus also had much stronger vocational identities.

THE BOTTOM LINE

Maintaining a positive attitude, including remaining hopeful, may help you engage more actively in your learning, earn higher grades, and gain the personal insights needed to make good career-related decisions.

REFLECTION QUESTIONS

1. How hopeful are you about your career future?
2. On a scale of 1 to 10, with 10 being the strongest, how would you rate your vocational identity? That is, how well do you understand your own career goals, interests, and strengths?
3. What steps could you take today to strengthen your vocational identity?

N. Amundson, S. Niles, H. J. Yoon, B. Smith, H. In, and L. Mills, "Hope-Centered Career Development for University/College Students: Final Project Report," last modified 2013, http://www.ceric.ca/ceric/files/pdf /CERIC_Hope-Centered-Career-Research-Final-Report.pdf.

Develop an Academic Plan

In college it's never too early to create an **academic plan**—a roadmap showing the steps you'll take to complete your degree or certificate. Recognizing your interests, values, and skills can help you create this plan, as can a solid understanding of your school's requirements—for instance, when you have to declare a major, the grade point average you need to be accepted into your chosen program, and whether you should document your plan electronically or on paper. To build your plan most effectively, you'll have to know what's expected—and when.

Your plan will also need to reflect your goals. For example, if you're attending a two-year college and you want to earn a four-year degree, it's crucial to determine which of your current classes will transfer to your next institution. And if you're attending school and want to get a job right after graduation, you'll focus on courses needed to obtain your degree and prepare for the job market.

Students have unique goals and schools have unique requirements, so your academic plan will likely differ from classmates' and those of students attending other types of institutions. This puts you in control—it's *your* academic plan, you own it, and you can make sure it works for you. If the idea of making these kinds of decisions right now seems overwhelming, trust that your critical thinking skills can help you gather, evaluate, and use the information to make good choices, and that many people at your school can help you do so. Your plan may change in the future, but developing a roadmap early gives you some initial clarity on your academic goals so that you can begin working to achieve them.

To get started on your plan, learn the basics: information about degree options, picking a major, and selecting courses, as well as the benefits of seeking support from an adviser (see Figure 13.1).

Academic Plan: A tool used by students and their advisers to plan and track a student's progress toward obtaining a degree or certificate.

FIGURE 13.1 Components of Academic Planning

Choose a Degree or Certificate

To choose a degree or certificate you have to know your options—and there are many! Schools across the country offer a wide range of degrees and certificates; Table 13.1 shows common examples. Generally, two-year colleges offer different types of degrees than do four-year colleges, though not always. For instance, some colleges that traditionally offered only two-year degrees now offer four-year bachelor's degrees in high-demand fields. And some four-year schools offer select two-year degrees.

As you research the options at your school, pay attention to terminology. For example, your school may use different terms to describe associate's degrees that prepare you to transfer to a four-year college and associate's degrees that prepare you to enter the workforce directly.

TABLE 13.1 Overview of Common Degrees and Certificates

Degree	Time required*	Schools offering degree	General purpose	Sample academic programs
Certificates	1–2 years	Two-year colleges, some four-year institutions, and specialty institutions	Prepare students with specialized skills for work	Automotive maintenance, construction technology, practical nursing, medical assisting
Associate of arts, associate of science, associate of applied science	2 years	Two-year colleges and some four-year institutions	Prepare students for work or for transfer to four-year colleges	Fire science, emergency medical technology, sports and fitness management, early childhood education, visual and performing arts, science, computer science
Bachelor of arts, bachelor of science	4 years	Four-year institutions and some two-year colleges	Prepare students for work or postgraduate education	Physics, psychology, literature, engineering, nursing, history, mathematics, dance, business, foreign languages
Master's degree	1–3 years (depending on degree type)	Four-year institutions and some specialty institutions	Prepare students for entry into fields requiring advanced training	Social work, counseling, accounting, business administration, geology, nursing and teaching specialties
Doctoral degree	3–6 years (depending on degree type)	Universities and some specialty institutions	Prepare students for entry into fields requiring a doctoral degree for teaching, research, or practice	School or university administration, psychology, science, pharmacy, physical therapy
Professional degree	3–5 years (depending on degree type)	Universities and some specialty institutions	Prepare students for entry into fields requiring advanced training for practice	Medicine (all specialties), law, chiropractic, audiology, veterinary, podiatry, optometry

*Note: Times listed to complete degrees are minimum times. Some students take longer, depending on their life circumstances.

In addition, remember that everyone's life circumstances are unique. Not all students graduate in exactly two or four years, even if they attend what's considered a two- or four-year school. For example, your time line may be different if you're going to school part-time (as do 37 percent of U.S. students[3]) or if you take foundational courses before you begin earning college credit. You can work with a professional adviser at your school to decide on a time frame and a degree or certificate program that make sense for you.

Choose a Major

A **college major** is a collection of courses organized around an academic theme. A major enables you to understand one area of scholarship or practice in depth. To select a major, you need to consider your own career goals and what's important to you and to understand some logistics—for example, by when your college expects you to make this decision.

Consider Your Career Goals and What's Important to You. If you have a particular career in mind, investigate what type of degree is generally required and whether that career requires a specific major. To enter fields such as nursing, engineering, education, and accounting, graduating with a pre-professional major is critical. And many academic programs in two-year colleges prepare you for immediate entry into a specific career, such as electrical technician, diesel mechanic, dental hygienist, and certified nursing assistant.

But other majors—such as sociology, English, psychology, and history—prepare you for a variety of careers by helping you build transferable skills valued by many employers. If your career of choice doesn't require a specific major, you can select a major based on other factors—for example, because of a class you enjoyed, because of your interests, or because you're skilled in a particular area (such as music or math).

As you weigh your options, it's also worth considering whether the career you have in mind calls for advanced schooling. Some careers (for example, doctor, lawyer, or school counselor) require a graduate or professional degree, so if you're planning to enter one of these fields, investigate whether related graduate programs recommend or require specific undergraduate majors. And if you're at a two-year school and plan to transfer to a four-year school, selecting certain majors may increase your chance of transferring, especially if you want to enter a specific program.

College Major:
A collection of courses organized around an academic theme.

A Passion for Science.
Marcus, a science major, holds up a model of a molecule. He selected his major because he's interested in jobs involving scientific research, which require specific degrees and majors. But Gloria, who's also taking this class, registered for the course simply because she has always been interested in science and wants to learn more. Noel Hendrickson/ Getty Images

Consider Time Frame and Qualifications. Many first-year students are undecided about which major to pursue, and that's okay—most schools have resources that can help students explore different academic and career pathways. However, you'll want to find out *by when* your school requires that decision to be made, so you can prepare yourself as best as possible.

In addition, you need to know your school's requirements for being admitted into a particular major so that you can plan how to meet those requirements. Take Nicolai, a first-year student attending a local two-year college. Nicolai wants to go into business and plans to transfer to a four-year college to complete his business degree. He knows that most business programs require a GPA of at least 3.3 to be admitted, but his current GPA is only 3.1. So he talks with his adviser about how he can improve his GPA (for example, he might go for tutoring) and discusses other options to pursue if he's unsuccessful in doing so.

Choose Your Courses

Depending on your school and program, you'll need a certain number of credits to graduate, and those credits usually come from two areas: courses required for your major and general-education (or *core*) course requirements.

To complete your major, certain courses will be required. For instance, if you major in outdoor education, you may have to take courses in teaching methods, child and adult development, and biology. Most majors also allow you to take electives—courses you choose to take based on your interests or career goals. If you're majoring in architecture, for example, you may decide to take electives in urban planning and art history.

General-education courses, which are common at both two- and four-year colleges, give students a broad liberal education in the natural and social sciences, humanities, arts, and mathematics. These courses are important because they help you develop critical thinking skills, use and evaluate data and numbers, and communicate through writing and speaking—all transferable skills. General-education courses also introduce you to a wide range of ideas and topics. Exposure to new knowledge can help you gain insight into your interests and values—which in turn can help you pick a major. In fact, you might find that you enjoy a course in your general-education curriculum so much that you end up selecting that area as a major.

Conveniently, sometimes you can satisfy general-education course requirements by taking courses related to your major (such as an architecture major who takes an art course). An adviser can strategize with you about which general-education courses will help prepare you for a particular career.

Get Help from an Academic Adviser or Counselor

As you can see, academic planning involves working with a lot of information. To make sure you're aware of everything you need to know, you'll want to meet with an **academic adviser** or, in some states, a **counselor**—a highly trained professional who can help you make effective academic decisions and refer you

---

**✎ CONNECT
TO MY CLASSES**

Consider the courses you're taking this term. Write down which courses satisfy your college's general-education requirements and which, if any, you're taking in your major.

General-Education Courses: A set of course requirements that gives all students a broad liberal education in the natural and social sciences, humanities, arts, and mathematics.

Academic Adviser/ Counselor: A highly trained professional who can help you make effective academic decisions and refer you to valuable campus resources.

SELECTING A MAJOR AND CHOOSING CLASSES

Courtesy of
Tony Kao

NAME: **Tony Kao**

SCHOOL: *University of Kentucky*

MAJOR: *Mechanical Engineering*

CAREER GOAL: *Mechanical Design*

I'm a first-generation college student. My parents immigrated to the United States so I could get a better education. It was always assumed that I would go to college, and my parents and advisers have supported me throughout the process. I want to find a career path that I'll enjoy, but also one that will make them proud.

The people who know me can tell you that I'm a very logical and analytical kind of person. I always like to figure out how things work and how each component of a product contributes to the overall design, regardless of what it is. I thought that since I enjoy learning about how things work, why not make a career of it? I could continue to learn, put my own knowledge to the test, *and* get paid for doing something I love and enjoy.

Because of this passion and because of my aptitude in math and science, I chose mechanical engineering as my major. This degree will allow me to be creative but also develop my technical skills and knowledge. For example, I recently completed an internship in an automobile assembly plant, which taught me the importance of product reliability, construction, and installation.

My university also has general-education requirements. I've tried to find elective courses that will not only fulfill requirements but also be useful in my career or daily life. I chose Technical Writing and Personal Finance. I think these courses will apply no matter what job I get after graduating. I also wanted to take a course that was fun, so I enrolled in a tennis class. I really enjoy this class, and it gives me a break between my engineering classes.

I hope to find a job that will provide me with financial stability, the potential for growth, and fulfillment. I want a sense of pride from the work that I do.

YOUR TURN: Have you chosen a major? If so, how does the process you used to select your major compare with the one that Tony used to select his? If your school offers electives, do any appeal to you? If so, which ones — and why?

> **"I've tried to find elective courses that will not only fulfill requirements but also be useful in my career or daily life."**

to valuable campus resources. Although ultimately you're responsible for your own academic plan, an adviser can provide the support and information you need to think critically about your options. He or she can also help you stay informed about your school's course, transfer, and degree requirements.

There are many types of advisers, and schools organize their advising programs in different ways. For example, some schools have a central academic advising office that specializes in working with first-year students, while at other schools this work is done in counseling centers. And in some cases, academic departments have advisers (some of whom are faculty members) who specialize in working with students who have declared a major.

Given the variety in how academic advising is structured, investigate your school's approach and find out which advisers are responsible for helping you right now. Schedule an appointment with an adviser at least once each term (including this term, if you haven't done so already) to assess your progress toward your academic goals, to get ideas for overcoming any challenges you encounter, and to refine your academic plan as needed.

Investigate Career Options

FIGURE 13.2
Investigating Career Options

So far you've explored your interests, work values, and skills, and you've learned how to create an academic plan. What's next? You can use these insights to investigate career options by conducting online research, talking with experts, and getting direct experience that will help you discover more about careers of interest (see Figure 13.2). You'll use your critical thinking skills to gather, evaluate, and use all this information in a way that makes the most sense for you.

As you gather information, try not to put too much pressure on yourself to pick the "right" career. For some students, making an initial career decision is a paralyzing process, because it feels like this one choice could dictate the rest of their lives. In reality, career decisions are more flexible: You make the choice, evaluate how it feels for you, and change it if you don't like it! In fact, many people change careers several times during the course of their lives. So view the information-gathering experience as just one step toward a satisfying career.

Get to Know the O*NET

Probably the best place to start researching different occupations is the O*NET (Occupational Network), an occupational database maintained by the U.S. Department of Labor. It's chock-full of helpful job-related facts, including how certain occupations match people's interests, work values, and skills. Drawing on your self-knowledge, you can search for jobs that meet the criteria you consider most important. You can also use the O*NET to research what level of education and experience is required for a particular occupation (a category called the Job Zone), how much the occupation pays, and its **occupational projection** for the next ten years, which predicts how many of those jobs may be available when you graduate. You can also search for occupations by keyword, such as the name of your college major.

Occupational Projection: The predicted rise or fall in the number of new jobs in a particular field.

For a more detailed look at the O*NET, see Figure 13.3, which shows how to search for occupations using the results of the Holland interest inventory. An activity at the end of the chapter also gives you a chance to explore the O*NET firsthand.

FIGURE 13.3 **Example O*NET Occupational Search Based on Interests**

These O*NET screenshots show a search for occupations by Holland interest type; a list of occupations sorted by Job Zone; and a summary report for a particular occupation. You can also search the O*NET by work values or skills.

Browse by O*NET Data

O*NET Data descriptors are categories of occupational information collected and available for O*NET-SOC occupations. Each descriptor contains more specific elements with data ratings.

[Interests ▾] [Go]

> You can browse occupations by Holland type.

Interests

Preferences for work environments and outcomes.

Realistic — Realistic occupations frequently involve work activities that include practical, hands-on problems and solutions. They often deal with plants, animals, and real-world materials like wood, tools, and machinery. Many of the occupations require working outside, and do not involve a lot of paperwork or working closely with others.

Investigative — Investigative occupations frequently involve working with ideas, and require an extensive amount of thinking. These occupations can involve searching for facts and figuring out problems mentally.

Artistic — Artistic occupations frequently involve working with forms, designs and patterns. They often require self-expression and the work can be done without following a clear set of rules.

Social — Social occupations frequently involve working with, communicating with, and teaching people. These occupations often involve helping or providing service to others.

Enterprising — Enterprising occupations frequently involve starting up and carrying out projects. These occupations can involve leading people and making many decisions. Sometimes they require risk taking and often deal with business.

Conventional — Conventional occupations frequently involve following set procedures and routines. These occupations can include working with data and details more than with ideas. Usually there is a clear line of authority to follow.

You have chosen: Realistic

More occupations | **Fewer occupations**   20 occupations displayed.

Job Zone [4 ▾]

	Code	Occupation
4	17-3021.00	Aerospace Engineering and Operations Technicians
4	53-2011.00	Airline Pilots, Copilots, and Flight Engineers
4	19-4021.00	Biological Technicians
4	17-1021.00	Cartographers and Photogrammetrists
4	17-2051.00	Civil Engineers ☀ Bright Outlook 🌿 Green

> If you click "Realistic," for example, you'll get a list of jobs in this category. You can then sort the jobs by "Job Zone." (Zone 4 requires a college degree.)

Summary Report for:

Updated 2014

Bright ☀ Outlook

🌿 green

17-2051.00 - Civil Engineers

Perform engineering duties in planning, designing, and overseeing construction and maintenance of building structures, and facilities, such as roads, railroads, airports, bridges, harbors, channels, dams, irrigation projects, pipelines, power plants, and water and sewage systems.

Sample of reported job titles: Bridge/Structure Inspection Team Leader, City Engineer, Civil Engineer, Civil Engineering Manager, County Engineer, Design Engineer, Project Engineer, Railroad Design Consultant, Structural Engineer, Traffic Engineer

Also see: Transportation Engineers

View report:	**Summary**	Details	Custom

Tasks | Tools & Technology | Knowledge | Skills | Abilities | Work Activities | Detailed Work Activities | Work Context | Job Zone | Education | Credentials | Interests | Work Styles | Work Values | Related Occupations | Wages & Employment | Job Openings | Additional Information

Tasks

➕➖ 5 of 17 displayed

- ✪ Inspect project sites to monitor progress and ensure conformance to design specifications and safety or sanitation standards.
- ✪ Compute load and grade requirements, water flow rates, or material stress factors to determine design specifications.
- ✪ Provide technical advice to industrial or managerial personnel regarding design, construction, or program modifications or structural repairs.
- ✪ Test soils or materials to determine the adequacy and strength of foundations, concrete, asphalt, or steel.
- ✪ Manage and direct the construction, operations, or maintenance activities at project site.

> Once you click on an occupation, you can access a wide array of related information — everything from tasks involved to applicable skills and work values.

> "Bright Outlook" jobs are those expected to grow rapidly in coming years. "Green Outlook" jobs are those that result from an emphasis on sustainability or that will change as a result of sustainability efforts.

Talk with Experts

As a college student, you have access to a wide range of experts who can help you with career planning, including career counselors on campus and people in the work world who can give you the "inside scoop" on particular types of jobs, employers, and careers.

Meet with a Career Counselor.

Career Counselor:
A specially trained professional who uses career assessments and other resources to help students explore career options and make career decisions.

Meet with a Career Counselor. Some students have a hard time defining a career path or feeling confident about the path they've chosen. Fortunately, many campuses employ **career counselors**, specially trained professionals who use career assessments and other resources to help students explore career options, make important career decisions, and manage any related stress they're experiencing. Career counselors, who usually work in the campus's counseling or career center, can connect you with all kinds of useful information. Services at these centers often include:

- Individual meetings with career counselors
- Workshops or groups designed to help you with specific concerns, such as how to structure your job search process
- Subscriptions to online career information resources (often based on the O*NET), which can include interest assessments and video interviews with people working in various occupations
- Tools for creating your résumé
- Tips for preparing for job interviews

Why not seize the day? Visit your school's counseling or career center this week to find out how counselors can help you investigate career options.

Conduct Informational Interviews. You can also get valuable job information from someone currently working in a career that interests you. By conducting an *informational interview*, or conversation, with a person working in a particular field, you can get "insider information" about what a job is really like from day to day.

To find someone working in a field of interest, get referrals from friends and family, ask your instructors, and review alumni mentor lists at your school's career center. When you first contact this person, be sure to explain that you're looking for an informational interview, either face-to-face or by phone. This is a fact-finding investigation—your purpose is not to job hunt but rather to find out what the work entails, what this person likes most and least about the job, and what benefits and opportunities for advancement this line of work offers. Table 13.2 shows questions you might ask during informational interviews.

Get Experience

Even while you're in college, you can gain experience that helps you learn more about careers of interest, and even start building the skills you'll need to succeed in those jobs. Consider these ideas:

- **Service learning.** Most colleges and universities offer *service learning* opportunities that pair a practical service experience with formal classroom discussions and assignments. For example, if Rhonda is interested in health care management and psychology, she could sign up for a ser-

TABLE 13.2   **Questions to Ask at an Informational Interview**

What kinds of tasks do you perform in a typical week?
How does this career affect your lifestyle?
What are some of the more difficult or frustrating parts of this career?
What are the best parts of your job?
Is this career changing? How?
Do you usually work independently or as part of a team?
Do you have any advice regarding how someone interested in this career should prepare?
What types of advancement opportunities are available for an entry-level worker in this career?
What is the average starting salary for someone in this career?

vice learning class working with senior citizens in a local nursing home. Through this experience, she would learn about nursing facility management while also helping the residents.

- **Internships.** Internships—formal programs that provide practical experience for beginners in an occupation or a profession—are another worthwhile option. In fact, recent research suggests that students who graduate with internship experiences receive more job offers and higher starting salaries than those without these experiences.[4] Internships are often available during the summer, though some come up during the academic year. Check with a career counselor at your school to find out which nearby organizations offer internship opportunities.

Growing Skills. The summer before Maria's second year in college, she planted strawberries as part of a paid internship at a community farm. The arrangement, financed by her college, helps Maria and other students build their skills. Meanwhile, the farm benefits from their energy, hard work, and fresh ideas. AP Photo/ Steven Senne

- **Co-ops.** College co-op programs offer alternating periods of academic study and periods of work experience in fields such as business, industry, government, and social services. These programs are a great way to learn about specific careers while also making a little money. In addition, during your work experiences you may forge helpful connections with people who can help you later—for example, when you're seeking job opportunities or when you need letters of recommendation for a potential employer.

- **Working.** Working while you're in college allows you to investigate career options as you build your skills and knowledge. The key is not to take on so many hours that you have difficulty juggling your coursework and your job.

Academic and Career Planning Milestones

Now that you've learned about the major components of academic planning and strategies for investigating career options, let's look at key milestones that come up in academic and career planning. Understanding these milestones can help you sketch out approximate times for completing them, which adds structure to your college experience.

- **Find your path.** Are you currently at a two-year college? If so, Table 13.3 offers two sets of suggested milestones: one for those who want to enter the workforce directly after graduating and another for those who plan to transfer to a four-year college. Are you currently at a four-year school? Table 13.4 offers suggested milestones for you to follow. Feel free to modify these models to suit your educational time line; if you'll be in school for more or less time than the models show, make adjustments to fit your specific circumstances. In addition, exactly what you do for each milestone (and when you do it) may vary depending on your school's requirements. So talk with an adviser or a career counselor to see whether there are campus-specific recommendations to keep in mind as you make your plans.

- **Get started.** As you look at the suggested milestones, consider which primary tasks you need to address right now—such as maintaining a strong GPA or planning a course of study with an adviser. Many of these tasks will be familiar, as they're discussed in previous sections in this chapter as well as in other chapters.

- **Consider tasks that are on the horizon.** Can you get a jump on some of these upcoming tasks now? If so, how? Take a particularly close look at the final year in the model plans. Except for students who are going on to further schooling, this is a time when most students begin searching for a job in their chosen field. This is a vital stage of your career development and it requires serious attention. Research suggests that students who take an active role in their job search are much better off than those who don't.[5]

- **Make connections.** Even if you're not looking for a job just yet, it's a good idea to start building relationships with counselors in the career center *now*. When the time comes, they can help you prepare for job interviews, review and critique your résumé, show you how to gather information about employers you'll be interviewing with, and give you tips on negotiating pay and other employment terms with an organization once you receive a job offer. (This book's Appendix also provides valuable tips on preparing for and conducting a job search.)

- **Revise as needed.** Finally, always remember: Academic and career planning is an ongoing process. As you go through college, you'll revisit your plans periodically and refine them as needed to reflect your most recent thoughts about your education and work life. By doing some reflecting and readjusting, you can be sure you're pursuing a path that's meaningful for you.

TABLE 13.3   Two-Year College Planning Milestones

Year 1: Transitioning, Exploring, and Planning
All
• Develop and practice the success skills discussed in this book.
• Focus on establishing a strong GPA.
• Begin to identify your career-related interests, skills, and values.
• Get involved in campus activities.
• Develop a preliminary résumé.
• Explore work or volunteer activities that will strengthen your résumé.
Transfer Option
• Plan your course of study with an academic adviser to maximize transfer credits.
• Discuss colleges and universities that you are considering transferring to.
• If possible, meet with an academic adviser at the schools to which you may apply.
• Identify the application deadlines for schools to which you may apply.
Work Option
• Document how the success skills you're using at school translate to future careers.
• Discuss with a career counselor what career opportunities are available for graduates with your degree.
• Conduct information interviews with people in your community who are employed in areas that interest you.

TABLE 13.3 (continued)

Year 2: Completing Your Program and Preparing for Another Transition

Transfer Option

- Prepare and submit applications for admission to four-year colleges.
- Gather information about the majors available at the schools to which you are applying.
- Meet with your adviser, or advisers at your target schools, to talk about declaring a major when you arrive.
- If possible, work with an adviser on your campus or an adviser at your target school to create a first-year course plan so that you can hit the ground running.
- Update your résumé annually.
- Continue to acquire practical experience through clubs and organizations, volunteering, and work.

Work Option

- Continue to develop the transferable skills that employers desire most.
- Meet with one or more instructors to discuss career options.
- Meet with a counselor at the career center to discuss the job search services the center provides.
- If available, register for on-campus interviews, or identify where employment opportunities are posted on your campus.
- Have a counselor at the career center critique your résumé.
- Conduct mock interviews with friends, colleagues, or a counselor at the career center.
- Continue to acquire practical experience through clubs and organizations, volunteering, and work.
- Consider leadership opportunities in clubs and organizations.

TABLE 13.4 Four-Year College Planning Milestones

Year 1: Transitioning and Exploring

- Develop and practice the success skills discussed in this book.
- Focus on establishing a strong GPA.
- Begin to identify your career-related interests, skills, and values.
- Reflect on which topics covered in your first-year courses you find interesting.
- Talk with an academic adviser about the majors you're considering.
- Talk with career counselors about the relationship between various majors and the careers you're considering.
- Get involved in campus activities.
- Develop a preliminary résumé.
- Explore work or volunteer activities that will strengthen your résumé.
- Conduct one or more informational interviews.

TABLE 13.4 (continued)

Year 2: Finding Your Direction

- Declare an academic major.
- Join a club or professional organization related to your academic major.
- Begin to develop relationships with instructors in your major who can later support your job search with letters of recommendation.
- Document how the success skills you're using at school translate to future careers.
- Consider volunteer or employment opportunities related to your academic major.
- Discuss with a career counselor what career opportunities are available for graduates with your major.
- Update your résumé annually.
- Research how to prepare for the careers that interest you.
- Consider conducting another informational interview with a recent graduate in your major. (The alumni center may help you find recent graduates who would be willing to talk with you.)

Year 3: Confirming Your Path and Gaining Experience

- Evaluate your satisfaction with the direction you have chosen. If you're not satisfied, meet with an academic adviser or career counselor to assist you in changing direction.
- Continue acquiring practical experience related to your major through clubs and organizations, volunteering, and work.
- Continue to develop the transferable skills that employers desire most.
- Consider whether you want to start working after getting your degree or enter a graduate or professional training program.
- If appropriate, determine graduate school testing and application deadlines.
- Begin researching graduate programs or employers related to the careers you are considering.
- Review syllabi in the courses in your academic major to identify possible career and graduate school specialty options.
- Update your résumé annually.
- Meet with instructors in your academic major to discuss career and graduate school options.
- Meet with a counselor in the career center to discuss the job search services the center provides.

Year 4: Preparing for Another Transition

- If you plan to continue your education, fill out graduate or professional school applications.
- If you are seeking employment, register for on-campus interviews.
- Meet with a counselor in the career center to polish your résumé.
- Research employers with whom you will interview.
- Conduct mock interviews with friends, colleagues, or a counselor at the career center.
- Continue to acquire practical experience through clubs and organizations, volunteering, and work.
- Find out what services the career center offers to students after graduation.

Keep Developing Your Career — Even While You Work!

Career planning doesn't end once you have a job. Rather, you can continue developing your career even while you work by seizing opportunities to master new skills, advance in your chosen profession, or even try a different career if your work values, interests, skills, or other life circumstances change. If you make a change, you'll be in good company: According to the U.S. Bureau of Labor Statistics, people change their jobs an average of eleven times before they approach retirement age.[6]

Advance in Your Chosen Career

As you refine your professional goals, you may find that making a career plan helps you rise in the ranks at your company or organization. Consider Sam, who had been working for two years as a clinical data manager at a regional hospital. One day, Sam learned that one of her coworkers, Elaine, was promoted to associate director of data management at an outpatient clinic in town. Sam wanted to get a similar promotion, so she did some career planning: She set out to learn what kinds of training and experience would best prepare her to take this next step in her professional life. Her plan included conducting informational interviews with her supervisor, Tomas, and with Elaine. As it turned out, Tomas was delighted to hear of her interest in advancement. He gave her new responsibilities to help her build her skills, such as managing the data-entry clerks in her office, and also recommended that she take online courses to develop the further skills she needed to advance in her career. And from Elaine, Sam learned a lot about the skills she'd need in order to excel in that more challenging, complex role.

Explore New Opportunities

For a different example of on-the-job career development, consider Seth's experience. As a gaming supervisor for a large casino in Las Vegas, Seth discovered that he liked working with people but wasn't happy with the job's unpredictable hours and stressful working conditions, which included constant noise, flashing lights, and dealing with disruptive customers. He thought about changing jobs but worried that he wouldn't make as much money in a new job without receiving considerable retraining. His work values had shifted: He had started a family, so financial security was important to him. And because being a parent was exhausting, he valued workplace settings that were quiet and relatively stress-free—a value that his current job didn't uphold.

So Seth logged onto the O*NET and researched occupations that would let him work with people but that had more predictable hours, less stressful working conditions, and acceptable pay. After reviewing the search results, he zeroed in on one option he found particularly interesting: dental hygienist.

Work Values: Fluid — Not Frozen. As you gain work experience, your work values may shift, possibly prompting career changes. For instance, maybe you originally valued the structure and comfort that came with a desk job but later realized you needed more physical challenge and fresh air in your work environment. If so, a job studying melting ice in the Arctic might be perfect for you! © Jenny E. Ross/Corbis

ON-THE-JOB CAREER PLANNING

NEIU

NAME:	**Bilal Malik**
PROFESSION:	*Associate Consultant*
SCHOOL:	*Northeastern Illinois University*
DEGREE:	*Bachelor of Science*
MAJOR:	*Computer Science*

I started figuring out my career plan back when I was in college. I had taken a few courses in computer security, and when I realized how much I liked them, I made that my focus and found ways to get experience. I participated in computer security–related events at school to network with information security professionals. One of my teachers, who also worked in the IT department, recognized my enthusiasm for the subject matter and recommended me for a Network Security Internship on campus.

I've since graduated and have a job in computer security, where I work on making credit card transactions more secure. While I'm off to a good start, in order to make sure my career develops the way I'd like it to, I picked up where I left off in college and went back to work on a career plan. I'm currently in year one of a three-year plan that I created. During this first year, I took some classes outside of college, picked up an extra certification, and started my first job. I also did some research and talked with colleagues in the information security field. I'm going to spend the second year of my plan gaining knowledge and expertise in the area of health care information security. I'll spend the third year building my skills and expertise around standards in the field. By creating and following a plan, I have a good handle on where my career will be in the next few years.

YOUR TURN: If you're currently working, where do you see your work life headed? Do you want to advance in your career? If so, could you build a multiyear plan for doing so, as Bilal did? What action steps would you include in your plan?

> " By creating and following a plan, I have a good handle on where my career will be in the next few years."

Then he did additional research to find out what training he'd need to move into this job.

Whether you want to advance in your chosen occupation or change careers entirely, you can use the skills you're developing this term to make smart work-related decisions in the future. What kinds of career decisions do you see yourself making in the next ten years? Do you feel better prepared to make those decisions now than you did at the start of the term? Why or why not?

my personal success plan

Are you inspired to set a new goal related to academic or career planning? If so, the Personal Success Plan can walk you through the goal-setting process. Read the advice and examples; then sketch out your ideas in the space provided.

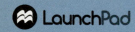 LaunchPad

To access the Personal Success Plan online, go to the LaunchPad for *Connections*.

1 GATHER INFORMATION

Think about your strengths and weaknesses related to academic and career planning, and revisit your Academic and Career Planning score on ACES. What realistic goal will you set now that will help you achieve your longer-term goal of graduating and preparing for a rewarding career? Reread the relevant sections of this chapter if you need ideas.

2 SET A SMART GOAL

Use the information you've gathered to create a SMART goal, making sure to use the SMART goal checklist.

SAMPLE: I'll schedule an appointment with my adviser next week to discuss my course plan for next year.

3 MAKE AN ACTION PLAN

Outline the specific steps you'll take to achieve your SMART goal, and note when you'll complete each step.

SAMPLE: I'll e-mail my adviser and let her know when I'm free for an appointment.

4 LIST BARRIERS AND SOLUTIONS

Think about possible barriers to your action steps; then brainstorm solutions for overcoming them.

SAMPLE: If my adviser doesn't reply to my e-mail, I'll send a second e-mail and leave a message on her voice mail.

5 ACT AND EVALUATE OUTCOMES

Now that your plan is in place, take action. Record each action step as you take it. Then evaluate whether you achieved your SMART goal, and make any adjustments needed to get better results in the future.

SAMPLE: I got an e-mail back from my adviser, scheduled an appointment, and met with her. I'm really feeling good about my course plan for next year.

6 CONNECT TO CAREER

List the skills you're building as you progress toward your SMART goal. How will you use these skills to land a job and succeed at work?

SAMPLE: I'm not sure yet what career I'll pursue, but scheduling appointments, following up if there's no response, and living up to my commitments are skills I'll need in any career.

my personal success plan

1 my information

2 my SMART goal

☐ **S**PECIFIC ☐ **M**EASURABLE ☐ **A**CHIEVABLE ☐ **R**ELEVANT ☐ **T**IME-LIMITED

3 my action plan

4 my barriers/ solutions

5 my actions/ outcomes

6 my career connection

13

CHAPTER SUMMARY

In this chapter you learned about the building blocks of academic and career planning, including the importance of refining your plans as you continue to gain experience and insights about yourself. Review the following key ideas and consider how you might use them to develop sound but adaptable plans for success as you go through college and take steps along a career path.

- Understanding yourself — your interests, values, and skills — helps you identify areas of study as well as lines of work that you may find rewarding.

- Taking an interest inventory can help you clarify your interests. Gaining experience in different jobs and work environments can help you define your work values, which can change over time. In assessing your skills, it's helpful to distinguish between specialized skills and transferable skills.

- An academic plan is a roadmap showing the steps you'll take to complete a degree or certificate. Most academic plans involve declaring a major and completing both college major and general-education requirements. An academic adviser (and others on campus) can review your plan and help you refine it as needed and ensure that you meet critical deadlines, such as the deadline for declaring a major.

- To investigate potential careers, you gather information about the available options and how they match up with your interests, work values, skills, and academic goals. You can gather information using the O*NET; talk with experts such as career counselors and people currently working in jobs that interest you; gain experience through service learning, co-op, and internship programs; and find employment.

- Career planning doesn't end when you graduate and start working. As your interests, values, skills, and goals change, you may change your plans several times to continue building a rewarding professional and personal life.

CHAPTER ACTIVITIES

Journal Entry

MAKING A GOOD CAREER DECISION

A good career decision draws on your insights about yourself and your evaluation of information about the world of work. Write a journal entry about an occupation that interests you, using the following questions to guide you.

- What interests you about this occupation?

- In what ways would this occupation align with your work values? In what ways wouldn't it align?

- What skills do you have that would help you succeed in this occupation?

- What skills would you need to develop to succeed in this occupation?

- What information would make you more confident that this occupation is right for you? How will you gain this information?

Adopting a Success Attitude

PERSISTING IN THE FACE OF OBSTACLES

As you put your academic and career plans into action, what obstacles might you encounter? For example, might you have difficulty fulfilling the requirements for completing your chosen degree? Might you identify a career that would be perfect for you — only to discover that by the time you graduate, few job opportunities will be available in that career? Identify three or four potential obstacles. Then, for each one, answer the following questions:

1. What strengths do you have that will help you overcome this obstacle?

2. How might you prevent this obstacle from becoming so overwhelming that you give up? For example, what could you say to yourself to stay hopeful and positive?

3. Who can support you or help you get past this obstacle? How?

4. What campus resources could help you deal with this obstacle? How, specifically, will you connect with these resources? For example, is there a campus career center that you plan to visit? If so, where is it located, what are its hours of operation, and what do you want to discuss during your visit?

Applying Your Skills

USING THE O*NET TO GATHER CAREER INFORMATION

This chapter introduced you to the O*NET, a comprehensive source of occupational information. For this activity, choose one occupation you'd like to learn more about. You may want to select something based on your interests, work values, and skills. Then follow these steps:

1. Type "O*NET OnLine" into your Web browser or go to http://online .onetcenter.org.

2. Under "Occupation Quick Search," type the name of the occupation you want to investigate.

3. Click on the occupational title.

4. Of the tasks listed for this occupation, which do you find most appealing? Least appealing?

5. Scroll to "Skills." Which skills in the list do you already possess? How did you acquire them? Which skills would you still need to develop to succeed in this occupation?

6. Scroll to "Interests." How does your Holland interest type (from your interest inventory) match the interest type or code for this occupation?

7. Scroll to "Work Values." How do your work values match those shown for this occupation?

8. Scroll to "Wages." What is the median annual wage (the middle number in a list of annual wages sorted from lowest to highest) for this occupation?

9. Select your state, and compare the national median annual wage for this occupation with the median annual wage for your state. Note which is higher.

10. Determine what, if any, additional information you'd like to gather about this occupation and how you will find it.

11. Analyze the information you've gathered, and use your critical thinking skills to determine whether this occupation would be a good match for you.

College Success = Career Success

CONDUCTING AN INFORMATIONAL INTERVIEW

Follow the advice for conducting an informational interview outlined in this chapter. Contact a person you'd like to speak with, and tell him or her that you'd like to spend twenty to thirty minutes asking questions to learn more about the person's career. Review the interview questions in Table 13.2 and bring them to the interview. To aid your memory, take notes on the person's responses to your questions. During your interview, pay close attention to the time, and don't go over. At the end, thank the interviewee for his or her time, and send a follow-up thank-you note or e-mail.

Then after the interview, write down your responses to the following questions:

1. Whom did you interview?

2. What did you learn from this person?

3. How did what you learned affect your feelings about pursuing this career?

14

Celebrating Your Success and Connecting to Your Future

Success, Then and Now: Assess Your ACES Progress

Dig Deeper: Reflect on the Specifics of Your Progress

Full Speed Ahead! Prepare for Continued Academic Success

Celebrate Success and Connect to Your Future — at Work

My Personal Success Plan

f you're reading this chapter, that means you're almost finished with the term. Congratulations! This is a good time to reflect on how much you've learned and to take pride in your successes. Think of all the goals you've set for yourself and achieved. Consider how well prepared you are for your remaining terms in college. Imagine what a great impression you'll make when you interview for an exciting new job. You have a lot to celebrate!

This is also a good time to think about your future. What challenges lie ahead for you, both in college and in your work life? Are you more excited about some courses than about others? Are there work experiences you'd like to gain?

In this class you've had the opportunity to spend time each week learning about yourself and developing the skills and attitudes critical to your success at school and at work. Chances are, you'll probably never take a course like this again. So how will you sustain the good habits you've developed?

The fact is, what you've learned in this class transfers over to other classes you take and to the jobs you pursue. If you keep practicing the skills and mind-sets you developed this term, you'll continue achieving successes. As a result, your confidence will keep growing. It won't always be easy, but the solid foundation you've built will carry you through even the toughest times. The key is to make connections between what you've learned in this class and the academic and career choices you'll make in the future.

This chapter helps you make those connections. First, we revisit many of the concepts we explored over the term, and you'll think metacognitively about your accomplishments and experiences. Then we turn to the challenges and choices that lie ahead of you — academically and professionally — and look at strategies for sustaining your success in the years to come. In fact, the structure of this chapter matches the structure you'll use to stay successful in life: Reflect on and learn from the past, then use the resulting insights to prepare for the future.

Success, Then and Now: Assess Your ACES Progress

At the beginning of the term, you completed ACES, and in each chapter of this book you've had a chance to reflect on your scores and use them to target areas where you want to develop your skills. Now that you've reached the end of the term, it's time to reflect on the ACES scales once more, but in a slightly different way. This time, we're not the ones providing results—*you* are! You'll assess how much you've progressed on the various skills during the term and use your assessment to celebrate improvement and identify areas for future growth. To do this, use Figure 14.1 as your guide and follow these steps.

1. Gather your ACES scores from the beginning of each chapter, or access your scores online using the LaunchPad for *Connections*.

2. On each scale in Figure 14.1, place an X where your corresponding ACES score falls. For example, if your Critical Thinking and Goal Setting score is 62 percent, mark the scale as follows.

Critical Thinking and Goal Setting

3. For each skill, ask yourself: Do I think my ability on this skill has improved since I took ACES at the start of the term? If so, what score would I give myself now? Do I think my ability is lower now than I thought it was at the start of the term? If so, what score would I give myself today?

4. Drawing on your honest responses to the questions in step 3, record a *new* score on each scale if you believe your abilities have changed. Place another X where the new score belongs.

5. For each skill, draw an arrow from your original score to your new score. For example, if you think that you've improved significantly in critical thinking and goal setting, you might mark the scale as follows.

Critical Thinking and Goal Setting

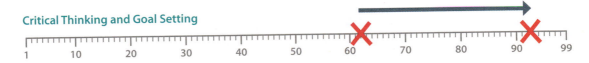

Resist any urge to rush through this activity. To really understand how your skills have changed, you need to trace what's happened over the term. For example, let's say that your initial score on the Reading scale was low. You weren't a confident reader when the term began, and you didn't enjoy reading. As time passed, though, you realized that you needed to read well in order to succeed in school, so you focused on improving. You previewed your reading materials before looking more closely at the content, and you mastered the art of crafting purposeful reading questions. Now you can feel good about giving yourself a higher score.

As another example, let's say that your original Organization and Time Management score was very high. At the beginning of the term, you were convinced that you were a time-management pro, but as the term progressed, you began to miss appointments and fall behind in your projects. As it turned out, managing your time was more challenging than you anticipated. Now that you've reached the end of the term, you realize that it's appropriate to give yourself a lower score for organization and time management than the score you had at the start of the term.

If you're uncomfortable at the thought of giving yourself a lower score, put your mind at ease: There are many logical reasons why your score might be lower now than it was at the beginning of the term. For example, you might have a more realistic understanding of yourself now than you did a few months ago. You've learned a lot about the attitudes and skills measured by ACES, so it's only natural that you're a better judge of your strengths and growth areas. Alternatively, maybe you misjudged the demands of college. You might have been a rock star at time management and organization in high school or at work, but now you need to step up your game in the more demanding college environment. So don't be afraid to lower your score if need be. Doing so shows that you're self-aware and allows you to more accurately gauge the progress you've made—or the skills you still need to strengthen.

After you complete Figure 14.1, you'll have a snapshot of the overall change in your skills from the start of the term to the end. To extract valuable insights from that snapshot, use these tips.

- **Identify any patterns in your results.** For example, are the scales on which you made the most progress related to one another? What about the ones on which you made the least progress? And in the areas where you made the most progress, did you set and achieve SMART goals? Students often see the most improvement in areas where they establish goals to improve a skill, carry out their action plans, and achieve their desired results.

- **Celebrate the major improvements you've made.** You've worked hard, and you deserve to reward yourself. As you take more difficult courses and make tougher academic and career decisions in upcoming terms, you can stay motivated by keeping your greatest successes in mind. And you can use the skills you've built to tackle each new challenge and make smart decisions.

- **Adopt a continual-learning mind-set.** For skills in which you've made less progress than you'd hoped, remind yourself that it's hard to develop many different skills at the same time. As you progress through college and have more work experiences, you can keep striving to build certain skills. By taking this course, you've armed yourself with the tools you need to learn and improve in whatever areas you target. If you use these tools during the rest of your college journey, you'll continue to "move the needle" in a positive direction.

FIGURE 14.1 Self-Assessment of Change

Place an X on each scale to represent your corresponding ACES score from the beginning of the term. Then place another X on each scale to signify where you rate yourself today. Finally, draw an arrow on each scale from the first X to the second to get a visual representation of how you've improved or to identify the skills you might need to strengthen in the future.

Critical Thinking and Goal Setting

1 10 20 30 40 50 60 70 80 90 99

Motivation, Decision Making, and Personal Responsibility

1 10 20 30 40 50 60 70 80 90 99

Learning Preferences

1 10 20 30 40 50 60 70 80 90 99

Organization and Time Management

1 10 20 30 40 50 60 70 80 90 99

Reading

1 10 20 30 40 50 60 70 80 90 99

Note Taking

1 10 20 30 40 50 60 70 80 90 99

Memory and Studying

1 10 20 30 40 50 60 70 80 90 99

Test Taking

1 10 20 30 40 50 60 70 80 90 99

Information Literacy and Communication

1 10 20 30 40 50 60 70 80 90 99

Connecting with Others

1 10 20 30 40 50 60 70 80 90 99

Personal and Financial Health

1 10 20 30 40 50 60 70 80 90 99

Academic and Career Planning

1 10 20 30 40 50 60 70 80 90 99

Dig Deeper: Reflect on the Specifics of Your Progress

Filling out Figure 14.1 gave you an overall view of how your abilities on key skills have changed over the term. Now you'll have a chance to reflect on your *specific* accomplishments in this class and what you've learned about yourself in the process. We'll revisit the key elements of college and career success, consider the impact they've made in your life, and celebrate everything you've learned during this term. Why? Because focusing on what you've accomplished strengthens your self-confidence and helps you stay motivated—and it just plain feels good!

What Did You Discover about Yourself?

In this class you've had many opportunities to strengthen your self-awareness—for example, by clarifying your interests, values, skills, and learning preferences. Self-awareness empowers you to take advantage of your strengths and address weaknesses. It's also a cornerstone of critical thinking and personal responsibility and an important first step in setting goals.

To prompt your thinking about self-awareness and the specifics of what you learned this term, let's begin with a quick exercise: In Table 14.1, identify the three most important insights you've gained about yourself in this class. Then write down why you consider each insight valuable and how you'll use it in your future classes and your future career. For example, perhaps you discovered how much you enjoy working with others in small groups. Now you can look for courses and volunteer opportunities that involve working with others, and you can investigate careers that involve collaboration. Concrete reflection like this—which you'll have a chance to do throughout the chapter—gives you a way to process all that you've experienced over this busy term.

This reflection is a great first step, but do remember that gaining self-knowledge is an ongoing process. You'll continue to learn more about your-

TABLE 14.1   Personal Reflection

What I learned about myself in this class	Why this knowledge is valuable	How I'll use this information in the future
1.		
2.		
3.		

self as you progress through college—and through life. In the coming terms, for example, you'll gain more insight into your academic and career interests as you take different courses or try out different jobs. You'll get better at interacting with various types of people as you work on group assignments for class or participate in school organizations. If you're working while going to school, you'll learn about yourself as a professional and a coworker. And once you've graduated, you'll continue building your self-knowledge as you face new opportunities and challenges in your professional and personal life. This course is only the beginning!

Keep Flying. This term, your career as a college student took off. You learned about yourself, started achieving important goals, wrestled with some tough challenges, and grew as a person. During the rest of your academic career, the skills you've built in this class will help you keep flying—reaching new heights while heading toward the bright horizon that's waiting for you. blackred/Getty Images

What Goals Did You Establish—and Achieve?

By now you've used the Personal Success Plan (PSP) many times to define goals and create action plans for achieving them. What did you think about this activity when you first tried it? Did simply setting a goal seem like a lot of work, or did it seem too easy? How do you feel about the PSP process now? Do the steps come more easily to you, or less so?

As the next step in your reflection, take a few moments now to review the PSPs you created and to consider the progress you've made toward your goals. Then, in Table 14.2, record three goals you're most proud of achieving, how achieving each goal helped you, and why you're proud of achieving it. For example, perhaps you became skilled at taking notes using an outline, which helped you stay organized when it was time to study for a test. And perhaps you're proud of achieving this goal because you practiced over and over before getting it right—which showed you the power of persistence and how good it feels to improve at a skill through hard work.

TABLE 14.2 Revisiting Your Goals

Goal I achieved	How achieving this goal helped me	Why I'm proud of achieving this goal
1.		
2.		
3.		

THE POWER OF UNDERSTANDING YOURSELF

NAME:	**Jennifer Field**
SCHOOL:	*Dixie Applied Technical College*
MAJOR:	*Drafting Technology Certificate*
CAREER GOAL:	*Residential Construction Consulting*

> **"I plan to maintain my success by taking what I know about myself and what I love and turning it into a successful career."**

High school was challenging for me, and I chose not to go to college right after I graduated. I tried going to college a few times over the years, but I always approached those attempts with a fear of failure and ended up leaving. Deep down, though, I knew that I really wanted to get my education. I wanted to show my family that I had what it takes to graduate from college. I also wanted to show our boys how important school really is. That's exactly what I did. I focused on what really mattered. I put my fears aside and I did it: I went back to school.

I'm so glad I did! Even though college is difficult for me now that I'm in my thirties and have a family to consider, I've found a school and a program that fit my style of learning and my career goals. I love the open learning and communication environment in the Drafting Technology Program. I'm able to interact daily with other students and instructors and to work at my own pace. The work is challenging at times and a breeze at other times. Being in this type of environment allows for hands-on and applied learning styles. We're encouraged to collaborate with other students on just about every project, and I think that's excellent training for my career field, where projects are almost always collaborative.

Knowing that I value collaborative work environments has helped me establish some longer-term goals related to my career. I know I want to be on the front line, work with people, and feel like I'm making a difference in people's lives.

Now that I've experienced success in school, I plan to maintain my success by taking what I know about myself and what I love and turning it into a successful career.

YOUR TURN: How has learning about yourself this term impacted your goals and your decisions? Like Jennifer, do you have a better sense of what you want to do for a career and why you want to do it? If so, what gave you this clarity?

What Kept You Motivated and Positive?

Motivation and positivity are key ingredients in success. Motivation keeps you moving forward—striving to reach your next goal, live your next dream, and build your next skill. Of course, motivation fluctuates depending on the goals involved, the rewards you expect to reap, and your academic and career priorities. It can also ebb and flow with the passage of time.

Now that you have some college experience, think about your motivation over the term. In which classes did you feel most motivated to work toward your goals? Why? Were they related to your major? Did they appeal to your interests? Did you believe those courses would best prepare you for your chosen career? Also think about times when you felt decidedly unmotivated, and consider how you handled the situation. Overall, do you think you're better at staying motivated, regardless of the task, than you used to be?

In Table 14.3, list three strategies that helped you maintain your motivation this term. Then describe why those strategies work so well for you and how you'll use them in future courses. For example, perhaps you stayed motivated by connecting your short-term goals to a long-term goal, such as landing a rewarding job. Each time you achieved a short-term goal and celebrated your progress toward the larger goal, it kept you energized. Now, if you're ever unmotivated to work on an assignment, you'll know that connecting it to a meaningful long-term goal will spur you on.

As you consider what motivates you, don't forget just how powerful a positive attitude can be—and how much it can drive you to succeed. To consider how positivity impacted you this term, think back over the last few months: Did you experience a setback during that time, such as performing poorly on a test or handing in an assignment late? How did you respond to the setback? Did you turn it into an opportunity for improvement, and if so, how? Now think of a time this term when you had a success. Maybe you achieved a PSP goal or received praise from an instructor about a project. How did you respond to this success? Did you gain confidence in your skills? Did your motivation grow? Consider what your responses to these questions suggest about how you'll handle setbacks in the future—and how you can use positivity to your best advantage.

TABLE 14.3   **Reflecting on Motivation**

Strategy for maintaining motivation	Why this strategy works for me	How I'll use this strategy in future courses
1.		
2.		
3.		

What Skills Did You Build?

Knowing yourself, establishing and achieving goals, and staying motivated and positive are all vital elements of success—but in themselves they're not enough. You also need to develop additional skills that will help you excel in college and beyond. The good news? During this term, you've done just that.

- You've developed critical thinking, decision-making, and metacognitive skills. All of these helped you reflect on your own values and interests, master course content, understand your learning preferences, *and* figure out which strategies are most effective in which learning situations.

- You've developed specific academic and life skills: managing your time, reading, taking notes, studying, taking exams, working with information, interacting effectively with others, and maintaining your personal and financial health.

- You've developed valuable *transferable skills*. You may already be using skills you've developed in this class to excel in your other classes, and you can apply those same skills to a job you have now and to your future career. (See the Appendix for tips on crafting résumés and cover letters that spotlight your key skills.)

Of all the many skills you've developed this term, list the three *most* important ones in Table 14.4. (For ideas, revisit Figure 14.1 or the Connect to Career skills you recorded in each PSP.) Describe how you developed each skill and why it's important to your success. For example, maybe you strengthened your public speaking skills by volunteering to deliver a group-project presentation in your world cultures class. You prepared your presentation in advance, rehearsed it until you knew it by heart, and then practiced delivering it to a family member to get feedback. The next time you have to present—either in future classes or at work—you'll be confident that you know what to do.

TABLE 14.4 Most Important Skills

Skill I developed this term	How I developed this skill	Why this skill is important to my success
1.		
2.		
3.		

Who Supported You?

Everyone needs help at times, and as you've learned in this class, getting help is a major component of success. Think back to all the campus resources you explored during this term, including tutoring programs, academic advising, counseling and career centers, and the financial aid office. Which of these resources did you find most useful? Why?

In addition to campus programs, consider especially helpful individuals who supported you during the term. For instance, think about your instructors.

Full Speed Ahead! Prepare for Continued Academic Success

345

Who was your biggest supporter? Why? How did you secure his or her support? And think about family members and friends who helped you this term. How did their encouragement differ from the help provided by your instructors or campus resources?

In Table 14.5, create your own supporter Hall of Fame. List three people who provided you with the most support this term, describe the support they provided, and explain how you benefited from their support.

For example, Tito doesn't make friends easily, but he knew when he met Matt at the campus gym that they'd get along. An excellent student, Matt freely shared tips on how he kept his life organized, managed his time, and handled stress—tips that Tito used to stay successful all term long. By being positive and encouraging, Matt snagged the top spot in Tito's Supporter Hall of Fame. Who gets the top spot on your list?

TABLE 14.5 Supporter Hall of Fame

Name of supporter	Support he or she provided	How I benefited from his or her support
1.		
2.		
3.		

Full Speed Ahead! Prepare for Continued Academic Success

You've learned a lot this term, scoring successes and facing challenges that gave you valuable new insights. But as a first-year college student, you've still got a long academic future ahead of you. As you take more courses, you'll continue strengthening the transferable skills and attitudes essential for success. This class has helped you lay a foundation that you can build on as you continue on your academic journey. But how, exactly, can you build on that foundation? Keep achieving goals. Adapt to new challenges. And stay connected with your supports.

Keep Achieving Goals

Goal setting is an ongoing process. You don't just set goals for one term, achieve them, congratulate yourself, and call it a day. Rather, as you go through college, you constantly define new goals, review your progress toward those goals, and revise them as needed. The following tips can help you remain a goal-setting pro, long after this class concludes.

- **Remember that *you're* in charge.** This term we've suggested setting goals related to the book's chapter topics, but as you move forward in your academic career, the goal-setting process won't be so structured. You'll be responsible for defining your own goals and tracking your own progress. If this sounds a little scary, remember: You have the resources, skills, and self-knowledge you need to define your own path. For example, you can use the PSP to guide you all the way to graduation—and beyond.

- **Connect your short- and long-term goals.** Step back occasionally from the day-to-day grind of college, and ask yourself what short-term goals you can accomplish now to keep working toward your long-term goals.

  Luis is a case in point. During the first term, his PSP goals included maintaining a high GPA, developing a strong support network of peers and faculty mentors, and gaining experiences that would prepare him to work in counseling. In the second term, Luis set a goal to practice the study skills he developed in his first term so that he could continue maintaining a high GPA. To support his goal of broadening his network, he set new goals to interview his psychology instructors about their research interests and attend student council meetings. And to support his long-term goal of working in counseling, he set a new goal to volunteer with his community's crisis hotline.

- **Reframe setbacks.** Did you have a perfect term, accomplishing all the goals you set for yourself? If so, you can skip to the next section! If not, remind yourself that most people experience a few setbacks as they work toward their goals. As you've seen throughout this book, instead of viewing setbacks as failures, you can reframe them as opportunities for future success by analyzing what caused you to fall short—and identifying changes you can make to get the results you want.

  In Table 14.6, list two goals that you were unable to achieve this term. For each goal, note something positive you learned about yourself as you tried to achieve the goal. And if you still want to achieve the goal, write down what you'll do differently next term to accomplish it.

TABLE 14.6 Identifying Ways to Improve

A goal I didn't achieve this term	Something positive I learned as I tried to achieve this goal	What I'll do differently to achieve this goal next term
1.		
2.		

Full Speed Ahead! Prepare for Continued Academic Success

347

Adapt to New Challenges

Now that you've spent time celebrating your successes and reflecting on the insights you gained from tackling challenges, it's time to consider how you'll keep learning and growing during the remainder of your college career. As you progress in school, you'll face new kinds of challenges: For one thing, your classes may not have the formal structure that this class had, so it may be harder to know how to prioritize your learning. What's more, as you take higher-level courses, your instructors will assign longer papers, and your tests and reading assignments will become more difficult.

Fortunately, during this term you've built foundational skills that you can use to adapt to the challenges you'll encounter during the rest of your academic career. Here are some tips.

- **Hit the "pause" button.** Research suggests that reflection is an important component of learning,[1] so schedule time throughout each term to reflect on your "big ticket" items: the demands you're facing, your goals and action plans, the barriers you're working to overcome, and the progress you're making. Think of these sessions as hitting the "pause" button so that you can focus on the major events in your life. Use this time to take stock of what's most meaningful to *you*. Your values, interests, skills, and goals can change over time; revisit them periodically to be certain that you're pursuing the major and courses that appeal to you most.

- **Take motivation time outs.** Once a week, stop for a moment to consider which tasks motivate you and which ones don't. Connect the nonmotivating tasks to a long-range goal—for example, "If I read this boring article carefully enough, I'll be better equipped to pass the test. If I pass enough tests, I'll pass the course, which I need for my major." Once you've completed those nonmotivating tasks, reward yourself.

- **Stay positive.** Celebrate your successes and look for positive life lessons when things don't go as you'd hoped. Remember: You can learn as much or more from setbacks and disappointments as you can from your successes.

Climb toward Your Goals. As you advance along your academic path, you'll encounter new challenges, including tougher courses and more demanding assignments. But if you start to feel overwhelmed, remember: You've built a strong foundation of vital skills this term. And by deploying these skills, you can keep climbing toward your goals, one step at a time. © Philip & Karen Smith/Ascent Xmedia/Corbis

THE POWER OF OPTIMISM

As we note in the chapter on personal and financial health, stress is a normal part of college life (as well as work life). Psychologists have long searched for insights on how to manage stress, and a recent study by Michelle Krypel and Donna Henderson-King suggests that *optimism*—having hope and confidence about your future—can help. The researchers asked more than three hundred undergraduate students from a midwestern university to complete measures of optimism, stress, and coping. Here's what they found.

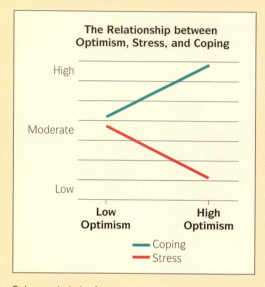

The Relationship between Optimism, Stress, and Coping

Being optimistic about your future is associated with developing and using effective coping strategies which, in turn, help you manage stress.

- Students with low levels of optimism were more likely to report being stressed in school than those with higher levels of optimism. Students who were more optimistic were more likely to report low levels of stress.

- The more optimistic students felt better equipped and more confident in their ability to manage—or cope with—their stress.

THE BOTTOM LINE

When you're optimistic about your future, you may feel *less* stressed overall and *more* confident in handling stress when it does occur.

REFLECTION QUESTIONS

1. Do you consider yourself an optimistic person? Why or why not?
2. How optimistic are you about your next term at college? About your life after graduation? Explain your answers.
3. Do you feel confident in your ability to manage the stress that happens in your life? Why or why not?

M. N. Krypel and D. Henderson-King, "Stress, Coping Styles, and Optimism: Are They Related to Meaning of Education in Students' Lives?," *Social Psychology of Education* 13 (2010): 409–24.

Stay Connected to Your Supports

Success is a team sport, and you've started building your all-star support team this term, including your instructors, an academic adviser, family, and friends. You'll continue building your team in college as you gain new experiences and as your needs change. For example, if you take a difficult math class next term, you might add a math tutor to your roster of connections. Or if you need help with a challenging term paper, you can visit the writing center. To keep building your support team, try these strategies.

- **Stay connected.** At the start of each term, list the resources you may need to help you manage your course schedule as well as the personal and professional priorities you're juggling. Each term, check in with an adviser to make sure you're on track to graduate.

- **Connect early.** Seek out help as soon as you recognize a need. For example, if you need more financial aid but you're not sure what's available and when the application has to be submitted, meet with someone in the financial aid office right away. Otherwise, you risk missing the deadline.

- **Find a mentor.** A mentor can provide you with the information, advice, guidance, and feedback you need to help you grow. If you're struggling with important academic decisions, such as what major to declare, a mentor can be a great sounding board. Mentors don't get paid—they agree to this relationship because they feel they have something to share. A good mentor might be someone who has already taken one of the classes you're in now (an advanced student), a person who knows the subject matter (an instructor), someone who graduated from your college (such as an older sibling or a neighbor), or an adviser.

- **Network.** Take every opportunity to *network*—to meet and get to know new people. They can share valuable insights on such topics as schools you might want to transfer to, interesting job opportunities, and contacts with whom you can discuss careers that interests you.

Nurture Your Network. The support network you started building this term will be crucial to you in later terms, so keep cultivating it. Maintain connections with your supports — mentors, advisers, career counselors, and others who have helped you. Forge connections with new people, too, and include them in your network if they can offer you additional forms of help. Peter Muller/Getty Images

Celebrate Success and Connect to Your Future — at Work

Celebrating your successes and connecting to your future are good ways to keep learning and growing in college. But these strategies will be equally valuable in your work life. Just as your values, interests, skills, and goals can change during college, they can shift in your professional life as well. Ongoing personal reflection, the ability to adapt as you encounter challenges, and a willingness to network will help you build a satisfying, successful career.

Keep Reflecting

When you celebrate your successes at work, you take stock of the new skills that you've acquired or talents you've strengthened, and these insights can help when you're seeking a promotion and refining your career path. Likewise, when you experience setbacks at work, you can take personal responsibility for analyzing what caused them and identifying the changes you'll make to get a better outcome in the future. Employers appreciate people who take initiative, turn setbacks into learning opportunities, and keep honing their skills. Ongoing personal reflection helps you do just that.

Adapt to Change

In the world of work, one thing's for certain: You can expect constant change. Over time, the job market for various careers can grow or shrink. Skills that employers value today may differ from those they'll want five years from now. The most pressing challenges and the most exciting opportunities that organizations face will also keep changing—thanks to new technologies, changes in consumers' preferences or needs, and radical moves by competitors.

By staying up-to-date on developments in your field, you can better anticipate what changes may be lurking on the horizon—and adapt as needed to take advantage of emerging opportunities or tackle fresh challenges. For instance, Paolo has just learned that his employer is installing new accounting software that requires some basic coding skills in SQL, a computer language for accessing and manipulating data. Proficiency in SQL would advance his career in any company, so Paolo purchases a book on SQL programming and creates a study schedule so he's prepared for the transition. By doing so, he is building valuable skills that will open up new doors for him.

Continue Networking

Networking is just as important in your professional life as in your academic life. So take just as much care to build and maintain your professional network as you do your academic network.[2] For example, if you've recently been hired at an organization, find out whether the company has a mentor program. A mentor can help you define career goals, connect you with people who know about job opportunities within the organization, and advise you on how to navigate the organization's political landscape.

The One Constant? It's Change. Change will be a constant not only in your academic career but also in your professional life. The organizations you work for will face major shifts in their environment — including technology advances that you'll need to adapt to. Take mobile phones — they've changed a lot already. Imagine what they'll look like in five or ten years! © Andrew Winning/Reuters/Corbis

THE VALUE OF CONTINUOUS PERSONAL REFLECTION

Courtesy of Rebecca Ratcliffe

NAME: **Matthew Gordon**

PROFESSION: *Author; future lawyer*

SCHOOLS: *Wilfrid Laurier University; Cornell University; University of Alberta*

DEGREES: *Bachelor of Arts; Master's; Juris Doctor (2015)*

MAJORS: *English and History; Industrial and Labor Relations; Law*

I'm a writer, and I very recently finished my third novel. As I worked many long nights, I focused on staying organized, maintaining my discipline, and achieving my long-term goals. I learned through experience that writing a novel is a test of endurance; I made progress little by little, not all at once. To stay on track and keep pushing myself, I constantly reflected on the progress I was making, how I handled different situations, and whether there were ways to improve.

My whole life, I knew I wanted to be an author. Although I've always liked academic writing and journalism, literature has been something I've loved for as long as I can remember. I spent my childhood and adolescence writing increasingly longer works until, during high school, I figured I was ready to write a novel. Each attempt since then has been better, leading up to the novel I just finished. It took me a year to write but, in some ways, vindicates all the effort I've put into reading and writing up to that point.

Now that I've finished this novel, I can step back, reflect on all my hard work, and celebrate how far I've come. It's a great feeling to be able to pick up my novel and enjoy the story that I wrote. Even though I know what happens next, I can still get lost in the story over and over again.

YOUR TURN: If you're currently employed, do you continuously reflect on your performance and progress, as Matthew does? Do you take time to celebrate your successes? Why or why not? If not, or if you're not yet employed, what strategies might you use to prompt self-reflection and appreciation in the future? How might these strategies benefit you as an employee?

> " To stay on track and keep pushing myself, I constantly reflected on the progress I was making."

Likewise, make sure your professional network is diverse. It should include people at higher and lower levels in the organization, peers in different divisions, and even individuals outside the organization, such as customers, suppliers, or members of a trade association. By gaining insights from people in your network, you can get a clearer picture of what's going on in your organization and where the best opportunities and sources of support are.

my personal success plan

LOOKING TO THE FUTURE

This is your final Personal Success Plan for this class! So far, each PSP you've completed has been related to the specific chapter content. This time, you're in charge of defining your own goal for *next* term on any topic you choose. Read the advice and examples; then sketch out your ideas in the space provided.

 LaunchPad

To access the Personal Success Plan online, go to the LaunchPad for *Connections*.

1 GATHER INFORMATION

Think about what you would like to accomplish next term. What new challenges might you face? Is there a goal you didn't achieve this term that you'd like another crack at? For more ideas, review your ACES scores and Figure 14.1. Is there a strength you'd like to develop further or a low score you'd like to improve?

2 SET A SMART GOAL

Don't be frustrated if you find it hard to decide on a good goal — this is the first time you've been asked to focus on developing a skill of your own choosing. Use the information you gathered in step 1 to create a SMART goal that makes sense for you.

SAMPLE: I'll spend one hour each week learning about career opportunities related to my major.

3 MAKE AN ACTION PLAN

Outline the specific steps you'll take to achieve your SMART goal, and note when you'll complete each step.

SAMPLE: The first week of next term, I'll interview an instructor in my major department about career options in this field.

4 LIST BARRIERS AND SOLUTIONS

Think about possible barriers to your action steps; then brainstorm solutions for overcoming them.

SAMPLE: If the instructor doesn't have much information, I'll make an appointment with a counselor in the career center to learn more.

5 ACT AND EVALUATE OUTCOMES

Because you're setting a goal for next term, you can't record your action steps and evaluate whether you have achieved your goal just yet. But you can make a commitment to pursue this goal. In fact, you can set a reminder in your calendar this very minute so that you'll follow up next term and implement your action steps.

6 CONNECT TO CAREER

List the skills you'll build as you progress toward your SMART goal. How will you use these skills to land a job and succeed at work?

SAMPLE: I'll learn how to network and locate important information, which will be useful skills in whatever career I decide to pursue.

1 my information

2 my SMART goal

☐ **S**PECIFIC ☐ **M**EASURABLE ☐ **A**CHIEVABLE ☐ **R**ELEVANT ☐ **T**IME-LIMITED

3 my action plan

4 my barriers/ solutions

5 my actions/ outcomes

6 my career connection

14

chapter review

CHAPTER SUMMARY

You've worked hard this term to build skills, score successes, and prepare for your future, regardless of what career you choose. Review the following list, celebrate your achievements in each area, and ask yourself what work still lies ahead.

- You've learned about your own interests and values.
- You've become skilled at critical thinking.
- You've learned an effective strategy for setting and achieving goals.
- You've become a motivated and active learner.
- You've discovered your own learning preferences.
- You've developed and strengthened academic skills.
- You've connected with others and explored the benefits of personal and financial health.
- You've launched academic and career plans.
- You've considered how you can strengthen and sustain all of this learning and all of these skills as you progress through your academic and work life.

CHAPTER ACTIVITIES

Journal Entry

CELEBRATING YOUR SUCCESSES

In this chapter you reflected on what you've accomplished this term and celebrated your successes. For your journal entry, describe one thing you're proud of accomplishing this term in each of the following areas: (1) school, (2) career, and (3) your personal life. In your description of each accomplishment, answer the following questions:

1. What did you do during the term to achieve this success?
2. What challenges did you encounter along the way? How did you overcome them?
3. What campus resources or personal supports helped you achieve this success?
4. How does this accomplishment make you feel? How will you celebrate it?

Adopting a Success Attitude

LOOKING TOWARD THE FUTURE WITH OPTIMISM

As you learned in this chapter, optimism means having hope and confidence about your future. Maintaining this success attitude will help you deal with stress and cope with challenges and will provide motivation when the going gets tough. Think optimistically by creating a list of your hopes for next term, using the following questions to brainstorm ideas.

- What do you hope to learn in each of your classes?
- What skills do you plan to build?
- How will you get involved in the campus community or meet new people?
- Do you plan to join any campus clubs or activities?
- Do you plan to use any campus resources?
- What faculty members, advisers, and counselors do you hope to connect with?
- How will you prepare for your future career?

These hopes for your future are more likely to become reality if you take personal responsibility for making them happen. Choose one of your hopes for the future, and describe in detail the steps you'll take to meet your goal.

Applying Your Skills

DESCRIBING YOUR SKILLS

During this term you've developed a wide range of skills, and you'll want to remember what these skills are, how you developed them, and what they helped you accomplish. Why? Describing your skills on a résumé, on a job application, on a scholarship application, or during an interview can help you stand out from the crowd. For practice describing your skills, both verbally and in writing, follow the steps below.

1. Begin by writing down three of your top skills. If you need ideas about which skills to spotlight, review Figure 14.1, Table 14.4, the Connect to Career skills you've recorded on your Personal Success Plans, or this book's table of contents.

2. For each skill you've listed, describe in detail how you demonstrate that skill. For example, if you select "working with others" as one of your top skills, write down what you do at school or work to show that you have this skill. Maybe you approach group work with an open mind, use conflict-management strategies to work through disagreements, and listen to the ideas of others.

3. Reflect on what each of the skills you've chosen to highlight has helped you accomplish. Continuing the example of "working with others," you might say, "This skill helped me successfully lead a project team that delivered high-quality work on time and earned the team members a glowing letter of recommendation."

4. In order to become more comfortable describing your skills and accomplishments out loud, ask a friend or family member to help you practice talking about your top skills.

College Success = Career Success

FINDING A MENTOR

Throughout this book we've talked about the importance of finding and using personal supports, and in this chapter we explored the value of having a mentor (both in college and at work) who can provide information, advice, guidance, and feedback to help you grow. In some cases these relationships can last a lifetime and become extremely meaningful to both the mentor and his or her protégé.

To get started finding an academic or a professional mentor, answer these questions:

- What would you like to learn from your mentor? What type of guidance or support could he or she offer you? Are these forms of support valuable to you? If so, why?

- How would you communicate with your mentor, including how often and where?

- How could you show appreciation to your mentor for his or her help?

- Do you have anyone specific in mind as a mentor? If so, how might you establish a mentoring relationship with this person? What would you say or do? If you don't have anyone specific in mind, how could you find someone who might make a good mentor?

Once you've answered these questions, take action: Establish your mentoring relationship. Then sustain it by making good use of your mentor's support while letting him or her know how much you appreciate the help.

APPENDIX
Your Career Search

Write a Résumé

Find Job Opportunities

Write a Cover Letter

Interview Effectively

You may be in the process of searching for a new job. Or, you may be anticipating how you'll enter the job market once you finish your academic program. No matter what your situation, we've designed this appendix to walk you through the steps of writing a résumé, locating a job, and presenting yourself in a cover letter and interview. Although this information comes at the end of the book, its importance shouldn't be minimized. The job market is competitive. You may be applying for jobs alongside 10, 100, or even 1,000 other people. Thus, we don't just want to help you prepare for the job search, we want to help you stand out and successfully sell employers on your skills and abilities.

Before digging into the details, let's begin with a few general suggestions, several of which you'll recognize as messages emphasized throughout this book. First, adopt a positive mindset. Recognize that you may not get offered the first, the second, or even the tenth job you apply for. The job search is a process, meaning it takes time and effort. Second, if you begin to feel frustrated or anxious, use your resources. Reach out to friends, family members, or those in your professional network to gain support, feedback, or advice. Third, take personal responsibility. The job search is an exciting opportunity for *you* to change the course of your future! Spend time reflecting on what type of job you're looking for based on your interests, skills, and values. Fourth, be proactive. Find job openings through multiple sources, including your professional networks. And fifth, remember that you're selling yourself in the résumé, cover letter, and interview. What do you bring to the company? Be sure to highlight the skills and experiences that make you a good fit for the job.

Write a Résumé

Résumé: A document that lists your education, work experience, and extracurricular activities.

At the most basic level, your **résumé** is a summary of your education, work experience, and extracurricular activities. It gives potential employers a sense of your prior experience and qualifications for the position you're targeting. Recruiters will often skim a candidate's résumé for this basic information before deciding whether to read more closely, so it's important that these basics be easy to find in the visual layout of your document.

At a deeper level, your résumé is an opportunity to detail your responsibilities, highlight accomplishments, and spell out transferable skills. It can be challenging to place all pertinent information on a page without it looking cluttered, but the key is to briefly list only the most critical information. You can provide greater details about your experiences in the cover letter or interview. Although most people prefer a one-page résumé, you may need to use two pages if you have a significant amount of work experience and accomplishments. Ultimately, your goal is to show how your qualifications align with the requirements of the job in a clear, professional way.

Résumé Basics

As you can see in Figure A.1, your name and contact information should appear prominently at the top of your résumé. You might also include a link to your LinkedIn profile, Twitter feed, or another element of your online presence if appropriate. And remember that your e-mail address should be professional—you may want to obtain a new one for the job search process.

Many job applicants choose to open their résumé with a summary section. Think of this as a place to tell employers what kind of professional you are. This description should highlight the characteristics and skills that you would bring to a job, while citing previous accomplishments as support for these points. Note that each statement in this section of Figure A.1 begins with a skill or quality that the student has chosen to emphasize. This puts the most important information in a prominent place and makes this section easy for a reader to digest, even if he or she is reading quickly.

Next, add your educational history. This should consist of all the institutions where you've completed undergraduate coursework, as well as any technical certifications you hold. On the first line of each entry, list the name of each institution, its location, and your dates of attendance. Underneath this, include your grade point average and area of study. Many students also choose to include their high school name, location, and year of graduation, and some students note the number of college credits they've earned, subjects in which they've completed substantial coursework, study abroad experience, scholarships, or even Honor Society membership. If you can fit them in, these kinds of details make your résumé more informative and help to spark conversation with an interviewer.

Marcus B. Student

2525 Market Street, #459
Springfield, WA 90546
403.555.1245

marcus.student@email.com
linkedin.com/marcusbstudent
@marcusontwitter

Qualifications Summary

Dedicated, hard-working professional with strong communication, leadership, and critical thinking skills. Demonstrated ability to organize and lead teams in workplace and education settings. Strong interest in and extensive experience with computer hardware, software, and social media applications. History of excellent customer service. Commitment to bringing demonstrable value to and delivering measurable outcomes for the organization.

- Promoted to team lead within 4 months of hire
- Commitment to volunteering and community service

- Elected treasurer of Marketing Club
- Tripled Marketing Club's Twitter followers through collaborative efforts within 2 months at Mountain College

Education

2015–present   Mountain College—Springfield, WA
GPA 3.75; completed 12 credit hours; major in Business Administration

2012–2013   Valley College—Hampton, OR
GPA 2.6; completed 18 credit hours; coursework in Accounting, English

2012   River High School—Carlisle, OR

Relevant Experience

2014–present   *Team Lead*—All Things Tech
Promoted to Team Lead after 4 months of outstanding work and customer service. Supervise 3 technicians. Monitor and respond to customer feedback regarding repair services. Provide outstanding customer service to promote repeat business. Collaborate with store manager to increase social media presence for store.

2014   *Technician*—All Things Tech
Provided excellent customer service in repairing customer computers, mobile phones, and tablets. Applied extensive background and expertise with computer and phone hardware to efficiently complete assigned repairs.

2013–present   *Big Brother*—Big Brothers and Big Sisters of Central Washington
Serve as Big Brother to now 13-year-old boy. Meet regularly, 3–4 times per month, to play games, hang out, talk about challenges of school and friends. Provide regular support and mentorship.

2011–2012   *Server & Cook*—Neugent's Burger Stand
Performed duties of server and cook. Demonstrated strong customer service in taking orders. Supported coworkers in responding to customer complaints. Quickly learned tasks of line cook. Performed well in fast-paced and stressful environment during lunch and dinner rush. Recognized as employee of the month 3 times, August and December 2011, July 2012.

Chronological or Functional

After your education section, list your work and extracurricular experience in one of two styles: chronological or functional. On a **chronological résumé**, entries simply appear in reverse chronological order, with your current or most recent experience first. Figure A.1 shows a chronological résumé, a style commonly used by college students. This format is a great choice for students who have taken on increasingly complex responsibilities over time, as it demonstrates this growth in a linear fashion. A chronological résumé also makes sense for students whose experiences are all somewhat relevant to the positions for which they're applying.

In a **functional résumé** entries are grouped based on the nature of the experience they reflect rather than the order in which they occurred. This style of résumé can be helpful when only some of your past experiences are directly related to the position you're seeking. For example, a student applying for a research assistant position may wish to highlight a summer research position from several years ago more prominently than her current part-time job in food service. To do so, she might develop a "Related Experience" section that includes work experience involving data collection and analysis, and then an "Other Experience" section that includes the rest of her work history. Functional résumés can also be useful for applicants applying for different types of positions. A student who is applying for both marketing and editing jobs, for example, might develop two different functional résumés: one for marketing positions in which the "Related Experience" section cites social media accomplishments, and another for editing positions in which the "Related Experience" section details his work in the college writing center and involvement with the school newspaper.

No matter which style you choose, you'll need to develop descriptions of your responsibilities and accomplishments in each position you've held. As you can see in Figure A.1, the style used for writing a résumé is quite different than the style used for written course assignments. Résumés use short phrases rather than complete sentences and begin each statement with an active verb. By describing what you accomplished in such vivid terms, you'll help employers visualize how your skills might apply to their open positions.

In addition to the sample résumé provided in this section, you can access résumé examples online through your career center or by doing your own online search (type "sample résumé" into a search engine). Your local library or bookstore may also have résumé-writing books with samples of both chronological and functional résumés.

Find Job Opportunities

Once your résumé is ready to go, what's the next step? Search for open positions that interest you. Just as the word *search* implies, this is an active process that often requires patience and persistence. The good news is that there are employers out there looking to hire students and recent graduates. In this section, we'll look at some of the places where employers advertise openings and interact with students who are interested in these opportunities.

Get Online

When employers have an open position to fill, they develop a description of responsibilities and qualifications the job requires. While few employers make use of newspaper classifieds in this digital age, some do list opportunities on online job boards like Monster.com, CareerBuilder, or Simply Hired. Keep in mind that while there will be some part-time and entry-level positions on these sites, online job boards will also have jobs for more experienced professionals. So do pay close attention to the qualifications and requirements listed in these postings.

If there are specific companies you'd like to work for—perhaps you admire their product or the way they run their organization—you might also look for job opportunities in the employment section of the organization's Web site. Keep in mind that these sites are updated as jobs become available, so if you don't see any openings the first time you look, don't lose hope! Instead, visit the site once or twice per week to look for new postings. You can also check out the target company's Twitter account or Facebook page, or look on LinkedIn. The federal government also advertises jobs online (www.usajobs.gov), as do some cities and states.

Use Campus and Community Resources

If your school has a career center, set up an appointment to get personalized guidance on your job search. Some college career counselors have vast networks of local and national hiring managers. They may be able to steer you toward specific companies or industries that are hiring. Additionally, your college career center may host on-campus interviews and have an online job search engine, free seminars on job search strategies, or other resources to help you in your job search.

Job fairs hosted by your school or in the community are another great place to network and learn about many open positions at once. Even if you aren't actively looking for a job at the time the fair is happening, take advantage of this opportunity to learn about employers in your area and make connections with recruiters.

When attending a job fair, dress professionally. This signals to recruiters that you're taking this process seriously and you want to make a good impression. In addition, print copies of your résumé on high-quality paper so you can provide them to employers whose opportunities interest you. And finally, to make the most of your time at the fair, develop a brief summary of the kinds of job you're looking for and your relevant experiences and skills.

Join a Professional Association

Affiliation with a **professional association** is another good source of employment information. Professional associations are nonprofit organizations through which individuals who share a specific trade or job function can network, share best practices, and promote their profession and its interests. Student memberships in these organizations are generally quite affordable, and provide access to job listings on members-only Web sites and listservs. More generally, professional associations allow you to learn about your chosen industry from insiders who may be hiring now or in the future. By attending

Professional Association: An organization through which individuals who share a trade or job function can network and promote the interests of their profession.

professional association meetings or events, you can introduce yourself and ask for advice on how to gain entry-level employment.

One way to identify appropriate professional associations is to consult your library's copy of *National Trade and Professional Associations of the United States*. This comprehensive directory of professional organizations includes membership and contact information, as well as dates and locations of upcoming conferences. You might also look for LinkedIn groups of professionals in your field, as this is another popular place to find job listings.

Network

As we've mentioned throughout the book, networking is a great way to find a job opening. Networking is really just about talking to people—everyone from fellow members of professional associations to instructors, classmates, friends, family members, neighbors, or those affiliated with your faith community, volunteer work, or recreational pursuits. Once you've identified the people you already know in your network, start contacting them. Explain that you're looking for a job, and be specific about what type of job or career field. Then ask them if they have any job leads or know anyone who could give you some advice on following your chosen path. If they give you a name, follow up with that person immediately.

When you get in touch with a contact, your best strategy is to ask him or her for advice or insight—*not* a job. Many people like to give advice, but if you ask for a job outright, you're putting them on the spot and they may feel ambushed. A better strategy is to meet with your contact and ask for insight into the field. If your contact does know of a job, he or she may tell you how to apply or give you an additional person to contact. Networking is about establishing relationships with people, so be sure to follow up any networking meeting with an electronic or handwritten thank you note.

Write a Cover Letter

Cover Letter: A formal letter in which you introduce yourself, your interest in a job, and your appropriate skills and qualifications.

Once you've identified an open position that interests you, it's time to work on a **cover letter** to accompany your résumé. Whereas your résumé can be somewhat generic—you might have a few versions highlighting different sorts of experiences—your cover letter should be highly tailored to the organization and position for which you're applying. This document is the place where you explain exactly how your previous experiences have prepared you to excel in this next job.

As you can see in Figure A.2, this document should be formatted like a formal business letter, with your name and contact information at the top, followed by the date and the address of the company to which you're sending your application. If there's a contact person associated with the job posting, address that person by name. If no contact information is provided, you can use "To Whom It May Concern." In the first sentence of your letter, identify the position that you're applying for and comment on your excitement about the position. You might follow this with another sentence that elaborates on why you're interested in working for this organization and why you're a good fit for the role.

Marcus B. Student

2525 Market Street, #459
Springfield, WA 90546
marcus.student@email.com
403.555.1245

April 27, 2016

Madeline Iverson
Director of Human Resources
Techstar Inc.
45983 Ocean Drive
Springfield, WA 09546

Dear Ms. Iverson:

I am excited to apply for the Enterprise Solutions Account Manager position at Techstar Inc. I have admired the work of Techstar Inc. for the past few years and I believe that I bring an optimal combination of experience, skills, and drive that will result in superb customer care and excellent sales within the division.

My past and current experiences are a strong match for the qualifications and skills you are seeking in your next Account Manager. As you can see from my résumé I have a demonstrated history of providing excellent customer service, and I have placed customer service as my highest priority. I believe that when clients are satisfied they are more likely to return and they are our strongest advertisers to generate referrals and sales. I also possess the technical skills to excel in this position, evidenced by my experience in repair and now as the leader of a team of repair technicians. Further, I have a demonstrated history of exceeding expectations.

- Completed 78% of customer repairs on or under time, highest rate in the branch
- Tripled number of followers on Marketing Club Twitter account
- 3-time employee of the month

Thank you for taking time to consider my application. I am very excited about implementing my current skill set at Techstar Inc. and believe that as I complete my Bachelor's degree at Mountain College, I will have even more to offer. If I can provide any additional information please do not hesitate to contact me. I look forward to discussing this position further.

Sincerely,

Marcus B. Student

glossary

Academic Adviser/Counselor: A highly trained professional who can help you make effective academic decisions and refer you to valuable campus resources.

Academic Plan: A tool used by students and their advisers to plan and track a student's progress toward obtaining a degree or certificate.

Accountable: Responsible for completing tasks and meeting obligations.

Action Plan: A list of steps you'll take to accomplish a goal and the order in which you'll take them.

Active Reading: A reading strategy that involves engaging with the material before, during, and after reading.

Barrier: A personal characteristic or something in your environment that prevents you from making progress toward a goal.

Behavioral Interview Questions: Specific interview questions designed to reveal information about how you act and react in certain situations.

Budget: A plan that documents income and expenses for a specific period of time.

Career Counselor: A specially trained professional who uses career assessments and other resources to help students explore career options and make career decisions.

Chronological Résumé: A résumé that lists work and extracurricular experiences in reverse chronological order, with the most recent appearing first.

Cite: To give another author credit when you include his or her ideas in your paper or project.

Cloud: A place on the Internet where you can store your files.

College Major: A collection of courses that are organized around an academic theme.

Cornell System: Method of note taking that organizes each page of content into sections: initial notes on the right, key points in a cue column on the left, and a summary section at the bottom of the page.

Cover Letter: A formal letter in which you introduce yourself, your interest in a job, and your appropriate skills and qualifications.

Critical Thinking: The ability to consider information in a thoughtful way, understand how to think logically and rationally, and apply those methods of thinking in your classes and your life.

Cumulative Exams: Exams that cover everything you've learned in the course up to that point in the term.

Discrimination: Treating people less favorably because of their membership in a particular group.

Diversity: Characteristics or attributes that make us different from one another and that can be the basis for membership in a group.

Elaborative Rehearsal: The process of making connections between new ideas and other information already stored in your memory.

Emotional Intelligence: The ability to recognize, understand, and manage your own and others' emotions.

Empathy: The ability to understand another person's emotions.

Encoding: Taking in information and changing it into signals in our brain.

Extrinsic Motivation: Motivation that derives from forces external to you, such as an expected reward or a negative outcome that you want to avoid.

Fixed Mindset: The belief that one cannot improve one's talents, skills, and abilities.

Functional Résumé: A résumé that groups entries by skills and experiences.

General-Education Courses: A set of course requirements that gives all students a broad liberal education in the natural and social sciences, humanities, arts, and mathematics.

Goal: An outcome you hope to achieve that guides and sustains your effort over time.

Growth Mindset: The belief that one can improve and further develop one's skills.

Information Literacy: Finding information, evaluating its quality, and effectively communicating it to others.

Integrity: Being honest and displaying behavior that is consistent with one's values.

Interpersonal Communication: An active exchange of information between two or more people.

Intrinsic Motivation: Motivation that stems from your inner desire to achieve a specific outcome.

Learning Preference: Your preferred method for acquiring and working with information. Also called a *learning style*.

Long-Term Memory: Memory that stores a potentially limitless amount of information for a long period of time.

Metacognition: Thinking about thinking or about learning.

Mnemonic: A learning strategy that helps you memorize specific material.

Multimodal Learner: Someone who uses many different learning strategies to adapt to the situation at hand.

Occupational Projection: The predicted rise or fall in the number of new jobs in a particular field.

Paralinguistics: Changes in the voice (such as volume or pitch) that convey emotion.

Paraphrase: To restate information in your own words.

Personal Success Plan (PSP): A tool that helps you establish SMART goals, build action plans, evaluate your outcomes, and revise your plans as needed.

Plagiarism: When one person presents another person's words or ideas as his or her own.

Positive Psychology: A branch of psychology that focuses on people's strengths rather than on their weaknesses and that views weaknesses as growth opportunities.

Prioritize: To give an activity or a goal a higher value relative to another activity or goal.

Procrastinate: To delay or put off an action that needs to be completed.

Professional Association: An organization through which individuals who share a trade or job function can network and promote the interests of their profession.

Purposeful Reading Questions: Specific questions you want to be able to answer when you've finished reading.

Resilience: The ability to cope with stress and setbacks.

Résumé: A document that lists your education, work experience, and extracurricular activities.

Rote Rehearsal: Memorization of specific information or facts by studying the information repeatedly.

Self-Efficacy: Your belief in your ability to carry out the actions needed to reach a particular goal.

Sensory Memory: Process that uses information from the senses to begin creating memories.

Service Learning: Classes that combine classroom instruction with volunteer experience in the community.

Sexually Transmitted Infections (STIs): Illnesses, some treatable and some incurable, that are spread through the exchange of bodily fluids during sexual activity.

Short-Term Memory: Memory that stores a small number of items for a short period of time.

SMART Goal: A goal that is specific, measurable, achievable, relevant to you personally, and time-limited.

Supplemental Instruction: A student-led study program for especially difficult classes.

Test Anxiety: Nervousness or worry about performance on an exam.

Thesis: The main idea or argument of a paper or an essay.

Transferable Skills: Skills that can be applied in many different settings, such as work, home, and school.

Work Values: The aspects of your work or your work environment that you consider important.

Working Memory: The part of short-term memory that actively processes memories and information.

endnotes

Chapter 1

[1]See, for example, Betsy O. Barefoot, Carrie L. Warnock, Michael P. Dickinson, Sharon E. Richardson, and Melissa R. Roberts, eds., *Exploring the Evidence: Reporting Outcomes of First-Year Seminars: The First-Year Experience*, vol. 2, Monograph Series, no. 25 (1998), http://eric.ed.gov/?id=ED433742.

[2]https://www.census.gov/hhes/socdemo/education/data/census/half-century/graphs.html.

[3]http://www.census.gov/hhes/socdemo/education/data/cps/2013/tables.html.

[4]https://trends.collegeboard.org/education-pays.

[5]http://cew.georgetown.edu/recovery2020.

[6]Edward M. Glaser, *An Experiment in the Development of Critical Thinking* (New York: Teachers College, Columbia University, 1941).

[7]http://www.heri.ucla.edu/briefs/TheAmericanFreshman2012-Brief.pdf.

[8]For more on positive psychology, see C. R. Snyder and Shane J. Lopez, eds., *Oxford Handbook of Positive Psychology*, 2nd ed. (New York: Oxford University Press, 2009); C. R. Snyder, Shane J. Lopez, and Jennifer Teramoto Pedrotti, *Positive Psychology: The Scientific and Practical Explorations of Human Strengths*, 2nd ed. (Thousand Oaks, CA: Sage, 2011).

[9]For more on resilience, see Jacqueline Aundree Baxter, "Who Am I and What Keeps Me Going? Profiling the Distance Learning Student in Higher Education," *International Review of Research in Open and Distance Learning* 13, no. 4 (2012): 107–29, http://www.irrodl.org/index.php/irrodl/article/view/1283; Robert Holloway, "From School to University: A Senior College Model," *Independence* 39, no. 1 (2014): 10–12; Steven M. Southwick and Dennis S. Charney, *Resilience: The Science of Mastering Life's Greatest Challenges* (Cambridge: Cambridge University Press, 2012); John W. Reich, Alex Zautra, and John Stuart Hall, eds., *Handbook of Adult Resilience* (New York: Guilford Press, 2010).

[10]C. R. Snyder, K. L. Rand, and D. R. Sigmon, "Hope Theory: A Member of the Positive Psychology Family," in *Handbook of Positive Psychology*, ed. C. R. Snyder and S. J. Lopez (New York: Oxford University Press, 2002), pp. 257–76.

[11]A. M. Wood, P. A. Linley, J. Maltby, T. B. Kashdan, and R. Hurling, "Using Personal and Psychological Strengths Leads to Increases in Well-being over Time: A Longitudinal Study and the Development of the Strengths Use Questionnaire," *Personality and Individual Differences* 50 (2011): 15–19; C. Proctor, J. Maltby, and P. A. Linley, "Strengths Use as a Predictor of Well-being and Health-Related Quality of Life," *Journal of Happiness Studies* 12 (2011): 153–69.

[12]S. A. Karabenick and R. S. Newman, *Help-Seeking in Academic Settings: Goals, Groups, and Contexts* (Mahwah, NJ: Erlbaum, 2006).

[13]http://www.aacu.org/leap/students/employerstopten.cfm; http://www.youtube.com/watch?v=ItL01G3Kovs.

[14]For example: Job Outlook 2015, National Association of Colleges and Employers. See more at https://www.naceweb.org/about-us/press/class-2015-skills-qualities-employers-want.aspx.

Chapter 2

[1]http://www.bls.gov/ooh/life-physical-and-social-science/forensic-science-technicians.htm#tab-6.

[2]Edward M. Glaser, *An Experiment in the Development of Critical Thinking* (New York: Teachers College, Columbia University, 1941).

[3]http://www.cdc.gov/flu/protect/keyfacts.htm. See the Vaccine Benefits section: "Flu vaccination can reduce the risk of more serious flu outcomes, like hospitalizations and deaths."

[4]For more on cognitive development in an educational setting, see Julie Dockrell, Leslie Smith, and Peter Tomlinson, eds., *Piaget, Vygotsky, and Beyond: Central Issues in Developmental Psychology and Education* (London: Taylor & Francis, 1997).

[5]For example:

B. S. Bloom, M. D. Engelhart, E. J. Furst, W. H. Hill, D. R. Krathwohl (1956). *Taxonomy of educational objectives: The classification of educational goals*. Handbook I: Cognitive domain. New York: David McKay Company.

Bloom, B. S. (1994). "Reflections on the development and use of the taxonomy." In Rehage, Kenneth J.; Anderson, Lorin W.; Sosniak, Lauren A. "Bloom's taxonomy: A forty-year retrospective." *Yearbook of the National Society for the Study of Education* (Chicago: National Society for the Study of Education) 93 (2).

[6]http://www.dominican.edu/dominicannews/study-highlights-strategies-for-achieving-goals.

Chapter 3

[1]See Albert Bandura, *Self-Efficacy: The Exercise of Control* (New York: W. H. Freeman, 1997), p. 382.

[2]S. G. Rogelberg et al., "The Executive Mind: Leader Self-Talk, Effectiveness, and Strain," *Journal of Managerial Psychology* 28 (2013): 183–201; Christopher A. Wolters, "Self-Regulated Learning and College Students' Regulation of Motivation," *Journal of Educational Psychology* 90, no. 2 (1998): 224–35.

[3]N. A. Vasquez and R. Buehler, "Seeing Future Success: Does Imagery Perspective Influence Achievement Motivation?," *Personality and Social Psychology Bulletin* 33, no. 10 (2007): 1392–1405.

[4]C. S. Dweck, *Mindset: The New Psychology of Success* (New York: Random House, 2006).

[5]H. S. Waters and W. Schneider, *Metacognition, Strategy Use, and Instruction* (New York: Guilford Press, 2010).

[6]For example, see Marylène Gagné, ed., *The Oxford Handbook of Work Engagement, Motivation, and Self-Determination Theory* (Oxford: Oxford University Press, 2014).

[7]Douglas J. Swanson, Ed.D., "Narratives of Job Satisfaction Offered by the '100 Best Companies to Work for in America,'" Annual Meeting of the Western Social Science Association, Denver, CO, April 2013, http://works.bepress.com/dswanson/69.

[8]http://www.linkedin.com/today/post/article/20130315141647-128811924-harnessing-career-power-the-beauty-of-personal-responsibility.

Chapter 4

[1]For more about the dimensions identified in the MBTI, see Isabel Briggs Myers and Peter B. Myers, *Gifts Differing: Understanding Personality Type* (Mountain View: CPP, 1995).

[2]N. D. Fleming and C. Mills, "Not Another Inventory, Rather a Catalyst for Reflection," *To Improve the Academy* 11 (1992): 137–55.

[3]National Survey of Student Engagement Report, *Engaged Learning: Fostering Success for All Students*, Annual Report (Bloomington: Center for Postsecondary Research, School of Education, Indiana University Bloomington, 2006).

[4]Job Outlook 2015, National Association of Colleges and Employers, https://www.naceweb.org/about-us/press/class-2015-skills-qualities-employers-want.aspx.

Chapter 5

[1]T. Yu, "E-portfolio: A Valuable Job Search Tool for College Students," *Campus-wide Information Systems* 29 (2012): 70–76.

[2]A. C. McCormick, "It's about Time: What to Make of Reported Declines in How Much College Students Study," *Liberal Education* 97 (2011): 30–39.

[3]N. J. Cepeda, N. Coburn, D. Rohrer, J. T. Wixted, M. C. Mozer, and H. Pashler, "Optimizing Distributed Practice: Theoretical Analysis and Practical Implications," *Experimental Psychology* 56 (2009): 236–46.

[4]Tony Schwartz, *The Way We're Working Isn't Working* (New York: Free Press, 2010).

Chapter 6

[1]R. Emanuel et al., "How College Students Spend Their Time Communicating," *International Journal of Listening* 22 (2008): 13–28.

[2]N. K. Duke and P. D. Pearson, "Effective Practices for Developing Reading Comprehension," *What Research Has to Say about Reading Instruction*, ed. A. E. Farstrup and S. J. Samuels (Newark, DE: International Reading Association, 2002).

[3]V. S. Gier, D. Herring, J. Hudnell, J. Montoya, and D. S. Kreiner, "Active Reading Procedures for Moderating the Effects of Poor Highlighting," *Reading Psychology* 31 (2010): 69–81.

[4]Act, Inc., *Workplace Essential Skills: Resources Related to the SCANS Competencies and Foundational Skills* (Iowa City, IA: Act, 2000).

Chapter 7

[1]N. D. Rahim and H. Meon, "Relationship between Study Skills and Academic Performance," *AIP Conference Proceedings* 1522 (2013): 1176–78.

[2]V. Slotte and K. Lonka, "Review and Process Effects of Spontaneous Note-Taking on Text Comprehension," *Contemporary Educational Psychology* 24 (1999): 1–20.

[3]D. Cohen, E. Kim, J. Tan, and M. Winkelmes, "A Note Re-structuring Intervention Increases Students' Exam Scores," *College Teaching* 61 (2013): 95–99.

[4]B. Christe, "The Importance of Faculty-Student Connections in STEM Disciplines: A Literature Review," *Journal of STEM Education: Innovations and Research* 14 (2013): 22–26.

Chapter 8

[1]R. C. Atkinson and R. M. Shiffrin, "Human Memory: A Proposed System and Its Control Processes," in *The Psychology of Learning and Motivation: Advances in Research and Theory*, vol. 2, ed. K. W. Spence and J. T. Spence (Waltham, MA: Academic Press, 1968).

[2]I. Winkler and N. Cowan, "From Sensory to Long-Term Memory: Evidence from Auditory Memory Reactivation Studies," *Experimental Psychology* 52 (2005): 3–20.

[3]N. Cowan, "The Magical Number 4 in Short-Term Memory: A Reconsideration of Mental Storage Capacity," *Behavioral and Brain Sciences* 24 (2000): 87–105; Y. Kareev, "Seven (Indeed, Plus or Minus Two) and the Detection of Correlations," *Psychological Review* 107 (2000): 397–402.

[4]Y. Hu, K. A. Ericsson, D. Yang, and C. Lu, "Superior Self-Paced Memorization of Digits in Spite of a Normal Digit Span: The Structure of a Memorist's Skill," *Journal of Experimental Psychology* 35 (2009): 1426–42.

[5]W. Klimesch, *The Structure of Long-Term Memory: A Connectivity Model of Semantic Processing* (Hoboken: Taylor and Francis, 2013).

[6]S. D. Gronlund and D. R. Kimball, "Remembering and Forgetting: From the Laboratory Looking Out," in *Individual and Team Skill Decay: The Science and Implications for Practice*, ed. W. Arthur Jr., E. Day, W. Bennett Jr., and A. M. Portrey (New York: Routledge/Taylor and Francis, 2013), pp. 14–52.

[7]N. J. Cepeda, N. Coburn, D. Rohrer, J. T. Wixted, M. C. Mozer, and H. Pashler, "Optimizing Distributed Practice: Theoretical Analysis and Practical Implications," *Experimental Psychology* 56 (2009): 236–46.

[8]C. Gillen-O'Neel, V. W. Huynh, and A. J. Fuligni, "To Study or to Sleep? The Academic Costs of Extra Studying at the Expense of Sleep," *Child Development* 84 (2013): 133–42.

[9]L. E. Levine, B. M. Waite, and L. L. Bowman, "Electronic Media Use, Reading, and Academic Distractibility in College Youth," *CyberPsychology and Behavior* 10 (2007): 560–66.

[10]G. D. Hendry, S. J. Hyde, and P. Davy, "Independent Student Study Groups," *Medical Education* 39 (2005): 672–79; D. S. Shaw, "Promoting Professional Student Learning through Study Groups: A Case Study," *College Teaching* 59(2), 85–92.

Chapter 9

[1] K. A. Rawson, J. Dunlosky, and S. M. Sciartelli, "The Power of Successive Relearning: Improving Performance on Course Exams and Long-Term Retention," 2013 *Educational Psychology Review* 25, 523–548.

[2] P. Baghaei and J. Cassady, "Validation of the Persian Translation of the Cognitive Test Anxiety Scale," *Sage Open* 4 (2014): 1–11.

[3] M. Mavilidi, V. Hoogerheide, and F. Paas, "A Quick and Easy Strategy to Reduce Test Anxiety and Enhance Test Performance." 2014 *Applied Cognitive Psychology* 28, 5, 720–726.

[4] J. C. Cassady, "The Influence of Cognitive Test Anxiety across the Learning-Testing Cycle," *Learning and Instruction* 14 (2004): 569–92.

Chapter 10

[1] "Michael Gorman vs. Web 2.0," *Chronicle of Higher Education* 53 (2007): B4.

[2] D. L. McCabe, L. K. Trevino, and K. D. Butterfield, "Cheating in Academic Institutions: A Decade of Research," *Ethics and Behavior* 11 (2001): 219–32.

[3] Hart Research Associates, "It Takes More Than a Major: Employer Priorities for College Learning and Student Success," *Liberal Education* 99, 22–29 (2013).

[4] C. B. Pull, "Current Status of Knowledge on Public-Speaking Anxiety," *Current Opinion in Psychiatry* 25 (2012): 32–38.

[5] Hart Research Associates, "It Takes More Than a Major."

Chapter 11

[1] National Education Association, "Build Better Listening Skills," last modified 2015, http://www.nea.org/tools/build-better-listening-skills.html.

[2] Emotional intelligence has been defined in various ways by different people. Our definition and model of emotional intelligence is a synthesis of the following works by Mayer and Salovey: J. D. Mayer and P. Salovey, "Emotional Intelligence: New Ability or Eclectic Traits?," *American Psychologist* 63, no. 6 (2008): 503–17; and J. D. Mayer and P. Salovey, "What Is Emotional Intelligence?," in *Emotional Development and Emotional Intelligence: Educational Implications*, ed. P. Salovey and D. Sluyter (New York: Basic Books, 1997), pp. 3–31.

[3] Mayer and Salovey, "Emotional Intelligence," pp. 503–17.

[4] M. Bayrami, "Effect of Assertiveness Training on General Health in the First Year of Students of Tabriz University," *Psychological Research* 14, no. 1 (2011): 47–64.

[5] J. Darrington and N. Brower, "Effective Communication Skills: 'I' Messages and Beyond," *Families and Communities*, April 2012, Utah State University Cooperative Extension.

[6] S. Miller and P. A. Miller, *Core Communication: Skills and Processes* (Evergreen, CO: Interpersonal Communication Programs, 1997).

[7] A. W. Astin, *Achieving Educational Excellence: A Critical Assessment of Priorities and Practices in Higher Education* (San Francisco: Jossey-Bass, 1985).

[8] Ibid.

[9] S. Uusiautti and K. Maatta, "I Am No Longer Alone—How Do University Students Perceive the Possibilities of Social Media?," *International Journal of Adolescence and Youth* 19, no. 3 (2014): 293–305.

[10] S. R. Ennis, M. Rios-Vargas, N. G. Albert, "The Hispanic Population: 2010," *2010 Census Briefs*, U.S. Census Bureau (May 2011). http://www.census.gov/prod/cen2010/briefs/c2010br-04.pdf.

[11] World Health Organization, "What Do We Mean by 'Sex' and 'Gender'?" (2015). http://www.who.int/gender/whatisgender/en/.

[12] *American Psychologist*, "Guidelines for Psychological Practice with Lesbian, Gay, and Bisexual Clients," 67 (January 2012), 10–42.

[13] Ibid.

[14] American Psychological Association, Task Force on Socioeconomic Status, *Report of the APA Task Force on Socioeconomic Status* (Washington, DC: American Psychological Association, 2007).

Chapter 12

[1] Mayo Clinic Staff, "Chronic Stress Puts Your Health at Risk," accessed February 11, 2015, http://www.mayoclinic.org/healthy-living/stress-management/in-depth/stress/art-20046037.

[2] Ibid.

[3] F. J. He, C. A. Nowson, M. Lucas, and G. A. MacGregor, "Increased Consumption of Fruit and Vegetables Is Related to a Reduced Risk of Coronary Heart Disease: Meta-analysis of Cohort Studies," *Journal of Human Hypertension* 21 (2007): 717–28.

[4] http://www.choosemyplate.gov/healthy-eating-tips/ten-tips.html.

[5] http://www.anad.org/get-information/about-eating-disorders/eating-disorders-statistics/.

[6] H. W. Bland, B. F. Melton, L. E. Bigham, and P. D. Welle, "Quantifying the Impact of Physical Activity on Stress Tolerance in College Students," *College Student Journal* 48 (2014): 559–568.

[7] World Health Organization, *Global Recommendations on Physical Activity for Health* (Geneva: WHO Press, 2010).

[8] D. C. Lee, R. R. Pate, C. J. Lavie, X. Sui, T. S. Church, and S. N. Blair, "Leisure-Time Running Reduces All-Cause and Cardiovascular Mortality Risk," *Journal of the American College of Cardiology* 64 (2014): 472–81.

[9] O. Pikovsky, M. Oron, A. Shiyovich, Z. Perry, and L. Nesher, "The Impact of Sleep Deprivation on Sleepiness, Risk Factors, and Professional Performance in Medical Residents," *Israel Medical Association Journal* 15 (2013): 739–44.

[10] National Alliance on Mental Illness, *College Students Speak: A Survey Report on Mental Health* (Arlington, VA: National Alliance on Mental Illness, 2012).

[11] http://core.siu.edu/results.

[12] http://www.cdc.gov/reproductivehealth/unintendedpregnancy/contraception.htm.

[13]American Psychological Association, *Stress in America: Paying with Our Health* (Washington, DC: American Psychological Association, 2014).

[14]http://nces.ed.gov/programs/coe/indicator_csb.asp.

[15]National Center for Education Statistics, *Undergraduates Who Work While Enrolled in Postsecondary Education, 1989–1990* (Washington, DC: National Center for Education Statistics, 1994).

[16]http://nces.ed.gov/fastfacts/display.asp?id=31.

[17]R. Crawford, "Financial Stress Impacts Work Productivity," *Employee Benefits* (2014): 3, http://www.employeebenefits.co.uk/.

Chapter 13

[1]J. L. Holland, *Making Vocational Choices: A Theory of Vocational Personalities and Work*, 3rd ed. (Odessa, FL: Psychological Assessment Resources, 1997).

[2]Based on O*NET Work Values, last modified 2014, http://www.onetonline.org/find/descriptor/browse/Work_Values/.

[3]http://completecollege.org/the-game-changers/#clickBoxGreen.

[4]J. Gault, E. Leach, and M. Dewey, "Effects of Business Internships on Job Marketability: An Employer's Perspective," *Education + Training* 52, no. 1 (2010): 76–88.

[5]Alan M. Saks, "Multiple Predictors and Criteria of Job Search Success," *Journal of Vocational Behavior*, 68 (2005), 400–12.

[6]http://www.bls.gov/nls/nlsfaqs.htm#anch41.

Chapter 14

[1]M. Shircore, K. Galloway, N. Corbett-Jarvis, and R. Daniel, "From the First Year to the Final Year Experience: Embedding Reflection for Work Integrated Learning in a Holistic Curriculum Framework—A Practice Report," *International Journal of the First Year in Higher Education* 4, no. 1 (2013): 125–33; S. Qinton and T. Smallbone, "Feeding Forward: Using Feedback to Promote Reflection and Learning—A Teaching Model," *Innovations in Education and Teaching International* 47, no. 1 (2010): 125–35.

[2]For more information on the importance of networking and how to do it effectively, see Ivan Misner and Michelle R. Donovan, *The 29% Solution: 52 Weekly Networking Success Strategies* (Austin, TX: Greenleaf Book Group Press, 2008).

Appendix

[1]For more information on the STAR approach to behavioral interviewing, go to http://www.igrad.com/articles/behavioral-interviewing-and-the-star-approach.

index